Entertainment Law Handbook

Related titles by Law Society Publishing:

Design Law: Protecting and Exploiting Rights
Margaret Briffa and Lee Gage

Intellectual Property Law Handbook (Due November 2007)
Bird & Bird, Edited by Lorna Brazell

Titles from Law Society Publishing can be ordered from all good legal bookshops or direct from our distributors, Prolog (email: **lawsociety@prolog.uk.com**; Tel: 0870 850 1422). For further information or a catalogue, email our editorial and marketing office at **publishing@lawsociety.org.uk**.

ENTERTAINMENT LAW HANDBOOK

Editor: Richard Verow

Nick Kanaar, Estelle Overs
and Vincent Scheurer

The Law Society

ISBN 10: 1–85328–977–9
ISBN 13: 978–1–85328–977–4

Published in 2007 by the Law Society
113 Chancery Lane, London WC2A 1PL

Typeset by J&L Composition, Filey, North Yorkshire
Printed by Antony Rowe Ltd, Chippenham, Wiltshire

Contents

About the editor and contributors

EDITOR

Richard Verow is a solicitor with experience of the sport, media and entertainment industries. He is currently Head of Legal and Business Affairs for the International Cricket Council. Richard has advised commercial clients including broadcasters, recording and publishing companies, managers and agents in sports and entertainment, licensing and merchandising businesses, sports rights holders and individuals.

CONTRIBUTORS

Nick Kanaar is a partner at Collyer Bristow where his practice, whilst specialised within the entertainment industry, has a wide commercial spread and his expertise is in the area of the transactional making of contracts and the contentious variation of them. He is a veteran in the music industry and in particular was responsible for the seminal case of *Macaulay (Instone)* v. *Schroeder*.

Estelle Overs is a Barrister and Attorney (California) specialising in film and television production and distribution. After practising for several years at the Bar she is now based in-house at one of the UK's leading film distribution and sales agent companies. She has a particular interest in film education and is a member of BAFTA.

Vincent Scheurer graduated in law at Oxford University in 1993, qualified as a barrister in 1994 and has practised law in the video games industry since 1997. Following the acquisition of Europress by Hasbro Interactive in 1999, he helped to build the interactive entertainment team at UK law firm Osborne Clarke. Vincent left Osborne Clarke to set up Sarassin LLP in August 2004. Sarassin LLP, is a London-based legal consultancy specialising in video game contracts. Sarassin LLP advises developers, publishers, financiers and intermediaries on all types of commercial agreements and related issues in the video games industry.

Preface

The first edition of this book came out during the last millennium in the form of a College of Law Legal Practice Course (LPC) Resource Book. It was co-authored by Richard Verow and Peter Carey who were both working at the College of Law, York, at the time. It accompanied the LPC Media and Entertainment law course. That course has since ended.

It was thought appropriate that the book should move on. The original book fulfilled its purpose as a text for trainee solicitors and to a lesser extent for business people working in the entertainment business. It was felt that a new edition should focus on the entertainment industry and should involve additional specialist practitioners to freshen up the base material created by Richard Verow and include the provision of precedent materials.

This new work builds on the original materials written by Richard Verow. There is an entirely new section contributed by Vincent Scheurer which deals with the interactive games industry and the legal and business issues that surround it. Nick Kanaar has contributed his enormous wealth of experience and knowledge to the music section. Estelle Overs has substantially rewritten the film and television section to take account of industry practice and legal and commercial developments.

The book is designed for those who advise and work within the entertainment business. It provides a general introduction to background law and moves on to consider in more detail the specifics of the music, film and television and the interactive game businesses. Whilst it cannot be a complete resource on all issues we have sought to find a balance between the essential needs of the lawyer and business person involved in the entertainment business and the other legal and business disciplines that are touched upon in the work.

As with any work of this nature, delivery of the final proofs to the publisher is cause for immense relief. There is, of course, a vast group of people comprising friends, family and colleagues to thank as well as the staff at Law Society Publishing and in particular Marie Gill and Simon Blackett. Fiona Starr of the International Cricket Council provided invaluable assistance with the text as did Daisy Gili, Jamie Ingram and Laura Oakes in proofreading certain sections of the work.

The law is stated as at 1 January 2007.

Richard Verow, Nick Kanaar,
Estelle Overs and Vincent Scheurer
February 2007

Table of cases

Table of statutes

Table of statutory instruments

Table of international treaties, conventions and directives

Abbreviations

AURA	Association of United Recording Artists
BBC	British Broadcasting Corporation
BBFC	British Board of Film Classification
BECTU	Broadcasting, Entertainment, Cinematographic and Theatre Union
BMR	British Music Rights
BPI	British Phonographic Industry
CDPA 1988	Copyright, Designs and Patents Act 1988
Code	Ofcom Broadcasting Code
Database Directive	Directive 96/9/EC
DCMS	Department for Culture, Media and Sport
DGA	Directors Guild of America
DGGB	Directors Guild of Great Britain
DRM	Digital Rights Management
E&O insurance	errors and omissions insurance
EIS	Equity Investment Scheme
European Convention	European Convention on Cinematographic Co-production
FRAPA	Format Recognition and Protection Association
IPA	interparty agreement
ITC	Independent Television Commission
ITV	Independent Television
MCPS	Mechanical Copyright Protection Society
MMF	Music Managers Forum
MMOG	massive multiplayer online game
MPA	Music Publishers Association
MU	Musicians' Union
NDA	non-disclosure agreement
Ofcom	Office of Communications
P&A	prints and advertising
PACT	Producers Alliance for Cinema and Television
PAMRA	Performing Artists' Media Rights Association
PFD agreement	production, finance and distribution agreement

Phonogram Convention	Convention for the Protection of Producers of Phonograms against Unauthorised Duplication of their Phonograms
PPL	Phonographic Performance Ltd
PRA	Producers' Rights Agency
PRS	Performing Right Society
QA	quality assurance
Rome Convention	International Convention for the Protection of Performers, Producers of Phonograms and Broadcasting Organisations 1961
SAG	Screen Actors Guild
TMA 1995	Trade Marks Act 1995
TUC	Trades Union Congress
UCC	Universal Copyright Convention
UKFC	UK Film Council
VPL	Video Performance Ltd
WGA	Writers Guild of America
WGGB	Writers Guild of Great Britain

PART 1

General

Richard Verow

CHAPTER 1

Commercial contracts

1.1 INTRODUCTION

This chapter introduces a number of important considerations in the negotiation, documentation and challenge of entertainment contracts.

1.2 REACHING AGREEMENT

1.2.1 General considerations

The basic structure of a commercial contract should include a statement of the parties, any recitals and the operative part of the document.

The operative part may contain a list of defined terms, any conditions precedent, the agreed rights and obligations of the parties, a list of representations and warranties, as well as the usual standard or boilerplate terms.

When negotiating rights and other matters in the media and entertainment business, the negotiator should ensure that all the points in the following checklist are dealt with in the basic terms of the contract:

- who the parties are;
- what rights are being granted;
- how exclusive the rights are;
- when or for how long the rights can be exercised and how the contract may terminate;
- where the rights can be exercised; and
- payment terms.

Each of these points is considered in turn below.

1.2.2 Parties

The contract should state clearly who the parties are and their capacity to enter into the contract.

3

1.2.3 Rights

The rights clause is fundamental and is often a grant of intellectual property rights such as copyright. The grant of rights may also relate to an individual's services such as those of an actor or a musician.

An agreement must specify what rights are being granted; it may (but does not have to) specifically reserve rights not otherwise granted. A specific reservation of rights is very common where a category of rights has already been granted to a third party and the rights owner does not want this fact to be in doubt.

The division of rights varies between different entertainment businesses and, when negotiating a contract, regard should be had to prevailing practice as well as the specific contract in point.

A rights clause can cause problems if it is not carefully drafted. For example, the rights clause may be too wide, impinging on other deals. Developments may take place which make new forms of exploitation possible. A recent example is the rise of Internet, electronic publishing and multimedia applications. It may not be clear who actually owns or controls the right to publish a work in electronic form as, until recently, these did not exist and therefore many contracts do not deal with them.

If rights clauses do not deal with these new methods of exploitation difficulties of interpretation may ensue, which may be resolved by negotiation or legal action as well as consideration of the contract and the intention of the parties. The leading cases in this area are the copyright cases referred to in **Chapter 2**.

1.2.4 Exclusivity

If the agreement is to take effect as an exclusive licence of copyright, the provisions of the Copyright, Designs and Patents Act 1988 (CDPA 1988) must be complied with (as discussed in **Chapter 2**).

Exclusivity is very important whatever rights or services are being considered. An actor's services must be exclusive for certain purposes during the filming and promotion of a film; an actor promoting a product may have to agree to provide an exclusive service which may mean that he cannot appear in other adverts.

There are potential legal problems with such arrangements since such exclusivity may amount to restraint of trade. It can also lead to breach of the freedom of goods and services provisions of the EU. An exclusive agreement may also be anti-competitive – which is possible where the distribution of goods or the exploitation of rights is concerned.

1.2.5 Term

The term or duration of an agreement may be a specified period of time, although an indefinite period may be used with a notice period exercisable by either party to the agreement to end the contract. Dealings with intellectual property rights are often tied to the length of protection given by law. If a contract deals with the personal services of an actor or musician, the term may vary between a day and a number of years.

The term of an agreement may be extended by an option clause allowing one party to give notice to the other extending the agreement on agreed terms. In this context, an option is a contractual term allowing a party to acquire a right or to extend the term of an agreement. Options are frequently found in entertainment agreements where an initial fixed period is followed by a number of contractual 'option' periods allowing an extension of the original term. A common alternative is for a lengthy fixed term with a number of 'opt out' provisions at agreed intervals.

All option clauses in agreements should set out the method by which, and the time-limit within which, they should be exercised. An option should also contain its own separate consideration upon exercise. Options when exercised should constitute valid binding contracts themselves. An option which is contingent upon terms of the subsequent contract being agreed may not constitute a binding contract at all, but may simply be an agreement to agree or an agreement to negotiate, both of which are unenforceable.

If an option is included in a contract, the person with the benefit of the option must call for its performance by notice in accordance with the terms of the agreement. There is only a right, not an obligation, to demand performance.

A right of first refusal, or a pre-emption right, gives a party the ability to make an offer on such terms as it sees fit, which the other party may choose to accept (or not) as it sees fit.

Some contracts grant 'matching' rights to a party. Upon termination, the party with the matching rights is entitled to match any offer the other party has obtained for the contract.

1.2.6 Territory

Most entertainment contracts contain a territorial restriction. The territorial limits commonly start with the world or the universe. They may also be restricted by language and country or 'territory'. It is common for rights, whether they are the rights to services or intellectual property rights, to be divided in this way, and a rights owner may try to maximise income and protect exclusivity by striking deals in a number of territories.

Legal problems relating to exploitation in this way may arise from the EU rules on freedom to provide goods and services, as well as competition law and the restrictions it can impose on contracts.

1.2.7   Payment terms

Contractual payment terms vary enormously. The contract may provide for a fee, a royalty or a profit share. A fee is normally a lump sum payment, which pays for all the rights under the contract.

A royalty payment is a percentage of income or the sale price of the product in question. Royalty rates can be altered and recalculated in many ways, as discussed in **Chapter 8**. If there is a royalty, there may also be an advance against royalties, which represents a payment on account of future earnings. Such an advance is always recoupable from future royalties although it is rarely returnable. This means that until enough royalties are earned to cover the amount of the advance from income from sales, no royalty is paid.

The contract may pay a share of profits. This may be a share of gross profits or net profits (as defined in the agreement), which usually means that once all the defined expenses are covered any profits are shared in an agreed way. In addition, there may be a guaranteed minimum payment due, whether or not the contract generates gross or net profits.

1.3   PROBLEMS IN FORMATION

1.3.1   General considerations

The terms necessary for the existence of a binding contract must be established by the parties to the contract. Although a contract may be oral, ideally the terms should be set out in a written agreement which is signed by both parties. There may be problems in formation where, before a full agreement is reached, the parties are negotiating terms. Negotiations should generally be conducted 'subject to contract'.

1.3.2   Lock-in and lock-out agreements

The terms of an agreement should be comprehensive and certain. Occasionally, situations arise where parties suggest that an 'agreement to agree' is entered into, or that they will 'negotiate in good faith', or that one party will not negotiate with anyone else. Such agreements must be carefully drafted if they are to be enforceable.

An agreement to agree or a duty to negotiate in good faith is contractually uncertain and therefore not binding on the parties. An agreement between the parties that one of them will not negotiate with anyone else for an agreed period of time is enforceable, provided consideration is given. This is a lock-out agreement. In such a case, the party agreeing to the restriction is not obliged to negotiate, it is simply saying that it will not go elsewhere. An agreement which requires them to negotiate with the other party, a lock-in agreement, is unenforceable being void for uncertainty (see *Walford and Others* v. *Miles and Another* [1992] 2 AC 128).

1.3.3 Renegotiation

Contractual renegotiations are common. The terms of a valid existing contract should be adhered to, as failure to do so by either party may result in a claim for breach of contract. There may be different reasons for a renegotiation. The artist may simply feel that he deserves more money, or he may have been advised that his contract is unenforceable on a legal ground such as restraint of trade. All renegotiations should be conducted 'without prejudice' to reserve a position in case of litigation.

If one party threatens proceedings for breach of contract and then subsequently settles the dispute, that party may not be able to reopen that dispute at a later date before the courts. Public policy prohibits the settlement of a previous dispute being reopened at a later date (see *Colchester Borough Council* v. *Smith and Others* [1992] Ch 421).

If a contract is successfully renegotiated, the new agreement should be recorded in writing to reflect its terms. A novation agreement or a variation should be executed to alter the previous agreement.

1.3.4 Letters of intent and heads of agreement

One party may not be willing to commit itself to a full agreement. This may be for a number of reasons, for example because a company wants to take more time to review the prospects of an artist or the viability of a project. A letter of intent may, in fact, be a binding contract if all the necessary elements for a contract are present. A letter of intent written 'subject to contract' may not be binding. It has been said that 'there can be no hard and fast answer to the question of whether a letter of intention is a binding agreement: everything must depend upon the circumstances of the particular case' (*British Steel Corporation* v. *Cleveland Bridge and Engineering Co. Ltd* [1984] 1 All ER 504).

A person who signs a letter of intent must consider the obligations to which he is being committed and whether or how he may be called upon to perform those obligations. Payment for work undertaken on the basis of a letter of intent may be recovered on a *quantum meruit* basis.

A heads of agreement may be a binding or non-binding document and is a useful short-form method to record the basic commercial terms of the agreement.

1.3.5 Independent advice

Although all the factors necessary to constitute a binding contract may be present, there may be other matters to consider before signing an agreement. Particular problems arise whenever artists enter any form of contract, and advice should always be taken on the terms of the contract. There are a number of minimum terms agreements in the entertainment industry. These agreements have been negotiated between various unions (such as Equity and the Musicians' Union) and major employers (such as the BBC).

The quality and availability of professional advice may be an important factor in any subsequent attempt to challenge a contract. Many agreements contain a specific declaration that the artist has been given independent professional advice but paying for such advice is often a problem for impecunious artists. Managers and record companies may advance the artist the amount of their reasonable professional fees against future income.

An independent adviser should explain the contract and the reasonableness of the obligations imposed. If necessary, terms should be varied by negotiation. All advice should be recorded in writing and if a client refuses to accept advice, that fact should also be recorded in writing.

If there is a later challenge to an agreement and one party can point to the fact that independent advice was taken, it is harder to establish that the artist did not understand the extent of his commitment. Independent advice is of particular value in cases where undue influence is alleged.

1.4 CHALLENGING AGREEMENTS

1.4.1 Introduction

Contracts in the entertainment business are occasionally susceptible to challenge. Some common reasons for such challenges are considered below.

1.4.2 Contracts with minors

Whilst all inexperienced artists need to be carefully and independently advised, minors or infants need special consideration. A minor is a person under 18 years of age. Any agreement with a minor is voidable at the instance of the minor on attaining the age of majority.

However, it is less likely that the contract will be voided at that time if the artist has either positively affirmed the contract (for example, by continuing to fulfil his contractual obligations) or done nothing to dispute the contract within a reasonable time (note that 'reasonable time' will vary according to the circumstances). The same will apply if the contract is manifestly advantageous to the artist, or if the artist had taken independent legal and financial advice prior to signing and so can be said to have understood fully the terms of the agreement. In general, the court will consider all relevant circumstances, and it is by no means the case that a contract can be voided solely because the minor has reached his eighteenth birthday.

To reduce the risk of the contract being terminated, the terms of the contract should be reasonable and allow a reasonable financial return for the minor. The contract should be for the minor's benefit so that it provides in some way for adequate training and other aids to a successful career. In addition, the terms of the contract should be properly explained to the minor, and preferably also to his parents or guardians, so that there can be no scope for future misunderstanding.

Where the contract provides for a guarantor of the performance of the minor's obligations, and the contract is held to be unenforceable against the minor, the guarantor is not obliged to fulfil the contract but may find himself liable to compensate the other party for loss caused by the non-performance of obligations by the artist. A guarantor should take independent advice on his obligations before committing himself and should ensure that those obligations cease when the minor attains the age of majority. As a rule, no one should guarantee the performance of a third party if he can reasonably avoid doing so.

There are a number of regulations concerning the employment of minors in the entertainment industry which are beyond the scope of this book.

1.4.3 Undue influence

A court will not hold someone to a bargain if undue influence can be established. This is an equitable doctrine. If a person enters an agreement where undue influence is presumed, the inference is that no free and deliberate judgement has been exercised upon entering the agreement and the agreement will be set aside.

A presumption of undue influence often arises with the existence of a fiduciary duty. In order for the presumption to arise, the party seeking to avoid the contract must prove that the other party involved acquired an influence over his mind which precluded his free consent. However, in cases where there is a fiduciary relationship, undue influence is presumed. A fiduciary relationship exists where one party relies on the guidance or advice of the other. There are certain categories of relationships which are by their very nature fiduciary. For example, the relationships between solicitor and client, doctor and patient, and trustee and beneficiary are all fiduciary relationships.

In the entertainment industry, this category may include the relationship between a manager and an artist.

Cases concerning undue influence have been concerned particularly with the relationship between husbands and wives and lenders (see, for example, *Barclays Bank* v. *O'Brien and Another* [1994] 1 AC 180). Where undue influence is presumed, rather than proved, the party seeking to avoid the contract must prove that the contract is manifestly disadvantageous to that party.

It is possible to rebut the presumption – most easily by showing that the weaker party took independent advice. In the context of an artist's contract, this should involve the terms of the agreement being explained to the artist by a truly independent third party adviser. One solicitor should not act for both parties in a negotiation (to avoid any conflict of interest) even if there appears to be complete accord between the parties. A separate solicitor from a different firm should be instructed. If the presumption of undue influence is to be rebutted successfully, it will also help if the independent adviser is experienced in the appropriate area of law. The 'weaker' party should also understand the terms of the agreement.

The relationship between artist and manager is one that may give rise to a presumption of undue influence. In the correct circumstances, it is also possible for the relationship between an artist and his record or publishing company (or, rather, the individuals involved in those companies) to give rise to such a presumption.

Not all relationships between an artist and a manager or a record company executive are fiduciary. This will be a question of fact. The age and experience of the artist and the extent to which the other party has taken control or otherwise of the artist's career are relevant factors. Coupled with this, the agreement entered into must involve some form of conflict of interest on the part of the other party. Accordingly, the artist must enter into an agreement with the party whose advice is being relied upon, which agreement is to some extent disadvantageous to the artist.

Examples

Armatrading v. *Stone* (1984) unreported, 17 September, QBD

The singer/songwriter Joan Armatrading entered into a management agreement with the Copeland Sherry Agency. The defendant was a partner in that firm. Initially, the Copeland Sherry Agency represented the claimant as her manager. However, during the term of the initial management agreement, the claimant was effectively represented by the defendant, Stone. When the initial agreement expired in March 1976, the claimant and defendant discussed between them employing the defendant as the claimant's personal manager. They both met a solicitor who prepared a draft agreement which they both signed. The bill for the agreement was sent to the defendant, and it appears that the solicitor was effectively acting for the defendant. The claimant did not receive, nor was it suggested that she should obtain, independent legal advice. One of the terms of the new management agreement was that the manager's commission should be perpetual for contracts negotiated or signed during the period of the management agreement. The agreement was to be for one year and the management commission was 20 per cent of all earnings.

The claimant successfully claimed that the agreement should be set aside on the grounds of undue influence. Towards the end of the 1976 agreement, she took independent legal advice and it became clear that she had not understood the commission clause and, in particular, the post-termination commission provisions of the agreement. In this case, the claimant was able to establish undue influence because she had not formed an independent judgement after full, free and informed thought.

O'Sullivan v. *Management Agency and Music Ltd and Others* [1981] QB 428, CA

The claimant, Gilbert O'Sullivan, signed management, publishing and recording agreements with companies controlled by his manager. His manager never suggested that the singer should take independent legal advice, and the evidence showed that at the time the agreements were signed the singer was commercially naive and trusted the manager implicitly. It transpired that the agreements which he signed with his manager's companies were not as advantageous as they would have been if they had been arm's length with independent third parties.

Because of the relationship between the singer and his manager, the agreements were presumed to be the result of undue influence and were voidable. In this case, the claimant recovered the copyrights in his compositions and the master tapes, and was also awarded damages based on an account of profits plus interest. In awarding damages, the court took some account of the time and effort that the defendants had spent in promoting the claimant. Essentially, the amount the claimant received was the difference between the arm's length rate he could have received with an independent company and the rate actually received from the defendants.

Elton John v. *Richard Leon James* [1991] FSR 397

The facts of this case were very similar to the *O'Sullivan* case. The claimant entered publishing agreements before signing a management agreement with the same company. Despite the fact that at the outset of the relationship the publishing and recording companies were not managing the claimant, a fiduciary relationship arose. The agreements were not the subject of negotiation although they were explained to the claimant by the defendant. However, no independent legal advice was taken on the original contract. The facts of this case showed that the claimant placed trust and confidence in the defendant and, accordingly, a presumption of undue influence arose.

It was held that the defendant had breached its fiduciary obligations and was ordered to account to the claimant for elements of its profit.

1.4.4 Restraint of trade

Many contracts are exclusive arrangements between the parties. An artist usually appoints only one manager. The artist is signed to one record company and one publishing company exclusively for all recorded performances and compositions. The reason given for the exclusive nature of many agreements is the risk and investment undertaken by the recording or publishing company in signing both established and unknown artists. A degree of exclusivity is acceptable in a contract, and most contracts involve a degree of exclusivity.

Restraint of trade is usually understood to mean or to involve a restriction on a person and his future ability to carry on a trade or profession. Such restrictions were originally regarded as unacceptable because of the monopolies they created in providing services or skills in industry. Restraint of trade makes all contracts or covenants which restrict trade unenforceable unless they are reasonable as between the parties and not injurious to the public interest. A distinction must be drawn between those contracts which are in restraint of trade and those which regulate the normal commercial relations between the parties to a contract.

Artists, individuals and businessmen often seek to challenge agreements not because they restrict them from carrying on their business once the agreement has ended (although some agreements contain post-contractual restrictions) but because during the course of the agreement they are committed exclusively to another party (usually a record or production company). That other party is not committed to them in a similar way. The company may not be obliged to record, exploit, publish or release an artist's compositions or recordings. During the course of the agreement, the artist cannot, it is argued, effectively carry on his business and as a result is prohibited from earning a living.

An artist's recording contract will commit the artist to a particular record company for an initial period which may then be extended for a number of option periods. During each period, there is usually a certain product requirement. The total period of such contracts may be anything between one and 10 years and involve the artist in a continuing obligation to record and perform, and thus provide recordings for the record company to exploit if it chooses.

Whenever an artist is exclusively contracted to another party, such as a record company, it may be open to the artist to challenge the agreement on the basis of restraint of trade.

The present law is largely based on the speeches of the House of Lords in *Esso Petroleum Co. Ltd* v. *Harper's Garage (Stourport) Ltd* [1968] AC 269. This case set out some of the main principles of the doctrine of restraint of trade.

Is the contract in restraint of trade?

The House of Lords refrained from laying down a rigid approach as to what constitutes a restraint of trade and stated that 'the doctrine of restraint of trade is one to be applied to factual situations with a broad and flexible rule of reason'.

At one end of the scale, there are contracts which 'merely regulate the normal commercial relations between parties' and, at the other end of the scale, there are contracts where the doctrine undoubtedly does apply. Examples of the latter include contracts where an employee restricts his ability to compete against his employer after he has left his employment, and contracts where the seller of a business agrees not to compete against the buyer of that business. The contracts with which this work is concerned, such as recording contracts, may also fall within this category. When considering a contract, all of the terms are important. If 'contractual restrictions appear unnecessary or to be reasonably capable of enforcement in an oppressive manner, then they must be justified before they can be enforced' (*Schroeder (A) Music Publishing Co. Ltd* v. *Macaulay (formerly Instone)* [1974] 1 WLR 1308, discussed at **para.1.4.5** below).

One way of looking at this is to consider whether the agreement is aimed at the absorption or the sterilisation of an artist's services. In other words, a certain amount of protection is permissible, but it must be limited to the amount necessary for the protection of a commercial interest.

Does it protect a legitimate interest?

The term which is in restraint of trade must protect a legitimate interest. What amounts to a legitimate interest for a record company in imposing restrictions in a recording contract varies. However, it seems that the commercial needs of the company in its desire to sell as many records as possible will be paramount. Such commercial considerations relate to the need to make a profit and a high quality product, and the ability to make informed and reliable business decisions based on the availability of products, as well as the company's ability to recover its investment in the contracted artist and any other artists.

A record company, like any other business, needs to be able to plan ahead for marketing, manufacturing and distribution purposes. Similar considerations will apply to publishing companies and managers involved in the entertainment business where exclusively signed performers seek to challenge

13

those agreements. These considerations all amount to a legitimate business interest.

Is it reasonable between the parties and is it in the public interest?

The term must also be reasonable between the parties and in the public interest (*Nordenfelt* v. *Maxim Nordenfelt Guns and Ammunition Co. Ltd* [1894] AC 535). In *Nordenfelt*, it was also stated that the claimant's motives in challenging the contract are not material.

If a term is to be reasonable between the parties, the restraint must be no more than is necessary for the adequate protection of the person in whose favour it is created. The balance is between protecting an investment and achieving a good return, and allowing the artist to pursue his career.

A number of terms should be scrutinised, for example the duration of the agreement, particularly with regard to any options to extend the term; provisions for assignment of the obligations and the ownership of rights created under the agreement; the consideration involved; provisions for terminating the agreement; and any obligations to promote and manufacture the product of the agreement. The fact that certain terms are not included in the agreement may be important, as is the relative bargaining position of the parties, their age and the availability of professional advice. The test laid down in *Schroeder (A) Music Publishing* (above) was 'is the agreement taken as a whole fair?'.

Not only must an agreement be reasonable as between the parties, but it should also satisfy the public policy test. The guiding principle is that 'everyone should be able to earn a living and give to the public the fruits of his particular abilities'. As long as the agreement does not conflict with this aim, it will satisfy the public policy requirement.

When considering an agreement it is necessary, first, to decide whether the contract is one that attracts the doctrine of restraint of trade at all. Secondly, if it is established that the contract is in restraint of trade it must then be determined whether it protects a legitimate interest and whether it is reasonable.

Effect of an agreement being in restraint of trade

If a contract is found to be in restraint of trade, it appears that the contract is voidable or unenforceable (*Schroeder (A) Music Publishing* (above)). A voidable or unenforceable contract ceases to exist for future purposes at the date of judgment. Prior to that date, the record or publishing company will retain the advantage of the contract.

It is possible that an offending clause could be severed from the contract. Severance involves separating the void part of the contract from the valid part. In principle, the courts will apply the 'blue pencil test' and sever an illegal promise only if this can be done by cutting words out of the contract so that the meaning of the remaining part of the contract is not affected. The court will not rewrite the contract, although it will delete offending terms provided that the other terms of the contract can remain sensibly intact. In principle, with exclusive entertainment contracts, the terms on which the parties will seek a declaration will be central to the contract and, accordingly, if the court is unwilling to rewrite the contract, the severance of those terms will leave no contract at all.

In claims involving restraint of trade and undue influence, it is common for the defendants to allege laches and/or acquiescence in the action.

Laches involves a delay in coming to court to seek a remedy for the alleged wrongdoing. The delay must not be one that takes the claimant outside the limitation period. However, even within a limitation period, action should be taken as promptly as possible. It is important to consider the length of the delay and the nature of acts done during the interval before action is taken which might cause a balance of injustice to one party or the other in the remedy sought.

In principle, a person should not be deprived of his legal rights unless he has acted in a way which would make it fraudulent for him to assert his rights.

1.4.5   Application of the doctrine of restraint of trade

The restraint of trade doctrine has been invoked in a number of cases involving performers and writers. It has also been used in cases involving sportsmen (see, for example, *Watson* v. *Prager and Another* [1991] 3 All ER 487 and *Eastham* v. *Newcastle United Football Club Ltd and Others* [1964] Ch 413), as well as in frequent cases involving employees.

Some examples of the application of the doctrine in the entertainment field are set out below.

Music publishing

Schroeder (A) Music Publishing Co. Ltd v. *Macaulay (formerly Instone)* [1974] 1 WLR 1308, [1974] 3 All ER 616

This case involved a young and unknown songwriter who entered into an agreement with a music publishing company. The agreement engaged the songwriter's exclusive services for a period of one year. The agreement was in the standard form used by the music publishing company. The songwriter assigned the full copyright for the whole world in each of his original songs created at any time during the period of the agreement. The publishers paid £10 to the songwriter as a general advance against royalties. When the first £10 was recouped from royalties, the publishers would then advance a further £10 which would be recouped from royalties in the same way. These advances would continue throughout the initial one-year period of the agreement. However, if the total royalties advanced to the songwriter equalled or exceeded £1,000, the agreement would be automatically extended for another one year. The music publishers could terminate the agreement by giving the songwriter one month's written notice. The songwriter was unable to terminate the agreement in similar fashion. Furthermore, the publishers were under no obligation to exploit any of the songwriter's compositions.

The songwriter sought a declaration that the agreement was contrary to public policy as being an unreasonable restraint of trade, and as a result was void.

This was an exclusive agreement which allowed the publishers to do as they wished with the copyrights. However, the songwriter could not assign any of his copyrights elsewhere during the term of the agreement. The agreement was in the publishers' standard form and was expressed to be non-negotiable.

The court held that all the terms of the agreement had to be considered. The court had to decide whether the bargain made was fair. In other words, the court had to decide whether the restrictions contained in the agreement were both reasonably necessary for the protection of the legitimate interest of the publisher and commensurate with the benefits that the songwriter received. In this case, the restrictions in the agreement were not fair and reasonable as they combined a lack of obligation on the part of the publishers with a total commitment from the songwriter. The publishers were not required to publish any of the songwriter's compositions. The songwriter could earn nothing from his abilities as a composer if his works were not published. The agreement amounted to an unreasonable restraint of trade contrary to public policy and was therefore void.

In reaching its decision, the court noted that under the agreement as originally drafted, the songwriter was tied to the publishers and could not recover the copyright in his works which the publishers refused to publish. Although the court did not consider that for the agreement to be reasonable the publishers should enter into a positive commitment to publish future works by an unknown songwriter, it felt that there should be some general undertaking to use their reasonable or best endeavours to promote the songwriter's work. There should also be some provision enabling the songwriter to terminate the agreement. The evidence in this case showed that there was no justification for the agreement being so one-sided.

The test of fairness is '. . . whether the restrictions are both reasonably necessary for the protection of the legitimate interests of the promisee and commensurate with the benefits secured to the promisor under the contract. For the purposes of this test, all the provisions of the contract must be taken into consideration' (at p.623H). Lord Diplock also made comments on the standard form of contract that the publishers used in this case. He described it as a 'take it or leave it' contract (at p.624D). The contract had not been the subject of negotiation between the parties or approved over the years by way of negotiation. A standard form contract or the usual terms of a publishing or record company will not stand the test of the courts' scrutiny unless they are considered in all the circumstances to be fair and reasonable.

Recording agreements

Zang Tumb Tuum Records Ltd and Another v. *Holly Johnson* [1993] EMLR 61 ('the Holly Johnson case')

An action was brought by the claimants, Zang Tumb Tuum, a recording company, and Perfect Songs Limited, a music publishing company, against the defendant, Holly Johnson. The defendant was lead singer of the group 'Frankie Goes to Hollywood'. He wanted to leave the group, and the claimants issued proceedings on the basis that the agreements the group had signed continued to be binding upon him both as an individual artist and as a composer.

The group had signed agreements in 1983 when they were young men with little business experience. The group were keen for Trevor Horn, the owner of the claimant companies, to produce their records. There was, however, no suggestion that the claimants exercised any undue influence over the group or the defendant or that they acted fraudulently or in bad faith. The group achieved some measure of success with a string of number one singles. Proceedings were bought by the claimant companies seeking to force Holly Johnson to record with them after he left the group. Holly Johnson resisted the proceedings on the basis that the contracts were so one-sided and unfair that they could not stand and could not be enforced. In addition, he counter-claimed for damages because the recording costs of the group's second album 'Liverpool' were excessive. Under the terms of the agreement, recording costs were recoupable from the royalties payable to the group.

Applying the principles laid down in *Schroeder (A) Music Publishing* (above) 'was the bargain fair?'. As part of the test, the court considered all the terms of the agreement.

In this case, the court found that the provisions of the recording contract which related to the duration of the agreement were grossly one-sided.

1. Group members were bound collectively and individually for up to seven 'option periods', and the agreement, if the record company had chosen to exercise these options, could have lasted for up to eight or nine years.
2. The claimants were free to terminate their obligations at any time, but the group was bound to record only for the claimants.
3. The claimants had the last word on all matters, including the approval of compositions and expenditure on recording costs.

4. The claimants also had an absolute discretion to refrain from releasing records and, even if records were not released, copyright in them would remain in the claimant companies.
5. Further, even though the group and the individual members were bound exclusively to the record companies, the companies were not exclusively bound to them. The record companies could record and promote other artists at will.

The court found that the recording contract was not a fair bargain and was in restraint of trade. In respect of the excessive recording costs claimed by the defendant, the court stated there was an implied obligation on the part of the record companies to keep such costs within reasonable bounds.

Silvertone Records v. *Mountfield* [1993] EMLR 152 ('the Stone Roses case')

The defendants were in dispute with their record company and music publishers. The claimants brought an action seeking a declaration that the recording and publishing agreements entered into with the defendants were enforceable and valid. The defendants contended that the agreements amounted to an unreasonable restraint of trade. At the time the agreements were negotiated it was made clear to the defendants that the recording and the publishing agreements were a package and were not separately negotiable. The defendants were advised by a manager and a lawyer at the time when they signed the contract. However, the manager was inexperienced, and the lawyer appeared to have little or no experience of the music industry. The agreement gave the record company exclusive control of the defendants for up to seven years. During that time, there was no obligation on the record company to release any records.

The court held that there was an immense inequality in bargaining power between the parties when the agreement was entered into. Considering all the terms of the agreement, if the defendants were prevented from reaching the public with their work over a prolonged period, then the agreement was a restraint of trade. The contract could lead to the sterilisation of the defendants' services. During the period of the contract, they could not work elsewhere. The lack of an experienced adviser will not always result in an unfair bargain. The court must always consider the contract itself to determine its fairness.

Panayiotou and Others v. *Sony Music Entertainment (UK) Ltd* [1994] EMLR 229 ('the George Michael case')

This case involved the singer George Michael, who sought to challenge an agreement entered into in 1988 with his recording company. This agreement was a renegotiation of an earlier agreement (signed in 1984) when George Michael was a member of the pop group 'Wham!'. The 1984 agreement was renegotiated when George Michael became a successful solo artist. The main improvement of the terms was in the advances and royalties that George Michael received. By 1991, the claimant had become dissatisfied with Sony and the 1988 agreement as he no longer regarded it as being in his interest. The claimant claimed that the 1988 agreement was unenforceable as an unreasonable restraint of trade or, alternatively, was rendered void by Art.81(2) of the EC Treaty.

The starting point for the court was to determine whether the contract was one which attracted the doctrine of restraint of trade at all. The second stage was to determine whether the contract satisfied the test set out in *Nordenfelt* (above), which involved reasonableness as between the parties and reasonableness in the public interest.

The court held that it could not regard the 1988 agreement as a new agreement, arising, as it did, out of the renegotiation of the 1984 agreement. The claimant failed on the basis that the compromise of the dispute relating to the 1984 agreement was genuine and bona fide and he had freely entered into it. Accordingly, he could not now seek to reopen issues which had been compromised at the time of the renegotiations for the 1988 agreement. There was, the court said, a public interest in upholding genuine and proper compromises. On this ground alone, the claimant failed in his action.

However, the court went on to consider whether the contract would have passed the reasonableness test as set out in *Nordenfelt*. The court held that the terms of the 1988 agreement were justified and the agreement was 'fair'. In reaching his decision, Parker J took account of the consideration received by the claimant, which was quite substantial. There was no risk, on the facts of this case, that the defendants would not exploit the claimant's works, although the claimant was exclusively bound to the defendants, who would own and be entitled to exploit all his master recordings during the term of the 1988 agreement. The court concluded that, taking into account all the terms of the 1988 agreement, the restrictions contained in that agreement were 'both reasonably necessary for the protection of the legitimate interests of Sony Music, and commensurate with the benefits secured to Mr Michael under it'.

Conclusions

These cases illustrate the doctrine of restraint of trade. Each case will turn on its own facts and, in particular, on the terms of the agreements entered into by the performers. The principles as set out in *Schroeder Music Publishing* (above) will be applied by the court. It is important to contrast the cases.

The Stone Roses and Holly Johnson cases illustrate that where young, inexperienced and unknown artists enter agreements which are capable of operating in a one-sided or oppressive manner then the court will be willing to set aside the agreements. In contrast, George Michael was an experienced and successful performer able to renegotiate an agreement on favourable terms – which involved the payment of substantial advances – and, on the facts before the court, it was unlikely that the contract would be operated oppressively. The agreement was capable of being fair despite its exclusivity. The George Michael case was decided mainly on the question of public interest in upholding genuine and proper compromises, and the court's comments on the reasonableness of the contract were obiter.

In assessing whether a contract falls foul of the restraint of trade doctrine, the factors considered above must be taken into account. In the *Schroeder Music Publishing* and Holly Johnson cases, the important factor supporting the decision was the duration of the exclusive term of the agreements in question. In the Stone Roses case, there were no obligations for the release of any records, whereas, in the George Michael case, if Sony did not release George Michael's recordings, George Michael could terminate the contract.

The financial terms for the artists in the *Schroeder Music Publishing*, Holly Johnson and the Stone Roses cases were poor, particularly when compared to those received by George Michael.

When considering entertainment contracts, the alleged restraint of trade generally relates to a contract's exclusivity and duration. Whether a contract is reasonable between the parties and reasonable in the public interest depends on the particular facts of the case. Guidelines were set out in the *Esso Petroleum* case (see **para.1.4.4** above), which are relevant to any examination of the reasonableness of the restraint of trade. For example, the consideration for the restraint, as well as any inequality of bargaining power must be considered. Also of relevance are any post-contractual restraints, whether standard forms of contract were used, and all the surrounding circumstances of the dispute.

Particular care must be taken where previous disputes have been settled and new contracts entered into, because it is in the public interest that settlements should not be challenged at a later date (*Colchester Borough Council* v. *Smith and Others* [1992] Ch 421). George Michael attempted to raise so-called 'counter equities' to challenge this equitable defence put forward by Sony. He claimed that during the course of his relationship with Sony, the record company had behaved unfairly towards him. The court found on the evidence that George Michael's complaints were not sufficient to counter Sony's claim that the 1988 agreement had been affirmed by George Michael.

1.5 REMEDIES AND TERMINATION

1.5.1 Damages

Damages recoverable are those which arise 'fairly and naturally . . . from such breach of contract or such as may reasonably be supposed to be in the contemplation of the parties at the time of the contract' (*Hadley* v. *Baxendale* (1854) 9 Exch 341). The general principle is that, where a contract has been breached and the damage is not too remote under the rule in *Hadley* v. *Baxendale*, the innocent party should be awarded damages to place it in the same position as if the contract had been performed.

Loss of profits and wasted expenditure

A claim may be made for loss of profits or for wasted expenditure. Both heads cannot be claimed and an election must be made. In certain circumstances, a claim for wasted expenditure may be better than one for loss of profits, which, particularly in the entertainment business, may be very difficult to prove (see, further, *Anglia Television Ltd* v. *Reed* [1972] 1 QB 60, and *CCC Films* v. *Impact Quadrant Films Ltd* [1981] QB 16).

Loss of publicity

There is an exception to the normal rule that a breach of contract gives rise only to a claim for damages for the loss arising from the breach. An artist engaged to perform is promised both a salary and the opportunity to enhance his reputation (*Withers* v. *General Theatre Corporation Ltd* [1933] 2 KB 536).

Accordingly, damages for breach of contract may be awarded to reflect both loss of earnings and loss of publicity. The damages in such cases are awarded on the basis of *Hadley* v. *Baxendale*, so they must be in the contemplation of the parties at the time of the agreement. A court may consider the stage of the artist's career, as well as the prominence and popularity of the venue. The publicity right appears to extend to performers as well as to writers and directors. In addition, professional sportsmen may be able to claim for loss of publicity if they lose the chance to compete in particular competitions or on specific occasions.

Inducement to breach contract

A typical claim for inducement to breach a contract arises where a third party attempts to entice someone away from his contract, perhaps by offering better terms. Alternatively, a claim may occur where a party cancels a contract with the result that a third party is no longer required to perform a service ancillary to the first contract. For example, if a singer cancels a show and the promoter of that show no longer needs the orchestra he hired, the orchestra may be able to claim that the singer induced the promoter to terminate his contract with them so leaving them without their full income for that performance.

It is an actionable wrong to induce a party to a contract to breach the contract. There are four elements to the tort:

21

(a)   a third party knows that a contract exists;

(b)   he persuades or induces or in some way acts so as to cause a breach of contract by one party to the detriment of the other party;

(c)   a breach of contract directly attributable to that interference results; and

(d)   damage is caused to the other party.

1.5.2   Enforcement of negative covenants

A contract which contains express negative terms or covenants may be enforced by injunction. However, an injunction to enforce a negative covenant will not be granted where it indirectly requires specific performance of a contract for personal services (such as a recording contract or a footballer's contract) because, effectively, an individual then has no choice but to go back to work for the 'employer'.

A singer may be restrained from performing for an impresario if she has already agreed to sing for another and nobody else (see *Lumley* v. *Wagner* (1852) 1 De GM & G 604). The court cannot compel her to sing under the original contract, but it can stop her singing elsewhere.

Where the terms of a contract are in restraint of trade, no injunction will be granted requiring performance of the contract. However, where the contract is a reasonable one, the court will grant an injunction unless in so doing it would amount to an order to perform the positive obligations in the contract (to work, record or play), as long as the employee or artist is left with some means of earning a living. This involves a careful evaluation of whether the employee or artist can actually work elsewhere or has to remain idle. In *Warren* v. *Mendy and Another* [1989] 1 WLR 853, the court set out the appropriate principles:

(a)   a court ought not to enforce the performance of negative obligations if that will compel performance of the contract;

(b)   the longer the term of the injunction, the more readily that compulsion will be inferred;

(c)   compulsion may be inferred where an injunction is sought against a particular third party or may be sought against any third party who attempts to replace the employer; and

(d)   an injunction will be less readily granted where there are obligations of mutual trust and confidence between the parties which have dissolved.

Nonetheless, in appropriate cases, the court will grant an injunction enforcing negative terms even where the injunction lasts for a long time as happened in the George Michael case (see above). It is also important that a party seeking to rely on a negative covenant must not itself have acted in breach of contract.

1.5.3 Termination

A contract may end for a number of reasons. Its fixed term may simply expire or an option may not be renewed. If there is a breach of the terms of a contract which does not or would not ordinarily entitle a party to end the contract, specific contractual provisions may be included to entitle a party to end the agreement.

A contract may be terminated because of a frustrating event, i.e. an event which occurs without the default of either party which renders the contractual obligations incapable of performance, or only capable of performance in a manner radically different from the original obligation. In *Gamerco SA v. ICM/Fair Warning (Agency) Ltd* [1991] 1 WLR 1226, a contract for 'Guns 'n' Roses' to perform at a rock concert was frustrated because the stadium in which they were to perform was unsafe. The claimants in the case were thus able to recover advances paid to the defendants on account of ticket sales. The ill-health or death of an individual may also frustrate a contract. In *Condor v. The Barron Knights Ltd* [1966] 1 WLR 87, the claimant drummer fell ill and was dismissed from the band. The drummer sued for wrongful dismissal, but it was held that because of his ill-health it was impossible for him to perform the terms of his contract with the group and therefore the contract was frustrated.

Well-drafted contracts should contain terms dealing with both termination and frustration. Frustration of a contract may thus occur in a defined set of circumstances, lasting for a specific period of time, after which the contract ends if a given procedure is followed. These are known as 'force majeure' clauses.

CHAPTER 2

Copyright

2.1 INTRODUCTION

Copyright is the cornerstone of the entertainment business. It is a property right which may be sold and exploited. It is a right to stop others from copying works without permission. There are many categories of copyright work which include applications as diverse as architecture, dress design and computer software.

The practical overlap between copyright, trade marks, passing off and the law of confidence is substantial. The law of contract is also of particular importance when considering the terms and enforceability of any contract which deals with copyright and any other intellectual property rights.

2.2 COPYRIGHT

The Copyright, Designs and Patents Act 1988 (CDPA 1988) is the principal statute governing UK copyright law. This statute has been amended on several occasions, most recently by the Copyright and Related Rights Regulations 2003, SI 2003/2498. This legislation applies not only to UK citizens but also to many other nationals by virtue of the reciprocal protection granted in various international conventions. The Act is supplemented by case law which has developed and interpreted the statute, and the previous Copyright Acts of 1911 and 1956 are still of considerable practical relevance. References in this Part are to CDPA 1988 unless otherwise indicated.

Two international copyright conventions lay down minimum standards of protection for copyright owners between those countries which have ratified the conventions. These are the Berne Convention and the Universal Copyright Convention (UCC). Both have many members, and some countries, such as the UK, have ratified both treaties. Whilst both conventions lay down general rules for copyright protection, there are some important differences for the formalities of protection. Under the UCC, the copyright work must contain the copyright symbol © along with the name of the copyright proprietor and the year of first publication. There is no requirement for such a mark under UK law, although it is essential for wide international protection. International aspects of copyright infringement are beyond the scope of this book. The English and Welsh courts will not hear disputes where no infringement has taken place within England and Wales, although contracts may require claims to be settled in accordance with UK law and in the courts of England and Wales.

The Act is applied to authors from foreign countries by statutory instrument and generally applies only to countries which give reciprocal protection to UK works. The countries specified in the statutory instrument are all members of one or other or both of the conventions.

The UK courts will not usually hear disputes where no infringement has taken place within the UK (*Tyburn Productions* v. *Conan Doyle* [1991] Ch 75), although contracts may require claims to be settled in accordance with UK law and in the courts of England and Wales.

The International Convention for the Protection of Performers, Producers of Phonograms and Broadcasting Organisations 1961 (the Rome Convention) gives international protection to makers and producers of sound recordings as well as performers and broadcasters. The Rome Convention (in conjunction with the Convention for the Protection of Producers of Phonograms against Unauthorised Duplication of their Phonograms (the Phonogram Convention)) requires the use of the p ℗ symbol (the letter p in a circle), together with the year of first publication, and the names of the owner of the producer's rights and of the performers, on the packaging and usually on the recording itself as well. The ℗ symbol is the equivalent of the © symbol for other copyright works.

2.3 THE SUBJECT MATTER OF COPYRIGHT

There are detailed rules that often need to be considered to determine whether copyright subsists in a given work.

As a starting point, s.1(1) provides that copyright may subsist in:

(a) original literary, dramatic, musical or artistic works;
(b) sound recordings, films or broadcasts; and
(c) the typographical arrangement of published editions.

There is no registration requirement for copyright to subsist in a work. The position is different in other countries, such as the USA, where rights should be registered for full protection. There are various qualifying provisions which must be met for copyright protection under UK law. Ownership of copyright is quite distinct from ownership of the material which records that copyright work. Although a consumer buys a CD or DVD, the copyright works are embodied on the discs owned by the record company or film studio concerned.

2.4   ORIGINAL LITERARY, DRAMATIC, MUSICAL AND ARTISTIC WORKS

Literary, dramatic, musical and artistic works are the cornerstone of subsequent exploitation in any publishing, music or film business. They must be recorded in writing or otherwise (s.2(2)). Writing is defined as any form of notation or code (s.178). It does not matter if the work is recorded by or with the permission of the author (s.2(2)); copyright subsists immediately. There is no notice requirement under UK law, although international law has different requirements. A prudent author dates and names a work and puts it in safe keeping. Section 2 elaborates on the meaning of literary, dramatic and musical works, and s.4 on that of artistic works. The courts have considered the requirement for 'originality' as it relates to literary, dramatic, musical and artistic works.

2.4.1   Originality

Literary, dramatic, musical and artistic works must be 'original' to acquire protection. The question therefore arises as to what is original. In *University of London Press* v. *University Tutorial Press* [1916] 2 Ch 601, it was held that 'original' does not mean that the work must be the expression of original or inventive thought. Except in the case of works of artistic craftsmanship, there is no requirement that a work should have any artistic or literary merit in order to obtain copyright protection.

Copyright is not concerned with the originality of ideas but with the expression of thought. In *Ladbroke (Football) Ltd* v. *William Hill (Football) Ltd* [1964] 1 WLR 272 the court held that the word 'original' requires only that 'the work should not be copied but should originate from the author'. An author needs in addition, however, to show he has expended his own skill and effort in order to justify protection. This requirement should be of little concern for most categories of work as they will obviously have the necessary originality. Skill and effort may lie in the selection and the obtaining of information, or the generation of information and ideas in the first place. This means an author may use the same source of information as another to create his own work, but he must not copy from another; he must use his own skill and effort.

Copyright is not a monopoly right. Two people could, in theory, write exactly the same work quite independently of each other. If it could be established that one author had not copied or known about the other's work, then the copyright in the work which was published first in time would not be infringed by the second. Both would be original. Copyright prevents one person from benefiting from another's skill and labour or directly copying

26

another's work. This can cause problems where a copyright owner refuses to license his copyright work, as in *Independent Television Publications* v. *Time Out Ltd* [1984] FSR 64, the result of which meant that no one else could publish TV schedules as the information could only be obtained from one source – the copyright work. This situation has since been rectified by the Broadcasting Act 1990 and the decision in *Re the Magill TV Guide; Radio Telefis Eireann and Others* v. *EC Commission (Magill TV Guide intervening)* [1991] 4 CMLR 586.

A work will not qualify for protection if it is too trivial or slight to warrant protection, as in the cases concerned with names and slogans dealt with at **para.2.4.3** below.

Whilst original works require skill and effort to justify protection, that protection extends only to the language or composition or the chosen form of expression. It is often said that copyright does not protect ideas but only the expression of ideas. The television presenter Hughie Green took action against a New Zealand broadcaster who broadcast a programme which was very similar to his own programme 'Opportunity Knocks'. He failed to stop the broadcast of the programme because his programme was too imprecise to qualify as a literary or dramatic work. Essentially, all that was copied was the idea for the programme (*Green* v. *Broadcasting Corporation of New Zealand* [1989] 2 All ER 1056).

2.4.2 Literary works

Section 2(1) provides that 'literary work' means any work, other than a dramatic or musical work, which is written, spoken or sung, and includes a table or compilation, a computer program and a database.

A common example of a literary work is a book – it may be a work of fiction or a textbook. Articles in a newspaper or magazine or on websites (effectively any original text) benefit from protection as literary works. A literary work does not need to have any particular literary merit. Accordingly, copyright protection is not limited to novels, poems, articles or the lyrics of a song. Case law has established categories of information which may be protectable such as examination papers (*University of London Press* v. *University Tutorial Press* [1916] 2 Ch 601); pools coupons (*Ladbroke (Football) Ltd* v. *William Hill (Football) Ltd* [1964] 1 WLR 272); television programme listings (*Independent Television Publications* v. *Time Out Ltd* [1984] FSR 64); and letters and business letters (*Donoghue* v. *Allied Newspapers Ltd* [1938] Ch 106).

2.4.3 Names and slogans

Various categories of works have been refused protection as literary works on a *de minimis* principle. In *Exxon Corporation* v. *Exxon Insurance Consultants*

International Ltd [1982] Ch 119 the claimant invested considerable time and money in finding a suitable name for its oil business only to find the defendant insurance business using the same name. In a subsequent copyright infringement action by the claimant, the court held that the word 'Exxon', even though it was original, did not qualify as a literary work. The name was simply an artificial combination of letters that provided no information, no instruction and gave no pleasure. It was not a literary 'work'.

The titles of books or magazines slogans, the names of events and individuals will not usually qualify for protection as literary works.

In *Francis Day & Hunter Ltd* v. *Twentieth Century Fox Corporation Ltd* [1940] AC 112, it was held that the copyright in the words of a song was not infringed by the use of the song's title as the title of a film. The film did not use any other parts of the song. In this case, the use of the title was not in itself substantial enough to constitute an infringement, especially when the song title was used in a very different context.

In such circumstances, a claimant may have recourse under the law of passing off or it may be appropriate to register a trade mark. In *Ladbroke (Football) Ltd* v. *William Hill (Football) Ltd* (above), it was said that, whilst as a general rule titles will not be protected, in a proper case a title would qualify for copyright protection. Similarly, there will rarely be copyright in an advertisement slogan such as 'youthful appearances are social necessities, not luxuries' (*Sinanide* v. *La Maison Kosmeo* (1928) 129 LT 265). Advertisements may be capable of copyright protection as literary or artistic works (see *Newsgroup Newspapers Ltd* v. *Mirror Group Newspapers* [1989] FSR 487) and, where appropriate, films, sound recordings and broadcasts also qualify.

2.4.4 Storylines

It is difficult to infringe copyright in a novel simply by adopting the same story. Whilst repeating the story or information used may result in a very similar creation, provided they are sufficiently original, copyright can exist in both works with no question of infringement. Two film makers proposing to make films of the life of World War One flying ace 'The Red Baron' can do so as long as one does not copy the other's film or script.

2.4.5 Copyright protection for characters

Common ideas and themes do not merit copyright protection of their own (see *Kelly* v. *Cinema House Ltd* [1928–1935] MacG Cop Cas 291). However, the author of a story may be able to claim copyright protection for particular elements of the story such as the character and order of incidents. A character existing in myth or legend, such as Robin Hood, will not warrant protection except to the extent that the precise dialogue written by the author of the work is reproduced elsewhere. A character created for the story or work in question may merit copyright protection. The approach suggested in *International Copyright Law and Practice* (Sweet & Maxwell, looseleaf) is to consider:

(a) whether the character as originally conceived was sufficiently developed to command copyright protection; and
(b) whether the alleged infringer copied the development and not merely a broader, or more abstract, outline.

A film or work recounting the exploits of a fictional English spy could not stop another producer or writer from using a similar theme. However, a producer or writer who creates a similar character doing similar things may, in the right circumstances, infringe the character's copyright. Of course, additional means of protection may be available through artistic and dramatic copyright, passing off and trade mark protection.

For that reason, there is an increasing use of trade mark registration in this area.

2.4.6 News and sports results

Whilst information itself is not subject to copyright, the actual expressions used to report the information are protected as literary or other copyright works. Accordingly, the actual results of an event or a series of games in a league are unlikely to qualify for copyright protection to the extent that they are not directly copied from another newspaper column or broadcast by simple photocopy or recording. Results will be in the public domain and as such not capable of protection.

In *Walter v. Steinkopff* [1892] 2 Ch 489 one news service copied verbatim the material from another news service. This was found to be an infringement of copyright. Where it is simply the same information which is used but not the wording, there is no copyright infringement. Provided the actual wording is not copied from someone else's reporting, no copyright problems should arise.

In the case of news items, there will usually be other sources available. If the information is publicly available (and there is no question of breach of confidence or contract), then there is no copyright reason why the news item cannot simply be recast in another form (which will in itself attract copyright protection) and be conveyed in that new form. It is common industry practice rather than a legal obligation to give an acknowledgement of the source of a story or news item.

Some news agencies provide a constant information service to subscribers who are then permitted to use the information received for news bulletins or in articles. In this situation, the recipient pays for the right to use the information and stories for certain permitted uses. The uses to which information can be put are defined in an agreement which governs the parties' relationship and may limit the rights they would otherwise have.

In any event, whilst the above constitutes the position in relation to copyright protection, the law of database rights has become much more important in this context. See **para.2.5** below.

2.4.7 Dramatic works

Section 2(1) defines a 'dramatic work' as including a work of dance or mime. A work cannot qualify as both a literary work and a dramatic work, although a dramatic work which contains musical elements may be protected under both dramatic and musical categories. A dramatic work is one which is capable of being performed, for example, by acting or dancing.

Once again, a *de minimis* principle applies. In *Green* v. *Broadcasting Corporation of New Zealand* [1989] 2 All ER 1056 the Privy Council held that the features which constituted the 'format' of a television show, which were simply accessories used in the presentation of, and additional to, other dramatic or musical performances, did not attract protection. A dramatic work must be one which is capable of being performed. In this case the features of the show for which protection was sought did not form a cohesive whole capable of performance. The format of the gameshow 'Opportunity Knocks' consisted of the use of a 'clapometer' and various catchphrases, which the court held did not amount to a dramatic work for the purposes of copyright protection. In *Tate* v. *Fullbrook* [1908] 1 KB 821, a character's acting style and the scenic effects used in a comedy sketch were not protected as dramatic works since they were not capable of being printed and published. It appears that here, as in *Green*, there was insufficient certainty in the dramatic format for which protection was sought. The decision in *Norowzian* v. *Arks Ltd and Others (No.2)* [2000] FSR 363 confirms the general approach where a dramatic work was defined as 'a work of action, with or without words or music, which is capable of being performed before an audience'.

The licensing of TV format rights is important for the international exploitation of many familiar TV game shows and situation comedies. Effectively, a form of gentlemen's agreement is in place between major TV producers and broadcasters ensuring that formats may be exploited by producers. This exploitation takes the form of a contractual licence by the owner of the format to the third party who wishes to use it. The protection is based as much in contract, confidentiality and know-how as in copyright law. Producers and broadcasters are advised to record the format with which they are dealing in as much detail as possible in order to establish its protection as a literary or dramatic work. The names of characters particularly associated with the show may also be protected using trade mark or passing off protection, and by adopting appropriate licensing and merchandising arrangements.

The relevance of dramatic works to the sporting context may be limited. However, it will be noted that when a work of 'dance or mime' is recorded using any form of notation it will have major resemblances to the charts used by coaches to record certain set moves or plays within games, which are then 'performed'. As such, the argument might run that the chart constitutes a dramatic work qualifying for copyright protection. It seems unlikely, however, that a move or a 'play' within a game will qualify as a dramatic work. Although the point has not been tested, despite the amount of work that coaches and players put into set piece moves in sport, and however 'dramatic' the effect may be, the lack of any certainty in the outcome of such a move and its status as a minor element in the total match, and the necessary interaction with opponents who are no part of the 'performance' and are actively trying to prevent it, will doubtless militate against such protection. However, given the nature of improvised drama and certain areas of performance art, and the potential application of certain of these comments to them, the point is not clear cut in principle. The general view, however, is that the legislation simply did not have sporting elements in its contemplation when providing protection.

2.4.8 Musical works

Section 2(1) defines a 'musical work' as a work consisting of music, exclusive of any words or action intended to be sung, spoken or performed with the music. The copyright for the music of a song is distinct from the literary copyright in the lyric and, indeed, any dramatic copyright if the music is accompanied by a dance or other type of performance. Copyright in musical works is in the composition itself. Quite separate rights arise in respect of any sound recording or broadcast of a musical work. There are separate copyrights, perhaps in separate ownership, for music, lyrics and recording.

2.4.9 Artistic works

Section 4(1) defines an 'artistic work' as:

(a) a graphic work, photograph, sculpture or collage, irrespective of artistic quality;
(b) a work of architecture, being a building or a model for a building; or
(c) a work of artistic craftsmanship.

Most artistic works are protected, irrespective of artistic quality. The result of this is that as long as some effort has been expended in making the artistic work original it is protected – personal taste will not matter. Section 4(2) defines a 'graphic work' as including a painting, drawing, diagram, map, chart or plan, and any engraving, etching, lithograph, woodcut or similar work.

A similar *de minimis* principle applies with artistic works as with other categories of copyright.

There are significant areas of overlap between copyright and design right in the area of industrial design, which are beyond the scope of this book. It is important to appreciate that copyright only protects three-dimensional works if they are sculptures, architectural works or works of artistic craftsmanship. Accordingly, industrial designs and purely functional articles must usually rely upon registered or unregistered design law for protection, as most articles exploited largely in their three-dimensional form (and thus open to infringement in that form) do not so qualify. The rules on three-dimensional copying of copyright works are complex but often occur in the context of merchandising items, or in the case of architectural designs.

The effect of s.51 is to prevent copyright, in the context of functional industrial articles, from extending into three dimensions. The design document or model used to manufacture the product is not infringed if the article is made to the design or if the product set out in it is 'reverse engineered' from the product itself. Save where the design document or model is a design document or model setting out designs for an artistic work (and therefore a graphic work, photograph, sculpture, work of architecture or work of artistic craftsmanship), s.51 provides that there is no copyright infringement by such action. There is, however, a potential design right infringement.

The overlap here between copyright and design right is problematical. Often the two coexist. An industrial designer making a sketch of a new design which would qualify for design right will also have copyright in that sketch. The sketch is an artistic work in two dimensions: the item sketched, in the three dimensions intended for it, may not qualify as an artistic work as a sculpture or a work of artistic craftsmanship. Section 226 provides that, where design right and copyright coexist under the rules provided in s.51, then copyright overrides design right and that item is protected by copyright alone. For instance, in a straightforward design drawing, if a copy were made of the design drawing, that would be a copyright infringement, even though there would simultaneously be a design right in that drawing for other purposes. The only infringement proceedings the designer could take would be in respect of infringement of the copyright.

In relation to artistic works (and subject to s.51 referred to above), s.17(2) provides that copying an artistic work includes the making of a copy in three dimensions of a two-dimensional work and the making of a copy in two dimensions of a three-dimensional work. Copyright in works of architecture, for example, may be infringed in this fashion.

However, s.62 provides that in relation to buildings, models for buildings, sculptures and works of artistic craftsmanship which are permanently situated in a public place or premises open to the public, copyright is not infringed by making a graphic work (such as a sketch or photograph) of it, making a film of it or broadcasting an image of it. However, to build a copy would infringe the copyright in the architectural work comprised in the building or any model for it under s.17(2), which is specifically preserved by s.51 above.

2.4.10 Photographs

A photograph is defined as 'a recording of light or other radiation on any medium on which an image is produced or from which an image may by any means be produced, and which is not part of a film' (s.4(2)). Single frames of a film are capable of protection as part of a film.

The definition of a photograph is wide enough to cover holograms. No artistic merit is required for copyright protection. Although photographs may not be copied, the scenes they represent can be independently photographed.

2.5 DATABASES

2.5.1 Introduction

Until (and including) 27 March 1996, 'databases' (broadly, collections of information such as directories) were protected under English law by copyright as a compilation if the compilation involved sufficient skill and labour according to the usual copyright requirements.

2.5.2 The new rules

Databases created after 27 March 1996 will now only receive copyright protection if they satisfy extra rules: Copyright and Rights in Databases Regulations 1997, SI 1997/3032, implementing EC Directive 96/9/EC (the Database Directive). The 1997 Regulations came into force on 1 January 1998.

2.5.3 What is a database?

Under s.2A a database is a collection of independent works, data or other materials which are:

(a) arranged in a systematic or methodical way; and
(b) individually accessible by electronic or other means.

A database should be considered as distinct from its contents – akin to the structure of a computer program.

Section 2(1) has been amended to add 'database' to the list of potentially 'literary' works and to exclude it from categorisation as a compilation.

2.5.4   Copyright protection

Under s.2A(2) the rules for full protection of a database by copyright are:

- as with any other literary work, a database must be original; but
- a database literary work will only be original if, by reason of selection and arrangement of the database contents, the database is the author's 'own intellectual creation'. No aesthetic, qualitative or other criteria are applicable (Database Directive, Recital 16).

This apparently increases the copyright threshold for 'databases' as defined.

2.5.5   The database right

The database right (s.3A) is separate from the copyright, if any, in the database. In principle this right saves many of the arguments that have gone on in the past about the protection of databases. The right applies to databases whether held as paper records or in electronic form.

Databases are protected by copyright but in addition to copyright also enjoy the protection of a comparatively new right known as 'database right'. This again is a right which comes into being automatically by operation of law rather than as a result of registration, and many elements of the right (which arose out of the incorporation into English law of the EC Directive on the Legal Protection of Databases) are yet to be worked out. The right protects the database against extraction or reutilisation of the whole or a substantial part of it without the consent of the owner. A full consideration is beyond the scope of this work.

2.6   SOUND RECORDINGS, FILMS, BROADCASTS AND CABLE PROGRAMMES

Sound recordings and films are, in most cases, 'derivative works', i.e. they are based on other copyright works. Broadcasts likewise are often derivative works, as they either consist entirely of previously recorded films or sound recordings, or they are live transmissions of copyright works. Broadcasts and films may also be of subject matter which is unprotectable under copyright law or the performers' rights legislation, such as sporting events.

The sale of broadcast rights to sporting events is based on contract law and a simple licence to enter property and is discussed elsewhere. In the absence of a contractual restriction on tickets, there is nothing to stop spectators or photographers from taking photographs or filming events (*Sports and General Press Agency Ltd* v. *'Our Dogs' Publishing Ltd* [1916] KB 880).

Originality is not a criterion for the protection of sound recordings, films, broadcasts and cable transmissions (s.1(1)(b)).

The distinction between derivative works and the underlying rights is important. A simple example is the recording of a song. There is copyright in the song itself and copyright in the sound recording of the song. The song itself is the underlying work. The permission of the copyright owner of the underlying rights (in this example, the song) must be obtained prior to recording of the underlying work.

2.6.1   Sound recordings

A 'sound recording' is defined in s.5(1) as:

(a)   a recording of sounds, from which the sounds may be reproduced; or
(b)   a recording of the whole or of any part of a literary, dramatic or musical work, from which sounds reproducing the work or part may be produced,

and this is regardless of the media on which the recording is made or the method by which the sounds are reproduced or produced.

2.6.2   Films

A 'film' is defined as a recording on any medium from which a moving image may by any means be produced.

This clearly covers video recordings and is wide enough to embrace new technology such as CD-ROM, interactive media and the visual aspects of computer games. Its relevance therefore will be immediately apparent to sport, as the footage of sporting events recorded in any manner will be protected by copyright law as a film.

Section 5(2) provides that copyright will not subsist in a sound recording or film which is a copy of a previous sound recording or film.

2.6.3   Broadcasts

A broadcast is defined (s.6) as an electronic transmission of visual images, sounds or other information which:

(a)   is transmitted for simultaneous reception by members of the public and is capable of being lawfully received by them; or
(b)   is transmitted at a time determined solely by a person making the transmission for presentation to members of the public

but excluding Internet transmissions save where they are 'simulcasts' transmitted simultaneously with transmissions of the same material by another means, concurrent transmissions of live events, or part of a programme service offered at scheduled times determined by the provider.

This is a new definition, introduced into the law by the Copyright and Related Rights Regulations 2003, and does away with the distinctions between broadcasts and cable programme services. It also, as can be seen, brings 'webcasting' in certain circumstances within the ambit of broadcasts.

Copyright will not subsist in a broadcast which infringes the copyright in another broadcast. It should be noted that the definition of broadcast here is for the purposes of determining whether the same is a work in which copyright subsists. Broadcasting is one of the acts restricted by copyright, and the changes made by the new Regulations in that regard, are dealt with below.

2.6.4 Cable programmes

Cable programmes are no longer recognised under CDPA 1988 but the following may assist for guidance in considering the role the definition played before their recent abolition, for the purpose of construction of documents and so forth.

A cable programme was defined as any item included in a cable programme service. 'Cable programme service' was defined as a service consisting wholly or mainly in sending visual images, sounds or other information by means of a telecommunications system, by electronic means.

2.7 PUBLISHED EDITIONS

Copyright also subsists in the typographical arrangement of published editions. A published edition is defined as 'the whole or any part of one or more literary, dramatic or musical works'. These provisions are aimed at giving a publisher of a work (whether in or out of copyright) some protection in the typesetting and arrangement of the published work.

2.7.1 Conditions for protection

Copyright does not subsist in a work unless the qualifying requirements are met (s.1(2)). The relevant requirements as to qualifying conditions for all works are contained in s.152. Copyright does not subsist unless qualifications are met as to (s.152(1)):

(a) the author; or
(b) the country of first publication; or
(c) in the case of broadcasts, the country from which the broadcast was sent, are met.

A work qualifying under any such category is protected.

2.7.2 Qualifying authors

A work qualifies for copyright protection if the author was at the 'material time' a 'qualifying person' (s.154(1)). A 'qualifying person' is defined as a British citizen, a British dependent territories citizen, a British national (overseas), a British overseas citizen, a British subject or a British protected person within the meaning of the British Nationality Act 1981, or an individual domiciled or resident in the UK or another country to which the relevant provisions of the Act extend, or a body incorporated under the law of a part of the UK or of another country to which the relevant provisions of the Act extend.

2.7.3 Material time

The 'material time' in relation to a literary, dramatic, musical or artistic work is defined in s.154(4) as:

(a) in the case of an unpublished work, when the work was made or, if the making of the work extended over a period, a substantial part of that period;
(b) in the case of a published work, when the work was first published or, if the author had died before that time, immediately before his death.

The material time in relation to other descriptions of work is defined in s.154(5) as:

(a) in the case of a sound recording or film, when it was made;
(b) in the case of a broadcast, when the broadcast was made;
(c) in the case of the typographical arrangement of a published edition, when the edition was first published.

2.7.4 The place of first publication

All types of works, except broadcasts, qualify for copyright protection under s.155(1) if they were first published in:

(a) the UK; or
(b) another country to which the relevant provisions of CDPA 1988 have been extended.

It is also possible for works to qualify for protection where they were first published in a country to which an order made under s.159 relates.

To qualify under this heading a work must be published. 'Publication' is defined as the issue of copies to the public (s.175(1)). Publication is also defined to include making copies available to the public by means of an electronic retrieval system. In *Francis Day & Hunter* v. *Feldman* [1914] 2 Ch 728, the sheet music of the song 'You Made Me Love You (I Didn't

Want to Do it)' was printed in the USA. Copies were sent to the UK and six copies were placed on sale in a shop in Charing Cross. The issue was whether this was sufficient to constitute publication. The anticipated demand for the song was small, and it was held that this was a good publication in the UK because it was intended to satisfy such demand as there was. However, a publication 'which is merely colourable and not intended to satisfy the reasonable requirements of the public' does not constitute publication.

2.7.5 The place of transmission

A broadcast qualifies for copyright protection if it is made from:

(a) the UK; or
(b) another country to which the relevant provisions of CDPA 1988 have been extended.

Likewise, it is also possible for broadcasts to qualify for protection if made from a country to which an order made under CDPA 1988, s.159 relates.

2.8   DURATION OF COPYRIGHT

There are various rules for the duration of copyright which depends on the type of work under consideration. These periods have been amended by the Duration of Copyright and Rights in Performances Regulations 1995, SI 1995/3297 which came into force on 1 January 1996, and which generally increase protection to 70 years, and by some provisions of subsequent regulations.

2.8.1   Literary, dramatic or musical works

Copyright lasts for 70 years from the end of the calendar year in which the author dies.

Copyright in a work of unknown authorship expires 70 years from the end of the year in which it was written, or 70 years from the end of the year in which it was made available to the public (s.12(2)). A number of presumptions operate to counter this potentially perpetual copyright. Section 57(1) provides that copyright is not infringed if it is not possible to ascertain by reasonable enquiry the identity of the author, and it is reasonable to assume that the copyright has expired or the author died 70 years or more before the beginning of the calendar year in which the act in relation to the work was done. Section 104(4) contains a presumption that where a work is anonymous, the publisher of the work as first published is presumed to be the owner of the copyright at that time.

2.8.2 Sound recordings

Copyright lasts for 50 years from the end of the year in which a sound recording was made and, if not released immediately, the copyright will expire at the end of the period of 50 years from the end of the calendar year in which it was first published, played in public, or communicated to the public (s.12A). Unauthorised acts are ignored. Publication is defined as being the issue of copies to the public.

2.8.3 Films

The term of copyright in films is increased to 70 years from the death of the last to survive of: the principal director, the author of the film screenplay; the author of the film dialogue; and the composer of music specifically created for and used in the film (s.12B).

The meaning of 'author' is extended beyond the definition in CDPA 1988, s.9(2) to include the principal director of the film. This does not apply to films made on or before 20 June 1994.

2.8.4 Broadcasts

For broadcasts, copyright expires 50 years from the end of the calendar year in which the broadcast was made.

Section 14(5) ensures that the copyright in repeats of broadcasts expires at the same time as the copyright in the original. Accordingly, no copyright arises in respect of a repeat broadcast where such is included in a service after the expiry of copyright in the original broadcast.

2.8.5 Typographical arrangement

The copyright in the typographical arrangement of a published edition expires at the end of the period of 25 years from the end of the calendar year in which the edition was first published.

2.8.6 Revived copyright

Since the regulations extend the term of copyright for various categories of work the possibility of extended and revived copyright exists. Copyright in works which had expired before 1 July 1995 subsists as if the regulations had been in effect at the date the work was made. This will affect the works of authors who died between 1925 and 1945. The provisions for ownership of the extended or revived copyright are as follows:

- in relation to existing works, the person who is the owner at 1 November 1995 owns the extended copyright;

- for a revived work:

    - where copyright was subject to an exclusive licence immediately before expiry of copyright, ownership vests in that licensee; and
    - in any other case, the person who was the owner immediately before expiry shall be first owner of the revived copyright;

- in relation to an existing work where the owner at 1 November 1995 is the owner by virtue of an assignment of the copyright and the assignment terminates earlier than the date on which the subsisting copyright expires, the person to whom copyright would have reverted thereafter shall, on 1 November 1995, be the first owner of copyright in that work, even though the date of termination of the assignment falls after 1 November 1995.

An agreement relating to:

(a) extended copyright entered into before 1 November 1995; or
(b) revived copyright prior to expiry of copyright,

makes provision for vesting of ownership of the extended or revived copyright upon the coming into existence of that right. Ownership of the copyright vests in accordance with that agreement.

Copyright is not infringed where:

- an act is done in relation to a copyright work pursuant to an agreement entered into before 1 January 1995;
- copies of a work are issued to the public where the copy was made before 1 July 1995 and copyright did not subsist at that time; or
- a restricted act is performed in pursuance of an arrangement made at a time when the name and address of a person entitled to authorise the act could not be ascertained by reasonable enquiry.

2.9   EXPLOITATION OF COPYRIGHT

2.9.1   Authorship

Authorship and ownership are distinct concepts in copyright. The author of a work is the person who creates it (s.9). The author of a work is the first owner of any copyright in it subject to the provisions relating to creation of copyright works in the course of employment dealt with below. The author of certain works (as distinct from the owner) is entitled to the moral rights in the work, the benefits of which remain with the author despite the fact that someone else may initially or subsequently own the work. Correctly identifying the author of a work and the first owner are essential if a work is to be successfully exploited.

Literary, dramatic, musical and artistic works

The author of a work is the person who creates it (s.9). Accordingly, it should usually be obvious who is the author of a given work. For example, the author of a novel is the person who wrote it, and the author of a piece of music is the person who composed it. For the purposes of copyright, the author of a photograph is the photographer.

The position of 'ghost writers' will usually be governed by a contract between the person who provides the material for the work and the actual writer of the work. In the absence of any such agreement, the position is that the author of the work is the person that fixes it and gives it form. However, where a work is simply dictated to a secretary or shorthand writer, the author is the person dictating the work and not the person transcribing it (see *Donoghue* v. *Allied Newspapers Ltd* [1938] Ch 106).

Sound recordings and films

The author of a sound recording is the producer (s.9(2)(aa)). The authors of a film are the producer and the principal director (s.9(2)(ab)). Accordingly, a film is treated as a work of joint authorship unless the producer and the principal director are the same person. The producer is defined as the person who makes the arrangements necessary for the creation of the work (s.178).

Broadcasts

The person making a broadcast, invariably a company, is the author of the broadcast. In the case of a broadcast which is received and re-transmitted from another broadcast, the person who made the first broadcast is the author. The person making a broadcast is the person who transmits it (s.6(2)) if he has responsibility to any extent for its content and any person who makes the arrangements necessary for the transmission of the programme. Broadcasts will often involve more than one party and, strictly speaking, there may be two makers of a broadcast for the purposes of the legislation. In such a case, the work will be treated as a work of joint authorship (see s.10(2)).

Published editions

In the context of copyright in the typographical arrangement of a published edition of whole or part of a work, the publisher is the author (s.9(2)(d)).

Joint authorship

Many works will be the result of more than one person's endeavours. A work of 'joint authorship' is defined as a work produced by the collaboration of two or more authors in which the contribution of each author is not distinct from that of the other author or authors.

The duration of the copyright in a work of joint authorship expires at the end of the period of 70 years from the end of the calendar year in which the last author dies.

In *Prior* v. *Lansdowne Press Ltd* [1977] RPC 511, three people claimed to be joint authors of a work, two of whom actually contributed to the writing and the other acted as a compiler of the work. Whilst the three were free to arrange ownership of the work as they wished, the actual writers were the authors for copyright purposes. Copyright distinguishes between joint authorship and joint ownership. As far as ownership is concerned, the parties can reach any agreement they like. It is a commercial right, to be dealt with commercially. Authorship is inalienable. The question of authorship relates to the contribution to the work. In joint authorship, each individual author must be an 'author' for the purposes of s.9(1). Each author must have been responsible to some degree for reducing the work to a material form.

Quite how ownership of the copyright is divided between joint authors will vary. Joint authors may be either tenants in common or joint tenants. The law usually presumes they are tenants in common. It is clear, however, from s.172 that if copyright in a work is owned by more than one person jointly then the agreement of all the owners is required for any dealing with the work.

In *Mail Newspapers plc* v. *Express Newspapers plc* [1987] FSR 90, a husband agreed that the claimants could publish wedding photographs, but the defendants published them instead. The claimants claimed an infringement of their exclusive rights. The defendants argued that the husband and the wife were joint owners of the copyright and, as joint owners, they both had to consent to any dealings with the photographs. The court held that both the owners had to consent to the exploitation of the work. Despite this, the defendants were prohibited from publishing on the grounds of breach of confidence.

2.9.2 Ownership of copyright

Author as first owner

The author of a work is the first owner of the copyright in the work subject to what appears hereafter. It is that first owner of the work who can deal with the copyright in the work. Authors frequently sign contracts granting rights to individuals and companies. These agreements may entitle others to some or all of the rights in a work.

Employees

There is an exception to this general rule. Section 11(2) provides that where a literary, dramatic, musical or artistic work, or a film, is made by an employee in the course of his employment, the employer is the first owner of any copyright in the work, subject to any agreement to the contrary. It is not enough that a literary, dramatic, musical or artistic work or film is made by an employee; it must also be made in the course of employment. If a work is made in the course of employment, then the employer will be the first owner of any copyright in the work, subject to an agreement to the contrary.

In industries which employ creative people such as the advertising, music, and film and TV industries, it is in the interests of the employer (and indeed the employee) to set out at the beginning of their relationship the arrangements which are to exist between them regarding works produced. Express assignments or licences of copyright are usually taken. Particular problems can arise where employees devote time to creating works in what they may well regard as being their 'spare time'. Cases turn on their own facts, and particular regard will be had to such matters as working hours, use of the employer's facilities, and whether the contract is viewed as a contract of service or a contract for services.

In *Byrne* v. *Statist Co.* [1914] 1 KB 622, an employee was on the regular staff of a newspaper but made a translation of a work in his spare time and for a separate fee. He was held to own the copyright in the translation because translations were not part of his normal duties. Where there is any doubt as to whether the employer owns the copyright, either an express assignment of rights should be taken or, alternatively, the employee should be joined as a claimant in any proceedings.

If an employee chooses outside his normal office hours to develop competing works, for example works of a similar nature to those that he would normally be employed to produce, then there may be a breach of contract or a breach of a fiduciary duty which prevents the employee from asserting that the work was not created in the course of employment (see *Missing Link Software* v. *Magee* [1989] FSR 361). Copyright would then vest in the employer. Any attempt by the employee to deal with the work would amount to conversion or theft in addition to a possible copyright infringement.

The first question to arise frequently is to determine whether the person in question was in fact an employee. A distinction is drawn between contracts for services (independent of the employer) and contracts of service (employees). The practical significance of the distinction in the creative industries is that an employer may find that rights in a piece of music or advertising copy or other copyright work are not owned by it and only a limited licence to use the work exists. Whilst there are potential theoretical difficulties with the distinction between a contract for services and a contract of service, the best advice is to make specific contractual arrangements for copyright ownership where any business is employing 'creative' staff in any capacity. In most cases, it should be made clear that copyright is owned by the employer whatever type of engagement contract exists. Failure to make proper provision can result in enormous problems and even litigation.

Likewise, whether or not a person who is an employee then acts 'in the course of his employment' is a question of fact. In most instances, it should be obvious whether or not the work is carried out in the course of employment by considering, for instance, what the employee is employed to do and whether the work produced falls within the employee's job description. This again is all the more reason for ownership of copyright to be dealt with expressly in the contract of employment, rather than simply to place reliance upon the implication under s.11(2).

Commissioned works

Where a work is commissioned from an independent third party, ownership of copyright should be dealt with at the time the work is commissioned. In the absence of an employer/employee relationship, s.11(2) does not apply. Express contractual provision should therefore be made dealing with the copyright, and CDPA 1988 makes no express provision for commissioned works. A written agreement evidencing any dealing with copyright is preferable, although not always essential.

A court may decide that owing to the circumstances of the commission and the true construction of the commissioning agreement or the relationship out of which the commission arises the substantive position between the parties is that the commissioning party has a beneficial interest, as in *Warner v. Gestetner Ltd* [1988] EIPRD 89, where the court held that there had been a beneficial assignment of copyright in a number of drawings.

Alternatively, there may, on the basis again of the true construction of the position, be an implied licence of copyright. A licence will not be implied between parties simply because it is reasonable to do so; it must be the intention of the parties. In one case, an architect was commissioned to draw building plans for the purpose of obtaining planning permission for some houses. The site was subsequently sold with the benefit of planning permission, and the plans physically transferred to the purchaser. The original commissioner and the purchaser both were considered to have an implied licence to use the plans for the purpose of building the houses. The court restricted the implied licence to use the plans for building houses on the site in question. If the purchasers had attempted to use the plans to build houses to those specifications on another site, they would have been prevented from so doing (see *Blair v. Osborne & Tompkins and Another* [1971] 2 WLR 502). A licence of copyright should be obtained in writing on terms agreed between the parties.

In *Ray* v. *Classic FM plc* [1998] FSR 622, the claimant developed a copyright database for the defendants. The defendants licensed the work overseas, and the claimant claimed that the defendants had no right to do so. The consultancy agreement between the parties contained no express terms as to ownership of the work. The claimant successfully claimed the defendants' rights were limited to a licence of copyright for the UK.

The advice given at the start of this discussion can only be repeated: any work commissioned should be covered by an agreement fully dealing with the copyright in the work.

Ownership of copyright and live events

As can be seen from the foregoing provisions, it is extremely unlikely that a sports 'rights owner' or events organiser will be the author and accordingly the first owner of copyright in a work. It is more likely that this will be the broadcaster or production company involved in a broadcast, the photographer at an event, the designer of a product or the writer of the relevant text. As has already been seen, however, authorship may subsequently be quite distinct from ownership of copyright in a work. It is important therefore that a sports rights owner or event organiser at the very least considers whether or not it should own the copyright in works which are created with its permission, such as films and broadcasts.

2.9.3 Exploitation

The methods of exploitation of copyright by owners vary widely. Copyright is, however, a form of personal property and may be dealt with by assignment, by licensing, by testamentary disposition or by operation of law (s.90).

The principal means of commercial exploitation of copyright are assignment or licence, and the terms of the agreements by which these deals are effected should always be recorded in writing.

The first and subsequent owners of copyright works have a number of options as to the manner of exploitation of the copyrights. For example, they may decide:

- to keep their rights and not to exploit them in any way; or
- to exploit the copyright material themselves (although this inevitably involves a third party's co-operation at some stage); or
- to assign rights to a third party; or
- to license third parties to do otherwise prohibited acts in relation to the work.

Copyright may be divided in a number of ways. The method of exploitation is frequently more dependent on the medium and the market than on the choice of the individual owner. The division of rights is extremely important in considering the most effective way of exploiting particular works. An author may be advised to appoint a UK publisher to exploit his novel within the UK, but that publisher may not be the best placed to exploit the novel in the US. Likewise, the UK publisher may not be the best placed to exploit the film rights or the dramatic rights in the novel. As technological advances take place, the author may have to decide who should exploit the CD-ROM and other electronic rights. Great care must be taken in defining the rights, territory and duration of the agreement.

Assignments and licences

An assignment is usually a sale of rights, whereas a licence is a contractual permission to use rights subject to ongoing obligations. An assignment may also be by way of gift or testamentary disposition. An assignment of copyright is not effective unless it is in writing and signed by, or on behalf of, the assignor (s.90(2)).

Assignments and licences may be limited in a number of ways. The dealing may be limited to:

- one or more, but not all, of the things which the owner has the exclusive right to do; and/or
- part, but not the whole, of the period of copyright protection (s.90).

An assignment or licence may thus be absolute or partial.

The assignor may also attempt to control where the rights will be enjoyed by the assignee, for example, only in the UK and not in Canada or the US. However, such territorial divisions are not contemplated by CDPA 1988. Although they are not specifically contemplated in terms of licensing either, one of the things the licensor may permit is the right to use in a given territory only, and so forth, thus in that way effectively creating the territorial division of rights. Accordingly, an assignment of copyright that limits exploitation on a territory by territory basis may be construed as a licence by the court.

An assignment may be of future as well as existing copyright (s.91), and in such a case, clarity is all-important.

Form of assignment

Although CDPA 1988, s.90(2) requires an assignment to be in writing to transfer the legal and beneficial title, the content of the document which forms the assignment is not specified by the statute. An assignment may be in very simple words or it may be a more complicated document containing a number of obligations. There are various problems that can arise with both assignments and licences, even though the s.90 requirements may have been followed.

The question of whether copyright has been assigned, and what form of words will suffice to do this, is sometimes problematic. A receipt stating that a sum of money was received 'inclusive of all copyrights' was deemed sufficient to assign the copyright in a number of card designs (see *Savory Ltd* v. *The World of Golf Ltd* [1914] 2 Ch 566).

It is usual commercial practice to include a more comprehensive assignment which also deals with various obligations, warranties and indemnities, together with the extent and duration of the rights granted and the consideration.

An assignment from the author of certain categories of work in which 'moral rights' arise should include consideration and treatment of such moral rights.

An effective assignment removes the copyright or the part of the copyright assigned from the control of the assignor. The assignor can, if necessary, be restrained from subsequently doing anything which infringes the rights of the assignee. If the rights to exploit given footage in a given way are assigned by an author, that author cannot then purport to grant the same rights to someone else without being in breach of contract and the subsequent exploitation being an infringement of the copyright which now belongs to the assignee.

Licences

A licence of copyright is a contractual right or permission from the owner of the copyright to do certain acts. A licence does not pass title in the copyright. It is a contractual right which generally ends if the contract expires or terminates. Likewise, any sub-licences also expire or 'terminate' (see *Python (Monty) Pictures Ltd* v. *Paragon Entertainment Corporation and Another* [1998] EMLR 640). There are various types of licence which can be granted. A licence may be exclusive or non-exclusive. An exclusive licence is one which authorises the licensee, to the exclusion of all other persons, including the licensor, to exercise a right that would otherwise be exercisable by the licensor. Such a licence must be in writing. The holder of a valid exclusive licence has rights which in many ways make it appear as if the licence were an assignment. Such an exclusive licence may, therefore, be construed as an assignment if it is indistinguishable in substance from an assignment. However, where an exclusive licence is used in connection with a territorial division of rights, it will stand as a valid licence. Likewise, a grant which is terminable upon failure to fulfil ongoing obligations is a licence not an assignment notwithstanding the exclusivity of the rights enjoyed by the licensee during its existence.

A bare licence (not being an exclusive licence) requires no formalities – it need not be in writing – yet it will bind the copyright owner who granted it and any assignees deriving title from that owner except a bona fide purchaser for valuable consideration without actual or constructive notice. A licence can even be implied from circumstances: for example, where an advertising agency designs a company logo, the company has an implied licence to use the logo. A licensee cannot usually restrict any other exploitation of the work by the licence owner unless the licence is an exclusive licence. A licensee has no direct right to assert the copyright against third parties; it must act through the licensor.

A licence may be distinguished from an assignment in a number of ways:

1. Ownership of rights is not transferred: an assignment gives a property right, a licence a contractual right.
2. An assignee has the right to sue to protect his copyright. A licensee does not usually have this right.
3. After assignment, the owner will usually have no more rights in the work.
4. A licence may be exclusive or non-exclusive.
5. Because a licence is a contractual right it is conditional on the performance of obligations by the licensee which, if breached, will lead to the termination of the contract.
6. On a licensee's insolvency, rights usually revert to the owner, whereas an assignee retains rights. In such a case the assignor can only sue to recover money owed on a debt and may rank as an unsecured creditor. The copyright remains with the assignee.
7. Assignments must be in writing (although an agreement to assign may be oral).
8. An assignee has the right to alter the work by way of correction and additions. A licensee does not automatically have such a right.

There are occasions when the distinction is particularly important. A non-exclusive licensee who wishes to sue is frequently precluded from doing so as he has no title; however, an exclusive licensee does have the right to sue, and there can be express grant even to a non-exclusive licensee of the rights to sue in relation to the acts it is licensed to perform.

Both assignments and licences may provide for the payment of a royalty to the copyright owner. For instance, in publishing it is standard practice for an assignment to be accompanied by an ongoing obligation on the part of the assignee to pay royalties. The payment of a royalty may however in the facts of a given case point to the document being a licence. This point has been considered in a number of cases. A presumption against there being an assignment and in favour of there being a licence between the parties may arise wherever there are continuing obligations between the parties. The case of *Jonathan Cape* v. *Consolidated Press* [1954] 1 WLR 1313 concerned the grant to a publisher of the exclusive right to publish a work in volume form. This was held to constitute an assignment. Conversely, in *Re Jude's Musical Compositions* [1907] 1 Ch 651, an agreement to publish in 'volume form', subject to payment of a royalty, constituted a licence. An agreement to publish a work subject to the performance of conditions is likely therefore to constitute a licence but all such matters will turn upon interpretation of all of the facts.

When drafting the documents, therefore, the extent of the rights granted, the exclusivity of the rights and the obligations imposed by the copyright owner are important to clarify the arrangement. An express provision stating that the agreement is 'by way of assignment/licence' only assists in the construction of the document. Modern precedents usually deal clearly with such matters.

There are two further problems which may arise where there are continuing obligations (such as royalty payments) contained in an agreement. If copyright is assigned in return for a royalty, the assignee should be prohibited from assigning the copyright to a third party or from granting rights, such as those frequently given by way of security, which may eventuate in an assignment. As there is no privity of contract between the original copyright owner and the third party, the royalty terms cannot be enforced against the third party, only against the original assignee. A restriction on assignment may be included or, alternatively, an express requirement may be made in the original agreement that, on any subsequent assignment to a third party, the assignee will enter into a direct written covenant with the original owner.

Barker v. *Stickney* [1919] 1 KB 121 considered the rights of an unpaid author whose copyrights had been assigned to a third party. The court concluded that the author had no right of action for royalties against a third party assignee. Appropriate contractual terms (as suggested above) must be included which limit such assignments. The best protection is to ensure that the agreement is not assignable and that the agreement is conditional on the payment of royalties.

In conclusion, therefore, because of the difficulties which have arisen in distinguishing between assignments on the one hand and licences on the other, great care should be taken in drafting the necessary contracts between the parties. Where any continuing obligations are envisaged, appropriate restrictions such as limitations on the right to assign the benefit of the contract and/or the rights transferred under it and termination provisions should be included in the contract. This ensures that, even where property has been transferred, there may still be a reassignment of rights in certain circumstances. This has become the norm for both assignments and licences.

Drafting the documents

Although the form of an assignment or a licence is prescribed, its contents are not. The most important consideration for an assignor or licensor is to transfer that which is intended and no more. This means that care must be taken with the rights definition in the agreement. A useful rule is for the assignor to give away as little in terms of rights as can accord with the parties' intentions and give the contract business efficacy. Except in the case of an outright assignment, the owner may retain control over other rights and exploit them as it sees fit.

All parties to an agreement will be concerned about precisely what rights are granted, in what territories, and for how long. A licensee must also ensure that the person granting rights has the ability to do so. Good title must be established, and account may have to be taken of the contractual matters discussed elsewhere in this book, such as duress and restraint of trade.

Most agreements deal with the exact rights granted, the territory and duration of the agreement. There should also be terms dealing with the exclusivity of the agreement. Basic warranties as to ownership and the 'basic' copyright warranties should be considered. Terms for payment should be included unless the dealing is by way of gift. Various boilerplate and termination provisions should always be included.

BASIC WARRANTIES

There are three basic warranties that should be included in a licence or assignment of copyright. These are that:

(a) the work is written by a qualifying person;
(b) it is original; and
(c) it is not defamatory or otherwise in breach of any third party rights (including infringement of the intellectual property rights of any other person).

Additionally, assignments and licences should be made with full or limited title guarantee (Law of Property (Miscellaneous Provisions) Act 1994). Full title guarantee means that:

(a) the person making the disposition has the right to dispose of it as he purports to and will at his own cost do all he reasonably can to give the person to whom he disposes of the property the title he purports to give;
(b) that the disposition is made of the property free from all charges and encumbrances and from any other rights exercisable by third parties other than charges, encumbrances or rights which the person disposing of the property did not and could not reasonably be expected to know about.

A disposition with limited title guarantee means:

(a) the person making the disposition has the right to dispose of it as he purports to and will at his own cost do all he reasonably can to give the person to whom he disposes of the property the title he purports to give;
(b) that the person making the disposition has not since the last disposition for value charged or encumbered the property with any charge or encum-

50

brance which subsists at the time the disposition is made or granted third party rights which are so subsisting or permitted such encumbrance and that he is not aware that anyone else has done so since the last disposition for value.

It is common for specific warranties to title to be included in any event whether a specific title guarantee is mentioned or not.

Construction of contracts: specific issues

As technology has developed, so have the ways in which copyright is exploited. This has had an important effect on the assignment and licensing of rights. Early cases involved the granting of film rights in novels and plays where, at the time of drafting the licence or assignment, innovations such as sound had not been envisaged. A more recent dispute involved the exploitation of a film by means of video where such rights did not exist at the time of the original assignment of performers' rights (see *Bourne* v. *Walt Disney Co.* (1995) US App Lexis).

The starting point in the construction of any contract is the document itself (see *Investors Compensation Scheme Ltd* v. *West Bromwich Building Society; Investors Compensation Scheme Ltd* v. *Hopkin & Sons (A Firm) and Another* [1998] 1 WLR 896). If the words used in the contract are clear and precise, then in the absence of fraud, mistake or other contractually significant circumstance, the contract stands. Despite what appears to be a perfectly clear document, disputes may arise where a novel form of exploitation is developed which did not exist at the time of the agreement. A current example is the development of interactive online and mobile technology products and platforms which incorporate or make use of various copyright works. It is often unclear whether an original assignment or licence was intended to include the right to exploit copyright in this way. This is a matter of interpretation.

The interpretation centres upon the form of words used by the parties in their agreement. If the words are wide enough to cover the new rights (for instance, the sending of images by way of mobile telephony) and those rights were at the least in the contemplation of the parties at the time of the agreement, then clearly those rights pass. A party may also seek to open up the document to wider consideration. Whilst a court looks to the document as a whole for its meaning, it is possible to use extrinsic evidence as an aid to construction of the contract by looking at what was properly in the consideration of the parties at the time of the agreement. In *Hospital for Sick Children (Board of Govenors)* v. *Walt Disney Productions Inc* [1966] 1 WLR 1055, the court had to consider the grant in 1919 by Sir James Barrie of a licence in all his literary and dramatic works to the defendants for the duration of the copyright term 'in cinematograph or moving picture films'. The court held that the proper construction of these words rested upon the view of the parties at the time of the agreement. The wording of the document itself provided no assistance (the words used being so wide), so the court looked at matters in the contemplation of the parties at the time of the agreement. Since silent films were the only means of commercial exploitation in the cinema at the time of the licence, a narrow view was taken and the talking rights were excluded from the licence.

Similar disputes may arise over licences granted to put films in video formats or standards as new formats are constantly being developed. Widely drawn definitions clauses in agreements cause problems for licensors, who now give more careful thought to the definitions in licences.

It appears construction of any contract will be dominated by two main principles:

1. The contract will be interpreted by what was in the minds of the parties at the time it was drafted, as evidenced by the words used in the agreement and facts that were then relevant: the majority view in *Hospital for Sick Children* (above).

2. The contract must also be looked at in the light of circumstances and conditions surrounding the agreement, as long as the parties have knowledge of the relevant circumstances and conditions. This may involve looking at the state of the art at the time of the agreement (see *JC Williamson Ltd* v. *Metro-Goldwyn-Mayer Theatres Ltd* [1927] 56 CLR 567).

2.10   COPYRIGHT INFRINGEMENT

2.10.1   Restricted acts

Copyright is infringed if a person does an act within the exclusive rights (set out in s.16) without the permission of the copyright owner. There are two categories of civil copyright infringement, known as primary and secondary infringements. There are also various criminal offences which can arise where rights are infringed.

The categories of primary infringement relate to infringement of the exclusive right to perform acts which only the owner of copyright can do or authorise, known as the acts restricted by copyright. These rights are dealt with in ss.16–21. Acts of secondary infringement involve dealing with or making commercial use of infringing copies of a copyright work. Secondary infringement is dealt with in ss.22–27.

There are various and complex provisions in ss.28–76 which provide that certain acts in certain circumstances, which might otherwise constitute infringement of the copyright, will not constitute infringement and which thus provide defences to any claim that infringement has taken place.

Frequently, as will be seen, these 'defences' relate closely to the nature of the works in relation to which they apply, and the nature of the user entitled to take advantage of them.

2.10.2   Exclusive rights

The exclusive rights set out in CDPA 1988, s.16 are the basis of protection for copyright owners. They are:

- the right to copy the work (s.17);
- the right to issue copies to the public (s.18);
- the right to rent or lend the work to the public (s.18A);
- the right to perform, show or play the work in public (s.19);
- the right to communicate the work to the public (s.20); and
- the right to make adaptations of the work or do any of the above in relation to an adaptation (s.21).

Copyright will be infringed where any of these acts are done without the consent of the copyright owner (s.16(2)). An act restricted by copyright may be done in relation to the work as a whole or any substantial part of it (s.16(2)). This means that infringement of copyright may take place not only where the whole of a work has been copied, but also where something less than the whole but nonetheless 'substantial' has been copied. The question of what amounts to a 'substantial part' of a copyright work is discussed above.

Section 16(4) provides that the restricted acts are subject to permitted acts (s.28 onwards) and the copyright licensing provisions of CDPA 1988 (s.116 onwards). The latter provisions are beyond the scope of this work.

Matters may be complicated where, in an action for copyright infringement, it is alleged that the defendant has copied a work or a substantial part of it but the defendant denies that in fact copying has taken place. Where an allegation of infringement is disputed, the courts have then to decide the matter on the basis of two elements that must be present:

1. There must be sufficient objective similarity between the infringing work and the copyright work, or a substantial part of it, for the former to be properly described, not necessarily as identical with, but as a reproduction or adaptation of the latter.
2. The copyright work must be the source from which the infringing work is derived (per Diplock LJ in *Francis Day & Hunter Ltd* v. *Bron* [1963] Ch 587). This case and the test adopted by Lord Diplock made the possibility of subconscious copying a possibility. If, in substance, there is a similarity between the copyright work and the infringing work, it must be proved that the maker of the infringing work had access to the copyright work, in which case a presumption will be raised that copying had taken

place. Such a presumption may of course be rebutted. If one author arrives by independent work at the same result as another author, there will be no infringement.

2.10.3 Substantial part

The copyright in a work is infringed where someone other than the copyright owner does any of the restricted acts in relation to the whole or a substantial part of a work. Whilst it is usually obvious what constitutes the whole of a work, the question of what constitutes a substantial part of a work can be problematic. The approach the court has adopted is that the question of what constitutes a 'substantial part' is a qualitative rather than a quantitative question. *Hawkes* v. *Paramount* [1934] Ch 592 concerned a newsreel that contained 20 seconds of a four-minute piece of music. However, the inclusion of such a piece of background music in a piece of film would now be permitted as incidental inclusion (s.21). The newsreel was held to infringe the copyright in the music. In *Ladbroke (Football) Ltd* v. *William Hill (Football) Ltd* [1964] 1 WLR 272 Lord Pearce said that the question as to what is substantial must be decided by quality rather than quantity. Additionally, the parts of a work copied will not amount to a substantial part if the parts copied were not in themselves original. The claimant in *Warwick Film Productions Ltd* v. *Eisinger and Others* [1969] 1 Ch 508 owned the copyright in a book which was essentially a compilation consisting of various court transcripts, an introduction and various appendices written by the claimant. Because of the amount of skill and effort the claimant had expended on the work, it was held that copyright subsisted in the collocation. However, the defendant copied parts of the work which had been taken from court transcripts. Accordingly, the court held that there was no substantial qualitative taking, since the claimant had merely copied those parts himself.

In *Ravenscroft* v. *Herbert and New English Library Ltd* [1980] RPC 192, the defendant wrote a novel entitled *The Spear*. A prologue to each of the chapters in the novel was based on the story of an actual spearhead, as told in the claimant's non-fiction work *The Spear of Destiny*. The defendant author admitted using these excerpts, but denied taking a substantial part of the work. It was held that the defendant had used more than common source material and, as such, had infringed copyright. Although it is open to another author to research common sources to develop a work, where the efforts of another are used, including their arrangements, or their efforts are simply adopted with colourable variations, this amounts to a breach of copyright.

In *EMI Music* v. *Evangelous Papathanasiou* [1987] 8 EIPR 244, the court considered the similarities between the defendant's piece 'Chariots of Fire', and the claimant's piece 'City of Violets'. There was not sufficient objective similarity between the works for infringement. The court reached this decision after hearing expert evidence from musicologists. The experts convinced the court that the similarities in the pieces were commonplace in music and not copied. The quality of evidence adduced in copyright litigation, together with the court's assessment of the similarity, frequently holds sway in such cases.

In the case of typographical works (s.1(1)(c)), the House of Lords has recently had to consider what amounts to the whole or a substantial part of a typographical arrangement (*Newspaper Licensing Agency Ltd* v. *Marks & Spencer plc* [2001] UKHL 38, [2001] 2 WLR 290). In this case, it held that the published edition was the entire newspaper in question. Accordingly, the typographical arrangement was the overall design of the newspaper. This would amount to a whole page of a newspaper at the very least. Copying individual articles was not therefore sufficient to constitute copying of a substantial part of the typographical arrangement. This case is of limited application, since Newspaper Licensing Agency Ltd only sued in respect of the infringement of the typographical arrangement and not the underlying copyright in the literary work.

2.10.4   Parodies

Parodies are a category of work which clearly owes something to the original work that is being parodied. Copyright works are often the subject of comical or satirical treatment. In essence, a parody of a copyright work is treated no differently from any other alleged infringement. The question is whether there has been a 'substantial taking' from the claimant's work. Parodies rely for some of their effect upon the association with the original work and, because of this, they are very susceptible to attack as infringing works. A parody will not usually incorporate the whole of a work, but rather an element of it which may be sufficient to identify the original and infringe the exclusive rights of the copyright owner. An attempt at parody will not of itself remove the work far enough away from the original.

Whether the parody is of a song, musical or dramatic work, the test will be the same. In *Williamson Music Ltd* v. *The Pearson Partnership Ltd* [1987] FSR 97, the Rogers and Hammerstein song 'There is Nothin' Like a Dame' had been parodied in an advertisement. In this case, there was a substantial taking of the music but not the lyrics for copyright purposes.

In *Schweppes Ltd and Others* v. *Wellingtons Ltd* [1984] FSR 210, the claimants claimed infringement of their tonic label. The defendants had used the phrase 'Schlurpps' instead of the claimants' 'Schweppes'. The defendants argued that their label was a joke in the nature of a caricature; however, it was held that the fact of a parody constituted no defence in an action for infringement of copyright.

2.10.5 Sampling

Sampling involves taking the whole or part of a sound recording. It may be a snatch of melody or a drum beat or sound. If the sample taken is of the whole or a substantial part of the copyright work, it may infringe that copyright, even though it has its own copyright protection. Samplers must take care not to use identifiable pieces of copyright material. Any sound recording which uses identifiable elements of other musical works or sound recordings may infringe copyright. It is usual for samplers to obtain a licence to use extracts from other copyright works.

The following guidelines may be useful in determining whether infringement has taken place.

1. Even short extracts of works may, when assessed qualitatively, be vital parts of a work and thus substantial. Even though there may be only a fleeting resemblance between two works, such as a melody line, or the selective use of scenes, incidents and language from another work, this does not preclude infringement of copyright.
2. The courts adopt a *de minimis* approach to some uses for copyright purposes, such as the use of a name or title, and will not hold that infringement of copyright has taken place. Alternative remedies such as passing off, defamation or trade mark infringement may be pursued.
3. The fact that the work in question is short does not preclude a conclusion of copying or substantial taking.
4. Some very simple ideas may only be represented in a limited number of ways – such as a photo of a view or a commonplace instruction. In such cases, a court will be reluctant to hold that infringement has taken place on the grounds that simultaneous creation of essentially the same work is more likely to have been the source of the similarity than copying.
5. A similar theme or plot for a literary work may be unprotectable as an idea – although care must be taken to avoid copying any text or dialogue. For infringement to be avoided the similarities must be of the unprotectable elements of the work: broadly speaking, the idea rather than the expression of the work.

In spite of all this, a good general guideline is that set out in *University of London Press* v. *University Tutorial Press* [1916] 2 Ch 601 'what is worth copying is worth protecting'.

2.10.6 Copying

Literary, dramatic, musical or artistic works

CDPA 1988, s.17(2) provides that copying in relation to any literary, dramatic, musical or artistic work means reproducing the work in any material form. This includes storing the work in any medium by electronic means.

At its simplest, copying will be very easy to prove: for example, where a compact disc is recorded on to a cassette, or the pages of a book are copied using a photocopier. In the case of artistic works, copying also occurs if a two-dimensional copy is made of a three-dimensional work, or a three-dimensional copy of a two-dimensional work.

In *Sony Music* v. *EasyInternet Café Ltd* (2002) unreported, 28 January, Sony was successful in its summary judgment application for infringement under ss.17 and 18. It was found that where material was downloaded from the Internet on to a central server by customers and then burnt on to CDs by EasyInternet for a fee of £2.50, this amounted to copyright infringement.

Films and broadcasts

In addition to the copying of the work as a whole or any substantial part of it, s.17(4) establishes that copyright in a film or broadcast is infringed if a photograph of the whole or any substantial part of any image forming part of the film or broadcast is made.

Typographical arrangements

Section 17(5) states that the copying of a typographical arrangement of a published edition means making a facsimile copy of it.

2.10.7 Issuing copies to the public

In the case of this restricted act, the issuing to the public of copies of a work means the act of putting into circulation copies not previously put into circulation in the EEA with the consent of the copyright owner. This restricted act does not apply to the subsequent distribution, sale, hiring or loaning of copies nor to any subsequent importation of such copies into the UK.

2.10.8 Rental or lending of copies to the public

The rental or lending of works to the public is a restricted act which applies to literary, dramatic, musical and artistic works as well as films and sound recordings. 'Rental' means making a copy available for use on terms that it will be returned for direct or indirect commercial advantage. This covers video rental shops. 'Lending' means making a copy of the work available through an establishment accessible to the public for use on terms that it will be returned but otherwise than for direct or indirect commercial advantage. This covers public libraries.

2.10.9 Rental rights

There are other provisions affecting authors' rental rights. An agreement for film production between an author and film producer is presumed to transfer any rental right the author has to the film producer. This is the case unless the agreement provides otherwise. The rental right may arise because the author's work is included in the film.

The author of a literary, dramatic, musical or artistic work and the principal director of a film have a right to equitable remuneration for the rental of their work. An agreement cannot exclude or restrict the right to equitable remuneration under the section. There are no guidelines as to what constitutes an equitable amount. Either party may apply to the Copyright Tribunal to determine the amount payable. It is also possible to vary any agreement as to the amount payable or vary a previous decision of the tribunal.

These provisions will apply as much to films and recordings of sports events as they do to films and recordings in the mainstream entertainment business.

2.10.10 Public performance

The performance of a literary, dramatic or musical work in public is an act restricted by copyright. 'Performance' of a work includes delivery of lectures, addresses, speeches and sermons, and, in general, includes any mode of visual or acoustic presentation, including presentation by means of a sound recording, film or broadcast of the works.

The playing or showing of a sound recording, film or broadcast in public is a restricted act, although s.72 provides some limited exceptions to this right in relation to broadcasts. Where the audience has not paid for admission directly or indirectly (for instance by paying more for goods and services upon the basis that the broadcast is available) to the place where the broadcast takes place the public showing of the broadcast (with important exceptions in relation to sound recordings of music which are beyond the scope of this work) will not infringe copyright in the broadcast or in the film or sound recording so broadcast.

When will a performance not be in public? Most times that will be fairly obvious. In the more obvious attempts to circumvent the section, an attempt may be made to perform 'behind closed doors' to a selected group of people for payment. It appears that such would not be sufficient to ensure that the performance is private. If payment is made to see a performance, the economic rights of the copyright owner are being affected, since an opportunity to exploit the work is being lost and, accordingly, the performance will be in public. For a performance not to be a public performance, it appears that the performance must be limited to a domestic situation. Playing records or having friends round to watch a film at home will not be a public performance of the work. If the film or music is played in a hall of residence at a university, however, it constitutes a public performance. If there is a degree of recurrence or regularity about such performances, a licence would also be required from the relevant licensing authority or copyright owner. (See further *Jennings* v. *Stephens* [1936] Ch 469, *Performing Right Society Ltd* v. *Harlequin Record Shops Ltd* [1979] 1 WLR 851, *Ernest Turner Electrical Instruments Ltd* v. *Performing Right Society Ltd*; *Performing Right Society Ltd* v. *Gillette Industries Ltd* [1943] Ch 167.)

Music played in shops, over telephones, in waiting rooms and in reception areas constitutes a public performance for which a licence is required. The playing of videos to guests in hotels or the transmission of cable or satellite programme services to guests will also constitute a public performance, and a licence will be required. The administration of the performance right in music and sound recordings is usually assigned by the relevant rights owners to collecting societies such as the Performing Right Society (PRS) and the Mechanical Copyright Protection Society (MCPS), which deal with the licensing of public performance and broadcast rights on behalf of their members in a manner beyond the scope of this work.

These provisions are important to the owners of sporting venues as well as to pubs and cafes where music is played.

2.10.11 Communication to the public

The owner of the copyright in a literary, dramatic, musical or artistic work, sound recording or film, or a broadcast may prohibit others from communicating the work to the public. Communication of the work to the public means first, the broadcast of the work, which means an electronic transmission of visual images, sounds or other information transmitted either for simultaneous reception by members of the public and capable of lawful reception by them, or at a time solely determined by the person making the transmissions. It excludes Internet transmissions unless they are 'simulcasts' transmitted simultaneously with transmissions of the same material by another means, concurrent transmissions of 'live' events, or part of a programme service offered at scheduled times determined by the provider. Secondly, it means the making available of the work to the public by electronic transmission in such a way that members of the public may access it from a place at a time individually chosen by them. This section does not apply to copyright in the typographical arrangements of published editions.

The infringement of copyright by communication to the public is another creation of the Copyright and Related Rights Regulations 2003 and should be seen largely as a response to the growing unhelpfulness of the old dichotomy between broadcasts as formerly defined and 'cable programme services'. It is clearly designed to cope with the new technologies enabling transmission of moving pictures and sounds by Internet and mobile telephony: observing whether these definitions prove able to keep track of technological change where others have not will be interesting. This is obviously of considerable relevance in sport, as sports footage is considered 'killer content' for any new audio-visual platform, and rights owners need to defend themselves against unauthorised use of this nature.

2.10.12 Adaptation

Making an adaptation of a literary, dramatic or musical work is restricted by copyright. Section 21(2) defines an 'adaptation' in relation to a literary or dramatic work as:

- a translation of the work;
- a version of a dramatic work in which it is converted into a non-dramatic work or, as the case may be, of a non-dramatic work in which it is converted into a dramatic work; or
- a version of the work in which the story or action is conveyed wholly or mainly by means of pictures in a form suitable for reproduction in a book, newspaper, magazine or similar periodical.

In relation to a musical work, 'adaptation' means an arrangement or transcription of the work.

An adaptation is 'made' when it is recorded in writing or otherwise. Section 21(2) states that the doing of any of the acts specified in ss.17–20 or s.21(1) in relation to an adaptation of the work is also an act restricted by copyright in a literary, dramatic or musical work. For the purposes of s.21(2), it is immaterial whether the adaptation has been recorded in writing or otherwise at the time the act is done.

'Writing' is defined as including any form of notational code, whether by hand or otherwise, regardless of the method by which, or medium in or on which, it is recorded (s.178).

Where an adaptation of a work has been made, subsequent dealing with it will infringe the other exclusive rights of the copyright owner (s.21(2)).

2.10.13 Secondary infringement of copyright

As well as the infringing acts restricted by the copyright in the work under ss.16–21, there is another category of infringing act known as 'secondary infringement'. The category of secondary infringement generally relates to commercial use of infringing copies of a copyright work. Secondary infringers are often also prosecuted in the criminal court.

In contrast to the position under ss.16–21, secondary infringement under ss.22–26 requires a mental element on the part of the infringer: the infringers must know or have reason to believe that they are dealing with infringing copies of a work.

In *LA Gear Inc* v. *Hi-Tec Sports plc* [1992] FSR 121 it was stated that the test as to what a defendant 'has reason to believe' is an objective one. It requires a consideration of whether the reasonable man, with knowledge of the facts that the defendant had knowledge of, would have formed the belief that the item was an infringing copy. This is important for many reasons, not least because, under s.97, if it can be shown in an action for infringement of copyright that at the time of the infringement the defendant did not know, and had no reason to believe, that copyright subsisted in the work to which the action relates, the claimant is not entitled to damages.

There is provision in s.97(2) for the court to award damages notwithstanding the defendant's lack of knowledge if the infringement is flagrant and the defendant has benefited from the infringing activity. In such a case, the court may award 'such additional damages as the justice of the case may require'.

Sections 22–26 set out the acts that constitute secondary infringement of a work.

Importing infringing copies

Importing an infringing copy of a work without the permission of the copyright owner, other than for private or domestic use, constitutes secondary infringement.

Possessing or dealing with infringing copies

Copyright in a work is infringed where, without the permission of the copyright owner, a person acting in the course of a business possesses, or exhibits in public or distributes, or (whether or not acting in the course of business) sells or lets for hire, or offers or exposes for sale or hire, or distributes otherwise than in the course of a business to such an extent as to affect prejudicially the owner of the copyright, an article which is and which that person knows or has reason to believe is an infringing copy of the work.

Providing the means for making infringing copies

Where a person makes, imports, possesses in the course of a business or sells or lets or offers to sell or let an article designed or adapted for making copies of a work, knowing or having reason to believe that it is to be used to make infringing copies of the work, he infringes copyright in the work. However, in *Amstrad Consumer Electronics* v. *BPI* [1986] FSR 159 similar provisions were not construed so as to hold the manufacturer of a twin deck tape recorder liable for subsequent breaches of copyright.

Copyright is also infringed where a person without permission transmits a work by means of a telecommunication system (this does not include broadcasting and so forth) if an infringing copy will be made at the point where the transmission is received. This captures or seeks to capture such things as electronic transmission by e-mail of a work, and will be invoked in relation to Internet downloads not captured by the communication to the public provisions.

Permitting the use of premises for infringing performance

If copyright in a literary, dramatic or musical work is infringed by a performance at a place of public entertainment, any person who gave permission for that place to be used for the performance is also liable for the infringement unless he believed on reasonable grounds that the performance would not infringe copyright.

Section 25(2) explains that 'places of public entertainment' includes premises which are occupied mainly for other purposes, but are from time to time made available for hire for the purposes of public entertainment. This might include a room in a pub which is occasionally used for performing plays or for live bands to perform.

Provision of apparatus for infringing performance

Supplying the apparatus to infringe the copyright in a sound recording or film or to receive visual images or sounds conveyed by electronic means in a manner which infringes copyright in a work will result in liability for the person who supplied the apparatus or any substantial part of it. An occupier of the premises who gave permission for the apparatus to be brought on to the premises may also be liable, as may any person who supplied the copy of the sound recording or film used to infringe the copyright in each case provided that the requisite mental element is in place.

Infringing copies

An article is an infringing copy if the making of that article constitutes an infringement of the copyright in the work in question. An article is also an infringing copy if it has been imported into the UK, and making it in the UK would have constituted an infringement of the copyright in the work. It must be shown that the article is a copy of a work and that copyright subsists in the work, in which case it is presumed until the contrary is proved that the article was made at a time when copyright subsisted in the work.

2.10.14 Presumptions

Sections 104–105 contain various presumptions relating to the proof of authorship and other matters relevant in proceedings. In relation to literary, dramatic, musical and artistic works, where an author is named on the published work, he is presumed, until the contrary is proved, to be the author of the work. Similar presumptions are made for sound recordings which bear the name of the copyright owner and year of first publication and for films which bear the name of the author or director, the name of the copyright owner, the date of issue and year of first publication. These presumptions can help to avoid the cost of proving title to copyright works.

2.11 TECHNICAL MEASURES

Section 296 includes detailed provisions which apply where either in relation to computer programs or in relation to other copyright works, a technical device (in relation to a computer program) or effective technological measures (in relation to another copyright work) have been applied to prevent copying or other use of the copyright work. Where a person knowingly circumvents those measures, that action is treated so that the person owning or controlling the copyright or rightfully exploiting it will have the same rights against the person who has performed that circumvention as if that circumvention constituted an infringement of the copyright.

In addition, it is an offence to manufacture for sale or hire, import or sell, offer for sale, advertise, possess or distribute in the course of business, or to distribute outside a business in such a way as to affect prejudicially the copyright owner, a device which is primarily designed, produced or adapted to enable or facilitate the circumvention of effective technological measures. The same offence effectively is committed if somebody provides a service with the same effect.

Those guilty of these offences are liable to imprisonment up to two years or to a fine at the statutory maximum.

Section 297 creates the offence of fraudulently receiving programmes. A person who dishonestly receives a programme included in a broadcasting service provided from a place in the UK with intent to avoid payment of any charge applicable to the reception of that programme commits an offence.

Section 297A states that a person commits an offence if he makes, imports, distributes, sells or lets for hire, or offers to do so, or has in his possession for commercial purposes, installs, maintains or replaces for commercial purposes or advertises for sale or hire or promotes any unauthorised decoder.

An unauthorised decoder is a decoder which is designed or adapted to enable encrypted transmissions or services of which that transmission forms part to be accessed in an intelligible form without payment of the fee which the person making the transmission charges for accessing it. 'Relevant transmission' includes transmissions provided from a place in the UK or any other member state or an information society service provided from a place in the UK or any other member state.

In addition to the provisions relating to criminal offences referred to above, s.298 provides to the person who makes a charge for reception of the programme, sends the transmission or provides conditional access services to the same, the same rights against the person committing the acts in relation to the unauthorised decoder as he has against an infringer of the copyright.

2.12   DEFENCES AND PERMITTED ACTS

2.12.1   Introduction

The provisions of s.16 take effect subject to the 'permitted acts' contained in ss.28–76. If a person can establish that what has been done in relation to the copyright work in fact falls within these provisions, there will be no infringement of the copyright in the work.

There are various categories of permitted acts grouped together under a number of headings.

2.12.2   Fair dealing

The first of these categories deals with the concept of fair dealing. This applies in a number of contexts, namely fair dealing for the purposes of research and private study, and fair dealing for criticism, review and news reporting.

The permitted acts centre around the concept of 'fair dealing'. This is a concept that has come before the courts on numerous occasions – for example, in a case involving the film 'A Clockwork Orange' (*Time Warner Entertainment Co.* v. *Channel Four Television Corp plc* [1994] EMLR 1) discussed further below. The copying of the work in question must be of the whole or a substantial part of the work to be an infringing act in the first place. The question of what amounts to a substantial part of a work and the application of the fair dealing defence are different issues.

Fair dealing for research and private study

The provisions of s.29 permit fair dealing with a literary, dramatic, musical or artistic work for the purposes of research for a non-commercial purpose. Copying in these circumstances does not infringe any copyright in the work provided it is accompanied by a sufficient acknowledgement. The copyright in a work is not infringed where fair dealing takes place for the purposes of private study.

The application of the provisions is not without difficulty. There is no rule or indication as to the amount of use which may constitute fair use of the work.

The application of the rules clearly relates to the quality as well as the quantity of the material used. It is clear that, in certain circumstances, a work may be copied.

The making of multiple copies or habitual copying of a work (because, for example, it is part of a syllabus) amounts to infringement. In the latter case, different rules apply and the copying should be licensed.

It is also clear that copying may be done by another person on behalf of the researcher as long as that copying does not result in copies of substantially the same material being made for more than one person at substantially the same time. The making of copies for research or study is thus limited to single and not multiple copies.

There are extensive provisions in ss.27–44 setting out the conditions upon which librarians (who may not be protected by s.29) may make copies of works for others. There are also provisions in ss.22–26 dealing with copyright works, and use and reproduction by educational establishments.

Fair dealing for the purposes of criticism, review and news reporting

Section 20(1) provides that fair dealing with a work for the purpose of criticism or review, of that or of another work or of a performance of a work, does not infringe any copyright in the work provided that a sufficient copyright acknowledgement is given and the work has been made available to the public with the authority of the copyright owner prior to such fair dealing. Section 20(2) states that fair dealing with a work (other than a photograph) for the purposes of reporting current events does not infringe copyright in the work. No acknowledgement is required if reporting takes place by means of a sound recording, film or broadcast, or where this is not possible for reasons of practicability or otherwise.

Fair dealing in this context is also problematical. Copyright will not be infringed if either the use does not amount to a substantial part or the fair dealing provisions apply. The question of what amounts to a substantial part is a vexed one. The fair dealing defence adds a significant weapon in cases of alleged infringement.

In *BBC* v. *British Satellite Broadcasting Ltd* [1991] 2 WLR 174, the defendants used excerpts from the claimants' World Cup football coverage in their news broadcasts. BSB gave an acknowledgement – which the legislation does not require – to the BBC for use of the excerpts. The court held that the use of the excerpts, even though it was of the interesting parts, mainly goals, amounted to fair use within the meaning of CDPA 1988. The limitation on the use suggested by the court related to the timing of the showing of the excerpts. As long as an item is current, its use will be covered by fair dealing.

This case resulted in an agreement between major broadcasters known as the 'Sports News Access Code of Practice' governing the use of excerpts from sports broadcasts.

The court will look at a number of factors in considering fair use. Lord Denning, in *Hubbard* v. *Vosper* [1972] 2 QB 84, described fair dealing as 'a matter of impression'. The factors to be considered include the following.

1. The amount of the work used will clearly be important. Fair dealing is not a carte blanche to reproduce copyright works.
2. The status of the work reproduced may also be important. If the material in question is confidential in nature, a claimant may have other remedies, but the availability of a defence of fair dealing may also be limited. In *Beloff* v. *Pressdram* [1973] 1 All ER 241, the reproduction of the contents of a 'leaked' memo could not be fair dealing. In contrast, the criticism of a work that is already in the public domain (even though not readily available to the public in this country) can, in principle, amount to fair dealing (see *Time Warner Entertainment Co.* v. *Channel Four Television Corp Plc* [1994] EMLR 1).
3. The purpose of, or the motive behind, the copying may also be relevant. The fact that the publication is for commercial gain may not be relevant – a reviewer may be keen to help sell copies of his paper – but if the use of the work will compete with the copied work, then that may be unfair. This applies whether the copying is for research or for criticism and review.

The *Time Warner* case (above) provides a good illustration of s.20l. The defendants had produced a programme that included excerpts from the claimants' film 'A Clockwork Orange'. The claimants had taken the film out of circulation in the UK because of incidents of copy-cat violence after its original release. At that time, the film had not been on authorised release in the UK since 1974, although it was available within the EC. The defendants bought a copy of the film in Paris and used extracts in their documentary. A total of 12 extracts were used, amounting to 12½ minutes, or about 8 per cent, of the film itself and 40 per cent of the programme.

The defendants appealed against an injunction prohibiting broadcast. The Court of Appeal lifted the injunction on a number of grounds.

1. The fact that, at the time, the film was not commercially available in the UK did not mean the fair dealing defence was unavailable.
2. The claimants claimed that the programme misrepresented the film as a whole, as the clips chosen were mainly violent ones. The court did not consider it necessary that the clips used were representative of the film as a whole. The fact that the criticism or review covers only one aspect of a work does not mean that the defence cannot be used.

3. The total length of the extracts used did not in this case go beyond the bounds of fair dealing. The question was a matter of fact and impression for the court. If use amounts to an 'illegitimate exploitation of the copyright holder's work' then it may be unacceptable.
4. The claimants contended that the purpose of the film was not criticism or review of the film, but criticism of the decision to withdraw the film from circulation. The court held that this did not appear to be the case, as the producers of the programme regarded the film as a work 'of long-term social significance'.

2.12.3 Incidental inclusion

Section 21 provides that copyright in a work is not infringed by the incidental inclusion of it in an artistic work, sound recording, film or broadcast, or by the exploitation of such artistic works, sound recordings, film or broadcasts.

Section 21(2) states that a musical work, words spoken or sung without music, or so much of a sound recording, broadcast or cable programme that includes a musical work or such words, shall not be regarded as incidentally included if it is deliberately included.

The incidental inclusion defence exists to permit programme makers and news broadcasters to show works that might otherwise be protected by copyright. A typical example might involve a film crew doing interviews or filming footage in the street. A number of works which are protected by the laws of copyright may be included in the film, such as buildings, advertising hoardings, music from cars or shops, and even other television broadcasts.

The exception to this is the use of musical works – most usually, records played over the radio – where the inclusion is deliberate. Thus, a film maker is presumed to have control over his set to the extent that any musical work playing in the background would then have to have clearance. Even a live broadcaster could find itself in breach of copyright. It will be a question of fact as to what constitutes deliberate inclusion. However, the existence of the PRS and Phonographic Performance Ltd (PPL) and the block licensing regimes should mean most broadcasters are granted permission under the terms of the relevant block licence. The inclusion of any copyright work should, nevertheless, be carefully considered.

What 'incidental' means in this context is difficult to define exactly. It has been said that it means something of secondary importance or something which is background or inessential to a work in which it appears. It will be noted that this section only applies to a comparatively small area of the works protected by copyright, being artistic works, sound recordings, films or broadcasts, and in each case those are the sorts of works which generate 'an impression'. Perhaps the most helpful recent formulation comes in a recent case, *The Football Association Premier League Limited* v. *Panini UK Ltd* [2003] EWCA Civ 995. Here Chadwick LJ suggested that the relevant test for whether something is incidentally included is the question as to why the work which it is suggested has been incidentally included appears in the other work. The answer to that will depend on an objective assessment of the work resulting from the inclusion and the manner in which it is exploited, not simply what was in the mind of the creator at the time of inclusion.

In this case, the defendants were responsible for the creation of stickers and albums which without licence from the Football Association Premier League Ltd or any of the Football Association Premier League Clubs depicted, both in stickers and in pages of the album, Club badges of certain Clubs and the logo of the Football Association Premier League, all of which were copyright works. The album was 'unofficial' and the depiction of those badges was principally in the form of photographs of players wearing kit on which the badges were included. In an action for copyright infringement in relation to those badges, Panini argued that the inclusion within the photographs of those badges amounted to 'incidental inclusion'.

The Court of Appeal said that it was not possible to say the inclusion of the badges was 'incidental' as it was essential to the object for which the images were used: these were intended to be full pictorial images of Premier League footballers showing them in their full and proper kit, thus having the authenticity conferred by such an image. It is in no way 'accidental' or 'incidental' to the image that it is a depiction of the player in that context and with the display of those copyright works which is selected, given that there would be an almost infinite number of alternative images which could have been selected, including those not showing the relevant copyright works or even in which the relevant copyright works were obscured or digitally removed. Essentially, what was perhaps incidental when the image was captured ceased to be incidental as a result of the manner in which that image was then exploited.

2.12.4 Other provisions

There are various other permitted acts listed in ss.57–62 which apply to certain categories of works, for instance, literary, dramatic and artistic works, as follows.

1. Section 57 covers acts done in relation to anonymous or pseudonymous works where it is not possible to trace the author and it is reasonable to assume that copyright no longer exists.
2. Section 58 is important for journalists using a recording of spoken words. As long as the recording is a direct record which is not prohibited by the speaker or copyright owner, and the owner of the recording allows the use, then the words may be used. This is most likely to be relevant where an interview has taken place. The interviewee has copyright in his

spoken words, and permission is required for their use. As long as the conditions are satisfied, the interview may be used.

2.12.5 Public interest defence

The public interest defence is not a statutory defence. This defence has been developed by the courts in a number of cases involving the publication of material which has been obtained illicitly. One example concerned the publication of the Thatcher diaries (*Times Newspapers* v. *MGN Ltd* [1993] EMLR 442). The copyright owner granted exclusive 'serialisation rights' to *The Times*. The *Daily Mirror* obtained and published excerpts from the book prior to its serialisation. In its defence to an action for infringement of copyright and breach of confidence, the defendant alleged that publication was in the public interest. It was held that the publication could go ahead as there were matters of legitimate public interest in publication. The claimants were left to a remedy in damages at a full trial or sooner settlement.

The defence applies in both the law of confidence and the law of copyright. In essence, a defendant argues that disclosure of the information in question is necessary.

The reasons vary, but the defence has applied where the publication relates to an iniquity (although wrongdoing is not essential), to religious matters and to persons in the public eye. The courts have also stated that there is a difference between what is interesting to the public and what is in the public interest.

The commercial interests of publishers and broadcasters must be distinguished from the public interest, which might be best served by giving the information to the police or some other responsible body. A leading case, *Lion Laboratories Ltd* v. *Evans and Others* [1985] 1 QB 526, concerned the publication of information relating to the reliability of intoximeters. The defendants argued successfully that it was in the public interest for the information to be published. The defence is a useful 'addition' to the fair dealing provisions of CDPA 1988.

2.13   REMEDIES

2.13.1   Civil remedies

The remedies available for primary and secondary infringement of copyright include damages, an account of profits, injunctive relief, as well as delivery up and destruction of infringing copyright materials.

2.13.2 Criminal remedies

In addition to the various civil remedies available for primary and secondary infringement of copyright, there are criminal remedies contained in ss.107–110.

CHAPTER 3

Moral rights

3.1 INTRODUCTION

This chapter considers moral rights, which were introduced into UK law by CDPA 1988. Moral rights exist alongside the copyright in certain types of work. Moral rights, generally, remain with the author of a work or pass to the author's estate on death (s.95). Unlike copyright, moral rights cannot be assigned (s.94), although they are frequently waived. Moral rights apply to joint authors (s.88) as well as to the whole or part of a work (s.89).

Moral rights are dealt with in Part IV under ss.77–89. Moral rights are divided into four categories as follows:

(a) the right to be identified as the author or director of a work – this is often known as the 'paternity right' (s.77);
(b) the right to object to derogatory treatment of a work – sometimes known as the 'integrity right' (s.80);
(c) the right to object to false attribution of a work (s.84); and
(d) the right to privacy of certain photographs and films (s.85).

These rights are new to UK law, and were introduced to bring UK law into line with the Berne Copyright Convention. The rights conferred by ss.77, 80 and 85 subsist for as long as copyright subsists in a work. In this respect, the moral rights are dependent upon the existence of copyright. The s.84 right subsists until 20 years after a person's death.

The existence of moral rights raises an important additional element in the negotiation and drafting of certain agreements. Unfortunately for many authors, the sale of rights is often accompanied by the insistence of the purchaser on the waiver of moral rights.

3.2 RIGHT TO BE IDENTIFIED AS AUTHOR OR DIRECTOR

3.2.1 Identification

The author of a copyright literary, dramatic, musical or artistic work, or the director of a copyright film, has the right to be identified as the author or director of the work. The right to be identified as author or director must be asserted. Generally, the right must be asserted in writing. The assertion may take place in an assignment of the copyright in the work by including a statement that the author or director asserts his right to be identified. Alternatively, the right may simply be asserted in writing by the author or director. In the latter case, a letter or other assertion by the author or director should be signed and sent to the person who will be dealing with copyright in the work.

If the right to be identified is asserted by the author or director, various people will be bound by such an assertion. Upon an assignment of copyright containing an assertion of moral rights, the assignee and anyone claiming title to copyright through the assignee will be bound, whether or not they have notice of the assertion of rights (s.78(4)). Where the right is simply asserted in writing by the author or director, anyone to whose notice that assertion is brought will be bound by it.

An author's right of paternity may be asserted as follows:

> The Author asserts his moral right of paternity to the Publisher, its assignees and licensees in accordance with sections 77 and 78 of the Copyright, Designs and Patents Act 1988.

It is common for an author to stipulate that every published copy of a work bears a notice stating:

> The right of the author to be identified as the author of this work has been asserted in accordance with sections 77 and 78 of the Copyright, Designs and Patents Act 1988.

Assuming an author or director fulfils the formal requirements and asserts his rights, if his work is published commercially, performed in public, broadcast or copies of the work are issued to the public, the author must be identified. Practically speaking, this means that the author of a book will be named on the cover of the book. If a film is based upon a book, then the author should be identified or given a credit in the film. Authors and directors are well advised to insist upon the s.77 right in any dealings with their copyright works.

3.2.2 Exceptions

There are various exceptions to this right. The right is not infringed in a number of situations (s.79), for example:

(a) it does not apply to computer programs, typefaces and any computer-generated works;

(b) it does not apply to employees whose employer is the first owner of the copyright in the work, or the director of a film where the director is not the author of the film for copyright purposes;

(c) it is not infringed where any of the defences to infringement apply (for example, fair dealing with the work or incidental inclusion of a work);

(d) it does not apply to any work made for the purposes of reporting current events; and, further,

(e) it does not apply in relation to the publication in a newspaper, magazine or similar periodical, or an encyclopedia, dictionary, year-book or other collective work of reference where the work was made for such a purpose, or the work was used with the author's consent.

3.3 DEROGATORY TREATMENT

3.3.1 Meaning

The author of a literary, dramatic, musical or artistic work and the director of a film have the right not to have their work subjected to 'derogatory treatment'. Section 80(2) defines treatment of a work as meaning 'any addition to, deletion from or alteration to or adaptation of the work, other than a translation of a literary or dramatic work or an arrangement of a musical work'. The treatment of a work will be derogatory if it amounts to 'distortion or mutilation of the work or is otherwise prejudicial to the honour or reputation of the author or director'.

It appears from s.80 that derogatory treatment must be in some way prejudicial to the reputation of the author. Although the author of a copyright work has assigned or otherwise dealt with the rights in the work, this does not give the new owner of copyright a carte blanche to deal with the work in any manner he thinks fit. The alteration of a storyline or significant alterations to the traits of main characters in a film based upon a book could amount to derogatory treatment of the work. It should also be borne in mind that an author may consent to or waive any right to object to derogatory treatment. Indeed, producers acquiring rights in novels or screenplays often obtain a waiver of the s.80 right as a matter of course. An employee author or director has the right under s.82 (assuming that the right has not been waived or consent is given to an act) not to have his work subjected to derogatory treatment as long as he is identified as author or director, either at the time of the infringing act or he has previously been identified in published copies of the work. An employee is thus able to object to derogatory treatment of his copyright work although he does not have the right to be identified as the author of a work. The right to object to derogatory treatment is dependent upon having been identified as the author or director of the work at some point.

Most commercial agreements which deal with the copyright in a work also contain waivers of the s.80 moral right. The British singer George Michael obtained an injunction asserting his 'integrity right' in some of his compositions. The singer alleged that some songs he recorded with his group 'Wham!' had been subjected to derogatory treatment when they were remixed and amended in other ways.

The rights under s.80 are infringed by commercial publication or the issuing of copies to the public of a work that has been subject to such derogatory treatment.

3.3.2 Exceptions

Various exceptions to the s.80 right are detailed in s.81. The right does not apply:

(a) to computer programs or computer-generated works; or

(b) to works made for the purpose of reporting current events; or

(c) to publication of a work in a newspaper, magazine, periodical or encyclopedia or other reference work where the work was made for such a purpose, or was used with the author's consent;

(d) where a work is altered to avoid committing an offence, complying with a duty imposed under an Act of Parliament, or, in the case of the BBC, avoiding the inclusion in a programme broadcast of anything which might offend against good taste and decency or which is likely to encourage or incite crime or lead to disorder or be offensive to public feeling. In such cases, a disclaimer should be included explaining that the author's or director's work has been altered in such a way.

There are no exceptions for fair dealing and, accordingly, despite the fact that a defence of fair dealing may be available in an action for infringement of copyright, an author or director may still have a cause of action under s.80 for breach of moral rights.

3.4 FALSE ATTRIBUTION

A person has a right not to have a literary, dramatic, musical or artistic work falsely attributed to him as author. A director also has a right not to have a film falsely attributed to him. Section 84(1) defines attribution as 'a statement (expressed or implied) as to who is the author or director of a work'. This right is infringed where copies of a work containing such a false attribution are issued to the public. The rights may be further infringed where such a falsely attributed work is performed in public or broadcast where a person knows, or has reason to believe, that the attribution is false. There are also categories of secondary infringement where, in the course of business, a person deals with or possesses copies of the work.

The right to object to false attribution was contained in earlier copyright legislation. In one case, *Moore* v. *News of the World Ltd and Another* [1972] 1 QB 441, the claimant obtained damages for false attribution of ownership where a reporter working for the *News of the World* made up quotations for an 'interview with the claimant'. In this case, the claimant also successfully pursued a libel action against the defendant. The remedy available under s.84 for false attribution is clearly useful where an author's name is attached to a work which is not his. Such an attribution may also amount to a passing off. The false attribution right exists until 20 years after a person's death. It is also possible that, where a work is adapted (perhaps in the transition from novel to screenplay to film), the work changes so fundamentally that in addition to a claim that this amounts to derogatory treatment, attaching the author's name to the final film also amounts to false attribution.

3.5 REMEDIES

The remedy for breach of moral rights is damages and injunctive relief. Defences to an action will include consent or waiver of moral rights in a work. In addition, s.87(4) states that the general law of contract and estoppel also applies where there are any dealings with moral rights. Authors and directors are advised to record any agreement relating to their work in writing, thus avoiding any later disputes.

3.6 WAIVER OF RIGHTS

There is no infringement of moral rights if consent has been given (s.87). Any waiver of rights should be in writing signed by the person giving up the rights. A waiver may be specific or general, and may relate to existing or future works. A waiver may also be conditional or unconditional, and may be expressed to be revocable. A form of waiver may read:

> The Author irrevocably and unconditionally waives his moral rights under section 77 and section 80 of the Copyright, Designs and Patents Act 1988.

A waiver may also be informal, in which case, the general law of contract or estoppel applies.

3.7   RIGHT TO PRIVACY OF CERTAIN PHOTOGRAPHS AND FILMS

The owner of copyright in a photograph is the photographer. The only exception to this exists for employees acting in the course of employment. Copyright in the photograph may be assigned or licensed by the owner. Whilst the copyright in the photograph may be assigned or licensed by the photographer, s.85 contains additional provisions to protect people who commission photographs or films for private and domestic purposes. It is unclear whether or not such commission must be for value. Such a person has the right not to have copies of the work issued, exhibited or shown in public or broadcast in public. Anyone who does or authorises the doing of any of those acts will infringe this right to privacy. Section 85(2) contains exceptions to the right where infringement will not occur. One example is incidental inclusion of such a photograph or film in an artistic work, film, broadcast or cable programme. The s.85 rights are enforceable by the commissioner of the work and not the subjects of it, although the subjects may have other remedies in contract or tort.

This right to privacy is of limited use to protect public individuals whose photograph has been taken. The work must have been commissioned and must be for private and domestic purposes to be of any use. Clearly, a newspaper wishing to publish wedding photographs which it obtains from the photographer at the wedding without the consent of the commissioner (perhaps the family of the bride or groom) could be liable for infringement of moral rights, despite the fact that the position in copyright law as to ownership is clear. As with the other moral rights, no infringement occurs where the person entitled to the right has consented or waived his right.

CHAPTER 4

Rights in performances

4.1 INTRODUCTION

This chapter is concerned with the existence and protection of performers' rights. The exploitation of performers' rights is generally a matter of contract law. Such contracts may be on standard terms and conditions, as negotiated by the Musicians' Union (MU) or Equity on behalf of their members, or may be a bespoke recording contract between a performer and a record company.

Section 180(4) provides that performers' rights exist quite independently of copyright and moral rights in any works and any other rights or obligations other than those arising under Part II of CDPA 1988. There is a distinction between the 'performance' of a copyright work (the right to perform a song in public) and the rights of the person who sings or performs that song. There are similarities in the form and duration of protection granted by performers' rights and copyright. Performers' rights are of particular importance to individuals who do not also own the copyright in the works performed.

As well as defining the ambit of performers' protection, Part II details the civil and criminal remedies available to performers and those with whom they have exclusive recording contracts.

4.2 PERFORMERS' RIGHTS

4.2.1 The rights

The Copyright, Designs and Patents Act 1988 (as amended by the Copyright and Related Rights Regulations 1996, SI 1996/2967, and the Duration of Copyright and Rights in Performances Regulations 1995, SI 1995/3297) sets out the regime for protection of performers' rights. The regime creates (in s.80(1)):

- statutory civil rights for performers by requiring their consent to the exploitation of their performances;

- rights for those with whom performers have exclusive recording contracts in relation to recordings made without their consent; and
- related offences which prohibit dealing with or using illicit recordings.

There are two performers' rights regimes under CDPA 1988 (as revised): performers' non-property rights and performers' property rights. The non-property right is a right to consent to the recording or live broadcast or transmission of a performance, or to the use, importation, possession or dealing with a recording of a performance (ss.182–184). The property right is the right to authorise the reproduction, distribution and rental and lending of copies of a recorded performance (ss.182A–182C).

There is an additional right to equitable remuneration whenever a commercial recording is played or broadcast (ss.182D–191G).

4.2.2 Meaning of 'performance'

A performance is defined in s.180(2) as any one of the following:

- a dramatic performance (which includes dance and mime);
- a musical performance;
- a reading or recitation of a literary work; or
- a performance of a variety act or any other similar presentation.

The performance in question must be a live performance by one or more individuals. The performance in question does not need to be in front of an audience – it can be in a studio or in a theatre or concert hall. There is also no qualitative test. The performance can be mundane or spectacular and original.

If the performance in question is also the first fixation or recording of a new work, then the work may also qualify for copyright protection.

It is worth noticing the limitation of the definition of 'performance'. Whilst protection clearly extends to actors, musicians, singers, dancers, etc., there are individuals who do not benefit from protection. The rights clearly do not extend to sportsmen as they are not, for the main part, performers as defined in the Act. Whilst ice dancing in the Torvill and Dean mode may well qualify as a performance, a footballer or athlete will not be able to stretch the definition of 'performance' to include his on-field sporting endeavours. Notwithstanding this, a form of consent is usually taken from sportsmen taking part in a recorded or broadcast event. Of course, if a sportsman takes part in (for example) a pantomime, then that performance is protected. In the main, any remedies sportsmen have rely on common law rights such as passing off or defamation, or on the registration of a trade mark. Sportsmen are best advised to take tight contractual control over commercial exploitation of their name and likeness.

4.2.3 Qualifying for protection

The only performances which qualify for protection are qualifying performances (s.181). These are performances given by a 'qualifying individual' or taking place in a 'qualifying country' (s.206):

- a 'qualifying individual' means a citizen or subject or an individual resident in a qualifying country;
- a 'qualifying person' is a qualifying individual or corporation formed in the UK or another qualifying country which has a place of business in the qualifying country at which substantial business is carried on;
- a 'qualifying country' means the UK or another EC Member State, or a country which is a party to a convention relating to performers' rights to which the UK is also a party. Section 208 allows the protection of CDPA 1988 to be extended to other countries if a statutory instrument designates it.

4.2.4 Performers' property rights

A performer's property rights are infringed when someone, without the performer's consent:

- makes, otherwise than for his private and domestic use, a copy of a recording of the whole or a substantial part of a qualifying performance (s.182A(1)) – the reproduction right;
- issues to the public copies of a recording of the whole or a substantial part of a qualifying performance (s.182B(1)) – the distribution right;
- rents or lends to the public copies of a recording of the whole or any substantial part of a qualifying performance (s.182C(1)) – the rental and lending right.

Performers' property rights may be dealt with by way of assignment or testamentary disposition or operation of law as personal or movable property (s.191B). In the same way as copyright, an assignment may be partial so it applies:

1. to one or more, but not all, of the things requiring the consent of the performer; and
2. to part, but not the whole, of the period for which the rights subsist (s.191B(2)).

Future performers' property rights may also be assigned (s.191C). It is also possible to grant an exclusive licence of a performer's property rights (s.191D). An assignment must be in writing (s.191B(3)) as must an exclusive licence (s.191D(1)).

An action for infringement of a performer's property rights is actionable by the rights owner (s.191I) and by an exclusive licensee (s.191L).

4.2.5 Equitable remuneration

Where a commercially published sound recording of a qualifying performance is either:

(a) played in public; or
(b) included in a broadcast or cable programme service,

the performer is entitled to equitable remuneration from the owner of the copyright in the sound recording (s.182D). There is a further right to equitable remuneration from the rental of sound recordings or films (s.191G).

Under s.182D, where a commercially published sound recording of the whole or any substantial part of a qualifying performance is played in public or included in a broadcast or cable programme service, the performer is entitled to equitable remuneration from the owner of the copyright in the sound recording. The right cannot be excluded or restricted (s.182D(7)). The Copyright Tribunal may vary or determine the amount payable by way of equitable remuneration (s.182D(5)).

In practice, these provisions mean that record companies now have to pay the artists a share of the income they receive by virtue of ss.9 and 20 which is collected by the Phonographic Performance Ltd (PPL). Performers now have the right to share an income stream to which they were not previously entitled. As far as the record companies are concerned, this is an income stream they may seek to control and use to recoup advances and recording costs. Performers will be keen to ensure they receive this money direct, thus avoiding recoupment. The PPL accounts for this income directly to performers who register with it either directly or through the Association of United Recording Artists (AURA).

In agreements concerning film production between a performer and a film producer the performer is assumed, unless the agreement provides to the contrary, to transfer the rental rights in his performance in the film to the film producer (s.191F). Most agreements will deal with this point explicitly. Although the rental right may be transferred, the performer retains the right to equitable remuneration for the rental of the film containing his performance (s.191G). The right to equitable remuneration may not be assigned by the performer other than to a collecting society (s.191G(2)) and it may not be waived (s.191G(5)).

An organisation such as the Performing Artists' Media Rights Association (PAMRA) may perform this function by collecting money for actors and musicians. The amount paid as equitable remuneration is to be agreed by or on behalf of the person to whom it is payable although applications to the Copyright Tribunal under s.191H are possible. Indeed, it is possible to go to the Tribunal to vary an agreement between parties or a previous decision of the Tribunal (s.191H(2)).

4.2.6 Performers' non-property rights

A performer's non-property rights are infringed where someone, without the performer's consent:

- makes a recording of the whole or any substantial part of a qualifying performance directly from the live performance (s.182(1)(a));
- broadcasts live, or includes live in a cable programme service, the whole or any substantial part of a qualifying performance (s.182(1)(b));
- makes a recording of the whole or any substantial part of a qualifying performance directly from a broadcast of, or cable programme recording including, the live performance,

otherwise than for private and domestic use (s.182(2)).

In the case of s.182 infringements damages will not be awarded if the defendant can show that he believed on reasonable grounds that consent has been given (s.182(3)).

Rights are also infringed where someone, without the performer's consent:

- shows or plays in public the whole or any substantial part of a qualifying performance (s.183(a));
- broadcasts or includes in a cable programme service the whole or any substantial part of a qualifying performance (s.183(b));
- imports into the UK other than for private and domestic use (s.184(1)(a)) or in the course of a business possesses, sells or lets for hire, offers or exposes for sale or hire, or distributes (s.184(1)(b)) a recording of a qualifying performance which is, and which that person knows or has reason to believe is, an illicit recording.

An illicit recording is a recording of the whole or any substantial part of a performance which was made otherwise than for private use without the performer's consent (s.197).

The requirement that the infringing act must be done in relation to the whole or a substantial part of the performance is similar to the infringement of copyright works. The test is a qualitative one and not a quantitative one. See further **para.2.10**.

4.2.7 Consent

The question of whether or not 'consent' has been given for exploitation of performers' non-property rights is fundamental to exploitation of these non-property rights.

Although CDPA 1988 does not specifically require consent to be in writing, this is obviously preferable. Consent may be inferred by conduct, such as where a recording is made with a performer's knowledge. There may also be a question of the amount of any payment to be made in return for the consent. This fact in itself should not preclude the exploitation of the recording. All contracts with performers must deal with and obtain the consent of the performer to record and also to exploit his performance. The absence of terms dealing with these matters can cause problems, as in *Bassey and Another* v. *Icon Entertainment plc and Another* [1995] EMLR 596 and *Mad Hat Music Ltd and Another* v. *Pulse 8 Records Ltd* [1993] EMLR 172.

4.3 RIGHTS OF PERSONS WITH RECORDING RIGHTS

Prior to the enactment of CDPA 1988, it was only the performers who had enforceable rights in their performances. Sections 185–188 create rights for those who have the benefit of exclusive recording contracts with performers.

Section 185 defines an 'exclusive recording contract' as a contract between a performer and another person under which that person is entitled exclusively to make recordings of the artist's performances for commercial exploitation. Commercial exploitation means 'with a view to the recordings being sold or let for hire, or shown or played in public' (s.185(4)).

Infringements of the rights relating to exclusive recording agreements relate to use of the whole or any substantial part of a recording in the following circumstances:

(a) showing or playing in public (s.187); or
(b) broadcasting or including in a cable programme (s.187); or
(c) importing into the UK other than for private or domestic use, or in the course of business possessing, selling or letting for hire, offering or exposing for sale or hire, or distributing, illicit recordings. The requirements of knowledge for these offences are similar to those set out under s.184.

A live broadcast is not an infringement of the rights of the person with an exclusive recording contract, although the broadcast of a recording will be an infringement of those rights.

Recording rights may be assigned (s.185(2)), although a performer may exclude such a possibility in any recording contract.

Consent is also important when considering recording rights infringements. Either the person with the benefit of the recording rights or the performer may consent to the making of the recording. Section 186 makes it clear that rights are infringed if consent was not obtained, unless the defendant can establish that he believed on reasonable grounds that consent had been given. In the situation where a record company has not consented to the recording but the performer has, the record company will have to rely on its contract with the performer for an effective remedy.

4.4   DURATION

Performers' rights last for 50 years from the end of the calendar year in which the performance takes place if a recording of that performance is released during that period, or for 50 years from the end of the year of release (s.191). A recording is released when it is first published, played or shown in public, broadcast or included in a cable programme service (s.191(3)).

4.5   REMEDIES

4.5.1   Civil remedies

The principal remedies are those of injunction and damages for breach of statutory duty (s.194).

Additional remedies provided by CDPA 1988 allow:

(a) an application for delivery up of illicit copies of a performance (s.195);
(b) seizure of illicit copies which are exposed or otherwise immediately offered for sale or hire as long as prior notice is given to the police (s.196). This right does not apply to anything offered for sale at a permanent place of business.

4.5.2   Criminal remedies

The offences relating to performers' rights are contained in s.198. These offences are very similar to those created by s.107. The s.198(1) offences are committed by a person who (without consent):

(a)   makes for sale or hire; or
(b)   imports into the UK otherwise than for his private or domestic use; or
(c)   possesses in the course of a business with a view to committing any act infringing the rights conferred by [Part II of CDPA 1988 (the provisions relating to performers' rights)]; or
(d)   in the course of a business –

    (i)   sells or lets for hire, or
    (ii)   offers or exposes for sale or hire, or
    (iii)   distributes,

    a recording which is, and which he knows or has reason to believe is, an illicit recording.

It is also an offence to show, play in public or broadcast a recording of a performance without sufficient consent (s.198(2)).

Offenders under s.198(1)(a), (b) or (d)(iii) are liable on summary conviction to imprisonment not exceeding six months or a fine, or both. On indictment, they are liable to a fine or imprisonment for up to two years, or both. The other offences are liable on summary conviction to a fine not exceeding level 5 or imprisonment not exceeding six months, or both.

An illicit recording is a recording of the whole or any substantial part of a performance made without consent. A recording made for private purposes is not illicit (s.197).

There are provisions relating to delivery up (s.199), search warrants (s.200) and corporate liability (s.202). There is also a separate offence relating to false representation of authority to give consent (s.201). A person guilty of this offence is liable on summary conviction to up to six months' imprisonment or a fine not exceeding level 5 on the scale, or both. An order may be made for forfeiture or destruction of illicit recordings (s.204).

It is the duty of local weights and measures authorities to enforce the provisions of s.198 (s.198A).

4.6 DEFENCES AND EXCEPTIONS TO RIGHTS

In certain circumstances, consent may be given by the Copyright Tribunal on behalf of a performer. An application to the Copyright Tribunal can be made where either:

(a) the identity or whereabouts of a performer cannot be ascertained by reasonable inquiry; or
(b) a performer unreasonably withholds his consent.

The Copyright Tribunal has power to make a suitable order for payment in the absence of agreement between the parties (s.190(6)). The criteria upon which the Tribunal may base its decision are set out in s.190. The Tribunal will not give consent where it is apparent that the performer is withholding consent for the protection of a legitimate interest. It is for the performer to show his reasons for withholding consent. If the performer does not give evidence, the Tribunal may draw such inferences as it sees fit (s.190(4)).

In any case, there are a number of factors which the Tribunal must take into account:

(a) whether the original recording was made with the performer's consent;
(b) whether the recording is lawfully in the possession or control of the person proposing to make the further recording;
(c) whether the making of the further recording is consistent with the obligations of the parties to the arrangements under which, or is otherwise consistent with the purposes for which, the original recording was made (s.190(5)).

It is important that any consent given by the performer covers the method of exploitation proposed for the work in question. The terms of any consent contained in a contract should be carefully considered before use is made of the performance in any new or unanticipated media. Similar considerations apply as with the construction of copyright licences discussed at **para.2.9.3.**

Section 189 and Sched.2 provide for a number of permitted acts which may be done in relation to a performer's rights. These are similar to the permitted acts done in relation to copyright works. There are 20 sections dealing with the various permitted acts, which include the following:

(a) fair dealing for the purposes of criticism or review;
(b) incidental inclusion of a performance or a recording;
(c) various exceptions allowing the playing, showing and recording of works, including performances for educational establishments; and
(d) free public showing or playing of broadcast or cable programmes.

4.7   EXPLOITATION

Most performers will, during the course of a professional career, sign a number of contracts. Contracts which relate to a performance, whether it is simply a live concert or a sound recording release, fall broadly into two categories: standard terms and individual contracts. The former category accounts for most of the day-to-day dealings between performers and businesses. For instance, the actors' union Equity has negotiated standard or collective terms with the BBC and the Independent Television Commission (ITC) relating to minimum fees and conditions of employment for its members. The MU has reached similar agreement with these broadcasters. The agreements provide for the payment of a basic fee for limited transmission rights. If further exploitation of a work is proposed, then repeat fees may be payable, together with fees for transmissions overseas and for other exploitation of the performance, such as video release.

Individual agreements are likely to be the subject of greater negotiation. Such agreements typically relate to longer-term exclusive contracts, such as for the services of a pop group or a well-known actor.

The terms of these collective and individual agreements are discussed where relevant in the music, and film and television sections of this book.

CHAPTER 5

Trade marks and passing off

5.1 TRADE MARKS

5.1.1 Definition

The law is mainly governed by the Trade Marks Act 1995 (TMA 1995). A trade mark is defined as:

> any sign capable of being represented graphically which is capable of distinguishing goods or services of one undertaking from those of other undertakings.

This includes, but is not limited to:

- words, including personal names;
- designs;
- letters;
- numerals;
- the shape of goods or their packaging, except those which consist exclusively of the shape which results from the nature of the goods themselves or which is necessary to obtain a technical result or which gives substantial value to the goods.

The definition is wide enough to cover distinctive colours and/or colour combinations, sounds and smells although the extent to which these will be relevant in sport varies.

5.1.2 Registration

A mark falling within the TMA 1995, s.1(1) definition should be registered unless there is a specific reason to the contrary. An application for registration of a mark may be refused on the basis of the absolute or the relative grounds for refusal.

5.1.3 Absolute grounds for refusal of registration

If the mark:

- is devoid of any distinctive character;
- consists of signs or indications which may serve, in the relevant trade, to designate the kind, quality, intended purpose, value, geographical origin, time of production or of rendering, or other characteristics of the relevant goods or services;
- consists exclusively of signs or indications which are customary in the current language or the bona fide and established practices of the trade;
- is contrary to public policy or accepted principles of morality;
- is likely to mislead the public, for example as to the nature, quality or geographical origin of the relevant goods or services;
- is prohibited from registration by UK statute or EU law;
- is a specially protected emblem, for example royal emblems or insignia, or national flags (subject to certain exceptions as described in TMA 1995, s.5);
- consists exclusively of the shape which results from the nature of the goods themselves, or the shape which is necessary to obtain a technical result, or the shape which gives substantial value to the goods; or
- is the subject of an application in bad faith, for example an application filed to block the application of another,

then it will be refused registration.

The first three of these grounds can be displaced if the applicant can prove to the satisfaction of the Registrar that the applicant for registration has conferred upon the mark 'a distinctive character' through use of the mark prior to the application. In those circumstances, the applicant must show that what otherwise would not be distinctive of any particular business has become so distinctive in use as to be broadly associated with the business of the applicant.

5.1.4 Relative grounds for refusal of registration

Registration will be refused on the relative grounds if:

- a mark is identical to an earlier mark and the application is in respect of identical goods or services;
- a mark is identical to an earlier mark and the application is in respect of similar goods or services, or is similar to an earlier trade mark and the application is in respect of identical or similar goods or services, provided (in each case) there is a likelihood of confusion between the marks in the public mind which includes likelihood of association with the earlier trade mark;

- a mark is identical or similar to an earlier trade mark in respect of any goods or services where the earlier mark has established a reputation and the later mark would take unfair advantage of or be detrimental to that reputation; or
- its use would be liable to be prevented because of prior rights belonging to another person, such as rights in relation to passing off, copyright or design rights.

Registration is initially for 10 years, and is then renewable for further periods of 10 years.

5.1.5 Infringement

A trade mark is an exclusive property right which is infringed by certain kinds of use of the mark, in the course of trade, without the proprietor's consent. The infringing acts reflect the relative grounds for refusal of registration dealt with above. The infringing acts are set out at TMA 1995, s.10 and are:

- using a mark which is identical to a registered mark in relation to identical goods or services to those for which the mark is registered (s.10(1)); or
- using a mark which is identical to a registered mark in relation to similar goods or services to those for which the mark is registered provided there is a likelihood of confusion on the part of the public, which includes the likelihood of association with the trade mark (s.10(2)); or
- using a mark which is similar to a registered mark in relation to similar goods or services to those for which the mark is registered or to identical goods or services to those for which the mark is registered where (in either case) there is a likelihood of confusion on the part of the public, which includes the likelihood of association with the trade mark (s.10(2)); or
- using a mark which is identical or similar to a registered mark in respect of any goods or services where the proprietor of the registered mark has established a reputation and the use of the later mark, being without due cause, would take unfair advantage of or be detrimental to that reputation or to the distinctive character of the mark (s.10(3)).

The meaning of 'likelihood of association' has been considered in a number of cases.

5.1.6 Trade mark use

A trade mark must be used for infringement to have taken place; 'use' of a mark includes:

- putting it on goods or packaging; or
- offering, marketing or stocking goods, or offering or supplying goods under the mark; or

- importing or exporting goods under the mark; or
- putting it on business papers or advertising material.

This definition does not purport to be conclusive or exhaustive.

The requirement of 'use' means that not every instance where a trade mark is seen or applied will constitute an infringement. For example, the mere appearance of a trade mark in a photograph used in a newspaper will not infringe the trade mark nor will the incidental appearance of a trade mark on an item of clothing or a piece of merchandise used in a film or an advertisement.

5.1.7   Criminal offence

There are also various criminal offences under TMA 1995 where identical and/or similar marks are applied to goods or used in advertising materials for goods.

5.1.8   Remedies

The right to bring proceedings vests in the proprietor from the date of filing of the application. However, no proceedings may be brought before the mark is actually registered.

An infringement is actionable by the registered proprietor, who has the right to such relief as would be appropriate in relation to infringement of any other property right, including damages, injunctions and accounts.

Specific remedies include:

- an order for erasure of the mark or destruction of the infringing goods, materials or articles; or
- an order for the delivery up of infringing goods, materials or articles, but subject to a six-year limitation period.

5.1.9   Exceptions to infringement

A trade mark is not infringed by use in accordance with honest practices where the use is:

- by a person of his own name or address; or
- to indicate the kind, quality, quantity, intended purpose, value, geographical origin, time of production of goods or of rendering of services, or other characteristics of goods or services; or
- necessary to indicate the intended purpose of goods and services, provided there is compliance with honest practices, for example, in the sale of spare parts or accessories for third party products.

Under s.11, there is no infringement by use in a particular locality of an earlier right applying only in that locality which would have enough goodwill to protect it by any rule of law, for example a passing off action.

5.1.10 Groundless threats

If an owner of a mark (or indeed its representatives) makes unjustified threats of proceedings against another for infringement other than the application of the mark to goods or their packaging, importation of goods so marked, or supply of services under the mark, it may be subject to:

- a declaration that the threats are unjustifiable; and
- injunctive relief; and/or
- damages,

unless the owner shows that the acts (or proposed acts) in response to which the threats were made infringed (or would infringe) the mark. Even if the owner establishes such actual or intended infringement, the other party can still get relief by showing that the registration of the mark is invalid or liable to be revoked.

5.1.11 Assignments and licences

A registered mark is a property right which can be transferred or charged by assignment, will or operation of law, so long as the disposition is in writing and signed by or on behalf of the assignor or (if appropriate) a personal representative.

5.1.12 Revocation and invalidity

A trade mark can be revoked on various grounds or may be declared invalid.

5.2 PASSING OFF

5.2.1 General

The passing off action is based on the premise that 'nobody has any right to represent his goods as the goods of somebody else'.

In *Warnink* v. *Townend* [1979] AC 731 Lord Diplock set out five characteristics necessary to launch a valid passing off action:

1. a misrepresentation;
2. made by a trader in the course of trade;
3. to prospective customers of his or ultimate customers of goods or services supplied by him;

4. which is calculated to injure the business or goodwill of another trader (in the sense that this is a reasonably foreseeable consequence); and
5. which causes actual damage to the business or goodwill of the trader by whom the action is brought or (in a *quia timet* action) will probably do so.

In *Consorzio del Prosciutto di Parma* v. *Marks & Spencer plc and Others* [1991] RPC 351, Nourse LJ reduced these characteristics to:

the classical trinity of:

(1) a reputation (or goodwill) acquired by the claimant in his goods, name, mark etc;
(2) a misrepresentation by the defendant leading to confusion (or deception); causing
(3) damage to the claimant.

The three characteristics will now be examined in turn.

5.2.2 Reputation or goodwill acquired by the claimant in his goods, name, mark, etc.

In order to acquire and maintain the type of goodwill which can be protected by a passing off action, the owner must:

- establish a reputation in a mark by using it in business (some kind of commercial activity is required);
- ensure the mark is associated with particular goods or services of the owner, or with the owner personally; and
- protect that reputation against misuse.

A mark is, very broadly, something which is used to try to give an identity to a supplier and/or its goods and services which is distinguishable from other, otherwise similar, suppliers and/or their goods and services.

The mark could be the:

- style of packaging;
- colour;
- 'get-up'.

It should be noted that this relates to the container, not the shape of the goods themselves.

Unlike the registrable trade mark, there are no restrictions for protection by a passing off action save that the mark must distinguish the owner and/or his goods and/or his services.

Where the claimant's business is locally based in one part of the country he may nevertheless get protection (and obtain an injunction) against persons using a similar name in other parts of the country. This will be more certain where the claimant can show some possibility of geographical expansion of his business at some future time. Where the claimant is outside the UK, he is not likely to succeed in a passing off action against a UK defendant unless he can show some business activity here. Such activity might be in the form of doing business through an agent in the UK or having customers here. However, goodwill may be established very quickly through advertising and/or actual sales and, indeed, it may be quite localised.

The following are examples of particular applications of the law.

5.2.3 Initials

Initials of themselves are hard to establish as a mark. There must be a distinctive presentation of them.

5.2.4 Place names

Place names are hard to protect unless they are associated in the public mind with goods or services – like Champagne – when a protectable mark may well arise. Such cases also show that it is possible, although not usual, for goodwill to be shared jointly (e.g. by those in the Champagne region).

5.2.5 Generic names

As with place names, if goods are marketed under a generic name and associated with standards of quality and production, then goodwill can be generated.

In *Warnink* (above), the manufacturers of Advocaat (a high quality product with a substantial reputation and which sold in large quantities) were able to stop sales of an allegedly inferior and cheaper liqueur called 'Keelings Old English Advocaat'.

The risk, however, is that extreme success of the genre may cause loss of distinctiveness. If the mark is not distinctive, it cannot be protected. 'Hoover' dominated the market when first sold by Mr Hoover, but now even an Electrolux vacuum cleaner is commonly described as a 'hoover'.

5.2.6 Descriptive names

It will be difficult to show a protectable interest in a name which is merely descriptive (e.g. corona applied to a cigar) until the name has been exclusively used for long enough to create a secondary meaning which relates only to the owner and not to any competitor.

Even when the secondary meaning is established, the courts will construe the name strictly unless fraud or misrepresentative intent is shown. This means that even a slightly different name used by the competitor may escape liability.

5.2.7   Character merchandising

Usually the name of a fictitious character (like Sherlock Holmes) cannot be protected as goodwill. But if it can be shown that a competitor intends to exploit the character's reputation and goodwill, and that a substantial number of people would believe the claimant was associated with the competitor then protection may be given.

Even then, it is normally necessary to show that the parties are in the same or similar fields of activity. If not, then the claim may fail, as in *Wombles Ltd* v. *Wombles Skip Hire Ltd* [1975] FSR 488. In that case, the claimant was the holder of copyright in books and drawings featuring the Wombles. These were characters known for collecting rubbish. The defendant was a skip hire company which had adopted the Wombles name. The claimant could not prove that there was confusion sufficient to lead to damage to his goodwill.

The courts have however recognised and protected 'character merchandising'. The *Ninja Turtles* case involved use of drawings (rather than the names) of turtle-like characters. Such use was restrained by interlocutory injunction. More recently though there has been a move away from granting such protection leaving most cases to turn on their own facts and claimants finding it increasingly difficult to stamp out 'unauthorised' merchandise. See, however, the discussion of *Irvine* v. *TalkSPORT* at **para.5.2.9** below.

5.2.8   Area of sale or operations

Cases about the geographical limits of goodwill are difficult to reconcile. On the one hand, the product must be available on the open market rather than amongst a small, defined and limited class. For example, the drinking of beers by UK-based American servicemen in private bars will not qualify. However, it is not necessary for the owner to set up a business in the UK, merely that the product is freely available here.

In 1967, the Crazy Horse Saloon of Paris (which had no UK base but was known in the UK) was unable to stop the opening of a similarly named, but otherwise unconnected club in the UK. In contrast, in 1965, the Sheraton hotel group (which again had no UK base but was known and took bookings for its overseas hotels from the UK) was able to stop the opening of a similarly named hotel in the UK. Finally, in 1977, Maxim's restaurant of Paris (owned by a UK company) was able to stop the opening of Maxim's restaurant of Norwich.

However, there can be no action for passing off if all the allegedly infringing acts – including production of products – take place entirely outside the UK. There may, of course, be a local action.

5.2.9 A misrepresentation by the defendant leading to confusion or deception

The representation may be express or implied. It does not matter that it is true if the overall effect is to mislead. A comparison with other goods is not a representation in this sense even if the comparative statements are false. There is no need for the misrepresentation to be a duplicate of the claimant's name and/or mark.

The misrepresentation must be made by a trader in the course of trade. Trade in this context (and in the context of those who may claim goodwill) includes business generally, the professions, service providers, charities and clubs. The misrepresentation must be made to prospective customers of his or ultimate customers of goods or services supplied by him.

A finding of fraud on the part of the person making the misrepresentation will put the evidential burden on the defendant but there is no need for the misrepresentation to be fraudulent. The essential precondition is the confusion of the customer by the representation. There is no need for the representation to be made by the defendant with the intention (or even the knowledge) that confusion would result. Innocence is no defence.

Normally it will be necessary for the claimant to show that he and the defendant are engaged in the same field of activity but this is not an absolute requirement. In *Stringfellow* v. *McCain Foods* [1984] RPC 501 there was held to be confusion between the claimant's night club (called Stringfellows) and the defendant's chips of the same name! The evidence of confusion was, no doubt, bolstered by the defendant's television advertising campaign which included a disco sequence. The claim was, however, unsuccessful as the claimant could not prove damage.

The real issue is the effect of the misrepresentation on customers. Will they believe that there is an association between the defendant's goods or services and the reputation of the claimant? That is a question of fact and may vary from case to case. In *Lego Systems A/S and Another* v. *Lego M. Lemelstrich* [1983] FSR 155 the toy brick manufacturers were able to stop the defendant's use of the 'Lego' name in connection with plastic irrigation and gardening equipment. This was largely because Lego is a household name associated with plastic.

Where the claimant is not yet involved in a particular field, it may be able to prevent use of its name if it has plans to go into the new field as soon as possible.

It must be likely that customers will be deceived by the representation. This is another question of fact. Expert evidence can be adduced. So, too, can evidence of market research, but this is likely to be criticised by the court for not being helpful, in which case the court may want to see all the individuals who took part in the survey as witnesses in court.

It need not be all or even the majority of customers who are confused, but it must be more than the 'moron in a hurry'. In *J. Bollinger* v. *Costa Brava Wine Co. Ltd (No.2)* [1960] Ch 262 the defendants claimed that only the ignorant would be confused by the sale of Spanish Champagne. The court said that a substantial part of the public, who did not know about wine, might be confused and that was enough for an injunction to be granted.

It does not matter that the confusion is transitory. In a retail case, first impressions count. The 'confusion' element will be satisfied if people 'conclude that the defendants are connected with the claimants, or are a branch of the claimants or in some way mixed up with them'.

Confusion alone is not enough to found an action for passing off. All the other characteristics must also be present. In particular, there must be a misrepresentation and loss. If confusion results simply from the 'collision of two independent rights' then neither party can complain. It is one of the misfortunes of life.

Examples of misrepresentation include the following.

1. A misdescription, provided there is a class of products or services to which the description can validly be applied (Champagne, for example, in relation to sparkling wine produced in the Champagne region of France) and provided the association of that description and the reputation of the claimant (Bollinger, for example) is established so that the customer expects such products and services to meet certain standards.
2. Claiming without reason a connection with some well-established business.
3. Using the claimant's advertising to give the impression that the defendant's goods or services are those advertised by the claimant or even that low quality goods of the claimant are the claimant's normal quality goods (e.g. where the defendant collects used razor blades manufactured by the claimant and resells them as new, having repackaged them in the claimant's distinctive containers).
4. Use of a mark similar to the claimant's mark.
5. Use of a name or trading name similar to that of the claimant. Distinctions here can be especially fine. Normally, no one can be stopped from using his own name (or one which has by association become his own: for example, in the way that Harry Webb has become known as Cliff Richard), but they must do so 'honestly' and 'not go beyond that'. However, it seems that if a person uses his natural or assumed name with the intention of taking business from another, then there can be a misrepresentation and such action may be restrained. Where the defendant's name is his own, the burden of proof on the claimant is usually heavy, but when it is an assumed name, the burden is lighter. Use by a company of its registered name may still amount to a misrepresentation. It should be remembered that all this assumes some misrepresentation on the

defendant's part, which will always turn on the facts of the individual case.

6. Alteration of or addition to the claimant's product.

7. Imputing that an operation or business has the authority or consent of the holder of the goodwill. This has a variety of guises, for example claiming membership of The Law Society or the British Medical Association. An interesting and novel example is *Associated Newspapers Group plc* v. *Insert Media Ltd* [1991] 1 WLR 571. The claimant published various magazines and wished to prevent retailers and distributors inserting advertising material between the pages of the magazines which the publisher had not authorised or arranging with third parties to make such insertions. It was held that insertion of advertising leaflets into newspapers would be a misrepresentation that the inserts were made or authorised by the publishers if there was also evidence that a substantial number of readers would believe the inserts were so made or authorised.

8. Substitution of rival goods.

A word needs to be said as to the nature of the confusion which the misrepresentation must evoke amongst members of the public in order for it to qualify for consideration as passing off. In many ways each of the elements of passing off is closely related to all the others and it is sometimes difficult to separate them conceptually. However, it has frequently been a problem in the area of merchandising or licensing, which is one of the principal areas of interest in the sports industry to which passing off is relevant, that because the goods using the goodwill of the proprietor were not the goods usually associated with that proprietor, passing off could not be established. An example would be *Lyngstad* v. *Annabas Products Ltd* [1977] FSR 62, in which t-shirts were produced picturing the pop group 'ABBA'. The court held that as ABBA was not the clothing business, there was not a common field of activity between the group and the defendants who produced the offending t-shirts and therefore passing off was not made out. That case is usually used in the context of considerations of goodwill and 'common field of activity': it is however related to other similar authorities such as *BBC Worldwide Ltd* v. *Pally Screen Printing Ltd* [1998] FSR 665 in which proceedings were taken in similar circumstances, once again against unauthorised printers of t-shirts, this time by the BBC in relation to unauthorised 'Teletubbies' t-shirts. The BBC here was denied summary judgment as it was considered to be possible that the public would not consider the shirts to have any relevant connection to the BBC. They would not have assumed that the BBC manufactured them or supervised their manufacture, and the shirts would be seen therefore merely to illustrate the characters. A recent authority which has caused some further interest in this context is *Irvine* v. *TalkSPORT Ltd* [2003] EWCA Civ 423. Here TalkSPORT, operating under its earlier trading name Talk Radio, wished to publicise its coverage of a Grand Prix and depicted the famous racing driver Eddie Irvine holding what appeared to be a radio with the words 'Talk Radio' printed on it. This was a doctored photograph originally showing Irvine holding a mobile telephone. It was used without Irvine's consent.

In the judgment, the court took formal notice of the common practice of famous sportsmen and other individuals exploiting their name and reputation by way of endorsement not only in the main areas of their expertise or competence but also more broadly. A distinction was drawn between 'endorsement' cases where the individual involved had specifically 'told' the relevant public that he approves of the product or service, and in 'merchandising' cases, where on the analogy of film merchandising, products using images from the film are sold to members of the public who want reminders of it.

Whether this is a simple dichotomy which can be followed in practice is perhaps open to doubt. However, it was decided that in the *Irvine* case the endorsement line of cases applied. In relation to the 'common field of activity' problems experienced by ABBA in the case cited above, and with particular reference to a previous character merchandising case *McCulloch* v. *May* [1947] 65 RPC 58, this line of thought was considered discredited in the context of 'character merchandising'.

It was determined therefore that where a defendant appears to be seeking to proceed on the basis that the product has been endorsed by the celebrity, that celebrity can take action in passing off if he can show that he enjoyed a valuable reputation and goodwill at the time, that the action of the defendant amounted to a representation to a significant section of the market that its goods had been endorsed by him and that damage had occurred which may be shown by reduction, blurring or diminishment of the exclusivity with which the goodwill referred to may be exploited. It is not necessary now to show a common field of activity in such 'endorsement' cases.

5.2.10 Damage

The final element of passing off which must be proven is damage. Without damage, there is no passing off – it is often said that damage is 'the essence of the tort'. The nature of damage which can qualify is not necessarily a closed category: it is clear that the straightforward damage by loss of sales, and damage to goodwill, for instance, by the sale of substandard goods, is sufficient to ground the action. *Irvine* (above) recognises other forms of damage which can ground the tort as set out there. Essentially, if the damage is clearly of an economic nature and not entirely speculative, there is the prospect of it being recognised by the court and the tort thus being made out.

PART 2

Music

Nick Kanaar

CHAPTER 6

The music business

6.1 INTRODUCTION

The music business is based on the exploitation of the separate copyright in the musical work, the sound recording of it and the activities of artists as performers (with spin-offs arising from the name and fame of the artist and their importance as personalities).

Each of the copyright owners of the song and of the recording expects to be paid for the exploitation of their rights. For artists/performers, this payment usually takes the form of a percentage of the copyright owner's receipts from exploitation of the recording.

The traditional method of exploitation of songs and sound recordings is by the sale of records, broadcast, cable diffusion and public performance. The copyright owners may also allow others to use their songs and recordings for use in films, fixed media, such as DVDs, and other commercial use. Use in films and advertisements may involve a new recording so that the original sound recording owner will not benefit, or it may involve the use of the original recording so that both original owners will benefit.

Developing technology presents new ways of exploiting copyright works. Songs and sound recordings are now included on computer games, in multimedia applications and in online and on-demand services, such as the Internet and 3G telephones, as well as the traditional methods such as sheet music and song books.

Most composers enter a contract with a music publisher, and performers will usually enter a contract with a record company. The contractual relations between composers and performers and their managers, agents, publishers and record companies are examined in the chapters which follow. The most effective way of exploiting a song is by recording, performing and broadcasting it. The separate creators/owners of copyright in the song and copyright in the recording try to maximise their return from the exploitation of the work, while the performers on the recording seek to receive a fair return for their performances.

This chapter broadly distinguishes between the creators and owners of songs and the creators and owners of recordings. The independent copyright (often in different ownership) and the industry-wide reliance on collecting societies to simplify the collection of payments for the use of songs and recordings provide a complex backdrop. Artists' live performing work is considered at **para.6.4** and as part of **Chapter 8**.

6.2 COMPOSERS AND PUBLISHERS

6.2.1 Introduction

The composer of a song (music and lyrics) is usually the author and the first owner of copyright in the work. Composers have to exploit their works effectively to achieve any degree of success. Exploitation is usually effected by giving permission for the public performance, cable and other new forms of diffusion and broadcast of a work (dealt with by the Performing Right Society (PRS)); by allowing people to record the song (dealt with by the Mechanical Copyright Protection Society (MCPS) and also by music publishers); by allowing the song to be synchronised with film, TV shows and advertisements (usually dealt with by either the MCPS or the music publisher) and through sales of sheet music (dealt with by the music publisher). There are other methods of exploiting songs, but these are the most important.

6.2.2 Publisher's function

Composers often assign or grant an exclusive licence of copyright to publishing companies of all the rights in a composition. If a work is a work of joint authorship, or if its constituent parts are written by different people, there may be more than one publishing company involved.

A music publisher does more than just arrange the printing, distribution and sale of printed sheet music. The publisher's main function is to promote the works of a composer and collect income from doing so. It includes arranging for the recording of songs, the use of the music on television, in films and in any appropriate media.

Much of the publisher's function relates to the 'mechanical rights' in a composition. The 'mechanical right' is an industry term of art simply referring to the restricted act of copying a work (CDPA 1988, s.17).

This right may be granted both by the MCPS and the publisher in respect of different media. The MCPS usually deals with the mechanical rights for the administration and payment of royalties on record sales whilst the publisher sanctions the recording of the work on film and in other media (synchronisation right) but roles change as the business develops and, for example, the MCPS now has a scheme whereby it deals with both the mechanical right and synchronisation right for DVDs.

6.2.3 Music Alliance

The Music Alliance brings together the PRS and the MCPS under one roof to share both office and administrative functions, as their membership consists of the same class of person – songwriters and publishers.

6.2.4 Performing Right Society (PRS)

The owner of the copyright in a work may control the public performance, cable diffusion and broadcast of the work. Collectively, this is known as 'the performing right'. Controlling the performance and broadcast of a work would be difficult, if not impossible, for any individual composer and music publisher because of the number of organisations which make use of musical works.

The function of the PRS is to do collectively for its members something they cannot effectively do as individuals. The PRS was founded in 1914 as a non-profit-making organisation. Its members consist of writers and publishers who assign the performing right in their works to the PRS.

Because of the cost of administration there are membership requirements for individuals and publishers which are reviewed and changed from time to time. Currently a composer must have a work which is being exploited in a way which is certain to produce a collectible fee and a publisher must have control of at least 15 such works. There are grades of membership based essentially on earning power and the grades affect the voting power of the member as do its earnings and volume of distributions.

The PRS administers the rights to perform a work in public, broadcast it (including via the Internet) or include it in a cable programme service. The PRS can only be involved in works which originate or are controlled by a member so that, for example, an American film producer may not be a member.

Blanket licences

By virtue of the assignment of copyright which is an integral part of membership the PRS owns in its own right the performing right as set out in the specific definition contained in its Articles of Association. It should be noticed that what are termed 'grand rights' (see **Chapter 9**) are not included and are retained by the original copyright owner. The PRS licenses the performing rights in its works in return for a royalty. Rights are licensed to broadcasters, cable operators and places where copyright works are performed (such as pubs, clubs and shops). The PRS then collects revenues on behalf of its members. Broadly, PRS has two categories of licence:

(a) blanket licences with broadcasters, cable operators and Internet service providers; and

(b) blanket and one-off licences for public performance of its members' works.

Blanket licences with broadcasting organisations facilitate the collection of money for PRS members. The agreements with organisations such as the BBC, the independent television companies and commercial radio, as well as satellite and cable broadcasters and operators, are separately negotiated by the PRS with the bodies concerned. The amount charged to such organisations is based upon a number of factors including the level of music usage and the revenue of the broadcaster. These broadcasters then provide returns to the PRS identifying the music used in films, television and radio programmes. This enables the PRS to distribute the royalties that it has collected to its members.

The PRS has various standard form agreements for public places such as bars and shops, with agreed tariffs for the use of its members' repertoire. The income from these licences is collected and distributed to members. Licences are granted to permit the playing of music, whether live or recorded (by means of juke-box or background music system) in premises including pubs, hotels, concert halls and discotheques. The PRS operates over 40 different tariffs which have been agreed with various organisations such as the brewers' associations.

An example of a specific licence would be the licensing of a show venue for a specific concert by a group where a fee based upon ticket sales will be agreed and attributed to the actual songs performed in accordance with their length in playing time.

PRS does not own or administer the so-called 'grand right'. There is some debate and no clear definition of grand right which is, for all practical purposes, the performance on stage in public of music where the music is not the only attraction, for example a West End or other musical play is the grand right as opposed to a concert or a group's appearance. This right is usually owned by the publisher in the usual way under a contract with the writer and is usually compensated for in the form of a share of the box office receipts for the production.

PRS fees

In order to distribute income to its own members and to members of affiliated societies whose repertoires have been licensed in the UK by the PRS (see below), the PRS will distribute in proportion to the use made of a member's work. Detailed returns are made by TV and radio broadcasters and, where music is performed live, programme returns are obtained from so-called 'significant venues' in respect of every concert or festival. These returns enable the PRS to identify the composer and publisher of each work performed or broadcast during the period, and to pay each interested party his appropriate share of the royalties. Radio logs, background music returns and music charts are used to estimate the fair proportion so that PRS may distribute the revenue from other public performance venues where it is not cost-effective to collect actual data.

The PRS also receives income from its overseas associates for the fees derived from overseas use of British works. This currently accounts for approximately one-third of PRS income. Collection of income from overseas performance and broadcast venues is made possible because the PRS is affiliated to performing rights bodies in other countries and operates in the UK to collect fees on their behalf. Fees from UK performance and broadcast venues are then distributed to these foreign affiliates by the PRS. The PRS distributes income quarterly to its members. Distribution takes place after the deduction of administration costs, which once amounted to some 19 per cent of total income from the UK and overseas, but following a drive for efficiency and computerisation it is now less than half of that.

The basic method of division of fees by PRS is on the basis of fractions of 12 or multiples of 12, but is sometimes on a percentage basis. If a composer has not assigned rights in a composition to a publisher, then the whole of the fee collected by the PRS will pass to the composer member. When a composer has assigned part of the rights to the publisher, then the fees are divided between the composer and the publisher in the proportion 8/12 to 4/12, unless there has been, as is normal, a variation agreed. PRS will not distribute more than 6/12 of a performing right fee to a publisher. Where there is more than one person involved in a composition, the fees will be divided by the PRS according to the publishing agreements. For example, if there is a lyric writer and a composer, it is common for the publisher to take 6/12 and for the composer and the lyric writer to take a share of 3/12 each.

PRS has a wide range of contracts and protocols with similar overseas collection societies whereby those associates will pay PRS for performing right use in their countries and will receive from PRS the income attributable to earnings in the UK of their members' performing right.

The EU is bringing changes to the territorial aspect of these activities and different relationships are beginning to emerge, especially in relation to Internet use where a provider can be licensed by one collection society for pan-European use of works controlled by it, rather than the previous more restricted method which required a separate licence for each country.

PRS maintains a scheme whereby the share of a deceased member may be passed to his successors.

A member is at liberty to resign on giving notice and in that event the performing right is reassigned. This might occur, for example, where a writer moves abroad and it becomes more convenient to join his new local society.

6.2.5 Mechanical Copyright Protection Society

The right to record a work is a separate right from the performance right in a song (CDPA 1988, s.17). Permission to record a song is the subject of a separate agreement with the person wishing to record the work. The MCPS was formed in 1924 to regulate the payment of royalties to publishers and composers for sales of recordings of their works. Acting as an agent for its member, the MCPS deals only with rights in underlying works not in the sound recordings themselves. The basis of membership is that the MCPS is appointed exclusively to grant the mechanical right and collect the fee but to some extent (which is reviewed and varies from time to time) there is an element of non-exclusivity.

Licences

Licences are granted by the MCPS to record companies and other bodies which wish to record works. If authorised by its members, the MCPS also issues licences to film companies and advertising producers to allow them to record members' works in films and commercials.

Through a series of licences, which are adapted from time to time in accordance with business reality, the MCPS grants licences on terms which vary upon the use and to some extent on the type of licensee. Thus companies with a good credit rating and which may be expected to manufacture copies in noticeable volume will be licensed on one basis whilst smaller companies or those with comparatively limited sales expectations will be licensed on a different basis, typically being authorised to manufacture a specific number of copies and being required to pay in advance. There are blanket licences to broadcasters covering the recording of music into programmes and detailed provisions for the reporting of actual usage so that income can be allocated equitably by the MCPS amongst its members. A separate form of licence has been developed for DVD use where the recording company needs a licence to cover not only the sale of copies but also a synchronisation licence for combining the sound with a visual image.

Complex other arrangements have been developed based upon the concept of 'central European licensing' prompted by the centralisation of manufacturing facilities by the large record companies and the legal obligation to allow a company to manufacture outside the UK and be free to import.

Income is also received by the MCPS from the use of its members' works abroad by means of various affiliations with over 50 foreign organisations. Similarly, the MCPS will collect in respect of overseas associates for the sale and use of their mechanical copyright in the UK. As with the PRS, pan-European licences for Internet and 3G uses are being developed.

Relationship with the British Phonographic Industry

The British Phonographic Industry (BPI) (see **para.6.3.4**) is the representative party on behalf of the recording industry charged with agreeing the rate of royalty to be paid for the mechanical right and, indeed, for all other uses. Formerly there was a rate specified by statute but currently the rate is negotiable and, in the event of a disagreement, it is settled by the Copyright Tribunal after hearing all the evidence. These rates are hotly contested by the publishers as the musical copyright owners (essentially represented by the Music Publishers Association (MPA) (see **para.6.2.6**).

A number of rates have been agreed from time to time without formal adjudication.

Music made available over the Internet

Currently the two sides in the industry, the publisher (music copyright owner) and the record companies (sound recording copyright owner), are at loggerheads over the use and sale of music over the Internet. In an area where there has been much unlawful use, with a large amount of copyright material being available on the Internet, the industry was, in a sense, dragged into the market and has found itself in a position of having to grant rights to service providers upon terms which might be said to have been dictated to them and which certainly have been the result of being agreed to from a very weak bargaining position. The fact of the matter is that there is much mystery as to the precise terms and conditions upon which authorised service providers are lawfully making available copyright recorded music to customers with a combination of subscription services (where the customer has a range of services for a flat fee) and specific fees for specific uses such as the ability to make a permanent copy of a record or only have it available for a limited number of plays or a limited time period.

The Internet provider which sells the music to its customers has been prepared to pay a specific sum as a payment for all copyright uses. The publishers (essentially represented by the MPA) and the record companies (essentially represented by the BPI) contest how that sum should be divided between them. It should be remembered that both sides will have an obligation to share whatever the income is with the writer/composer on the one side and the recording artist on the other.

6.2.6 Music Publishers Association

The Music Publishers Association (MPA) is the music publisher's industry representative and its members comprise nearly all the music publishers active in the UK. It celebrated its 125th anniversary in 2006 and its concerns include the protection of copyright and the safeguarding and improvement of the legal environment within which its members operate. It operates an educational programme about copyright and the music publishing industry, actively lobbies parliament and the European Commission, liaises with the PRS, the MCPS and their associates internationally, conducts negotiations upon commercial matters and leads the industry applications to the Copyright Tribunal.

6.2.7 British Music Rights

British Music Rights (BMR) is an umbrella organisation which represents the interests of composers, songwriters and music publishers. Formed in 1996, its members and founders are the British Academy of Composers and Songwriters, the MPA, the PRS and the MCPS. BMR pursues and lobbies for all matters of common interest to its members.

6.3 THE RECORD INDUSTRY

6.3.1 Introduction

A separate copyright exists in recordings as opposed to the copyright in underlying material such as songs and compositions. The copyright in a sound recording is an important independent copyright which is exploited by producers and record companies. As has been seen, the life of copyright in a record is much shorter than that of a musical copyright, being 50 years from first publication. The popular music industry is now over 50 years old and this period has given great cause for concern. A movement is afoot to change the law not only in the UK but across Europe, but the attempt appears to have failed in the UK.

A record company must obtain a licence or assignment of copyright before it can record a song. This licence may be obtained from the MCPS or directly from the music publisher concerned.

The exploitation of sound recordings, whether by the sale of CDs, by broadcasting or by the authority to undertake any other act restricted by CDPA 1988, is as important to the record company and the performer as the recording and exploitation of the original song is to the composers and publishers. The record company pays a royalty (the mechanical royalty) to the composer and publishers of the song, and a separate royalty to the performers on the recording in consideration for their services. The agreement with the performers will be embodied in a record contract or a session musicians' agreement. These agreements are considered in **Chapter 8**.

The record companies are members of their own organisations, Phonographic Performance Ltd (PPL) and Video Performance Ltd (VPL), as well as the BPI.

Record companies take the recorded product and release it for sale and broadcast to the public. Various promotional and marketing activities are undertaken to try to gain as much exposure as possible for the work. Depending upon where the record company is based and its resources, it may conduct each stage of the manufacturing and distribution process itself. If a recording is to be exploited abroad, arrangements will be made to license a foreign company to undertake all the necessary commercial steps to promote and distribute it. The larger companies are now international and will have subsidiary or same group companies to fulfil such functions but may still license separate independent companies.

6.3.2 Phonographic Performance Ltd

Phonographic Performance Ltd (PPL) is a non-profit-making organisation established by record companies and record producers to control broadcasting and public use of recordings. Members assign the usage rights in all their works to PPL. PPL negotiates and issues licences for the broadcasting and public performance of sound recordings in a similar way to the PRS. Fees are based upon the value to the user derived from the recordings.

Thus, radio and television broadcasters in the UK pay licence fees to PPL for the use of their members' recordings. In addition, PPL issues licences to performance venues such as discotheques, clubs, dance halls and juke-box operators to permit the public performance of sound recordings. PPL divides the licence fees between its members in proportion to the amount of use made of the relevant records. Detailed returns are made by broadcasters, and sample returns are taken from venues where sound recordings are performed publicly. PPL has set up a complex and unique database of works which comprises much detail of the featured artists and of the paid session musicians.

PPL was for many years regarded as an inefficient organisation but over the last few years it has had a thorough overhaul and is now highly regarded. Historically it made ex gratia payments to featured artists but much has changed since the introduction of equitable remuneration which created a legal entitlement of featured artists and session musicians. Following that legal entitlement two additional bodies were set up to pursue such rights and to ensure collection and distribution of moneys to those entitled. They were PAMRA (which mainly represented the featured artists) and AURA (which mainly featured the unfettered session musicians).

So complex has the subject become, and thanks to the work of PPL in compiling its database and to its efficiency and reputation, the position has just been reached where PAMRA and AURA are to be merged with PPL as one body. This merger has occurred with DTI approval, which was necessary because of the monopoly implications.

Although PPL has not yet incorporated Internet use in its activities this can be expected in the future and might be considered a logical step for many record companies.

PPL also has reciprocal arrangements with other similar bodies overseas to collect income due to them and to collect income due from any public performance of the recording copyrights administered by it. PPL has already moved into digital licensing for some of its members and has licensed Internet radio use and some ringtone usage. It can be expected to increase such activity.

The fees collected by PPL for year ended December 2005 amounted to some £87.5 million.

6.3.3   Video Performance Ltd

Another method of exploiting sound recordings and songs is to make short promotional visual programmes accompanying the release of the recording. In recent years these have increasingly been made available on discs as DVDs instead of video tapes. Video Performance Ltd (VPL) grants licences for the broadcasting and performance of such music and visual programmes. In much the same way as the agreements set up by PPL and the PRS, blanket agreements with television stations, such as MTV, and other programme providers, as well as other public performances, allow full use of the VPL repertoire in return for a fee.

6.3.4   British Phonographic Industry (BPI)

The BPI is a non-profit-making organisation whose members comprise record companies. Its current membership accounts for approximately 90 per cent of the sound recordings sold in the UK. The BPI oversees the official UK charts and organises the annual Brit Awards which are televised internationally. As part of its trade function, the BPI negotiates agreements on behalf of the record industry relating to the payment of session musicians and covering the rate of mechanical royalties paid to composers when their works are recorded. This contract is negotiated with the MCPS. Principally, the BPI acts as a trade association for the record industry and represents the industry in negotiations with the Government, trade unions, retailers and other sections of the music industry. Another of its functions is to combat bootleg recordings (sales of unauthorised recordings) as well as counterfeit recordings (i.e. illegal copies of recordings) in the music industry. The BPI has an established anti-piracy unit set up to fight the counterfeiting and bootlegging of sound recordings belonging to its members. The BPI also works with PPL.

As has been seen above (**para.6.2.5**), the expansion of the use of the Internet has caused problems, and negotiations between the BPI and the MPA have foundered and been referred to the Copyright Tribunal.

The Internet has created the serious problem of copyright infringement as copyright recordings are readily available to anyone who has access to a computer and a connection to the Internet. Whilst BPI has long maintained a piracy unit which polices copyright infringements, the Internet presents special challenges. Simple policing was difficult enough but the illicit use was accompanied initially by claims that it was not an infringement of copyright, accompanied by a general lack of public comprehension that something so easy to access could be illegal. Through a process of public education and litigation, BPI has made great strides to assist the furtherance of legitimate business. It has not been an easy process especially as access to a computer is not necessarily restricted to the owner of the equipment, for example, it may belong to an Internet cafe, or children may be using a family computer at home.

6.3.5 Music Managers Forum

Formed only in 1999 the Music Managers Forum (MMF) is, as its name suggests, an organisation formed by and for artist managers. Through frequent activities and the provision of standards and codes for managers, with the provision of educational courses concerning the business and with the lobbying of government and the European Commission it has quickly established itself as a body whose position is to be taken into account.

It is associated internationally with like bodies. Partially, at least, its purpose is to emphasise the rights and interests of the artists whom its members represent.

6.3.6 Musicians' Union

The Musicians' Union (MU) is the only trade union in the UK which solely represents musicians. Its objective is to advance and protect musicians in a number of ways. Its functions include setting minimum rates of pay for its members, and the provision of standard terms of engagement. It has produced a number of standard contracts for things such as session work in recording studios and for club or cabaret engagements.

6.4 LIVE WORK, FAME, IMAGE AND PERSONALITY

Apart from recording and songwriting activities, the remainder of the music industry and the income of performers is derived from live performances on stage in pubs, clubs, ballrooms, concert halls, arenas and stadiums and on radio and television, and the other ancillary aspects of show business. These activities revolve around the efforts of the manager and booking agents.

Booking agents work on a commission basis calculated on the gross income of the engagements arranged. For many years their commission was 10 per cent but in the popular music field in respect of the bulk of artists this rate has crept up to 15 per cent because, until an artist has achieved success and is able to command large fees, it is simply not a viable business for an agent at the lower rate. Booking agents are necessary and must be paid enough to stay in business. Contracts are comparatively simple and short and are not subject to a great deal of negotiation. An agent will be appointed for a fixed period which is likely to continue automatically until terminated by either side. An agent will wish to be appointed on an exclusive basis and, provided that there are safeguards built in requiring him to produce a requisite number of engagements, that will normally be acceptable to an artist.

A successful artist can generate substantial additional income through the sale of branded merchandise. The activity will usually be conducted by separate firms who specialise in the field and the artist will usually receive a percentage share of the goods sold. A variety of formulae apply so that sometimes the merchandising company will take all the risk of manufacturing, stocking and selling the goods and sometimes the risk will be shared by the artist who may also provide a sales team. Obviously the potential return is higher to the party that undertakes the risk. When negotiating rates it is also worth knowing that many venues demand by contract and as a condition of hire that they receive a share of the proceeds of sale. Sales will usually also take place by mail order either through the merchandiser's catalogue or through a fan club or on the Internet and, to some extent, by retail sale in regular shops.

The really successful artist can also look forward to reward from activities which result from his fame or personality, for example by appearing in advertisements or endorsing products.

CHAPTER 7

Management agreements

7.1 INTRODUCTION

This chapter considers the choice of business medium for an artist in the music business, as well as the need for and role of a manager in the development and representation of a group or individual artists. In particular, some of the more common terms of management agreements will be considered, together with the more usual pitfalls. A typical form of agreement is set out in **Appendix A1**.

7.2 CHOICE OF BUSINESS MEDIUM

It is important that the business, as well as the artistic, side of a performer's career is managed professionally and conducted properly, just as in any other business. There must be proper financial accounting records and the principals in the business must be aware of their responsibilities to each other. It is for this reason that, like all businesses, musicians should put a workable structure in place to help them manage their affairs. One of the initial considerations relates to the choice of business medium.

The music business is a business like any other and thus the usual considerations are relevant.

Section 1 of the Partnership Act 1890 will almost certainly apply to groups of performers in that they will be carrying on a business in common with the intention of making a profit. Accordingly, the implied terms of the Partnership Act 1890 apply when the group forms unless another structure is specifically put in place.

The other structures are the normal ones which exist under English law, namely incorporation or possibly a series of individual sole traders. Taxation advice will help in a decision as to structure between a number of choices such as incorporation into a traditional limited liability company with a share capital or a limited liability partnership, or a series of companies utilising the services of the individual. It should be remembered that complicated structures may lead to confusion and expense and careful consideration needs to be given to all the implications.

Put simply, a record company asked to sign an unknown band may not be prepared to involve itself if it is required to accommodate an unusual structure at the behest of a group especially if this involves the record company in departing from its usual way of doing business or in having to take its own professional tax or legal advice because of the group's business structure.

Whatever structure is adopted there must be a clear statement of the respective rights and obligations of all involved and these should be reduced into a written agreement. It strongly advisable to set out the relevant aspects and mutual obligations in a written agreement. An important element which applies to a musical group (of two or more) is to establish the position if and when a member wishes to leave or perhaps the majority wish to part company from others. A period of notice needs to be agreed, along with the proposed treatment of any valuation of goodwill and the terms upon which any capital can be withdrawn.

A particular problem arises in connection with the future use of the group name and this has been a fertile ground of litigation over the years. It is strongly recommended that this be considered in some detail and with an understanding of the many possible permutations. It should also be remembered that during the life of a recording contract (especially with a major record label) it will usually be a term of the contract that the record company will designate which member or members may use the name and which members can be prevented from doing so. That is because of the considerable investment that will be made by the company, and such a provision will override the partnership agreement.

Another potential problem is the ongoing income deriving from records made together or songs composed together, especially the latter where initial enthusiasm and goodwill may have resulted in credit being given in excess of the contribution of any one. In this sense there is often considerable unhappiness on behalf of the continuing members who find that they have to carry on with the hard work of creating and sustaining success, including heavy touring commitments (in both financial and effort terms) and then see a noticeable part of the rewards going to a former member free of this involvement.

7.3 APPOINTMENT OF A MANAGER

7.3.1 Why appoint a manager?

An artist rarely has the time or expertise to manage himself, and a good manager may already have experience of management and useful contacts within the music business. The manager should help the artist find venues to perform in, and to secure recording and publishing contracts. A manager can actively promote an artist's business interests. Depending upon the terms of appointment, the manager will be responsible for the artist's whole entertainment career, although this may be limited to his career in the music business. This commonly involves negotiating and agreeing terms for recording contracts, publishing deals and the live performance of the artist. An experienced manager with good contacts in the business can at least make the record and publishing companies aware of the artist through those contacts. The artist is left to concentrate on his music, while the manager concentrates on financial and contractual matters.

7.3.2   Role of a manager

In law, the manager acts as an agent for the artist. The relationship is one based on mutual trust and confidence and fidelity. This is all the more so in the music business because of the degree of responsibility most managers assume for the development of the artist's career. A manager performs a personal service for an artist and acts on his behalf in dealings with third parties.

The essence of the role is to help develop and sustain the career of the artist. Initially this will entail the negotiation of recording and publishing contracts and thereafter following those through to success.

Prior to the appointment of a manager, both parties should be separately represented. There have been a number of cases where management contracts have been successfully challenged on the basis of undue influence being exercised by the manager over the artist or because arrangements have been in restraint of trade. If the artist obtains independent legal advice before signing an agreement with a manager, it should ensure both that the agreement is less open to challenge at a later stage by the artist, and also that the terms negotiated on the artist's behalf are not unduly restrictive or financially onerous.

If an artist is keen to sign an agreement contrary to advice, the legal adviser should record his advice in writing and, if necessary, particularly onerous clauses should be drawn to the attention of the artist to avoid any liability at a later stage. If a management agreement is subject to analysis by a court, the availability and experience of the legal advice given to the artist may be a major factor in the court's decision. A well-advised artist warned against an onerous contract may find it difficult to set the contract aside. It is perhaps for this reason that many managers see the wisdom in complying with a request from an impecunious artist that the manager should meet the legal costs of the artist.

The manager should be responsible for a number of matters.

1.   He should plan the artist's career (in consultation with the artist).
2.   He should deal with all necessary administrative steps as appropriate for

the touring and promotional arrangements. This may include the arranging of insurance, work permits and visas, as well as appointing touring agents and arranging meetings with third parties involved in the artist's career.

3. He should agree to negotiate any necessary recording or appearance contracts on behalf of the artist. The artist must approve and sign such contracts.

4. Whilst the provision of the manager's service is usually non-exclusive to the artist, it is important that the manager does not take on too much other work thus disabling him from carrying out his duties under this agreement effectively. An obligation should be included in an agreement ensuring that the manager does not create a conflict of interest between one managed artist and another and possibly that the management services of a named 'key' individual are provided to the artist.

5. There should be an all-inclusive obligation requiring the manager to provide any necessary advice and services which are customarily required or expected of a manager.

6. If a company is the manager, the personal services of the individual enjoying the artists' confidence should be available as a condition of the contract.

7.3.3 Manager's authority

The legal basis of the contract between artist and manager is usually that of principal and agent. The artist gives the manager authority to act on his behalf. The usual agency rule applies in that the agent is not liable in any way under any contract negotiated with a third party, and cannot, in the normal course of business, be sued by a third party for the principal's default. It is important that most, if not all, obligations incurred by the manager on the artist's behalf are approved and signed by the artist. In particular, all performance, recording and publishing obligations should be understood, explained to and signed by the artist as well as the manager. Further, in accordance with normal agency law there should be a provision ensuring that the artist shall not act for himself.

The artist should define carefully the nature and extent of the manager's authority, his duties and obligations. A valid contract will not arise between a principal, in this case the artist, and a third party, unless the manager has authority to bind the principal.

In the absence of actual or apparent authority, the artist, as principal, is not bound or liable to a third party for the acts of his manager acting as agent. It will be appropriate to consider whether the manager was acting in accordance with accepted practices of the music business, and also whether or not it is known or there has been any form of representation that a manager acts for a particular artist. A prudent third party would usually require some evidence that the artist is interested in the engagement or obligation before signing an agreement. If there is any dispute as to an agent's authority (whether actual or apparent), it is open to the principal to rectify an unauthorised act and thereby legitimise the contract with the third party.

7.3.4 Implied obligations of the manager

The management agreement should set out the specific obligations of the manager to the artist. In the absence of any express prohibitions to the contrary in the contract, there are a number of implied obligations which arise because in law the relationship is that of principal and agent. The most important of these implied duties are as follows.

(a) Where the manager agrees to act for the artist he must carry out the terms of the agreement as agreed and, unless the agreement states otherwise, carry out the artist's lawful instructions.

(b) The manager must exercise due care and skill in acting on behalf of the artist. A straightforward example of this is to negotiate and contract on the best terms available for the artist.

(c) Unless otherwise agreed, the manager must also act personally for his principal. Whether or not a manager is obliged to act personally or is permitted to delegate will depend upon the arrangements with the artist. Where the management services are provided by a company, then the artist should specify or agree who is responsible for management.

(d) The manager has a duty to act in good faith towards the principal. The relationship between manager and artist has a fiduciary nature. Accordingly, the manager should not permit a conflict of interest between himself and the artist and, if any does arise, he must disclose that conflict to the artist. The manager must not make any secret profit or take a bribe from a third party. Any benefit that accrues to the manager for himself as a result of his agency will be a breach of this duty of good faith. If this trust breaks down, the artist may be able to terminate the management agreement (see *Denmark Productions Ltd* v. *Boscobel Productions Ltd* [1969] 1 QB 699).

(e) The manager must not misuse confidential information for his own or a third party's benefit. This applies even after an agency ceases. 'What the butler saw' revelations by managers and employees of famous people are not uncommon and, in an appropriate case, the courts may prohibit such disclosure (see *Ash and another* v. *McKennitt and others* [2006] EWCA Civ 1714).

(f) The manager is under a duty to account to the artist. This involves a duty on the manager, as agent, to keep proper accounts of all transactions, and, in principle, the manager should keep the artist's money separate from his own. An artist should avoid the risk of trying to recover money from an insolvent manager. Any money the manager keeps on the artist's behalf should be placed in a separate trust account. Notwithstanding that, there is an increasing tendency for the accounting matters to be delegated to an accountant representing the artist and for the accountant to control the bank account into which all moneys must be paid by the manager.

A number of implied terms affect the manager:

1. The manager has the right to be indemnified by the artist for any expenses incurred acting on the artist's behalf. Once again, it is usual to include express terms in a management agreement detailing the amount and type of expenses that a manager can incur without having to seek express authorisation from the artist.

2. Unless otherwise agreed, there is no right for an agent or manager to claim any remuneration from the artist as principal. Such a right must be expressly or impliedly agreed between the parties and, accordingly the management agreements will deal with payment of the manager by way of commission on an artist's gross or net earnings.

3. Once a manager's contract is terminated, no further commission will be payable by the artist to the manager. It is very important that any continuing obligation to pay commission to a manager is carefully worded so that if one management agreement is terminated and replaced by another, there is no element of double payment. It is conceivable that the terms of the original management agreement provide for ongoing commission and that the new management agreement also provides for commission or remuneration on similar categories of earnings.

7.4 TERMS OF AGREEMENT

7.4.1 General

There are a number of areas which need to be covered in the terms of any management agreement. There is no industry standard, and there is inevitably a great difference in the terms that a manager would like to see in a finished agreement and the terms that the artist is well advised to insist upon. Although a good manager is important to an artist and may be able to influence his career path, terms should not be discussed on a 'take it or leave it' basis. The artist is engaging the manager's services and should retain some influence and control over his affairs; this is to be contrasted with the position which arose in the infancy of the business when the ostensible 'manager' employed the services of the artist and, effectively, took any profit that he could generate after paying the artist a set wage.

7.4.2 Key terms

The areas that need to be set out are:

- the appointment and the extent of the artist's activities to be managed;
- the geographic territory of the appointment;
- the period of the appointment;
- the remuneration payable;
- the treatment of expenses; and
- accounting and control matters.

The relationship between artist and manager is a business arrangement and, accordingly, the terms of the agreement should be reflected in writing. This is to ensure certainty and to avoid any later dispute as to the actual terms of the agreement. Whilst subsequent disputes may arise as to what those terms on their natural construction cover, the use of a written agreement is preferable to an oral arrangement.

Before entering into negotiations there are a number of fundamental points which need to be clarified in the interests of both sides:

- Are there any existing contracts signed by the artist which affect his ongoing activities?
- What recordings or songs of or by the artist currently exist (whether alone or with a group)?
- Was there a previous management agreement which will affect the future income of the artist?
- Is the artist of full age or a minor?

7.4.3 Appointment and exclusivity

It is usual for a group to appoint only one manager or management company to deal with their affairs, although it is unusual for a manager to agree to manage only one artist. If the manager is free to manage other artists then it is important that the manager is able to fulfil his obligations under the agreement. A manager who fails to provide the necessary time and commitment may breach the terms of the agreement and, accordingly, entitle the artist to terminate the agreement. It is important that both parties consider this before signing the agreement. The artist wants to maximise the benefit from representation, and, equally, the manager wants to maximise his return by way of commission or royalties on the artist's earnings. A clause requiring the manager to use his best endeavours to further the artist's career is important.

The agreement should deal with the particular fields of the entertainment business in which the manager is appointed to represent the artist. This may depend upon the skill and experience of the manager, although consideration should be given to the future aspirations of the artist as well as any current activities. For example, the manager's representation may include an artist who later turns to acting, or who decides to publish a novel or poetry collection. A catch-all appointment which deals with any activity or performance by the artist in the 'entertainment industry' should be avoided. Quite apart from the fact that such a clause may be too wide and (if ever challenged) could be void for uncertainty, the activities of a manager should be directed at particular sectors of the industry. In the case of a musical artist, this representation should include all aspects of the making of sound and promotional video recordings of musical works, live performances whether in concerts, on radio, on TV or other broadcasts, as well as the writing and composing of musical works. Some artists also become involved with the mixing and production of recordings, and this may also be covered by the management agreement. Many successful artists also engage in widespread commercial promotions, usually by way of merchandising and product endorsement. The income from such activities may also be included in the scope of the manager's representation.

The manager's role is a matter for negotiation and agreement. A manager will not accept a role which is so narrow and well defined that his earning potential from the artist is severely limited; likewise, an artist should not grant a manager rights over every aspect or potential aspect of his career at a stage when he does not know in what way his career may develop.

7.4.4 Geographical territory

As well as the exclusivity of the appointment, it must also be ascertained to what extent the manager can effectively represent the artist throughout the world. It may be more practical for the manager's appointment to be limited to, say, Great Britain, Northern Ireland and the EU. Separate representation might be obtained for the US, Japan, etc. Again, this is a matter for consideration in the light of the manager's experience and expertise. A well-connected manager with representation abroad may well be able to fulfil the obligations in a very wide territory and, accordingly, all countries throughout the world might be appropriate territory. Most managers insist upon exclusive worldwide representation.

The foregoing is particularly relevant to North America. It is a generally held view that in relation to the US (which arguably is the largest potential market for English speaking artists) it is necessary to have a manager who has strong connections there, including a knowledge of the local market and a full-time presence there.

There are a number of ways in negotiations of dealing with this aspect. It may be possible to exclude North America from the manager's appointment or to provide him with authority to subcontract some or all of his obligations. If he is to subcontract then any remuneration payable should be paid by the manager from his commission and should not be an extra charge.

7.4.5 Period of the appointment

The management agreement may be for a fixed term with options to renew; or it may be indefinite, terminable upon notice by one or other party; or it may be approached by considering that a career proceeds in cycles linked to record release. The last is the current norm. Thus the appointment may be for such period as passes until after the release of a second long-playing record. There should be provisions dealing with termination if there is no record contract in place, when obviously there will be no album release.

There should also be termination provisions in the agreement which deal with breaches of contract by the parties.

The period of an agreement is open to negotiation. As an alternative to the term being related to album release it can be a simple period of time. A manager will require a reasonable period of time – three years is acceptable – both to give him time to plan the affairs of the artist and to give him a substantial period over which to gain a return. In either case there should be provisions allowing the termination of the contract if no progress is being made. Progress may be gauged in terms of minimum income levels derived from the career or the existence of satisfactory recording contracts.

A management agreement may contain an option to renew the term for further periods exercisable by the manager. Ideally, the notice should be served some time before the end of the agreement enabling the artist to plan ahead. An artist should avoid being tied to a manager indefinitely. Exercise of the option should be predicated upon the artist's career having progressed satisfactorily, again, probably by reference to earning targets and the existence of a suitable recording contract.

Managers are usually content with some such provision, as long as they are expressed as conditions of the entitlement for the contract to continue and not in the form of a guarantee from the manager.

7.4.6 Remuneration of the manager

The manager provides his services in return for a commission which is usually based upon the artist's income from specified activities. The definition of 'income' is important and is discussed below.

The first issue between the parties must be the agreed percentage of commission for the manager. This varies, although 20 per cent is quite common, and depends upon the experience of the manager as well as the extent of his representation. Many artists, particularly in the early stages of their careers, are an unknown quantity and, accordingly, a manager will demand, and usually receive, a higher commission than for an established artist signing a new management agreement. Some agreements allow for an escalation of the commission percentage as income grows. The converse is also possible.

The second issue is the source of the income which will be the subject of the commission. A manager appointed only in respect of musical recordings and performances can only claim a commission on receipts from those activities. It is possible to exclude certain categories of income from the manager's commission. Commission should be paid only on income arising from contracts agreed or negotiated during the term of the agreement although if the artist is already established it may also attach to actual income even if the relevant contract under which the income arises was already in existence when the management agreement was signed.

'Net' deals

Given that the cost and expense of touring and recording in particular can be very high it is normal to agree that at least an element of these should be deducted before calculating the management commission. In a net deal, if the artist makes a loss, the manager makes no money. The manager will want to control closely the categories of deductible expenditure for a net agreement.

The management agreement should set out the income and deductions for commission purposes.

Artist's income

An artist's income for commission purposes is all the money he receives from the defined management activities. This includes income from recording, publishing, performing, merchandising and any other professional entertainment activities. Artists sometimes receive gifts and payments in kind. It is usual for gifts to be excluded from the category of income on which commission can be charged. However, a payment in kind which is clearly meant as consideration for services would be included in the income of the artist and thus subject to commission.

Advances

Advances from most sources are subject to the manager's commission as long as they are income for the artist. An advance which is a payment on account of royalties is thus subject to the manager's commission and is a valuable source of income for both artist and manager.

Recording and video costs

Advances made by record companies for recording costs or promotional video costs should not be subject to commission. Such sums are not income or earnings for the artist. Usually the royalty provided for under a recording contract will be inclusive of the royalty payable to the individual creative record producer. That third party money paid to a producer by the artist should not be included in income. However, money an artist receives as a producer will be subject to commission.

Tour income

A tour undertaken by a comparatively unknown or novice artist may produce little or no profit. Manager's commission on tours and personal appearances should be based upon a net profit figure, the net profit being the money left over after the deduction of certain agreed categories of expenditure, such as lighting, staffing, travel and accommodation which are reasonably incurred and directly attributable to the tour.

A separate agent is usually appointed to book tours and venues, and that agent receives commission on gross fees for the tour. Such commission varies and typically amounts to 10 or 15 per cent of gross receipts. Agent's commission should be excluded from the manager's commissionable figure.

Tour support is money provided by a third party, often a record company, to offset a touring loss. This money should be excluded from tour income in calculating a manager's commission.

If litigation is required to recover money then the cost should be deducted from any recovery before calculating commission.

Actual receipts

It is important that commission is payable to the manager only on the basis of moneys actually received. An artist should be concerned to ensure that the manager is only entitled to commission on moneys received and not moneys which are simply due to the artist, otherwise the manager may be entitled to his commission before there is any income available to pay it.

7.4.7 Commission and termination of the agreement

Ideally, an artist will cease paying commission to a manager as soon as an agreement is terminated. Negotiation rarely achieves that position.

The manager will usually negotiate a provision whereby he continues to be entitled to receive commission on income arising from records recorded or works composed during the term of his agreement. The artist will want to be bound only to pay commission if the records are released during or shortly after the term of the management agreement and similarly in relation to the songs.

The period during which ongoing commission is to be paid may be short-term, long-term or, in exceptional circumstances only, indefinite. It may reduce over time so that, for example commission would continue at full rate for three to five years and be at half rate for a further three to five years before ceasing altogether. Under this type of arrangement, a new manager can be engaged with fewer complications. The artist may consider paying ongoing commission if an album has been recorded but not released, or a song written but not published or recorded at the date of termination. An indefinite obligation to pay commission once the agreement has ended, even on deals negotiated by the manager, should be avoided.

Agreements which contain provisions which entitle the manager to commission on income from deals negotiated by him during the term of the agreement are frowned upon and are likely to be avoidable. Under such an agreement a manager would ostensibly be entitled to receive commission on each album under a three, four, or even five album record deal negotiated by him even though, in an extreme case, the management agreement finished a few days after the contract was signed and the manager performed no further services and in circumstances where the artist engaged a new manager who also was to receive commission on the same future income. Attention must be paid to this subject so that a new manager can be engaged after the term with the prospect of some earnings for his commission.

It is important to explain to the members of a group that the terms of the agreement may apply to them if they depart and seek a different career. There may also be other matters to be addressed upon departure of a member. These will relate particularly to the internal management of the group members as well as to the manner in which joint, but perhaps unrecorded, material will be dealt with. Regard should also be had to the terms of any recording agreements, which may similarly seek to bind the departing member to recording with the same company.

7.5   MANAGER'S EXPENSES

The manager should be primarily responsible for his own business expenses, just as the artist is responsible for his own business expenses. There is certain expenditure the manager might seek to recover, namely expenditure which is directly referable to the management of the artist. This might include transportation, travel and accommodation, as well as associated office and professional fees.

If any such deductions are to be allowed, they should be within specified limits, and all such expenses incurred by the manager must relate directly to the management of the artist. The deduction or recovery of such expenses is something that an artist will normally seek to resist. Some expenditure will clearly be in an artist's best interests and not expenditure which a manager would otherwise be expected to incur on his own account.

Wherever the manager has authority to incur expenses on the artist's behalf, there must be an upper limit on expenditure on any particular item. The manager should seek the prior approval of the artist for expenses exceeding this limit. It is important, however, that the agreement is workable. No manager will want to be continually answerable to an artist for every single item of expenditure. Essentially, any expenditure that the manager incurs should be directly attributable to the promotion of the artist. If that is the case, and the expenses are reasonable, then there is no reason why an artist should complain at a later stage that the manager has exceeded his authority or incurred unnecessary or excessive expenditure. If litigation is required to recover money, those costs should be deducted from income before commission.

7.6 MANAGER'S WARRANTIES AND OBLIGATIONS

The purpose of a management agreement is that the manager agrees to the best of his ability to promote the artist. Failure by a manager to promote the artist using his best skill and endeavours may give the artist cause to terminate the agreement. Whilst the obligation to promote the artist underpins the manager's obligations, it is impossible for management to guarantee success. It is clearly in everyone's best interests for an artist to record, perform and generate income.

The manager should be careful to ensure that he complies with any statutory obligations since otherwise he may acting unlawfully, in which case his contract may be void for illegality. In this connection, historically a poor form of management contract used to use words suggesting that it was part of the management obligation to obtain engagements. In London at least that meant that, as a matter of strict interpretation of the law, the manager was required to obtain an employment licence or to be acting unlawfully. There is some confusion under the Conduct of Employment Agencies and Employment Businesses Regulations 2003, SI 2003/3319 but the better view is that the manager should comply. This is not a matter of obtaining a licence but of being obliged to follow the strict code of conduct or to be held to be acting unlawfully. In real terms this only means that he has to put in writing his terms of business, so a full written management agreement will probably suffice.

7.7 ACCOUNTING

A prudent artist will ensure that all income is paid directly into a bank account controlled by himself or his accountant. Commission is then paid with the artist's authority to the manager by an accountant or other third party. The manager must take appropriate steps to ensure that all moneys are paid to the designated account. If this involves legal action, the artist should be consulted prior to proceedings being issued.

There may be reasons why such an arrangement is not suitable and in such a situation matters should be arranged so that the manager establishes a separate designated account through which to conduct the business of the artist. It should be made clear that the manager receives all moneys in trust for the artist, with the exception of the manager's commission. Arrangements should be in place for the artist to be able to inspect or audit all books and records maintained by the manager and to be entitled to copies.

In respect of the income which he controls the manager must provide full, accurate and regular statements of account to the artist. These statements must deal with all income received by the manager on behalf of the artist. Whilst it would not be usual to require the manager to provide audited accounts, the keeping of up-to-date accurate books is important. Without such information, the artist's accountant is unable to prepare tax returns. The manager should prepare cash-flow forecasts as well as estimates of expenditure. The manager must then provide brief but regular accounts and other financial information to keep the artist up to date with his financial situation. This may involve monthly accounting. The manager should also provide more detailed accounts on a half-yearly basis.

7.8 ARTIST'S OBLIGATIONS

The fundamental obligation for the artist is to provide his services in accordance with the agreed career plan. A refusal to do so will prevent the manager from performing his obligations and, accordingly, there may be a breach of the terms of the agreement. That is not to say that an artist should do everything that a manager requests, but he should do so if this is in conformity with an agreed career plan. The types of services the artist should perform relate only to the scope of the manager's appointment. Typically, for a musician this involves performing, recording, composing and promoting his work.

An artist will usually also agree not to provide services for any third party without the manager's permission. The artist is exclusively represented by the manager and, accordingly, performing or recording with someone else without the manager's consent will be a breach. It will be a matter of law based upon the specific facts as to the legal effect of such a breach and whether it will be repudiatory or whether it gives rise only to a claim for damages. If the latter the assessment of the quantum of damages will not be easy.

Frequently, agreements will be signed obliging new members of a group to sign a management agreement with the group's manager. Similarly, departing members will often be obliged under the terms of the agreement to use the manager in any new or solo career which they undertake.

It is usual for management agreements to be signed jointly and severally by the individual members of the group. In such a case, each member will be liable for the acts and defaults of the others. In principle, such joint and several liability also means that each individual is bound to the manager. An express clause dealing with the situation where one member of a group leaves to pursue a different career will normally be included in an agreement for the avoidance of doubt. In such a situation, a clause will specify what rights a manager has. Once again, this is a matter for agreement between the parties.

It is important for departing members of a band that they are fully indemnified against any risks or liabilities which might have arisen whilst they were part of the band. Usually, a group's partnership agreement will deal with this, often by way of an indemnity from the remaining members. If the group is a partnership then the usual steps upon departure or retirement of a partner should be taken, for example placing appropriate advertisements, and altering the group stationery and bank accounts.

A departing member may simply assume – despite a clause in the contract to the contrary – that the manager will have no interest in his new career. In such a case, the departing member cannot rely on the fact that a manager may have done nothing to assert his rights. If the rights are contained in the contract, then it will usually be some time before the manager is deemed to forego rights. It is possible that a failure by the manager to promote a departing member is a breach of his best endeavours obligation. However, this cannot be relied upon by the departing member and, if necessary, a specific release should be sought from the manager.

7.9 MISCELLANEOUS

The manager must confirm that he has not entered into any conflicting agreements or arrangements which would in any way limit or hinder his ability to provide services as agreed under the terms of the agreement.

The manager should also undertake not to assign or attempt to assign the benefit of the agreement to any third party. An artist may consider agreeing to such an assignment; however, any assignment must be made with his prior written consent. Ideally, an artist should take independent advice in such a situation.

It is preferable for an acknowledgement to be placed in the agreement on the part of the manager stating that no copyright or performance rights are vested in the manager. Furthermore, no rights in the name or likenesses of the artist will vest in the manager. Accordingly, all intellectual property rights should, unless specifically assigned elsewhere (e.g. in publishing agreements), remain in the ownership of the artist. It is not usual for an artist to assign such rights to a manager, and he should resist such a requirement.

There are a number of provisions relating to termination which may be included in the agreement.

A force majeure clause will deal with unforeseen circumstances beyond the control of the parties which would otherwise frustrate the contract by preventing one or both of the parties to the agreement from fulfilling their obligations.

Failure by the manager to perform any of his obligations could also give a right to terminate the agreement, for example where the following situations arise.

1. An allegation is made that the manager is not using best endeavours to promote the artist and, accordingly, is not performing his side of the bargain. In such a situation, the artist should keep careful records of evidence which, if necessary, could be produced before a court to help substantiate such allegations. Minor breaches should be remedied quickly. Persistent breaches, although minor in nature, should give the parties the right to terminate the agreement.
2. There is a failure to account or render accounts as required by the agreement. This should be a specific breach of obligation on the part of the manager which could result in termination.
3. Automatic termination of the agreement if the manager becomes insolvent or is in any way unable to meet his debts as they fall due. In such a situation, the right to commission under the terms of the agreement should also cease.

A time-limit should be set within which the artist must complain or serve notice on the manager terminating the agreement. A distinction will usually be drawn between a breach of contract which brings or gives a right to terminate and minor breaches of contract which are more easily remedied. In any event, an artist may, by conduct, affirm the contract despite a breach by a manager. In such a case, an artist would not subsequently be entitled to terminate an agreement unless there was a new breach of agreement giving the right to termination.

Other boilerplate clauses dealing with assignment of rights, confidentiality, choice of law and jurisdiction, service of notices and other relevant matters, for example arbitration, should be included as appropriate. There should be a ban on assignment by either party at least without formal written consent.

CHAPTER 8

Recording contracts

8.1 INTRODUCTION

8.1.1 Recording agreements

A recording agreement is the cornerstone of a successful career for 'popular' performers. Although live performances can create an enthusiastic following, the money and recognition created by recording and releasing work is the basis of wider popularity. The number, quality and popularity of artists signed on recording contracts to record labels are a basic asset for most successful record companies. This chapter considers some of the important clauses and considerations which must be borne in mind when drafting or reviewing recording contracts.

It is unusual for all but the most established artists to have a choice of record company and recording contracts. It is often the case that an unsigned band will accept any deals offered. This will be because it is a simple fact that if there are no records on the market there can be no success. As is said in other areas, you have to be in it to win it. The terms of all offers can be made more acceptable with negotiation between the artist and the record company. The artist should always be advised by someone who is independent and experienced in the music industry (for the problems that can arise if this does not happen, see, e.g. *Silvertone Records* v. *Mountfield* [1993] EMLR 152 discussed at **para.1.4.5**). The absence of such advisers may, in the event of a subsequent dispute, prove fatal to the agreement. Whilst this may not be of immediate concern to the artist, record companies are best advised to ensure that the artist is aware of the need for and takes competent professional advice.

8.1.2 Categories of contracts

For many reasons which are not the concern of this book the recording industry has changed quite dramatically in relation to current popular music. The number of large record companies has shrunk as a result of mergers prompted by the fall in volume sales of singles and lower profit margins all round (although that is probably not the full answer by any means).

129

The first category of contracts is that between artist and major record company. The second is a variety of formats of agreements between artists and either small independent record companies or independent producers who can also operate in part as small record companies.

Under the first category, the deal is with a fully functioning company with the full infrastructure needed for the more successful artists internationally including identifying the material to be recorded, recording that material, and the full range of promotion, advertising, manufacturing, distribution and general career development.

The second category has a number of differences but the essential ones are that the operation will not be as well funded and a great number of the elements involved will have to be subcontracted, and any activity outside the UK will have to be subcontracted to others. An independent company may have success and then be taken over by a major one. Within this area are also a number of much smaller companies that are in business with the underlying knowledge that they only expect to be able to have enough success to attract the interest of a major in any given artist. They hope that the major will sign a contract subcontracting the services of the artist but with an ongoing involvement of the independent.

This chapter looks at the provisions in the full recording contract but most if not all of the same principles will apply to contracts with the independent sector. The reason is that the company that is a genuine full service independent record company will need the same basic rights as the major because it will need to enjoy the fruits of its success and will need to be vested of the rights to enable it to licence abroad. The small company looking to create an interest will need to be able to offer to the major record label the relevant rights and controls over an artist if the major does become attracted. The independent will need some longevity built in so that it may benefit from its foresight and commitment.

The form of contract for a major will be drafted by the record company and it is not appropriate to supply a suggested format within this book. A form of contract relating to the independent sector appears at **Appendix A3**. The format for a full recording contract reflects most of what will typically be found in the contract prepared by the major. It will not be uncommon for the independent to utilise the form provided at **Appendix A2**, and to prefer to use the concept of sharing the net profit with an artist rather than providing for complicated royalty provisions. Not only will this shorten negotiations considerably but it also removes some of the risks and shares some of the financial burdens. It does this by reason of the fact that the independent does not know the precise royalty rate it will get from its licensees and therefore it does not risk, for example, having to pay the artist a royalty of 10 per cent if it only receives that percentage or a lower sum. It is also safer for the independent because rather than having to pay a royalty on each record sold it only pays a royalty once the project has shown a profit overall.

There will be other contracts applicable to a record company and this book does not attempt to deal with the whole range. The most common will be that between the company and the individual producer of records. The producer is the person who works in the studio with the artist. He will make his own creative contribution to the recording affecting its presentation, structure and style. The producer will receive a fee and a share of royalty which should be computed in the same way as the royalty payable to the artist. There is one exception to that as a producer, properly advised, will require what is called an 'A Side' provision. That is a clause that requires that the royalty payable to him is not reduced if the two sides of a single carry tracks produced by different producers. There are no contractual principles which differ in the producers' contracts from any others.

Apart from normal suppliers' contracts the other main contracts which will be relevant are those whereby the company licenses use of its records outside the UK. The principal elements of those contracts are:

- parties;
- territory;
- term (including options);
- definition of records included in the contract;
- advances;
- royalty rate;
- post term rights; and
- assignment and other provisions.

Such contracts are not further discussed in this chapter because the same elements and legal principles apply to these as apply in the contract between artist and record company (be it major or independent) and those that apply and are discussed as between a publisher and its sub-publishers elsewhere in this book (see **Chapter 9**).

8.1.3 Performers' rights

The record company will wish to acquire the exclusive rights to the recording services of an artist so that its success cannot benefit another. It will also acquire the right to exploit and promote the results of those services.

The statutory performers' rights contained in Part II of CDPA 1988 and the consent necessary for the exploitation of performances are important aspects of a recording contract. The 1988 Act also recognised the existence of 'exclusive recording contracts' between performers and record companies, and for the first time, gave rights to the company to the artist services which could be asserted against third parties. The performances in question usually take place in a recording studio with other musicians, a sound engineer and a record producer. Explicit consent to record and exploit performances should be given in the contract.

In return for the grant of exclusive recording rights to a record company, an artist expects to receive payment. An artist's remuneration is paid either as a royalty based on sales of recordings or as a share of the net profit made from the exploitation of his recordings.

In addition, it is common for an advance against royalties to be paid to the artist. The record company will also pay recording costs. Both sums are recouped from income. In the case of a royalty deal they will be treated as an advance of the potential royalty and recovered out of it. In the case of a net profit deal they may either be deducted from the gross income or even from the artist's share only. The artist's right to equitable remuneration is dealt with by receipt of a share of a recording's public performance income – the income collected by PPL.

8.2 SOUND RECORDINGS

The Copyright, Designs and Patents Act 1988 defines a sound recording as a recording of sounds on any medium from which the sounds may be reproduced. For the purposes of a recording agreement, it is important to define exactly what sound recordings the company has the rights to and, in particular, what types of recording the artist gives his consent to the company to exploit. The agreement must define what is meant by a 'recording'; for example, a recording may be defined in the agreement as:

> an audio or audio-visual recording made for the Company by the Artist on any format known now or arising in the future under this agreement.

The company will own and exploit the recordings. The agreement should stipulate the medium on which the recordings can be exploited, otherwise the artist may be able to argue at a later date that no consent was given for a particular form of exploitation. A record company should reserve the right to 'distribute and sell the recordings in any configuration and all media whether now known or known in the future'. Such a clause will include CDs, tapes, LPs and singles, Internet use, ringtones as well as audio-visual products. The definition should, from the record company's point of view, be wide enough to include methods of exploiting sound recordings which have not yet been invented but which may become popular in the future. An interesting example of this is the development of the compact disc over the last 16 years, with the prospect of developments such as the mini disc and the DAT tape continuing in the future. Forms of multi-media exploitation such as CD-ROM and other computer formats may also be considered, as well as interactive products, web casts and broadband exploitation. Online distribution and exploitation of recordings has also developed and record companies now exploit these rights. The extent to which the artist will be able to negotiate royalties on unusual exploitation of the sound recording depends on the status of the artist and on the precise wording of the contract which may not have taken account of some technological advances and thus have no royalty rate in place for them. Although the definition of a 'recording' may cover a new technological advance, the contract may not provide a royalty rate for that new format. The company and the artist may then have to agree a rate for the format or the company may claim the artist is not entitled to further payment. Generally, a record contract provides a 'catch-all' royalty rate for all new technologies/formats.

8.3   COPYRIGHT

The copyright in a sound recording is distinct from the copyright in any underlying material such as the song itself. The exploitation of an underlying work and the collection of income due from an artist's original compositions is a matter for the artist's music publisher, the PRS and the MCPS. In any sound recording, there will be a number of rights involved. The copyright in the song (music and lyrics) will either be with the original composer or authors of the work or it may have been assigned to a music publishing company. The ownership of copyright in a sound recording is dealt with by s.9(2)(a) of CDPA 1988, under which the author is the person by whom the arrangements necessary for the making of the recording are undertaken. This is often the producer of the sound recording or the record company itself. The performance right in this copyright is dealt with by PPL on behalf of individual record and production companies.

The recording contract will deal with ownership of copyright in sound recordings. It is usual for the contract to contain an express declaration that the record company owns copyright as well as for the artist to make an assignment of such copyright to the record or production company. Such an assignment will be included in the agreement so as to avoid any later arguments over copyright ownership in the recordings. This is quite distinct from copyright ownership in the underlying works, use of which requires permission from the songwriter or publisher. Many record companies will agree a provision whereby after a period of time their rights shall cease and all rights shall revert to or be assigned to the artist. This is true of most record companies, not just the smaller independent companies.

8.4   MORAL RIGHTS

Moral rights relate mainly to the underlying works in a sound recording (such as the song itself) and thus relate to the composer of works that are recorded. The scope of and need for any provisions in the recording contract dealing with moral rights must be carefully considered. However, in 2006 moral rights were extended to actual performances by artists.

8.5 CONTRACT CONSIDERATIONS

Apart from matters dealt with expressly as a result of copyright, performers' rights, rental rights and moral rights, the recording agreement is mainly a matter of commercial agreement and contract law. It is important that the terms of the agreement are all expressly included in writing in the document signed by the parties. Enforceability of a recording contract, together with the construction of its terms, is a matter for rules established under the common law. There have been particular problems with entertainment contracts over the years, which have resulted in extensive litigation. In particular, courts have been asked to look at contracts that are allegedly in restraint of trade or have been made as a result of undue influence. It is also important that where an artist is a minor, due regard is had to the common law governing contracts with minors.

The major terms of recording contracts are considered in this chapter. Matters that are purely contractual, and not particular to recording contracts, are considered in **Chapter 1**, which includes such considerations as undue influence and restraint of trade.

Before signing a recording contract an artist should be properly and independently advised.

An independent, experienced manager can be appointed to help promote the artist and negotiate agreements on his behalf. It is important that the manager does not have any conflict of interest. For example, if the manager owns or has a holding in the production or record company with whom the artist is signing, he should not wear both those hats in any negotiation.

Independent legal advice explaining the terms and effects of any agreements should be obtained before such agreements are signed. Although such advice should be of assistance, there have been instances where, despite the provision of experienced legal advice at the outset, the courts have been willing to set aside or vary agreements. The fact is that many artists will sign with a record or production company despite adverse advice because of the difficulty in obtaining any contract at all.

As far as possible, the terms of the agreement should be fair and reasonable and not unduly onerous. If possible, the obligations placed on both parties should contain the minimum restrictions necessary to give the contract business efficacy.

8.6 DURATION OF THE AGREEMENT

The duration of a recording contract should be as certain as possible. However, the term of the agreement, whether fixed or not, will be referable to a 'minimum recording commitment'. The agreement is also likely to be separated into a number of separate contractual periods. Each period will usually be tied to an option on the part of the company to renew the contract once the minimum recording commitment for the period has been satisfied. The number of contractual periods and therefore the number of recordings is negotiable. It will be longer for major companies and shorter for the independents, and for established artists it may be as many as five or six albums.

For example, an agreement may provide that it is to last one year during which time the artist has to make enough recordings to satisfy a minimum recording commitment. This commitment will almost certainly be for material previously unrecorded by the artist. It may also have to be for material written by the artist.

The term may be referable to the delivery of recordings and an additional period to allow the company to release and exploit the recording in order to gauge the potential for success before the risk of entering into a new contractual period. Thus, an initial period may last until 180 days after delivery of the recording for that period, but for not less than a year or 18 months in total. When considering the term of any contract, regard must be had to the potential length of the agreement including any options and other extensions (such as for late delivery) included in the agreement. It will be normal to specify a maximum time for each period come what may. This is of interest to the artist in order to bring some certainty and acceptable to the record company to avoid any risk that the contract will be attacked as being perpetual.

Late delivery of an album may allow the company to extend the term of the agreement by a certain number of days. Any extensions which are possible under the agreement should only be for reasons which are referable to the artist's default. As long as the artist satisfies his minimum recording commitment, there should be no extension or effective penalty for events that are out of the artist's control.

The contract may also require the artist to deliver the recordings within a certain period of time after which the record company may be able to terminate the agreement. This is to prevent long delays by previously successful artists subsequently wishing to resume a career. In addition, the artist is usually restricted to the delivery of one recording at a time. This prevents the total contractual commitment from being delivered by the artist at once in order to end the contract.

Marketing requirements also call for additional recordings which can be made available as various incentives and these so called 'bonus' records will be additional and part of the minimum commitment for the period.

The duration of an agreement is one of the matters that the courts have considered in a number of the cases dealing with restraint of trade in music contracts. The contract should specify as clearly as possible when the term commences and the date on which it ends.

If an artist fails to satisfy the minimum commitment during the agreement (and any extensions) it will amount to a breach of contract allowing the company to terminate its obligations under the agreement.

The minimum commitment should be for a definite number of master recordings. The number should be attainable, and the company should be obliged to provide the means for the artist to meet the commitment. This involves the allocation of a budget and the booking of studio time. Compositions must be chosen for the recording sessions. If necessary, a producer must be agreed. The terms upon which a producer is employed are usually a matter for the company to negotiate, although a producer royalty is often deducted from the artist's income. The minimum commitment may be for a certain number of singles or albums as defined in the agreement. The terms of the agreement should also deal with the obligation of the record company to promote, distribute and commercially exploit the master recordings. Ideally failure to release would result in termination of the contract and return of the recordings to the artist, but this may not be achievable.

8.7   OPTIONS

It is usual for a record company to include either an option to extend the length of the term or a number of break clauses at various points in the contract. Indeed, there may be an option to extend the term several times or a break clause exercisable on a different number of occasions. Each extension of the term of the agreement should be for a certain or defined period and for a certain recording commitment during that time. If the term of the contract, or the options granted under it, result in the artist being bound to the record company for a long period of time, this may be a factor in a subsequent challenge by an artist to the validity of the contract on the grounds of it being in restraint of trade.

There is no standard formula for the inclusion of an option or break clauses within an agreement. A new signing is unlikely to be given a long-term commitment from a record company until the artist has achieved some success. For the record company, the purpose of an option or break clauses is to enable it to retain successful artists and release those who are unsuccessful.

The option, or each successive period of the contract, should be accompanied by a payment, which may be an advance on royalties, and, as such, recoupable by the record company from the artist. Any option must clearly set out the conditions and terms of the extended contract. An artist who feels that the contract, if extended, does not reflect his status and success may seek to renegotiate terms. Any renegotiation inevitably centres on the amount of money (in terms of advance and royalties) the artist expects to receive and the duration of the agreement (in terms of the number of recordings the company may now commit itself to call on during each period of the agreement). Accordingly, the artist should negotiate increased advances and stepped royalties for each option or successive period of the agreement.

Record companies often cite the use of break clauses over options as preferable, because a company cannot 'inadvertently' neglect to exercise an option. The converse is also true – it may neglect to terminate. Frequently the drafting technique to deal with this is to provide that there are options to continue but if they are not exercised the term is automatically extended until the artist makes a written enquiry as to whether the company in fact wishes to renew.

8.8 ARTIST'S WARRANTIES AND OBLIGATIONS

8.8.1 Standard terms

Reference in this paragraph to 'standard' terms and conditions is to the common or usual terms normally found in a recording agreement. Although there is enormous variation from record company to record company, there are a number of matters that it is usual to find in an agreement.

8.8.2 Artist's obligations

Central to the recording contract is a promise by the artist to provide exclusive services (performances) to the record company in return for money. The exclusivity provisions are fundamental to the record company. An artist cannot record elsewhere without the record company's permission. Typically, there is also a re-recording restriction which is discussed at **para.8.8.3**.

It is important that the artist – whether an individual or a member of a band – is not bound by any previous agreement which could affect the contract that is being offered. The artist is normally required to warrant that there are no existing obligations which would restrict his freedom to enter into the contract. The record company will require a number of warranties from the artist relating to this point.

In particular, a record company usually requires the artist to state that:

(a) he is free to enter into the contract;
(b) he has the right to assign any rights granted to the company;
(c) he has not entered and will not enter into any other conflicting arrangements; and
(d) there are no recordings by him which have not already been released by other recognised record companies.

Alternatively, if an artist is still bound by a previous contract, this should be disclosed to the company. The new contract will almost certainly conflict with any previous exclusive recording agreement. The record company should not sign the artist unless and until the artist is released from the previous contract. All previous contracts should be disclosed to the record company to ensure that there are no existing obligations that conflict with the new agreement.

The record company will require a number of other obligations from the artist. For example, he may have to agree:

(a) that his performances will not be obscene, blasphemous or defamatory of anybody;
(b) to join and remain a member of the MU or other similar organisation, if legally necessary;
(c) not to do anything that would prejudice his standing or that of the record company or damage either party's reputation;
(d) to take reasonable practical steps to stay in good health and not put himself at any risk;
(e) to perform to the best of his abilities;
(f) not to grant any other person the right to record a live or other performance, including any one-off performance he may give which could, nonetheless, be exploited;
(g) to do what the record company reasonably requires to promote the recordings including personal appearances free of charge;
(h) to attend recording sessions and rehearsal promptly and in a fit state to perform and rehearse;
(i) not to perform with any other artist without the record company's permission;
(j) that he is not a minor; and
(k) that he is a qualifying person for the purposes of CDPA 1988.

The artist might also be obliged to use his own name or his stage name, as appropriate, and not to change it except with the company's permission. Part of the artist's goodwill is in his name. This is the easiest way for the buying public to identify the artist and buy his recordings. There may be an obligation on the artist to keep the company informed of his whereabouts at all times. Some of the more onerous terms might relate to the look or style the artist adopts. The company will be concerned that an artist does not abandon a successful image in favour of an untried one without proper consultation. An artist may warrant that he will not carry on any anti-social activity or be convicted of a crime, although such restrictions should be avoided as being unduly onerous. A mutual obligation may be imposed by the record company to ensure confidentiality so that the terms of its agreements are not disclosed.

The artist should avoid giving any warranty or entering into any obligation that is either unduly onerous or difficult to perform. Once again, this is a matter for considered advice and discussion.

The artist will usually allow the company to use his likeness and name for promotional purposes and he should require that such is in a form previously approved by him. It may be appropriate for the artist to be given the opportunity to approve any promotional or advertising material in advance of publication. This permission should be limited so that it covers only the right to use the artist's likeness for promoting records and not for any merchandising purposes. Merchandising rights should be the subject of separate agreements and negotiation.

Obligations to promote recordings and to tour may also be included in a recording contract, although the details of such obligations will be agreed between the management, the artist and the company.

8.8.3 Re-recording restrictions

The record company is likely to require a restriction of a few (perhaps five) years from the end of the agreement on the re-recording of any of the master recordings or any individual compositions contained on them. This restriction only binds the artist and does not stop third parties (who have the publisher's permission) from producing other versions of a previously recorded song. The restriction would apply to live as well as studio versions of recordings, but does not hinder an artist from performing his recordings live. This restriction should be tempered so that it only applies if the record company has released the composition in question either during the term of the agreement or within a specified period (of perhaps one or two years) after the end of the agreement.

Such a restriction exists to allow the company to exploit its catalogue of original recordings to its best ability. It is quite common for recordings to enjoy a resurgence of popularity some time after the original release because of an advertising campaign or a wave of nostalgia. It does not prohibit an artist from re-recording with the consent of the company although that consent may not be forthcoming. Such restrictions may be in restraint of trade.

8.9 COMPANY'S WARRANTIES AND OBLIGATIONS

8.9.1 Recording and release

It is important, if the artist is obliged to perform and record material, that there is some obligation on the company to fund, release and exploit those works. If the company is in no way obliged to do so, then the artist has no way of making a living. An agreement which places no obligation or no substantial obligation on a record company to release material may be challenged as being in restraint of trade. Whilst the artist is signed exclusively to the company, the company may effectively have no reciprocal obligations of its own. This obligation should include overseas release.

An artist should ensure that the record company is obliged to provide the money for him to record a specified number of master recordings, whether singles or albums. Without this commitment from the record company, the artist has no way of fulfilling the minimum recording commitment. On the other hand, record companies are concerned that they are not obliged to fund and release a large number of recordings where the artist in question is, as yet, unproven. In this case, the record company will usually be willing to commit itself to a certain minimum of product – perhaps two singles or one album – and then to have an option to extend the term of the agreement, as discussed at **para.8.7**, depending upon the success or otherwise of those recordings.

Most companies are unwilling to give an undertaking to release a record and, indeed, such an obligation may be somewhat meaningless in reality since a release without enthusiasm and proper marketing is of little value to an artist. The solution is to agree terms that provide for the artist to call for a release and if the company is not prepared to release and promote the record, for the artist to be at liberty to seek another company. This should provide that in this event the contract term ceases because without the ongoing exclusive services of the artist any other company is likely to refuse to become involved.

Similar provisions should apply to other countries, or at least to important ones, but in this case the termination will not apply to the whole territory but only to the rights of the company in the given country as to future recordings.

Acceptability of recordings

The artist will be concerned to ensure that the record company, having paid for and received master tapes of a recorded performance, is then obliged to manufacture and make those recordings commercially available to the public. The record company will be unwilling to undertake any minimum release commitment and will be allowed to use its own commercial judgement as to the date and manner of release. The record company will reserve the right to refuse recordings if they are not deemed to be suitable for its purposes. This suitability relates to technical matters (such as the quality of the equipment the performances have been recorded on) as well as the commercial suitability of the product. This latter requirement is likely to be the more controversial of the two as it involves the record company making an artistic judgement. If the artist and the record company have collaborated sufficiently in the making of the recordings, there should be no problem. The agreement should reflect this collaboration by requiring the company to consult the artist over the choice of material, approval of a budget, appointment of a producer and any other matters which are important to the parties.

Release

Some of the cases which have considered music industry agreements (such as *Silvertone Records* v. *Mountfield* [1993] EMLR 152, discussed at **para.1.4.5**) have commented on the lack of obligation on the part of a record company to release or exploit recordings. If there is no such obligation, the contract may be challenged as being in restraint of trade. Such a challenge would usually only enable the artist to be released from the contract with an award of damages. Ideally, an artist would like to see a record company actively manufacturing, promoting and selling his work to the public.

Unfortunately, there is no guarantee that any works will be successful, however much money has been spent on making and promoting them. A record company cannot make the public buy a record, although there are certain steps that can be taken to ensure that recordings come to the attention of the public. Manufacturing recordings is the first step in this process, after which the work needs to be 'plugged' and marketed to receive as much broadcast coverage or 'air-time' and other publicity as possible. This involves giving copies of new releases out to disc jockeys, TV stations and the music press to encourage their broadcast and purchase. As a result of broadcasting, reviewing and appropriate promotional dissemination, public interest may arise sufficiently to stimulate sales of the work.

A record company must agree to release or procure the release of the master recordings delivered by the artist under the terms of the contract. It should do so within a reasonable time of delivery. A time should be stated in the contract. This time may vary, but must be at least long enough for the company to make all the necessary arrangements for the release of the recording. A provision requiring the company to use its best or reasonable endeavours to promote the recording should be considered. A company may not agree to the best endeavours clause, but, nevertheless, some commitment should be extracted. A period of between four and six months between recording and release is quite reasonable. The effects of the company's failure to release the recordings should also be dealt with in the agreement. If there is a legitimate reason (such as an event of force majeure), the artist may have no cause for complaint. If the company has simply been dilatory in fulfilling its obligations, the artist may consider serving a notice requiring it to fulfil its obligations within a specific time. If the company fails to do so, the termination provisions of the agreement could take effect. If the company never releases a recording, the artist may sue for breach of contract. In the event of no release, the artist should also ask for a reassignment of copyright in the recording.

8.9.2 Recording costs

An artist will generally be financed by the record company, which should provide the necessary means to fund studio time, payment for session musicians, studio engineers and, in certain circumstances, the producer. Recording costs are part of general advances which are recoupable from royalties. The recording costs are the record company's investment risk. If an album is not successful, it does not recover its investment. Although a record company is usually entitled under the terms of the recording contract to recover recording costs as a first charge on royalties in the same way as advances are recoverable, if an artist fails to break even in terms of recording costs alone after his first album, then the record company may not renew its options or release any further material by that artist.

The record company recovers recording costs (as it does advances) from all royalties payable to the artist on the sales of that artist's recordings. Effectively, the artist subsidises his unsuccessful recordings with his successful ones.

Recording costs can often be a bone of contention between an artist and a record company. Generally, it is in both parties' interests to control recording costs so that they do not escalate unduly. Excessive recording expenditure may be the difference between a recording being profitable and never recouping its costs. It is in both parties' interests to obtain the best results possible from the available budget. In *Zang Tumb Tuum Records Ltd and Another* v. *Holly Johnson* [1993] EMLR 61, the court looked unfavourably upon the level of expenditure incurred in producing the second album by the group 'Frankie Goes to Hollywood', especially as the costs were largely spent in hiring the company's studios. In the circumstances, the court was prepared to state that there was a duty on the production company not to spend an excessive amount on production costs. This should be borne in mind by company and artist alike at the time of recording.

It is important that the artist limits the actual recording costs which can be recovered from royalties by ensuring that the way in which recording costs are defined is limited to actual direct costs incurred by the record company in producing the album. For example, an artist will not wish recording costs to include other productional packaging costs of the recording itself, such as the commissioning of artwork or sleeve design or the payment of royalties to third parties associated with the production of the recording. These are costs which should be borne by the record company, and not the artist.

The record company will recoup from royalties the total of an artist's costs and expenses over the whole course of the agreement and sometimes from previous agreements. Thus, a successful back catalogue of recordings can subsidise an unsuccessful future recording. Cross-recoupment from music publishing deals and income from anything other than recordings should be avoided. The artist should police cross-recoupment from other contracts carefully, as terms allowing this can sometimes slip into deals.

8.9.3   Music publishing royalties

In addition to the payment of royalties to the artist for his performance, there are payments due from the record company to the owners of the underlying works. Underlying works in the case of popular music are usually the songs used and recorded by the performers. These songs may or may not be written and composed by the performers themselves and may include cover versions of previous songs, or songs specially written and submitted to the artist for recording.

The sale of records which contain copyright works attract a royalty, known as the 'mechanical royalty', which is due to the owner of the copyright in the song. The MCPS administers this right under an agreement reached with the BPI. These payments are unrelated to the royalty due to the artist as performer of a work. Overseas the mechanical royalty income of the publisher may be dealt with by the MCPS collecting this from its associate, or more usually it will be dealt with by the sub-publisher.

It is important that the artist royalty rate payable under the recording contract does not allow for any deductions from the dealer price in respect of such royalties payable by the record company for use of the underlying copyright material. This is an expense properly borne by and accounted for by the record company (subject to the limitations of the 'controlled composition' clause).

8.9.4   Controlled composition clause

The payment of mechanical royalties in North American proceeds on a different basis from that in the UK. The American copyright law provides for a statutory rate for the mechanical royalty but also allows the parties to negotiate a variation. Record companies argue that the statutory rate is too high and they require a negotiated variation as an almost invariable condition. Very successful artists are able to avoid this but it is an exception rather than the rule. In somewhat simplistic terms the required variation is that the artist agrees that on sales in America the mechanical royalty will be three-quarters of the statutory rate applicable at the date of the recording or of the release of the record (without increase over the years) and that it is limited to the amount which would have been paid on the usual album of 10 or 12 songs even though the album may contain more. This is a complex and specialist area where advice will be necessary but against a background of a reluctance on the record companies to negotiate. The independent will very much reduce its chances of securing a licensee for its records in North America if there is no controlled composition clause.

Accordingly the contract with the artist will provide that in relation to songs written in whole or in part by him (and other songs if the artist chooses them) there will be the special rate of mechanical royalty granted for North America.

There will also be a provision for the grant of synchronisation licences for visual programmes of the artist on terms favourable to the record company.

8.10   OTHER OBLIGATIONS

8.10.1   Promotion

The promotion of the artist's recordings should primarily be undertaken by the company. The costs of the promotion should also be borne by the company. The company should undertake a certain basic level of promotion, which should ensure that the recording is promoted to the public. The cost of any higher or unusual promotion may be recoupable from the artist, although this must be agreed with the artist if not included in the agreement.

A typical method of promoting new recordings includes making visual programmes for the so-called promotional video. The company may retain the right to request the artist to make a promotional video. The exploitation of the video is left in the hands of the company. Record companies may release promotional videos in a similar way to tapes and CDs for sale to the public and will increasingly do so as multi-use and sound with vision use including DVD become more popular. The costs of such videos are usually treated as recording costs and deducted from royalties. The usual term is for 50 per cent to be attributable to the artist's general recording costs and the remaining 50 per cent to income from the exploitation of the video and recouped from such income. The exploitation of promotional videos by broadcast and sale should attract royalty payments. The agreement will enable the company to call upon the artist to make a video. The storyline, budget and all production matters of the video should be agreed with the artist before production.

As part of its promotional activity, the record company may institute advertising campaigns, perhaps by way of newsprint advertisements or sometimes by broadcast advertising. There are often provisions in recording agreements stating that where a recording is advertised by means of a broadcast medium (such as television or radio) then the royalty rates payable on sales of that sound recording may be reduced to one-half or two-thirds of the normal royalties. The artist will be concerned to see that an excessive amount is not spent on any such broadcast campaign. The costs of such promotion should also be split between the artist and the record company. An artist may also contest the inclusion of such a clause in the first place. If a recording is to be advertised in such a way, then the budget for this should be predetermined. Whilst both the artist and record company should recognise that promotion of the artist generally and of sound recordings particularly is an

144

investment, restrictions should be maintained and budgets imposed on any such advertising or promotional campaign. It is usual to limit the reduction by relation to sales during a period related to the country of the TV campaign and to the period of the campaign and further to a point where the royalty forgone equals one-half of the costs of the campaign.

8.10.2   Tour support

Traditionally, artists have promoted recordings by touring and other live appearances as well as by the release of singles from albums. Tours are usually undertaken to coincide with the release of recordings in order to maximise their impact and publicity. Whilst record companies are unlikely to underwrite the cost of a tour, they often provide support for tours. A record company may agree to contribute an unspecified amount of money to a loss-making tour (known as 'tour support'), as part of the recording's promotional expenses. The amount of tour support will be capped to a maximum figure, and the company will expect the artist and his management to manage the tour so as not to produce a loss if possible.

The artist and the company will agree which expenses are deductible from tour income in calculating any loss. Management and agent's commission is unlikely to be included as an expense of the tour. Any tour support should not be considered as commissionable income for the purposes of management or agent's commission. It is also important that tour support is not treated as a recoupable advance for royalty purposes.

8.10.3   Websites

With the growth of the Internet, the majors in particular utilise web pages as an integral part of promotion. Thanks to complicated computer programmes this use extends far beyond simple awareness advertising. 'Hits' can be analysed and the information used as marketing tools not just for the artist in question but to provide a wealth of data which the company can use in other areas. As a result the majors insist upon controlling and owning artist websites. This has become a non-negotiable aspect but the artist should at least make arrangements that the underlying fan base material is available to him and passed to him upon expiration of the term of the contract. The Data Protection Act 1998 is often cited as a reason not to agree this but careful thought can remove that obstacle.

There are costs involved in running websites and thought should be given to any suggestion that the artist should bear any of that cost and to the possibility that the artist should be able to share in any ancillary income generated, such as from the sale of merchandise.

8.11 ADVANCES

The record or production company normally provides all the money for an artist to record a work. Such an investment is almost entirely speculative on the part of the record or production company. It has been estimated by the BPI that the cost of launching a new pop single is in the region of £250,000, but it is further estimated that only one in 10 of all new releases is ever actually profitable. Because of this, to a great extent, the record company's successful artists are indirectly funding the unsuccessful ones. Whilst every artist wants to get the best terms possible from a record company, it is unusual for a new signing to receive a large advance or to obtain a particularly advantageous royalty rate. At best, an artist may come to a company with a solid live following, but translating that into substantial record sales is a different matter. Such a risk is reduced where a company re-signs an existing artist, as the company already has a back catalogue from which it can continue to recoup advances and recording costs.

A record company should advance money to an artist. An advance is a payment made upon signing the contract on account of future royalties. The size of an advance is usually either based upon the success of an established band or reflects the record company's estimate of the artist's potential. A new signing is unlikely to attract a significant advance. In most cases, an advance is payment against future earnings from record sales. As such, it is recovered by the record company from future royalties; this is known as recoupment. Advances are usually recouped from all royalties received by the record company under the artist's contract. Thus, successful albums pay for unsuccessful albums. An artist's advance attracts manager's commission at the agreed rate.

Before an artist receives any royalties, the company will be able to recoup any advance paid on signing the recording agreement, as well as the actual costs of recording. The contract will contain detailed provisions dealing with these aspects.

The majority of artists receive advances on a non-returnable, but recoupable basis. That is to say, they will be required (in the normal scheme of things) to repay the advance, but only from royalties due to sales. If an artist accepts an advance fraudulently or otherwise in breach of contract, the advance may become repayable after litigation.

In addition to an initial advance, there should be further advances if the record company exercises options to renew the contract.

The artist must appreciate that an advance is usually on account of royalties and is not to be thought of as a gift. In effect, the advance has to be earned at some point. The advance is deducted as a first charge from any royalties due if the recording sells. It is effectively a loan, although it is nearly always non-returnable and it does not bear interest.

8.12   OBLIGATION TO PAY ROYALTIES

The obligation to pay royalties is of considerable importance to the artist as it relates directly to his income-earning capacity and livelihood. A record company must be obliged to pay a royalty to the performer. Royalties are based upon a percentage of income from sales and exploitation of the artist's recorded performance. Before any royalty income reaches an artist, payments on the artist's account made by the record company, including recording costs, recoupable advances and other agreed expenses must be paid back in full from this income. The amount of royalty payments and the method of calculation will vary from record company to record company and from artist to artist. A new artist would not normally expect to receive as attractive a deal as an established artist negotiating a new contract.

An artist who is also a composer receives income from the PRS and the MCPS, which may be dealt with by a music publisher, for use of his compositions. The royalty from the recording contract is solely in respect of exploitation of performers' rights and is additional to these other payments. Publishing income is generated by use of songs embodied in sound recordings exploited by record companies. The record company has a payment obligation to the MCPS for use of the underlying works.

The record company is free to exploit the copyright in the sound recording itself, subject to its obligation to make payments to other people such as the artist and music publishers.

8.13   ROYALTY RATES

8.13.1   Factors influencing the rate offered

The royalty rate offered by a record company varies. A previously successful artist renegotiating a contract or entering into a new contract may demand and receive a higher rate than an unknown artist. What the artist may regard as being fair in all the circumstances will undoubtedly differ from the record company's perception. Although there is no 'standard' rate offered to artists, the norm is for a rate somewhere in the region of between 12 and 20 per cent and will vary upon the perceived prospects, with established artists receiving more. Such a rate is based on the published dealer price of recordings; that is to say, the price at which the company lets it be known that it will sell to the dealer (which will then add its own mark up before selling to the public). That price will be defined in the contract and subject to negotiation be adjusted for the purposes of royalty calculation.

The real adjustment is a deduction for royalty calculation purposes of any discount allowed to the dealer. This is of major importance since following the growth of multiple stores it has become common for very substantial discounts to be given. Historically the artist's royalty used to be based on the published retail price but following the abolition of fixed retail prices that is abnormal. Different rates (perhaps half or two-thirds of the basic contract rate) apply to records released with special prices such as 'mid price' and 'budget line' labels, record clubs and compilations which include an artist's work (see further **para.8.14**).

It appears to have been accepted by the courts in the George Michael case (*Panayiotou and Others* v. *Sony Music Entertainment (UK) Ltd* [1994] EMLR 229) that the similarities between record companies in terms of royalty rates offered (as well as the similarities in other contractual terms they offer) are not due to any lack of competition between record companies. Instead, the royalty rate is a commercial rate which reflects the risk and investment the company makes.

8.13.2 Flat rates and sliding scales

The rate offered by a company may be a flat rate on all sales regardless of the success of the artist. Alternatively, the rate may be set at a comparatively modest level for a certain volume of sales and then operate on a sliding scale if and when sales escalate. An artist is thus effectively rewarded for success in a way which he would not have been under a flat rate arrangement. A sliding scale arrangement is a useful mechanism to represent the increasing popularity of an artist as reflected in increased sales. Increased royalty rates often apply on recordings achieving silver, gold and platinum sales.

The artist is usually concerned to establish whether any increased rate applies only to sales above a certain limit or to all sales once the limit has been reached. Obviously, this can have a major effect on the income of the artist, especially if there are a number of steps in the sliding scale as sales increase.

An artist and his advisers will be trying to obtain as high a rate as possible. It is very unlikely that a company will accept an increase retrospectively on earlier sales. The increased rate will normally only apply on sales reported in the accounting period following the account showing the trigger sales as having been achieved. There may, however, be scope for agreeing that once an artist has achieved a given level of sales on recordings, the higher rate then applies to all subsequent sales of all records both existing and future. This ensures that each new recording does not have to climb the scale before the higher rate applies.

Other alternatives include an annual incremental increase in the rate, although this is unlikely to be offered by a recording company as it does not reflect the popularity of the artist and may reward nothing more than longevity.

As an alternative to a sliding scale royalty based on sales of any given record, the royalty could increase on subsequent releases if an earlier release attains a stated minimum in terms of sales. The most attractive arrangement for an artist is either an initially high rate or a sliding scale arrangement to reflect modest and exceptional levels of sales. Given the enormous unpredictability of the record-buying public, an artist is clearly best advised to seek a higher return on those records which are actually successful rather than on future records which may or may not be successful.

8.14 ROYALTY RATES ON SALES AT REDUCED PRICES

8.14.1 Record clubs

Not all sales of a record are full-price sales. There are various mail order and record club organisations which advertise records variously at full price or reduced price, and often include introductory promotions as well as bonus offers once a minimum purchase level has been reached. Most artists would not expect to have their recordings offered immediately through such mail order facilities, although this may sometimes take place quite soon after release. However, mail order sales can provide a large source of income to recording artists and record companies.

An artist's royalty rate on records sold in this way is usually reduced. The reduction in royalties may be to one-half or two-thirds of the full rates and, indeed, no royalty may be payable at all if an artist's recordings are offered as part of an introductory offer or a free or bonus record to the record club or mail order company. Reduced royalty rates are controversial on items such as this. The record companies argue that, since the purchase price is lower, there is effectively less to share between the record company and the artist, as other costs (such as the production costs and mechanical royalties for copyright owners in the underlying works) remain the same. This means that record companies take a bigger slice of the sale price of reduced price sales. In addition, record companies provide a large number of free goods to the clubs, often on a one-for-one basis.

8.14.2 Budget line labels

Most record companies have budget line labels. These are used as a means of selling records at a lower price. These are 'oldies but goldies' which may be part of a record company's back catalogue. These albums can then be rediscovered by purchasers or be released on new sound recording configurations, such as CD, and offered on slightly more competitive terms than new releases as a means of encouraging people to replace their old versions on vinyl or cassette.

Artists are usually concerned to prohibit the sale of their products on budget labels for a reasonable time after the first release of the recording.

Record companies insist on a lower royalty rate in respect of budget line recordings for the simple reason that their selling price is lower resulting in a lower profit margin. Since many of these recordings are only released well after their original release and at a time when the company may have recovered all the initial costs associated with release, the reduced rate seems harsh. Once again, the reduced royalty rate will be in the region of one-half or two-thirds of the full rate.

8.14.3 Compilations

There are two main categories of compilation albums. The first are compilations of an artist's old work (such as 'Greatest Hits' albums) and, secondly, there are compilation albums which may include hits from a given year or hits by particular types of artists (for example, the 'Now That's What I Call Music . . .' compilations). Such compilation albums are often very popular with the public.

The royalties received by an artist on compilations of his own works, such as a 'Greatest Hits' album, should be at the full royalty rate. The release of a 'Greatest Hits' album will not count towards the minimum commitment under the artist's recording contract, nor will it usually attract an advance. Once tracks have been recorded, it is generally open to the record company to do with them as they wish, although the artist may limit the number of 'Greatest Hits' compilations released by the record company. There is unlikely to be any obligation to re-release a recording. Generally, the release of a 'Greatest Hits' or compilation album will be in addition to any other recording commitment as required by the recording contract. The royalty paid for the 'Greatest Hits' album may be calculated in a number of ways and varies from deal to deal.

If a single recording is included on a compilation album or film soundtrack, the rate offered should be pro rata to the other tracks on the album. This compilation may be of the record company's own artists, or it may be a compilation album produced by a wholly independent company which specialises in producing compilation albums containing hits of this year or yesteryear or particular styles of popular songs. On such an occasion, the artist may not be entitled to a royalty based on the full retail selling price of the compilation. Instead, the royalty is based on the artist's proportional contribution to the compilation. The artist will not usually receive more than a proportion of the total royalty based upon his contribution.

8.14.4 Overseas sales

Royalties offered on overseas sales are usually a percentage, perhaps 75–85 per cent of the artist's full rate. Many record companies use licensees or subsidiaries in other countries to promote and distribute recordings. The company should be permitted in its discretion to do so. Full royalties on the sale of recordings overseas are unlikely unless an artist signs direct with an overseas label. In addition, the royalty rate for overseas sales may vary depending on whether the sales are in a major or minor territory. The exchange rate applied to payment should ideally be the same as that applied when the record company receives payments from abroad to ensure that the artist does not suffer as a result.

8.14.5 Online exploitation and other categories

After many years of confusion, sale over the Internet is now an established part of the music business. The record companies, after a slow start, now widely license their recordings for sale over the Internet in various ways. However, there is considerable debate as to whether the sums being charged and paid to publishers and record companies are the right ones.

Be that as it may, there are moneys being paid and record companies are not directly involved in the selling effort and do not have to manufacture, package, store or transport copies of the recordings. Nevertheless the industry standard imposed by the major companies seems to be that the artist will be paid the applicable record royalty rate based not upon the 'dealer' price or even the end user customer price but on the net sum actually received by the record company. The generally prevalent price paid for a download is in the region of 79 pence (including VAT). This figure is also subject to a fee deducted by the credit card companies (and possibly also a fee deducted by the service provider) and in addition has to be shared with the publisher. Surprisingly, there are record companies that actually make a packaging deduction from the net receipt before calculating the artist royalty. Careful attention needs to be paid to the contract in such areas.

There are other forms of exploitation of recording copyright, most noticeably in the form of use in advertisements and in films. The contract should contain provisions for a payment to the artist. One-half of net receipts is usual but it should be remembered to include a provision for the artist to be paid a share of income for any use not covered elsewhere in the contract and specifically attracting a royalty or share of income.

8.14.6 Free goods

Where a record company does not receive payment for a record the contract will provide that the artist receives no royalty on the recordings in question. This is understandable as long as the contract provides that there is a bona fide reason. Records given away in reasonable quantities for promotion is acceptable but such marketing plans as giving away free the records of a sought after artist on condition that the dealer buys the records of another artist is not. Equally there comes a point where the company will sell records at bargain basement prices to get rid of dead stock. Assuming this is a bona fide step and not undertaken for another reason and there is little or no profit for the company this too may be acceptable. Suitable protections and limits should be written into the contract.

8.14.7 Producer's royalties

Producer's agreements are not considered in this book except where they impinge upon an artist's recording agreement. The main consideration is whether the artist is responsible for the producer's royalty. If this is the case, the producer's royalty will be accounted for from the artist's royalty. A producer's royalty is usually in the region of 3–4 per cent. The main difference with producers is that they may not have to bear any recording costs, which means that they are entitled to royalties from the first sales of recordings. The artist, however, is not entitled to any royalties until recording costs have been recouped. Both artist and producer may have received an advance against royalties from the record company. The artist's royalty is thus reduced by the amount of the producer's royalty.

The situation is complicated because the obligation to pay the producer is often placed on the artist, not the record company. The producer may be entitled to further royalties well before all recording costs have been recouped. This arises because the producer only has to recoup the producer advance and not the recording costs. A better arrangement is for agreements to provide that the producer is not entitled to any further royalty until recording costs (which will include his fee) have been recouped.

8.15 CALCULATING ROYALTIES

8.15.1 Establishing price and number sold

The royalty rate, once agreed, is then used to calculate the amount due to an artist by the record company. The royalty payment will be based upon the price and the number of recordings sold.

The rate an artist receives is usually based upon a notional wholesale price that the record company charges dealers after allowing for discounts and VAT. There are also likely to be risks of a sale or exchange arrangement or discounts by way of free goods rather than a straight reduction in purchase price. Careful consideration must be given to all these provisions in the agreement.

There are still some contracts which base royalties on the retail price of records. It is not realistic to establish the actual retail price in each shop since the same record will be sold at different prices in different shops. The industry has resolved this by adopting a policy of creating a 'deemed' retail price being a company's dealer price uplifted by a notional figure to give a retail price upon which the royalty is based. This figure is usually 131 per cent for cassettes and 129 per cent for CDs. Thus, a 10 per cent royalty under the 'old' system is replaced by a 13.1 per cent royalty under the 'new' system.

The artist will want the same royalty rate whatever the product configuration – whether it is compact disc, pre-recorded tape or vinyl long-play or single record disc. Record companies reduce the royalty rate for certain types of recordings, particularly CDs and pre-recorded tapes, on the basis that they are more expensive to produce. Any such reduction should be resisted by the artist. A solution to any problem over this is to attribute a slightly higher packaging cost to such sound recordings. This will reduce the retail selling price upon which royalties are payable (see **8.15.2**). Further there is frequently a reduction in the rate in relation to sales of singles.

8.15.2 Deductions

Packaging costs

Packaging costs are the costs of the album sleeve, the tape cassette, the container and inserted printed material for the compact disc or other medium in which the final retail product is packaged for sale. The most popular format is currently CD although the vinyl disc is still produced. The packaging charge is expressed as a percentage amount of the dealer price (but note not the net dealer price) of the various configurations. The recording agreement may define packaging charges in respect of the various sound recording configurations, for example, pre-recorded cassette (20 per cent) and CD (25 per cent). The packaging charge is then deducted from the dealer price prior to the royalties being calculated. There will normally be no packaging deduction for singles unless there is some special packaging used.

VAT and other taxes

Value added tax (VAT) and any other sales taxes are also deducted from the royalty base price. In allowing such deductions the artist must ensure that the taxes were included in the price in the first place. If this is not the case, then the record company is creating an extra level of profit for itself at the expense of the artist.

The record company will also have to deduct any tax as directed by any legislation which will apply usually in relation only to artists who are not resident in the UK. In receiving accountings from abroad the company may suffer tax deductions especially in relation to income from countries where the UK does not have double tax provisions. The contract should provide that only a fair and equitable proportion is to be deducted from the artist and the necessary documents provided so that the artist may seek repayment or credit for that tax. Additionally the contract should provide that in the event of the company receiving repayment or tax credit the artist should receive the equitable credit.

8.15.3 Net sales

The royalty rate is applied to the sale price of the recordings less deductions. This figure must then be applied to the number of recordings actually sold.

It is at this stage that the record company should be able to account to the artist for royalties actually due on sales.

8.16 ACCOUNTING

8.16.1 Maintaining accounts

The company must undertake to maintain proper and accurate accounts. It should also account to the artist and pay royalties at regular intervals. The normal is for accounting statements showing sales and other income to be made up to 30 June and 31 December in each year and for this statement to be sent with the money shown due within 90 days. There is some tendency to accelerate these periods, the more especially since computerisation makes accounting much easier. The accounting should include all UK and overseas receipts. The record company will be entitled to retain allowable deductions under the agreement and credit income against advances and recording costs. After deductions, the artist can expect to receive his royalties, although this may take some time.

The actual calculation of the royalties due to the artist will be performed by the record company itself. The agreement sets out standard accounting periods in which the company is obliged to account to the artist with a cheque and statement of account.

The artist may be given a period within which to challenge any account and may have the right to audit it. This represents a reduction of the limitation period and should be resisted. If there have been any mistakes in the calculations, then the agreement should require the company to make good any such payment. It may also be appropriate for the artist to direct the record company to pay royalties to the manager or into a particular bank account. The arrangements between the artist and the manager as to payment will be of no concern to the record company. The record company's only concern is that once money has been paid over at the direction of the artist, it incurs no liability if the recipient then acts improperly with that cash. That is a matter for the artist to safeguard himself against.

The artist should obtain a right to inspect and audit the books and records of the record company and to take copies. This is usually agreed so long as the inspection is by a professional accountant who does not seek an advantage by inspecting for more than one artist at a time. If the inspection reveals errors then the cost should be reimbursed but this is usually negotiated only to apply if the error is substantial. Record companies try to limit the inspection to exclude manufacturing records and clearly such a limit effectively hampers the inspection.

Ideally the right of inspection should be obtained to apply to the records of overseas companies especially where the large companies have their own associated companies. At the least, the artist is advised to secure a covenant by the record company that it itself will carry out inspections of its overseas licensees and make available the benefit of any errors discovered.

8.16.2   Reserves

Because records are sold on the basis that a retailer can return them if they do not sell, most agreements contain royalty reserve provisions. This is to ensure that record companies do not pay their artists more royalties than the artist has ultimately earned. The company retains a certain percentage of the total royalties payable to an artist on the basis that some of the records sold will be returned. Reserves for new artists are higher than for established ones and may amount to 25 per cent of the royalties due. The company is entitled to keep the reserve for a certain amount of time after which it must be liquidated and paid to the artist. If the recordings are returned by the retailer, the artist will not have earned the royalty and it will not be paid to him.

8.17   DEPARTING MEMBERS

8.17.1   Group provisions

The recording agreement for a group (or a partnership) will contain provisions dealing with the position if one member of the group leaves. A group should have a partnership agreement or a company dealing with their collective arrangements, as well as a management agreement with their manager. All departing member provisions may be susceptible to challenge on the basis of a restraint of trade as they can tie up an individual's services with a company for a long period.

8.17.2   Services of departing member

The record company will include a clause in a group's agreement stating that any departing members must give notice of their intention to depart to the record company. This may be in addition to any notice to the band itself under their agreement. The record company may reserve itself a number of options.

1. The company may be able to terminate the whole agreement (this should be resisted).
2. The remaining members may be required to continue their services under the contract.
3. The departing member may also be required (at the record company's option) to provide the same services as before, on his own for the company. If the record company is interested in the artist as an individual, it may require the departing member to produce a demonstration recording with one or two original compositions performed by him. This helps the company to assess the potential of the departing individual. A time-limit should be placed upon the company requiring it to make its decision as soon as practically possible. If the company does not wish to use the departing member, a release should be obtained.

The treatment of the group name will be of fundamental importance to the record company which will consider that its investment will have been an integral part of building the goodwill in the name. The record company will wish to have final say in who may or may not use the name upon leaving the group and the right to designate who shall do so. This is likely to take precedence over any agreement made between the individuals.

8.17.3 Departing member's income

The departing member is entitled to receive his share of income from recordings he appeared on during his time with the band. The income is subject to any charges attributable to the departing member. Thus, account will be taken of advances and other deductible costs before the departing member receives his share. The remaining members of a group have their income and expenses as a separate 'account' with the record company. Any provisions that enable the record company to apply income from both the departing member and the remaining group members to the group deficit or, alternatively, the individual's deficit from group income must be resisted. Only a pro rata share of the income should be charged to the group or to the individual's deficit with the company. Thus, the departing member takes his debt with him from which his share of the group income is then attributed to pay it off. The remaining members of the group retain the remainder of the debt, which their share of the income pays off.

Income and costs from future recordings should not affect the royalties of the departing member from previous recordings. The member's entitlement to income as an individual continues despite the fact that he is no longer part of the group, although the group may continue to record.

8.17.4   Group name

The provisions in the contract dealing with use of the group name should be considered. It is most likely that in any contract with a major there will be provisions providing that it will be the company that will control use of the name and such a provision will be binding and will prevail over any other arrangement which the group may have made. Control of use of the name should in any event be restricted to use during the term of the recording contract so that afterwards the partnership arrangement will again apply.

8.18   TERMINATION PROVISIONS

All recording agreements should contain termination provisions. If differences cannot be resolved, the agreement may then be terminated according to these provisions. It is important that the company cannot simply suspend the agreement indefinitely because of an alleged breach. In particular, the obligation to account for income should not cease.

During the course of the agreement, it is quite common for artists to fall out with their record company. This may result in litigation on a number of grounds. Many artists argue that the agreement they entered into was in restraint of trade. They also often argue that the record company has not fulfilled its side of the bargain and is in breach of contract. Record companies often drop artists due to poor sales and do not exercise their option to extend the agreement.

Once an agreement has ended, the artist is free to move on or renegotiate an agreement. The copyright in the sound recordings is owned by the record company for the agreed period. Some or part of the recordings may, in the course of time, be deleted from its active list, sold and licensed to others or become part of its back catalogue. This depends upon the success of the artist and the continued popularity of his recordings.

The company should continue to account for income due to the artist and the publishers on sales of recordings. The artist must also comply with any enforceable re-recording restrictions in the agreement. If the artist moves to another record company, the terms and conditions of that agreement should be considered in light of the matters raised in this chapter. In particular, a release should be obtained from the previous company confirming that the artist is no longer bound by the former agreement.

8.19   OTHER PROVISIONS

As in all contracts there will be the so-called 'boilerplate' clauses dealing with such matters as the giving of notices, the applicable law and jurisdiction and assignability. A major company will expect no restriction on assignability but the artist should insist that all assignees must as a condition of assignment undertake a binding contractual obligation to observe and perform the obligations of the company under the contract to avoid possible arguments as to liability and obligation in the absence of privity of contract.

CHAPTER 9

Music publishing

9.1 INTRODUCTION

9.1.1 The origins

The exploitation of the separate copyright in a musical composition is usually carried out by a music publisher in the interests of both itself and the writer(s)/composer(s). The writer/composer will usually have a written contract with the publisher pursuant to which the income arising from the exploitation will be shared between them on an agreed formula, expressed as a percentage of the actual receipts.

The traditional source of publishing income was the sale of printed editions of a song which were used by bands and orchestras at shows and concerts and by individuals making entertainment for themselves at home. In the early days that and modest sums from the performing right were the sole source of income. The publisher who undertook the expense and risk of printing was the conduit to the bands and orchestras. As with many forms of exploitation relevant to today the writer could represent himself but not many were in a position to have the right contacts or wanted to take the risks. In an undeveloped industry of comparatively small turnover it was also common for the writer to sell outright all his rights for a small fee. Nevertheless it was not uncommon and soon became the norm for there to be an arrangement for a royalty to be paid.

Clearly things have moved on and although there remains a substantial business in the sale and use of printed copies other areas have become more important in terms of generating income. The popular music industry has become a truly international one with the need to exploit copyrights internationally and to protect them by registration and prevention of copyright infringement, and to ensure that correct payment is received for any usage.

9.1.2 Applicable contracts

There are, then, two essential aspects where contracts need to be entered into between the various parties involved in the creation, exploitation and protection of musical works.

The first aspect is the contract between the writer/composer and the publisher. This will set out the extent of the rights of the publisher and its duties and obligations and the commercial terms agreed between the parties. A sample contract is set out in **Appendix A4**.

The second aspect is the contract necessary to ensure exploitation and protection and the disposition of moneys arising from that exploitation. This will be necessary to ensure that international activity is conducted on agreed and authorised terms. Whilst much use of copyrights in various countries internationally can be overseen by the publisher in England (especially in terms of collection of moneys through the international arrangements by the MCPS and the PRS) there are many risks with which only a local company can anticipate and deal. Arguably, for established songs all that is required is the collection of moneys. That is not generally an approved view, not least because there will be copyright registration requirements and because it is advisable that there be someone in place to ensure day-to-day use and exploitation of songs.

A sample of a sub-publishing agreement is set out in **Appendix A5**. The arrangements between the publisher and the PRS and the MCPS are contractual and are industry standard set terms which are not reproduced in this book.

This chapter looks at the basic contracts which deal with ongoing relationships. The more usual relationship between a writer and publisher is by means of an agreement whereby the copyrights created will be vested in the publisher on an exclusive basis for a period of time. The relationship between a publisher and its international representatives will be for a fixed period of time and will relate to all the songs owned or controlled by the publisher (which is known as its 'catalogue') during that period.

9.2 SONGWRITERS' AGREEMENTS

9.2.1 The scope of the agreement

Agreements between writers and composers and music publishers are known as 'songwriters' agreements'. It is possible for the relationship to be limited to a small number of specified songs and in that event they will be dealt with in a format known colloquially as 'a single song assignment'. Many of the comments below will apply to such limited agreements and the only real difference is that there will be no element of ongoing exclusivity to the services of the writer or the products of those services.

Songwriters' agreements are designed to set out a long-term relationship between the writer and publisher and should have the intent of assisting and nurturing the writer in the development of his creative and professional activities and talents.

The agreement will need to deal with the following aspects:

- the parties;
- the precise copyrights affected;
- the extent of the rights of the publisher;
- the extent of the obligations of the publisher;
- the extent of the obligations of the writer;
- the financial terms;
- any territorial limitations; and
- the extent in terms of length of period of the rights granted.

9.2.2   The parties

As in any contract it is important to understand precisely who the contracting parties are. If the writer is a member of a group or habitually writes jointly with others then the publisher is likely to proceed only if all members of the group or all other prospective co-writers also join into the contract. This is because there are practical problems if there are two publishers representing separate parts of one overall copyright work and also because the publisher will wish to avoid future arguments as to the respective entitlements of all the contributors to a work. The writer will need to identify that his contracting party is a company of substance and to ensure that the company is the actual operating company and that it will not subcontract the actual trading activity.

As we saw in **para.7.2** the writer artist will have elected the business operating vehicle. If he has not followed the incorporation route he will personally enter into the contract. If he has incorporated then his songwriting services are likely to be owned by the company. In such a case it will be the company that will enter into the agreement with the publisher, but it will be a requirement that the writer will also contract by way of a so-called inducement letter whereby he will confirm the rights of the company and will effectively guarantee that the company will fulfil its obligations to provide the relevant copyrights so that the publisher will enjoy the intended rights. The letter will go on to provide that if the company fails to deliver the copyrights for any reason then the writer will personally do so.

9.2.3   Identity of copyrights

The underlying subject matter of a songwriting agreement is the rights in copyrights to which it is subject and these will need definition. The first thing to identify will be whether there are any already existing songs which will fall under its provisions. Often with a new group the publishing deal will be struck based upon a number of songs which have been produced as demonstration records which have attracted the interest of a record company and in that case those songs will be required by the publisher to fall under the deal. In general terms the publisher will wish to include all songs written by the writer which have not already been assigned to another publisher. This is reasonable and is consistent with the ethos of a mutual collaboration to develop and nurture a writer.

The agreement will define the relevant songs as being all those written during its term (or any part of any songs which may be co-written) together with any already written or partially written if not already assigned to another publisher. This latter provision also has the effect of preventing a writer claiming later that a song does not fall within the provisions of the agreement because it was written before commencement of the term.

9.2.4 Minimum commitment

If there are to be substantial advances the contract will require that the writer promises that a minimum number of new songs under it are written, recorded and released. This may include an obligation that the release will be by one of the major labels (since it is generally perceived that there is more likelihood of success with a major). That promise may also require that the release shall be in certain countries where there is a prospect of volume sales and earnings. The provision is usually written as a condition and not a guarantee by the writer. The usual sanction for the failure to release is an extension of the then current term until the expectation has been fulfilled or it may be that the advances are not paid until that event. The writer should seek to negotiate a provision that he can satisfy the publisher by way of an alternative of achieving enough success to recoup the advance out of income. For example, a song might be successful because it is used in an advertisement so that once the publisher has recouped any advance it cannot impose any sanction.

9.2.5 Term of the agreement

The term may be expressed in actual years or, as has been seen in connection with management contracts, in the form of a career cycle related to release on sale to the public of albums. If there is to be an advance on the potential earnings (see **para.9.3**) the contract will make provision for this in addition to a requirement that there be a minimum number of songs released on record. A writer should consider these definitions and their construction.

Whether the term is simply expressed in years or by reference to the career cycle it will provide that the period will automatically extend until the minimum number of releases with applicable songs has been achieved. In accordance with normal contract law it is advisable to have a provision that come what may any given period has a reasonable and finite time-limit.

Most negotiations will provide for the publisher to have options to renew and extend the term for additional periods. This is normal in accordance with the ethos mentioned above and because the publisher will wish to see a return for its initial faith and investment in the writer/composer.

The investment and risk undertaken by the publisher is likely to be less than that of a record company which has to risk not only any advance paid but also the considerable cost of recording, advertising and promotion of an artist. As a result there are strong arguments in negotiation for ensuring that the potential overall length of a songwriting agreement should be less than that for a recording contract. The negotiations can meet those objections in part at least by adjusting the advances payable in future years upwards and by adjusting in the writer's favour the division of earnings in future years either in relation to the actual earnings across all songs or perhaps only for new songs written during the extended option periods of the contract.

9.3 ADVANCES

In all probability the writer will have been attracted to any given publisher not only by its reputation and belief in the writer but because the publisher is prepared to pay to the writer an advance of his potential share of income under the contract. Such advances are recoupable from the share of income when it is payable but should be expressed to be otherwise non-repayable. The amount of advance will be negotiable as a commercial matter and will vary according to the publisher's assessment of the commercial potential of the song. That view will be guided by creative assessment of the song itself, by knowledge of the degree of interest from other publishers who may wish to negotiate with the writer, as well as by the publisher's view of the strength and enthusiasm of any record company which may be involved.

It should be remembered that recording artists who will record and promote their own songs are not the only writers who may secure contracts with publishers. Frequently a writer will not be a recording artist but instead he writes songs which a publisher hopes will be recorded by unconnected artists or by artists with whom the writer is associated. The publisher may already be working with a writer who will wish to co-write. The same considerations need to be given to contracts for pure writers in such circumstances and perhaps with a need to consider more carefully some of the royalty calculation provisions discussed in **para.9.5** and especially those relating to so-called 'cover versions' of songs.

The agreed advance may be paid in one sum on signature or may be paid in stages related to the release of records which reproduce songs that fall under the contract. This may be further refined by reference to release in specific countries, typically as to payment of part on UK release and part on US release and perhaps part on mainland Europe or Japanese releases. Further refinement may be discussed based upon whether the release is just of a single play record or an album. Care should be taken to define what amounts to a release especially as Internet release becomes more and more prevalent.

The negotiations will include those as to future advances if there are options on the part of the publisher. If it exercises an option those future year advances will also be predicated upon stage payments in the same way as the initial release. A writer will wish to incorporate a provision that the release commitment will no longer apply if in fact such exploitation as does take place has been successful enough to recoup the advance in the same way as was discussed in relation to the minimum contract requirements at **para.9.2.4** above. It is possible that one single could have a runaway success or perhaps some success coupled with use in an advertisement so that the writer's share of earnings will have recouped the advance and removed the risk and will have shown the publisher a profit.

9.4 ROYALTIES

9.4.1 General basis

The share of income generated by the sale, use and exploitation of a copyright payable to a writer is designated the royalty. Historically the publisher paid to the writer an agreed share of the actual income received by it. Regrettably certain publishers devised an arrangement whereby the actual sum received by any given company could be artificially reduced to the detriment of the writer but not the publisher. The seminal case of *Schroeder* v. *Macaulay (formerly Instone)* [1974] 1 WLR 1308, HL exposed this to public scrutiny and resulted in substantial changes to the industry. In that case it appeared to the court that a company in England signed a writer on the basis of paying to the writer 50 per cent of its net receipts from the relevant songs. There then came a series of publishing companies in various countries abroad which established an internal accounting procedure so that many countries around the world sent their publishing earnings to an American holding company after deducting a share locally. America then deducted a share and sent the balance to the English company which paid the writer one-half of that. Thus on paper at least (and always denied by the publishers) the strict contractual position appeared, by way of example, that after a deduction in Germany and then in America and then by the English company the writer received not half of the earnings of the song but one-eighth whilst the publishing companies involved received seven-eighths. Publishers no longer put forward contracts which allow for that device but it remains necessary for a writer to enquire about and understand how the earnings of a song are to be treated.

As far as income generated by use of a song in England is concerned the contract should spell out whether or not there is to be any deduction. A writer will find it quite acceptable that the costs and expenses of the MCPS, being an independent third party, should be allowed as a deduction so that the share is based upon the income net of such costs. It may well be that a writer will not agree a deduction for any third party administrator's fees nor for any element of the overhead or staff expenses of the publisher, although he might agree the deduction of some specific expense (perhaps a recording studio) if he is to be consulted in advance.

So far as moneys generated abroad are concerned the following considerations should be taken into account.

In common with the recording industry the publishing business is dominated by the major companies who are essentially international. They have their own operating companies in most countries of the world. Those companies offer to the writers the very real attraction of a share of royalties calculated 'at source'. That is to say they treat the moneys generated in each country (less the collection fees of bona fide third party collection societies and local unavoidable taxes) as if they were earned and received in England. There is no deduction for the costs of maintaining and running the local business and only the provisions relating to 'covers' (see **para.9.5.2**) which have to be borne in mind.

The music publishing industry has long been host to many independent operators and this continues. It is physically impossible for a few majors to manage the whole business. For such independent companies it is not economically viable to offer a full share of royalties 'at source' without reducing the royalty share to be paid. In a limited sense this is only a semantic distribution in that to calculate 60 per cent of income 'at source' gives the same actual sum as a calculation of 75 per cent of net receipts if net receipts are calculated after receiving from a sub-publisher 80 per cent of the gross 'at source' income. By the same token, undertaking the same calculation with any noticeably higher share of gross at source income than 60 per cent will mean such a small sum to be retained by the independent that it is simply not worth being involved.

In relation to an independent publisher which will itself appoint sub-publishers in other countries it will be necessary to negotiate the effective net rate to allow the publisher to remunerate the sub-publisher and yet itself make an income.

The advantages to a writer of signing with an independent are normally that he is signed to an active publisher who will devote more energy and focus to a smaller catalogue and will hope to achieve a greater chance of success. In such circumstances the contract should specify the maximum deduction that may be allowed to a sub-publisher for the purposes of calculation of royalties.

9.5   ROYALTY FORMULA

9.5.1   Royalty bearing income

The royalty part to the songwriter will be based upon net income and the contract will set the rate after negotiation. This is likely to differ in relation to different sources of income. The basic approach will vary according to the importance of the artist and his songs and to the risk undertaken by the publisher. In this sense the underlying rate is likely to be higher if the publisher is not making any substantial advance payment. The varying rates in relation to various types of income should also increase in favour of the writer as the option years come into effect, but this is a matter of negotiation.

The usual types of income which are royalty bearing are as follows:

- *Mechanical income.* This is the sum paid by the record company to the songwriter for each disc sold.
- *Performing income.* This is the income collected by PRS for public performance, such as radio and television air plays whether of a record made of the song or a musician or group or orchestra playing live on air or in live venues.
- *Printed sheet music copies.*
- *Synchronisation licence fees.* This will be paid if a song is used in an advertisement or in a film or a video.
- *Grand rights.* Grand rights are for all practical purposes the performing right relating to music which is utilised in a stage musical show. Usually expressed as a share of ticket sales or 'box office'.
- *Other income not covered above.* There is potential for a myriad of examples now known or to be invented, but an example is the fees for the use of lyrics which are printed in a book or newspaper or in a confused rights area such as ringtones.

There will be a basic rate negotiated for each use and it will depend upon the relative strengths of each party in the negotiation and upon the level of advance payment to be made against future earnings of the writer. It is unlikely to be less than 60 per cent for mechanical income and should be at least that for other areas.

There will be negotiations for variations as time goes on allowing for a greater share to be paid to the writer following success or even simply in the event that the publisher exercises an option to continue the term of the contract.

PRS will normally pay 50 per cent of the performance moneys directly to the writers but it is usual for the contract to provide that the publisher will account to the writer for a share of the publisher's share of a like sum of 50 per cent, but any such additional share will be subject to recoupment by the publisher of any advance.

9.5.2 Covers

The other substantial area of negotiation is in relation to so-called 'covers' which need to be considered and negotiated very carefully. 'Covers' is the expression used for use of a song which is not the recording made by the writer. The basic concept is that any income which is not actually mechanical income from a recording made by the writer is to be subject to a smaller share to the writer. The usual arrangement is that the publisher should be required to demonstrate that it actually did something directly related to causing or securing the relevant activity in order to obtain a greater retained share for itself. Negotiations should also provide that there should be no 'double dipping' so that, for example, if a sub-publisher is to retain a greater share for a cover it must show that it actually was instrumental in obtaining the new activity on the song and the original publisher should not also be entitled to a greater retained share for the same income.

Particular care needs to be given to the position of a writer who is not a recording artist because in such a situation every single act in relation to the song must be a 'cover' and this may not lead to equity in the relationship.

9.5.3 Controlled compositions

Almost invariably a contract between an artist and a writer will have provisions relating to the mechanical royalty payable in respect of sales of copies of the record in North America. Those provisions will apply to all songs recorded by the artist. In North America unless the parties agree to opt out there is a statutory rate of mechanical royalty payable to the publisher. In negotiations with publishers in the case of writers who also record their own songs full disclosure of the terms of the contract with the record company should be made. In cases where there is not yet a recording contract in place the writer should ensure that the publisher will accept and allow for the fact that the writer will be required to contract out and guarantee to the publisher that on sales in North America a reduced mechanical rate will be payable. (See **para.8.9.4**.)

Negotiation should provide that the publisher is prepared to accept the special rate required, failing which the writer will be obliged himself to bear the difference either by a contractual obligation to reimburse the record company its 'loss' or at the very least to have the cash sum deducted from his record royalties.

Such special provisions apply in the recording contract also to the grant of a synchronisation licence for videos. There will be a requirement by the record company that synchronisation licences will be granted on a predetermined basis which will be less than a normal commercial rate. This aspect should be disclosed to and agreed by the publisher.

In both events if such terms are not included the writer alone will pay when usually such activities are designed to boost overall sales and therefore the general publishing income.

9.6 GRANT OF RIGHTS

The contract will vest in the publisher certain rights and the extent of those rights will have to be negotiated. The starting position for a publisher is that it will wish to have an assignment for the full term's copyright (the life of the composer and an additional 70 years). The contract is usually expressed also to be an assignment in perpetuity as a precaution against the possibility of a lengthening of the term of copyright. The assignment of copyright is still requested but perhaps the better view now being accepted is that the grant of rights should be for a limited time. For technical reasons and for the purposes of protection and enforcement of rights it may still be advisable to formally assign the copyright but with provisions for it to be reassigned after the agreed period. The actual period is a matter for negotiation and will range, for example, for the term of the contract from anything between 5 and 20 years thereafter. It may additionally depend upon the position of the recoupment of any advance but it is hard to justify any extension on the grounds that there are still moneys outstanding. If songs have not recouped an advance after, say, 20 years it is a little optimistic to expect them ever to do so.

9.7 PUBLISHER OBLIGATIONS

In accordance with normal contract law the contract should contain consideration and the publisher should give contractual obligations. The publisher should:

- agree to make payments of advances and royalties under the contract;
- undertake to make all reasonable endeavours to exploit the songs;
- undertake to maintain an efficient accounting, administration and collection system;
- undertake to make all appropriate copyright and collection society registrations and to cause those to be done in other countries as appropriate.

One of the reasons that decided the *Schroeder* v. *Macaulay* case (see **para.9.4** above) was that the contract operated as an assignment of copyright of all songs written by the writer over a potentially long period but there was no obligation on the publisher to exploit them. It was considered to be in undue restraint of trade for a publisher to be able to lock up the writer's talent in this way.

The contract should contain the usual provisions for rendering accounting statements and payments and should afford the writer a reasonable right of audit and inspection. A writer should also seek the right to audit the books and records of sub-publishers or at least obtain a covenant from the publisher that it will take all reasonable steps to ensure prompt and accurate payment from its licensees, sub-publishers and subcontractors.

The principles applicable to these matters are the same as those discussed in **Chapter 8** in relation to recording contracts.

9.8 TERMINATION PROVISIONS

As in all contracts for services the agreement should obtain provisions for termination for breach or insolvency. It will be of particular importance to the writer to ensure that his rights are returned to him if the publisher becomes insolvent or ceases to carry on business. It should be noted that there are considerable difficulties as a matter of law of securing a re-assignment of copyrights in the case of insolvency since the general view is that such an arrangement is void as a matter of public policy.

Whilst there will be provisions allowing the publisher to subcontract its activities outside England such provisions should be carefully drafted so that any subcontractor will not obtain rights independently of the publisher and so that termination of the contract with the publisher also operates to terminate the contract with the sub-publisher.

There should also be provisions prohibiting the publisher from assigning any rights or transferring its obligations under the contract. At the very least the contract should provide that any assignment whether voluntary or by operation of law should be conditioned upon the assignee (and successors in title) being legally bound to observe and perform the obligations of the publisher under the contract.

9.9 SUB-PUBLISHING ABROAD

Whilst there are some circumstances (such as in the case of an established body of works only recorded by one artist or group) where no sub-publisher will be relevant it will normally be prudent to appoint a sub-publisher for the purposes of copyright protection and for promotional purposes and collection and administration purposes. The rare case where no sub-publishers are necessary is only possible by reason of the international network of collection societies. However, a local and motivated representative should be considered necessary.

In the case of the international major companies there is likely to be a standing agreement which will be a private internal matter. In other cases there will be a bespoke agreement put into place between the publisher and the overseas 'sub-publisher'. The independent publisher will require a written agreement with its licensee which will give it authority to deal in the works and specify the mutual rights and obligations. The contract will have essentially the same commercial legal and financial provisions as the contract between the writer and the publisher.

The agreement will contain provisions dealing with the following matters:

- the works covered;
- the territory;
- the length of the contract and any retained rights after expiry such as any continuing rights to administer or the right to collect earned but not yet received income;
- the extent of the right to authorise use of the works; for example the right to grant any or only local or worldwide synchronisation licences for films or advertisements or the right to alter or adapt any of the works;
- the advances payable;
- the calculation of royalties in full detail of the various sources of income with special attention to 'covers';
- clarifying that the contract is personal and not assignable or the subject of subcontracting and that any change of control is a ground for termination;
- specific obligations to protect and register copyrights and efficiently administer the same and collect income;
- accounting obligations with the provision of statements and the right of audit;
- inclusion of any 'key man clause';
- termination for breach or insolvency or cessation of business; and
- choice of law and jurisdiction of courts.

9.10 ADDITIONAL SPECIFIC ASPECTS

The publisher will need to deal with the possibility of any changes in the songs, for example local translations of lyrics. In many countries there may be the need to provide lyrics in the local language. Frequently this is authorised by the local society rules and cannot be prevented but the publisher will need to limit as much as possible any payments to third parties. In this regard it is usual for the local society to insist on a share of royalties being paid to the local lyricist but limited to income which can be demonstrated as having been generated by use of the lyrics and not in relation to any use of the original.

The publisher should also investigate local custom and practice to establish whether there are any other differences applicable to the local territory. It is frequently found that the local societies have systems which might favour payment for local songs or might favour local publishers. The outstanding example is what is known as 'black box' income. In simplistic terms this is a fund of money accumulated or collected by the local society which cannot be identified and attributed specifically to any particular work. This is distributed to local publishers and since it cannot be related to any particular song the original publisher will not receive a share of it. A solution which might be agreed is that the local publisher will declare all such sums and then pay a proportion to the regular publisher. That proportion will be in the ratio which the local general income overall bears to the income which can be identified as relating to the original publisher's catalogue.

PART 3

Film and television

Estelle Overs

CHAPTER 10

Introduction and pre-production

10.1   INTRODUCTION

The production financing of feature films in the UK is largely based around equity investment, distribution advances by way of pre-sales to distributors, tax relief (tax credits replaced sale and leaseback and film tax partnerships in the UK in 2007) and co-productions. This allows independent film production companies to piece together the 'jigsaw' of film financing, necessary in the absence of a studio system in the UK to produce and distribute feature films throughout the world in various windows from theatrical through to free television broadcast, as well as exploit any ancillary rights. The production of television programmes in the UK is largely based around the major terrestrial, satellite and cable broadcasters (BBC, ITV, Channel 4, Five and BSkyB) who commission and broadcast television programmes in the UK and worldwide. The BBC and Channel 4 are also involved in the financing of a limited number of feature films per year. Cable and satellite channels, as well as new methods of distribution such as video-on-demand via the Internet and to mobile telephones, have created opportunities to exploit first run feature films on subscription channels or for a one-off fee prior to free television broadcast, as well as exploit older television programmes, sport and specialist channels. Since the Broadcasting Act 1990 the BBC, ITV, Channel 4 and Five have been under a statutory duty to commission at least 25 per cent of their programmes from independent producers. As the 25 per cent threshold is a minimum, not a maximum, the BBC has recently decided to reduce its in-house production to 50 per cent. Under the Broadcasting Act 1996 digital terrestrial television channels are also subject to the same arrangements but with a lower percentage of 10 per cent. Satellite and cable channels must 'where reasonably practicable' reserve at least 10 per cent of their transmission time for programmes made by independent productions pursuant to the EU 'Television Without Frontiers Directive'.

Development finance is the most difficult finance to source in film and television production, particularly in relation to the development of feature film screenplays as it is a risky investment with limited opportunity to recoup the investment. Film production companies often have to use their own equity or apply to third party financiers such as the UK Film Council for development funds. It is normal for production companies involved in feature film production to set up a special purpose vehicle company that will own and license the rights relating to an individual feature film, rather than the production company itself. Some small television companies are reliant on larger production companies and broadcasters for their development finance in order to develop their own ideas into television programmes. The sums of money and number of different parties involved with feature film development and production are usually greater than for television production.

There are three main stages to film and television production:

(a) the development stage during which screenplay/script development takes place, performers and crew are engaged, rights and content clearance takes place and production finance is sourced (pre-production);
(b) principal photography of the feature film or television programme (production); and
(c) distribution of the finished 'product' and exploitation of any ancillary rights.

A lawyer's contribution to feature film and television production relates to the negotiation and drafting of the agreements necessary to set out the respective rights and obligations of the parties involved in the financing, production and distribution of the feature film or television programme, as well as agreements relating to the exploitation of any ancillary rights. The lawyer for the production also ensures that the content of the feature film or television programme is cleared, for example it is not defamatory of any living person or in breach of third party rights such as trade marks or (in respect of television programmes) does not breach the Ofcom Broadcasting Code.

Some feature film and television production agreements are in a standard form pre-negotiated between representative bodies in the UK film and television industry such as Equity (the actors' trade union) and the Producers Alliance for Cinema and Television (PACT) (the producers' UK trade association). Other agreements such as development or production agreements contain many terms that are based upon industry custom and standard format although the commercial terms will vary depending upon the financier or broadcaster in question. For example, the UK Film Council, the BBC and Channel 4 have a set of working practices that are used whenever a project is developed or commissioned by their organisations. It is customary for a financier or broadcaster providing development finance to a production company to enter into a development agreement with the production company setting out the terms of the loan of development finance and provisions for repayment. The main agreement in relation to the production of feature films is the production finance and distribution (PFD) agreement or interparty agreement (IPA); and for television programmes it is the production agreement or acquisition agreement.

Few production companies have the financial resources to produce a feature film or television programme without external finance. Raising production finance is always difficult, and production companies invariably have to raise finance from more than one source. Each financier will require repayment of the initial equity investment and interest, plus security over the copyright in the feature film or television programme and any other assets of the production company such as money in production accounts. Alternatively, they may require ownership of a percentage of the copyright in the screenplay or script or a licence of particular distribution or exploitation rights. They may also require a share of net profits or producer's net profits.

Equity investment by financiers, pre-sales to distributors and broadcasters and international co-productions inevitably involve splitting up the rights in the completed feature film or television programme territory by territory in order to finance the production, which greatly reduces the value to the production company of the completed production in the long term. (A typical co-production agreement is provided at **Appendix B3**.) Recent changes to the financing of feature films in the UK and the commissioning guidelines for UK broadcasters have been made with this problem in mind, with the aim of assisting production companies in retaining rights in completed projects in order to add value to their companies by building libraries of titles.

The distribution of a completed feature film or television programme is the means by which the production company recoups and repays the investment made by all financiers to the project, pays any use fees or residuals to performers and crew and generates profits once recoupment has taken place. This is done in a number of ways: theatrical exploitation, DVD sales, video-on-demand and television broadcast. Ancillary rights such as publication of the screenplay or script, radio or stage productions and merchandising can also be exploited by the production company to recoup investment, as well as generate profits.

10.2 PRODUCTION ORGANISATIONS

There are a number of organisations and professional bodies involved in feature film and television production and broadcasting in the UK. The UK Film Council, the Department for Culture, Media and Sport and HM Revenue and Customs are all involved in policy and legislation relating to the production and financing of UK feature films. The main television commissioning and broadcasting bodies in the UK are under an obligation to commission independent programming from independent production companies. The Office of Communications, Ofcom, is responsible for guidelines relating to taste, decency, fairness and privacy in the UK media, including in respect of television broadcasting. There are also several professional bodies that represent those working in the film and television industry in the UK. PACT is the main trade association for independent film and television producers in the UK. The Broadcasting, Entertainment, Cinematographic and Theatre Union (BECTU) represents crew working on film and television productions.

10.2.1 Film policy and legislative bodies

UK Film Council (UKFC)

The UK Film Council (UKFC) was established by the Department for Culture, Media and Sport in 2000 and is the Government-backed strategic body for film in the UK. It aims to develop a sustainable UK film industry.

The UKFC invests government grant-in-aid and National Lottery money to UK and EU production companies by way of three separate funds designed to cater to different types of film maker and levels of development and production finance: the Development Fund, the New Cinema Fund and the Premiere Fund. It also has a Training Fund providing funding for training programmes aimed at those working in the UK film industry and a fund for theatrical distribution of certain genres of film in order to help develop audiences in the UK.

The UKFC has responsibility for the Arts Council of England's Lottery Film Department, the British Film Institute and the British Film Commission (now the International Department of the UK Film Council). It also funds British Screen Finance and the British Screen European Co-Production Fund, as well as regional film throughout the UK (for example Film London, Scottish Screen and the Northern Ireland Film and Television Commission).

Department for Culture, Media and Sport (DCMS)

The Department for Culture, Media and Sport (DCMS) is the Government department responsible for certifying British feature films, those feature films produced either entirely by way of UK finance or via international co-productions.

The DCMS issues two types of certificate to production companies in respect of a British feature film: an EC Certificate of Nationality and a Certificate of a British Film. A Certificate of a British Film may be granted to a production company by the DCMS pursuant to the revised Sched.1 to the Films Act 1985 (which introduces a new Cultural Test for British Films) or by satisfying the terms of one of the UK co-production treaties with other countries in Europe and Canada (see **para.12.2.4**).

Certification as a British film is necessary in order for UK production companies to access UK tax relief, an important part of piecing together independent feature film financing in the UK (see **para.12.2.4**).

HM Revenue and Customs

Policy and regulations relating to UK tax relief for feature film makers is under the remit of HM Revenue and Customs.

In the 2005 Budget the Chancellor of the Exchequer announced that the Government would introduce a new tax relief for feature film production in the UK to replace the existing legislation (Finance (No.2) Act 1992, s.42 and Finance (No.2) Act 1997, s.48 which facilitated sale and leaseback and film tax partnerships). The new legislation is set out in Chapter 3 of Part 3 of, and Scheds.4 and 5 to, the Finance Bill 2006 and is available in respect of British feature films intended for theatrical release which commence principal photography on or after 1 January 2007 (see **para.12.2.4**).

10.2.2   Television broadcasters and Ofcom

British Broadcasting Corporation (BBC)

The British Broadcasting Corporation (BBC) is a programme maker and broadcaster. Its income is derived from the television licence fee and commercial exploitation of its catalogue of programmes through overseas sales, DVDs, licences to UK cable and satellite networks (such as UK Gold) and secondary rights such as publishing and merchandising. Through BBC Worldwide it also acts as a distributor of programmes throughout the world. The BBC commissions programmes from independent producers, produces programmes in-house and licenses programmes from third parties.

When the BBC commissions programmes from independent producers, it will generally require a full assignment of copyright in the completed programme, in exchange for which the production company will receive a production fee based on the programme budget and a share of profits. The budget of the programme will usually be met by the BBC which will also cash flow the production and treat the production cost as a fee for the UK broadcast rights. Sometimes BBC Worldwide will advance funds to the production budget; in such cases, the advance must be recouped from distribution income before the BBC and the production company are paid profits.

BBC Film is the feature film making arm of the BBC. It co-produces approximately eight films per year and works in partnership with major international and UK distributors.

Independent Television (ITV)

The Independent Television (ITV) network consists of regional companies and the ITV Network Centre. It commissions, schedules and broadcasts programmes across the entire ITV network. Programmes produced for or acquired by the ITV network may be for regional broadcast only or for broadcast over the entire ITV network. Most independent production companies use a regional company to finance their productions. The regional ITV company will usually take an assignment of rights in the programme in return for providing production finance. ITV is currently in negotiations with PACT to agree new terms of trade for direct access commissions following a recent Ofcom review of television production in the UK.

Channel 4, Five and BSkyB

Channel 4 commissions programmes from independent producers for broadcast. Channel 4's income arises from the sale of advertising, as well as the exercise of distribution rights in commissioned programmes. FilmFour is the film arm of Channel 4. It invests around £10 million a year in development and co-finances six to eight feature films per year through a part-equity, part-UK television licence fee arrangement. FilmFour works with a range of co-finance partners, international sales agents and distributors.

Five and BSkyB operate in a similar manner, with a mixture of commissioned and acquired programming, although they do not invest in feature film production.

Office of Communications (Ofcom)

The Office of Communications (Ofcom) is the regulator for the UK communications industries. It was granted statutory duties under the Communications Act 2003 and has responsibilities across television, radio, telecommunications and wireless services. Its objectives are set out in s.319(2) of the Communications Act 2003, which include protecting persons under the age of 18, ensuring that news is presented with due impartiality and reported with due accuracy, and applying standards to protect the public from offensive and harmful conduct.

Ofcom has taken over the responsibilities and powers of the regulators it has replaced (the Broadcasting Standards Commission, the Independent Television Commission, Oftel, the Radio Authority and the Radiocommunications Agency). It seeks to protect the interests of consumers in areas such as mobile telephones and the digital switchover of television and has drawn up the Ofcom Broadcasting Code (the Code) for television (with certain exceptions for the BBC) and radio, covering standards, sponsorship, fairness and privacy. The Code came into effect on 25 July 2005 and replaces the previous codes of the redundant regulators. The Code has relaxed the rules on sponsorship of television programmes but still prohibits product placement in television, although this is likely to change in the future. It does not deal with 'two way' delivery services such as video-on-demand and the Internet, although this is likely to fall under the remit of

Ofcom in the future. The Code has been drafted in the light of the Human Rights Act 1998 and the European Convention on Human Rights.

10.2.3 Professional bodies

Several professional bodies in the UK have worked together over the years to agree minimum terms and conditions of service in collectively bargained agreements for 'above the line' (creative) and 'below the line' (crew) professionals in the film and television industry.

The main US professional guilds, being the Writers Guild of America (WGA), the Directors Guild of America (DGA) and the Screen Actors Guild (SAG) may also be involved in film and television production in the UK if any of their members are engaged in a UK production.

Writers' Guild of Great Britain (WGGB)

The Writers' Guild of Great Britain is the trade union in the UK that represents writers of screenplays for feature films and scripts for television programmes. It has negotiated and entered into agreements with the BBC, ITV and PACT in respect of minimum terms upon which a writer may be commissioned to write a script for a television programme by a production company. The terms guarantee writers minimum payment rates and repeat fees and specify the rights assigned by the writer to the production company.

The Writers' Guild of Great Britain agreement in respect of feature film screenplays has not been renegotiated with PACT since 1992. The majority of production companies and financiers engaged in the development and production of feature films in the UK negotiate contractual and commercial terms with writers without reference to the minimum terms specified in the 1992 Film Agreement, with the exception of the on-screen credit obligations set out in the Screenwriting Credits Agreement 1974 which is incorporated into the 1992 Film Agreement.

Directors Guild of Great Britain (DGGB)

The Directors Guild of Great Britain is the trade union in the UK that represents directors of feature films and television programmes. Although there is no collectively bargained agreement in force between directors and PACT or UK television broadcasters, the Directors Guild of Great Britain surveys its members in order to produce rate cards for feature film and television programmes that can be used in negotiation with production and provides an advisory service to its members in relation to legal and business issues such as assignment of rights.

Equity

Equity is the performers' trade union, representing artists in the entertainment and arts industries in the UK such as actors, singers and variety artists. There are equivalent organisations throughout the world, for example the Screen Actors Guild (SAG) in the US and the Canadian Actors' Equity Association in Canada. Equity has negotiated minimum terms on behalf of its members in collectively bargained agreements with the BBC, ITV and PACT in respect of feature films and television programmes. Whenever a production company employs an Equity member, it is obliged to use the minimum terms as a starting point for negotiations. Terms relating to pay, overtime, holiday entitlement, travel, confidentiality, pensions and merchandising are also included.

Musicians' Union (MU)

The Musicians' Union (MU) is the only trade union in the UK that represents and advises musicians. The MU is a member of the Trades Union Congress (TUC) and the International Federation of Musicians and agrees standard terms of engagement for its members with production companies, broadcasters and record companies when engaged on feature film and television productions, as well as providing advice to members on related issues such as minimum fees and tax.

Producers Alliance for Cinema and Television (PACT)

The Producers Alliance for Cinema and Television (PACT) is the trade association that represents the commercial interests of independent producers operating in the film and television industry in the UK. Although based in London, PACT has an office in Scotland and is active throughout the UK in order to represent its regional members. It lobbies the Government, regulators and public agencies in the media industry on issues affecting its members and also maintains working relationships with the UKFC and Government departments such as HM Revenue and Customs in order to argue for a properly structured and funded UK feature film industry.

PACT provides support and information services to its members by way of training and events. The Producers' Rights Agency (PRA), PACT's industrial relations arm, negotiates and maintains terms of trade with the Writers' Guild of Great Britain, Equity, the MU and the BECTU and provides PACT members with pro forma production agreements and advice about industrial relations issues.

Broadcasting, Entertainment, Cinematographic and Theatre Union (BECTU)

The Broadcasting, Entertainment, Cinematographic and Theatre Union (BECTU) is the independent union that represents employed, contract and freelance crew involved in feature film and television productions, from runners and art department assistants to casting directors, set decorators and production accountants. It has entered into a collectively bargained agreement with PACT and negotiates pay, conditions, safety and contracts with employers as well as providing personal advice and representation to its individual members.

10.3 SCREENPLAY/SCRIPT DEVELOPMENT

10.3.1 Protecting an idea

Whether the feature film or television programme is a drama, documentary or a television format such as a game show or comedy, the idea for the project should be sufficiently developed to warrant copyright protection before the search for development and production finance begins. The development process can be a lengthy one, often taking place over a period of years from initial idea to commencement of principal photography. As there is no copyright in an idea, proposals for projects should be kept confidential by the writer or production company at all times and circulation of any documents be restricted until the idea is sufficiently developed (by way of a treatment, outline, screenplay, script or format) into a work that attracts copyright protection in order to ensure competitors cannot use the idea.

Studios, larger production companies and broadcasters developing their own feature films and television programmes often receive submissions by independent writers and production companies for programmes that are very similar to those they are developing themselves. Writers and production companies approaching such organisations for development finance should carefully consider the terms of any submission agreement they are required to sign, as they may find they have waived any right to take action for breach of copyright if the studio or production company develops a screenplay, script or format similar to that which they have submitted.

It is also very important for writers or production companies to keep accurate records and dates of the inception of their copyrightable work. It is useful to send a copy of any treatment, outline, screenplay, script or format by registered post to a bank, lawyer, accountant or professional body for safe keeping and as evidence of the date when the copyrightable work was written in the event of a dispute over ownership. The Writers Guild of America and the US Library of Congress Copyright Office both offer registration services upon payment of a fee. Some writers send their screenplays or scripts to themselves by registered post to prove the date of inception, although an independent recipient is better evidence should the matter be serious enough to reach court. The copyright symbol (©), year of the work and the name of the production company should be prominently placed on all copies of treatments, outlines, screenplays, scripts or formats to put third party contributors on notice of copyright ownership. Writers and production companies should take particular care during development or brainstorming sessions by ensuring that third parties assign their copyright and waive their moral rights in respect of any contribution they may make to the screenplay, script or format.

The law of confidence may also be used to protect an 'idea' or project. This is particularly helpful in relation to formats for game shows or comedies where the idea for the format will not attract copyright protection. In the case of *Green* v. *Broadcasting Corporation of New Zealand* [1989] RPC 700 (PC) Hughie Green, the creator and host of a talent search programme in the UK called 'Opportunity Knocks', unsuccessfully sued a television broadcaster in New Zealand for copyright infringement and passing off in respect of a talent search programme that used many of the same elements of 'Opportunity Knocks' such as the same name and catchphrases. Green was unable to demonstrate that the rival programme was based upon scripts or other material that amounted to copyrightable literary work. More recently, several cases relating to so-called 'Reality TV' programmes that have been alleged to have infringed the rights of the owner and broadcasters of the television programme 'Survivor' have also been dismissed by the courts (CBS unsuccessfully sued Fox over 'Boot Camp' and ABC over 'I'm A Celebrity Get Me Out of Here' in the US and Endemol over 'Big Brother' in The Netherlands). As the law appears to be out of date with the commercial interests of makers of television programmes that involve formats, production companies have striven to protect their interests by forming a self-regulatory body called the Format Recognition and Protection Association (FRAPA) which has put in place a format registration system, regulates disputes and provides advice on protecting formats. The law of copyright can also be used to a certain extent by production companies who create detailed scripts, music, artwork and merchandising as well as production bibles and lists of contracts, as each is a copyrightable element of the programme or material that may also be subject to the laws of confidence. The format creator should request the commissioning production company, broadcaster or financier to sign a confidentiality agreement acknowledging that discussions relating to the idea are confidential to the creator of the format and that no use may be made of the idea without the permission of the originator. The courts have also recognised the protection of confidential information even without the existence of a confidentiality agreement: see *Fraser and Others* v. *Thames Television and Others* [1984] QB 44 where a writer who gave a television company an idea in confidence that was subsequently used by the television company without the involvement of the writer was successful in an action for damages for breach of confidence.

10.3.2 Developing an idea

The usual development steps for a project involve:

- entering into development agreement(s) with development financiers;
- taking an option over any existing work that will be used as source material for the screenplay or script such as a novel, magazine article or play;
- engaging a writer or writers to write the screenplay or script;
- undertaking the rights and content clearance exercise;
- engaging performers and crew, whether under the terms of collectively bargained agreements (such as Equity) or otherwise;
- setting the budget and putting together production finance;
- seeking co-production partners;
- considering distribution margins, the genre of the production and sourcing pre-sales from distributors;
- scouting for locations and entering into location agreements;
- obtaining professional advice from lawyers and accountants; and
- setting a production timetable.

10.3.3 Development agreements

A development agreement should deal with the matters set out below.

The project

The project should be clearly defined so that the production company and development financier know what they are developing. The name and specifications of the feature film or television programme should be set out.

Finance

The development budget provided by the financier to develop the project should be set out in detail, specifying whether it is to be paid to the production company in stages or in one payment (for example upon signature of the development agreement). The production company may be required to open a joint bank account with the financier into which the development finance is deposited, held on trust and used in the way specified in the development agreement. The financier will wish to see receipts and bank statements in order to establish that the development finance has been spent as agreed. Sometime a producer's fee may be paid to the individual producer responsible for the development of the project, which may be separate from the development finance.

Development steps

The development agreement should set out what the financier requires the production company to do and how the development budget can be used. The development steps will vary according to the project, but will normally include those set out in **para.10.3.2** above.

Rights

The financier will almost certainly require the production company to assign some or all the copyright in the project to the financier. Although the production company will wish to resist granting this form of security, there is very little else a financier can take by way of security in exchange for the development finance. Assigning the copyright to the development financier means that the production company effectively loses control of some or all of the rights in the project until the development finance is repaid. This puts the production company at a disadvantage in any subsequent negotiations when seeking production finance for the feature film or television programme as it will be unable to demonstrate a clean chain of title for the project and will be unable to assign the copyright in the screenplay or script to production financiers in exchange for production finance.

The production company should therefore seek to limit the copyright it grants to the development financier. It should seek to grant, for example, only 50 per cent of the copyright in the development work or the screenplay to the development financier, not the copyright in the feature film or the television programme itself or any of the distribution rights or ancillary rights. Alternatively, the production company may grant the development financier a charge or mortgage against the production company itself which can be registered at Companies House rather than a percentage of the copyright in the screenplay or script.

The production company should also ensure that the development finance is included as a line item in the production budget so that it can be sourced from production financiers (rather than be repaid by the production company itself or drawn from producer's fees) and repaid to the development financier on the first day of principal photography (the date the production finance is normally drawn down) in order to reassign the rights in the screenplay or script to the production company and provide a clean chain of title to production financiers.

If it is envisaged that the development financier will also provide production finance for the project, or if the production company wishes to have the opportunity to reacquire the rights in the project from the development financier, the production company should ensure there is a turnaround clause in the development agreement. This allows for the reassignment of the rights to the production company upon repayment of the development finance (plus interest if necessary) if the development financier does not provide production finance within a specified time period. The production company may then take the project to another production financier as sole owner of the copyright in the development work and/or the screenplay or script.

10.3.4   Underlying rights

The production company must acquire the rights to all underlying rights used in the production during the pre-production period. As well as considering the matters set out below, a full rights and content clearance exercise as set out in **Chapter 11** should also be undertaken by the production company in order to ensure that there are no copyright or legal issues.

Existing works – option and assignment agreements

An existing copyright work such as a novel, magazine article, play or existing screenplay or script cannot be 'adapted' or rewritten without the permission of the rights owner (CDPA 1988, s.21). It is common in the film and television industry for a production company to take an option over an existing work for a smaller fee instead of acquiring all the rights in an existing work for the full purchase price. An option and assignment agreement grants to the production company on an exclusive basis for a limited period of time all rights in the existing work which the production company will require in order to develop the project (such as the right to write a screenplay based upon the novel) in exchange for an option fee, as well as the right to exercise the option at the end of the option period in order to acquire the rights in perpetuity in exchange for the purchase price if the project proceeds to production.

A careful examination should always be made of the rights owner's claim to own the rights before the option and assignment agreement is entered into, particularly as there is no copyright registration system in the UK equivalent to the US Library of Congress Copyright Office. The production company will only have the right to claim for damages to cover any costs of development and loss of profits (if they can be proved) if it transpires at a later stage that the rights owner does not in fact own the rights to the underlying work.

The option and assignment should include the following.

1.   The length of the option period (usually one or two years), any extensions of the option period and the rights that may be exercised by the production company during the option period (such as the right to engage a writer to write a screenplay or to seek production finance).

2. The option fee (and any fees for extensions of the option period) and the purchase price to be paid upon exercising the option. The option fee is, as a rule of thumb, 10 per cent of the purchase price and is often payable on account of (i.e. is included in) the purchase price. The purchase price itself may be a fixed sum or a percentage of the final budget (for example 2–5 per cent of the final budget) with a 'floor' and a 'ceiling' of certain specified sums.

3. The rights granted to the production company upon exercise of the option. This will usually be all rights the production company needs to produce and distribute the feature film or television programme. The production company will often require the rights owner to sign the assignment at the same time as the option in order that further signatures are not required if the production company decides to exercise the option.

4. Warranties from the rights owner that he is the original author of or owns all the rights in the existing work to be granted to the production company.

5. A waiver of moral rights and an assignment of rental and lending rights.

6. Any net profits or producer's net profits granted to the rights owner.

A typical option agreement is provided at **Appendix B1**.

Commissioned works – writer's agreement

If the production company intends to engage a writer to write a treatment, outline, screenplay or script based upon the existing work over which the option has been taken, the production company should also enter into a writer's agreement.

The production company may commission an original screenplay or script, a screenplay or script based on a treatment or outline provided by the production company or a screenplay or script based on an existing work in respect of which the production company has entered into an option and assignment agreement.

The terms of the writer's contract of engagement should include the following.

1. Payments to the writer for each stage of the screenplay or script delivered to the production company, for example a first draft screenplay and revisions, a second draft screenplay and revisions and a polish. Minimum rates are set out in the collectively bargained agreement between the Writers' Guild of Great Britain and PACT in respect of the commission of television scripts.

2. Delivery dates and reading time by the production company for each draft of the screenplay or script.

3. An assignment of copyright to the production company in respect of the entire copyright in the screenplay or script or an assignment of specific

rights, for example the right to produce one feature film or television programme based on the screenplay or script.

4. Any rights reserved to the writer, for example publication of the screenplay or script, radio or stage productions and merchandising.
5. A waiver of moral rights and an assignment of rental and lending rights.
6. Screen credits (which may be a specific commercial term or pursuant to the Screenwriting Credits Agreement 1974).
7. Use fees entitlement (for UK repeats and foreign distribution).
8. Any net profits or producer's net profits granted to the writer.

Third party rights – clearance

A full rights and content clearance exercise as set out in **Chapter 11** should be undertaken in respect of any third party rights in order to ensure there are no copyright or legal issues.

Public domain material

There is no need to acquire rights in material that is not subject to copyright protection.

Material in the public domain such as news, facts or information does not require rights clearance or acquisition. However, great care must be taken when basing a screenplay or script upon an existing work such as a biography that makes reference to public domain material such as historical facts or news as the existing work itself will have copyright protection. In such circumstances, the production company should either acquire rights in the existing work or commission a screenplay or script based solely on material in the public domain. *Harman Pictures NV* v. *Osborne and Others* [1967] 1 WLR 723 illustrates the problem. In this case, a film producer was unable to agree terms with the rights owner of a book concerning the events leading up to and culminating in the Charge of the Light Brigade. The producer commissioned a script similar to the claimant's work in its choice of incidents. An injunction was granted to the claimant because similarities in the works were not explained or accounted for by the producer.

It is important that a work in which copyright previously existed and is now out of the public domain is out of copyright in all the countries where the finished feature film or television programme will be distributed or ancillary rights exploited.

10.4 ENGAGEMENT OF PERFORMERS AND CREW

Feature film and television productions may engage employees of the production company or the broadcaster or self-employed contractors. Employees will be allocated to productions by their employer and generally no separate agreement will be required. For self-employed contractors separate contracts of engagement should be entered into specifying their obligations, assigning their copyright and rental and lending rights, waiving their moral rights and agreeing terms for payment. As well as considering the matters set out below, a full rights and content clearance exercise as set out in **Chapter 11** should be undertaken in order to ensure there are no copyright or legal issues.

10.4.1 Performers

Actors are usually (although not always) employed on the basis of the collectively bargained terms agreed by Equity (or the SAG in the case of US actors).

Equity agreements contain terms relating to the obligations upon the cast member during production and the rights, consents and the fees payable for use of their performance in the feature film or television programme.

The agreement should set out the name of the feature film or television programme and the period of engagement. The actor will be required to prioritise his commitment to the production. The production company will specify a guaranteed period when the actor will be needed for pre-production, principal photography and promotional periods during distribution of the completed production. The level of commitment required from the actor during these periods is known as 'first call' (priority to the production) and 'second call' (can finish other work).

Conditions relating to the actor's engagement such as rehearsals, accommodation, transport, clothing and make-up, attendance at premieres or film festivals, the actor's screen credit and any approvals should be specified. The agreed fee and time for payment should also be specified. For a feature film production on Equity rates a performer is entitled to a daily minimum rate of £100 or a weekly minimum rate of £400 plus a pre-purchase payment against theatrical, television, videogram and pay, cable and satellite rights and either:

(a) a percentage of income from all sources once the initial investment in the feature film has been recouped, or to be shared among the performers on a points system; or

(b) a percentage of gross receipts from sales to television broadcasters and from sales of videos and DVDs, in line with the SAG agreement, to be shared among the performers on a points system.

10.4.2 Director

The director has overall artistic and creative responsibility for the production. The director's obligations should be set out in the contract of engagement and should include liaising with the writer, working with the producer in relation to the budget, locations and shooting schedule, working with performers and crew, directing the feature film or television programme and editing and delivering the final version (although not the director's cut, as the producer has the right to make the final edit) of the feature film or television programme. The director may also be required for promotional services after completion of the production. The agreement should also specify the name of the feature film or television programme, the period of engagement, the agreed fee and payment provisions, the director's screen credit, attendance at premieres or festivals and any net profits or producer's net profits. The contract of engagement should assign the copyright in the director's contribution and the rental and lending rights, as well as waiving moral rights. A model agreement is provided in **Appendix B2**.

10.4.3 Producers

An individual producer will be appointed by the production company in relation to the production with responsibility for the day-to-day running of the production and completing it within budget and on schedule. Individual producers may be engaged on separate contractual terms setting out their responsibilities and obligations or may be employees of the production company. An assignment of copyright, rental and lending rights and waiver of moral rights should be included in the contract of engagement, as well as the agreed fee, payment provisions, screen credit, attendance at premieres or festivals and any net profits or producer's net profits.

Line producers (responsible for working with the crew and locations during principal photography) and executive producers (usually responsible for finding or providing production finance) should also enter into agreements with the production company.

10.4.4 Composers and musicians

If original music is required for a production, a composer should be engaged by the production company to compose suitable music on the minimum terms agreed by the MU. An agreement with a composer should take account of any previous publishing and recording agreements the composer has entered into as they will usually be exclusive in nature. The production company should agree suitable terms with the composer for the writing of the music such as fee, delivery date and an assignment of rights in the music to the production company. If the composer performs, produces and records his work an agreement similar to a recording agreement must be entered into and the production company must obtain permission to synchronise the music and recording with the feature film or television programme. Where a musician is already subject to an exclusive recording agreement a release should be sought from the organisation with the benefit of that agreement (usually the record company) permitting the use and exploitation of the musician's services in the feature film or television programme.

CHAPTER 11

Rights and content clearance

11.1 INTRODUCTION

Rights clearance involves ensuring that the production company has taken an assignment or licence of all the underlying rights and derivative works used in the production and those of all parties who have contributed towards the feature film or television programme (such as writers, performers, directors, producers, composers, musicians and any creative crew such as editors and production designers). This is sometimes referred to as the 'chain of title' of the feature film or the television programme, i.e. the transfer of ownership of the various rights to the production company rather than the name of the feature film or television programme such as 'The Godfather' or 'Top Gear'. Financiers will not finance a feature film until they have seen a chain of title report and are satisfied that the chain of title is clear.

Content clearance involves checking the screenplay or script to ensure that no third party rights such as trade marks have been infringed and no defamatory or obscene statements have been made. Rights of privacy or 'image' or 'personality' do not have to be cleared as in general no such rights exist in UK law. Other jurisdictions may have different requirements and standards.

Wherever problems arise it is important that the production company takes steps as soon as possible to avoid an action for damages or an injunction to prevent distribution of the feature film or broadcast of the television programme. In certain circumstances distribution or broadcast may take place despite a serious legal problem if the production company, distributor or broadcaster concerned considers the commercial or public interest in distribution or broadcast is greater than the risk of legal action.

11.2 COPYRIGHT

11.2.1 Use and fees

The production company should clear copyright at the earliest stage of production. This can be done either by acquiring rights outright (an

193

assignment) or by making use of the rights for a specified period of time (a licence). An irrevocable assignment of copyright in the work from the contributor to the production company is always preferable to a licence of rights, as it will be in perpetuity and exclusive rather than for a limited time and possibly on a non-exclusive basis.

Whether an assignment or a licence of the copyright is taken by the production company, the copyright owner will be paid a fee for specific use or exploitation of his work, for example the right to make a feature film of a writer's screenplay or the right to broadcast an actor's performance. If a different type of use or exploitation occurs, for example the right to make a sequel to a feature film based on the writer's screenplay or the right to use an actor's image from the television programme in merchandising, the production company must acquire or licence such additional rights and pay a further fee to the copyright owner. If there is insufficient finance available to pre-purchase all rights, or if only certain types of use or exploitation are envisaged, a production company may choose to acquire or license limited rights only. Other uses or exploitation may then be cleared and paid for by the production company as and when they occur. However, if possible it is best for the production company to buy out as many rights as possible at the outset of production rather than pay for further use or exploitation if and when it occurs as there is always a risk that the copyright owner will refuse permission or ask for an increased fee, particularly if the feature film or television programme is successful. If permission has not been obtained for a specific use, for example the rights have only been cleared to make a feature film for television broadcast but it is then decided to distribute the feature film theatrically or on DVD, the production company will be unable to use the uncleared rights. If it does so there will be infringement of copyright and breach of contract, thereby exposing the production company to the risk of litigation.

As well as paying attention to the extent of the copyright granted to the production company, care must also be taken to ensure that the agreement between the production company and the copyright owner does not contain any onerous termination provisions that would make future distribution or broadcast and exploitation of the finished feature film or television programme and any ancillary rights impossible. The right to terminate an agreement by the copyright owner should be restricted in the event of a breach by the production company to a right to damages, not automatic reversion of the rights to the copyright owner or the right to injunct the distribution or broadcast and exploitation of the feature film or television programme and any ancillary rights.

The production company should seek to use the copyright for the full term of copyright, all revivals or renewals and thereafter in perpetuity. If a licence is granted this should be for the longest period possible in order for the production company to fully distribute or broadcast and exploit the feature film or television programme and any ancillary rights. The production company should also ensure that the assignment of copyright is for the widest territory, for example the world or the universe and not just the UK as it will not be possible to distribute or broadcast and exploit the feature film or television programme and any ancillary rights in countries which are not specifically set out in the agreement.

11.2.2 Underlying rights and derivative works

The production company may wish to use many underlying rights or derivative works subject to copyright protection in a feature film or television production such as books, screenplays or scripts, magazine articles, poems, dance, works of art, songs, sound recordings and clips from other films. All must be cleared by the production company with the owner of the copyright work before they can be used. The copyright owner will invariably require a fee for use and may request a credit or other acknowledgement for inclusion of the copyright work in the feature film or television programme. The production company must ensure that permission is obtained at pre-production stage before using the copyright work in order to avoid the risk of the copyright owner refusing permission, requesting an increased fee or issuing legal proceedings against the production company.

Underlying rights – literary works and dramatic works

The production company may base the feature film or television programme on an existing book, magazine article or play, or commission a screenplay or a script from a writer. The permission of the copyright owner in respect of such underlying rights should be obtained before seeking production finance or the commencement of principal photography. The production company may take an option over the underlying work for a limited period of time in order to allow pre-production steps such as engaging performers and crew, budgeting and sourcing locations to take place until sufficient finance has been raised by the production company to pay the purchase price for the book, screenplay or script. This is discussed further in **para.10.3.4**.

Underlying rights and derivative works – musical works and sound recordings

Incorporating existing songs into films and television programmes requires the permission of the copyright owner. Identifying the rights owner of the song itself (which may be the writer of the tune and the lyrics or the music publisher) is the first step; PRS, MCPS and PPL are useful starting points for identifying the rights owner. Permission will also be required from the record company in order to use the copyright in the sound recording of the song in the feature film or television programme. The rights owner and the owner of the sound recording will both require payment of a fee. A synchronisation licence will also be required to synchronise the song with the soundtrack and to distribute the feature film or television programme, for example in cinemas, on DVD or by television broadcast.

Derivative works – excerpts from feature films and television programmes

Incorporating excerpts or clips from other feature films and television programmes into a new feature film or television programme production will require permission from the production company or broadcaster which is the copyright owner of the original feature film or television programme.

The production company should enter into a licence agreement with the rights owner and should ensure that the owner of the original feature film or television programme gives a full warranty and an indemnity that the owners of any underlying rights in the original feature film or television programme granted their permission for use of their work. Otherwise, the production company must seek permission from the underlying rights owners as well as the owner of the original feature film or television programme in order to use the extract or clip. In relation to television programmes such as news or live sport, the production company should enter into a licence agreement with the broadcaster which will have copyright ownership of the broadcast itself.

Use without permission and defences

If a production company uses material without obtaining the necessary clearances from the copyright owner, there may be a risk of legal proceedings unless one of the copyright exceptions or defences applies.

The fair dealing exception is available to production companies making feature films or television programmes where extracts of a work are used for criticism, review or news reporting. There is no requirement for a sufficient acknowledgement. The extent to which use is 'fair' is not defined in CDPA 1988. The fair dealing for purposes of news reporting exception does not apply to photographs; permission for their use must be obtained from the copyright owner.

The incidental inclusion exception (CDPA 1988, s.31) is also available to production companies in limited circumstances. Whenever the production company has control or choice over the filmed environment, care should be taken that copyright works are not included without the owner's permission. However buildings, sculptures, models for buildings and works of artistic craftsmanship permanently situated in public places or in premises open to the public may be included in films, photographs or broadcast or included in a cable service (CDPA 1988, s.62).

196

11.2.3   Rights of contributors to the production

The production company must ensure that all parties who have contributed towards the feature film or television programme such as writers, performers, directors, producers, composers, musicians and any creative crew such as editors and production designers have assigned the copyright in their contribution to the production company.

Directors

Under CPDA 1988 the author of a feature film or television programme is the producer, being 'the person by whom the arrangements necessary for the making of the film are undertaken' (CPDA 1988, s.178) and the principal director (CPDA 1988, s.9(2)(ab)). The production company must take an assignment of the copyright of the contribution of the director to the feature film or television programme in order to own, control, distribute and exploit all rights in the feature film or television programme.

Performers

Although performers do not have a copyright in their performance, they have a performance right which is the equivalent of copyright. The production company must obtain the written consent of all performers in the feature film or television programme to the recording and distribution and exploitation of their performance by the production company. It is also prudent to require all performers to assign to the production company any copyright which may arise in respect of their contribution to the production, such as any changes they may make to the screenplay or script or any interviews relating to the production that are written down or given on film, as the performer will own the copyright in the spoken words.

Actors are generally employed on the basis of the collectively bargained terms agreed by Equity (or the SAG in the case of US actors) which set out the relevant assignment of rights and agreed minimum fees for distribution or broadcast of the feature film or television programme and exploitation of any ancillary rights. Although there is an exception in CPDA 1988 which means there is no requirement to seek the permission of those whose performance is in the background or incidental to the principal matters in the feature film or television programme, it is good practice to ask all extras or background artists to sign a short release assigning all copyright in the contribution to the production company. Likewise when filming on the street or in public it is good practice to place a prominent sign next to the set indicating that filming is taking place and that by walking past or through the area members of the public grant permission for them to be filmed and recorded.

197

Composers and musicians

A composer of music for a feature film or television programme may have existing agreements with a publishing company and a recording company which restrict his ability to compose and record for third parties. For example, the composer may be obligated contractually to assign or license the copyright in any of his compositions to the publishing company, or may be prohibited from recording compositions for anyone other than the recording company without permission. In such circumstances it will be necessary for the production company to reach agreement with these parties in order to engage the composer for the production and distribute the feature film or television programme.

If the composer has no existing publishing or recording agreements the production company should seek an assignment or licence of the rights in the composition and the recording in exchange for a royalty payable to the composer. The assignment or licence will usually grant the right to the production company to include the composition in the soundtrack of the feature film or television programme as well use the compositions on CDs and DVDs. Musicians engaged to perform the music should also enter into an agreement with the production company on similar terms.

11.3 MORAL RIGHTS WAIVERS

Whenever a production company undertakes the exercise of acquiring the copyright in any works used in the development or production of a feature film or television programme, it is important that the moral rights of any author, director, performer and other creative crew are also irrevocably and unconditionally waived in writing in the contract of engagement.

An author of a screenplay or script and director of a feature film or television programme is entitled to be identified as the author of his work (the paternity right). The production company should always ensure that the moral right of paternity is waived by the author and director in the contract of engagement in favour of a contractual obligation to be given a credit in the on-screen titles to the feature film or television programme and any paid advertising and publicity. The credit should be in an agreed form that binds the production company as well as subsequent purchaser of the rights in the feature film or television programme and licensees of any rights in the feature film or television programme, such as a distributor or broadcaster.

The moral right to object to derogatory treatment of a work of an author of a screenplay or script or director of a feature film or television programme must also be waived in writing (the integrity right). Any changes made by a production company to a screenplay or script, to the title of the feature film or television programme or any cutting or editing of a feature film or television programme may be 'derogatory treatment' as defined in CDPA 1988 if it amounts to distortion or mutilation of the work or is otherwise prejudicial to the honour or reputation of the author or director. An example of what is likely to amount to derogatory treatment is to turn a drama into a comedy or to make it sexually explicit. The production company will need to have flexibility in rewriting a screenplay or script, changing the title or cutting or editing a feature film or television programme. The production company must also be entitled as part of the licence of distribution rights to a distribution company or broadcaster to entitle the distribution company or broadcaster to submit a feature film or television programme for censorship, prepare foreign language versions and broadcast with commercial breaks or sponsorship.

The moral rights of paternity and integrity rights apply to all authors of copyright works. This includes any creative crew such as set designers, special effects personnel, composers, choreographers and anyone else who has contributed towards the screenplay or script such as an individual producer or story editor. The production company should therefore ensure it obtains an irrevocable and unconditional waiver of moral rights in writing in the contract of engagement from all these individuals. Moral rights are now also enjoyed by performers under UK law as a result of the Performances (Moral Rights, etc.) Regulations 2006, SI 2006/18 which came into effect on 1 February 2006 and amend CPDA 1988, although it has been customary for some time to include a written waiver in the collectively bargained contracts of engagement used in the film and television industry.

11.4 COPYRIGHT AND RELATED RIGHTS REGULATIONS 1996

The Copyright and Related Rights Regulations 1996, SI 1996/2967 implemented into UK law an EC Directive which created additional rental rights for writers, directors and performers in relation to feature films and television programmes. Under the Regulations writers, directors and performers who have transferred their rental rights to the producer of a feature film or television programme are entitled to 'equitable remuneration' payable by the distributor or broadcaster for the rental of productions in which those persons were involved.

There is no specific guidance on what amounts to 'equitable remuneration'. A writer, director or performer cannot waive his right to equitable remuneration, although he can assign his rental right to the production company. Of concern to the production company is ensuring that the rental right is assigned to the production company in the contract of engagement along with any other rights such as copyright and performers' rights and that the agreed fee payable to the writer, director or performers for their work includes a remuneration which is equitable for the purposes of the

Regulations. This avoids the need for production companies, distribution companies and broadcasters to pay any further fees to the writer, director or performers in the future.

11.5   CONTENT CLEARANCE

Content clearance involves checking the screenplay or script and the completed feature film or television programme to ensure no third party rights have been infringed or legislation breached, thereby avoiding any civil or criminal liability. This will include:

- defamation;
- productions based upon living persons;
- obscenity and indecency;
- official secrets;
- breach of confidence;
- contempt of court;
- trade marks;
- product placement;
- passing off;
- negative entry checks; and
- the Ofcom Broadcasting Code (see **para.10.2.2**).

11.5.1   Screenplay or script clearance reports

The production company should engage a lawyer or rights clearance agency to read the screenplay or script, prepare a screenplay or script clearance report and undertake the clearance exercise. Great care should be taken when basing productions on living persons. Comments that may be regarded as defamatory should be avoided and releases from living persons should be obtained from anyone who is fictionalised in the production. Likewise, any living person who gives an interview upon which the screenplay or script is based or which is used as source material should sign an interview agreement with the production company assigning all copyright and waiving moral rights in the contents of the interview to the production company. Negative entry checks should be carried out on all names, address and telephone numbers used in the production in order to avoid accidental reference to a real person or their personal contact details. Although there is no right of privacy, 'image' or 'personality' in UK law, care should be taken to avoid using famous individuals to endorse a feature film or television programme or any related merchandising without permission, as the tort of passing off may be used to argue that the public were deceived into believing that goods relating to the feature film or television programme bearing the name or image of the 'celebrity' were endorsed by that person (see *Irvine & Ors* v. *TalkSPORT Ltd* [2003] EWCA Civ 423, CA, 1 April 2003, Lawtel, discussed at **para.5.2.9**).

Television broadcasters usually require production companies to complete a 'Programme as Completed' or 'Programme as Transmitted' form, which requires the production company to set out all third party rights and clearances obtained in relation to the television programme before broadcast.

11.5.2   Errors and omissions insurance (E&O) and clearance warranties

Once the rights and content clearance exercise has been undertaken and a screenplay or script clearance report has been prepared, full disclosure of any potential problems should be given by the production company to the provider of errors and omissions (E&O) insurance for the production. This is a form of insurance that provides cover for any potential infringement of third party rights as long as they have been disclosed in advance and are related to intellectual property or founded in tort (for example defamation). Errors and ommissions insurance does not cover breach of contract such as failure to pay moneys due under a contract of engagement with a writer or failure of a feature film to qualify as British or be granted a certificate by the British Board of Film Classification (BBFC). Depending upon the degree of risk involved, the insurer will set a premium and an excess and may exclude certain claims from the cover.

In respect of feature films, the financiers and the completion guarantor will require E&O insurance for the production in the event of any future claim of infringement. Insurance is bought up to certain levels (usually $1 million per occurrence and $3 million in the aggregate) for a minimum of three years after production.

In relation to television programmes, the ITV networks will usually add individual production companies to their blanket policy when individual programmes are commissioned. The BBC does not require E&O insurance.

The production company will be obliged under the interparty agreement (IPA) and distribution agreements (in respect of feature films) and the production agreement or acquisition agreement (in respect of television programmes) to warrant and indemnify that it is not in breach of any third party rights and regulations. In certain cases, the production company and broadcaster may assess the risk of action by a third party and take an informed view to broadcast. This is the type of situation which occurred with the Clockwork Orange case (*Time Warner Entertainment Co.* v. *Channel Four Television Corp plc* [1994] EMLR 1, discussed at **para.2.12.2**) where the broadcast of excerpts from the banned film 'A Clockwork Orange' was ultimately justified by the courts.

CHAPTER 12

Finance and production

12.1 INTRODUCTION

Because of the difficulty of putting together independent finance particularly in relation to feature films, financial closing, i.e. when the production moneys used to cash-flow the feature film or television programmes are drawn down from the lending bank into the production account, very often does not take place until the first day of principal photography. Cash-flow is extremely important because all productions incur costs such as outstanding payments for the purchase of underlying rights, writers' fees and weekly wages for cast and crew which cannot be deferred (i.e. remain unpaid) until after the production is complete.

This chapter discusses some of the most common methods of financing a feature film or television production in the UK, the most important terms set out in the financing agreements, and common terms in production agreements. A lawyer's contribution to the finance and production process relates to the negotiation and preparation of relevant documentation with the financiers, distribution companies, broadcaster and any outstanding content and rights clearance issues that may arise during production. (For the rights and content clearance exercise, see **Chapter 11.**)

Finance, production and distribution agreements are usually separate agreements, although they may be dealt with in one document, especially where a distribution company or broadcaster fully commissions a production and acquires all the rights in the production. In feature film production, if a bank is involved in the financing (which is usually the case) there is normally one controlling document setting out the rights and obligations of the production company, the bank and the financiers. This is called the interparty agreement (IPA) and in the event of a dispute this supersedes all other finance, production and distribution agreements. In television production, the main document is the production agreement or acquisition agreement.

Once fully developed and financed, a feature film or television programme proceeds to production. This is the point at which the screenplay or script, producers, director, budget, schedules, locations and cast and crew come together and principal photography takes place.

12.2   METHODS OF FINANCE

There are a number of sources of production finance for UK productions. The production of feature films is largely based around equity investment, distribution advances by way of pre-sales to distribution companies, tax relief and co-productions. The production of television programmes is largely based around the major terrestrial, satellite and cable broadcasters (BBC, ITV, Channel 4, Five, and BSkyB) who commission and broadcast television programmes. The BBC and Channel 4 are also involved in the financing of a limited number of feature films per year. Each method of funding the production budget is flexible and it is common for a production company out of necessity to acquire production finance from a number of different sources. Each source is likely to provide finance on a different basis and have different requirements for repayment of the initial investment, the rights it is granted and any profit entitlement.

Raising finance will be less of an issue for in-house television production with a commission by a broadcaster, as the production company will usually be granted development funding from the broadcaster, which will also generally finance and cash-flow the production.

In order to interest financiers in providing finance for a production the production company will have to convince financiers that the production is likely to be successful enough to return the initial investment in the budget and possibly make a profit.

12.2.1   Equity investment

Investment of equity (i.e. a cash amount) in a feature film or television programme is a risky investment by a financier because the success of a production can never be guaranteed. Unlike other opportunities for investment such as property or FTSE companies where the likely level of return can be assessed, it is virtually impossible (as the Hollywood studios have discovered many times) to predict whether a feature film or television programme is likely to be a success.

In relation to feature films, the Hollywood studios and larger production companies invest large sums in pre-release marketing and screenings, sometimes changing the ending of a film if preview audiences do not like it, in order to maximise the likelihood of return on their investment. As the Hollywood studios distribute their own films, they are also able to invest large sums of money (often equivalent to the actual budget of the film itself) in prints and advertising (P&A) in order to release the film on a large number of screens and draw the film to the attention of as many members of the cinema-going public as possible. Independent production companies do not have the luxury of being able to undertake large marketing exercises and usually work with smaller independent distribution companies who are not in a position to guarantee a large P&A spend. However, there are some ways that independent production companies can increase the likelihood of being able to recoup the finance invested in the production of the film. Genre films such as horror or thrillers are often more successful than dramas as they tend to be more 'critic-proof' and a star name will often bring more success at the box office as distribution companies find such films easier to market. Appropriate distribution margins (i.e. the budget of the film should not be greater than the likely level of return at the box office) is also something production companies should try to ensure.

Equity investors therefore take great care to protect their position in order to ensure the return of their initial investment in the production, which will be generated from the receipts of the feature film or television programme, and guarantee any share of profits the feature film or television programme may make once the investment in the production budget has been repaid. The receipts and profits of the feature film or television programme will be generated from sales of the feature film or television programme in all forms of distribution and exploitation (for example theatrical, video/DVD, television and merchandising worldwide) or specific rights or territories only as determined by the production company in agreement with the relevant financier (for example theatrical and soundtrack only excluding the USA).

Any equity investment will be based on the budgeted cost of the feature film or television programme and will be loaned on specific terms set out in an investment agreement between the financier and the production company which will provide for repayment, any interest and a share of profits (if granted by the production company). Where there are a number of equity financiers the production company should agree the order of priority of repayment from the receipts of the feature film or television programme which will be set out in a recoupment schedule in the production, finance and distribution (PFD) agreement or the IPA if a bank is involved in the financing of the production.

There may also be a separate collection agreement between the production company, the financiers, all those entitled to profit participation, and the organisation appointed by the production company to collect the receipts for the feature film or television programme throughout the world. The collection agent may be a Hollywood studio (if it is distributing the film), the bank involved in the production or a specialised collection agent. The collection agreement will specify that all receipts from the distribution and exploitation of the production must be paid into a collection account opened specifically for the feature film or television programme. Each financier will be repaid from the collection account either in strict order (for example financier number one is repaid its entire investment and then financier number two is repaid its entire investment) or 'pari passu and pro rata' (i.e. without preference and in proportion to their respective contributions) as moneys are received into the collection account until each is repaid and the film then begins to make a profit. Once the feature film or television programme begins to make a profit, the collection agent will account to and pay any person or organisation entitled to a profit participation, for example the writer, director, lead cast and any financiers in their respective proportions. If the production company has limited the rights or territories from which repayment of the production budget to financiers and profits shall be paid, this should also be set out in the PFD agreement or the IPA and the collection agreement.

There are limited opportunities for production companies to seek equity investment in a feature film or television programme in the UK. The UK Film Council and regional film organisations (for example Film London, Scottish Screen and the Northern Ireland Film and Television Commission) provide equity investment in UK feature films on specific terms. The television broadcasters have funds available for investment in the production of television programmes and in the case of the BBC and FilmFour a limited number of feature films each year. Private investors are however increasingly prepared to risk investment as a result of an interest in the film and television industry. Previously, film tax partnership equity funds consisting of investment by high net worth individuals able to benefit from tax breaks as a result of their investment were available to UK feature film production companies but these tax advantages have been eroded by recent changes in tax legislation by the Government. Opportunities are now found in hedge funds and from venture capitalists. Often an independent production company with a smaller budget will have to seek several small investments from other companies and even friends and family in order to fund the production.

It is also possible for production companies to seek investment for feature films and television programmes by way of a capital investment in the production company itself. This form of investment may take place by way of the purchase of shares in the production company or a loan. Investment may be made by private individuals, banks, venture capitalists or other production companies, although they are generally for the setting up and running of a production company rather than a particular production. It is also possible to set up a production company as an Equity Investment Scheme (EIS) company, a Government initiative for small companies (not just those in the film and television industry) which allows investment in shares in the company by individuals up to certain specified levels in exchange for tax breaks. Production companies in the television industry seeking investment should be careful to maintain their independent status for the purposes of the Broadcasting Act if they are providing programmes for UK broadcasters.

12.2.2 Distribution advances by way of pre-sales to distributors

The pre-sale of rights in a feature film or television programme to a distributor under the terms of a distribution agreement is a common method of raising production finance in the film and television industry. Using this method of finance, at pre-production stage a distribution company agrees to take a licence of certain distribution rights in the completed production in exchange for payment of a fee for the distribution rights known as a distribution advance or minimum guarantee. Unlike an equity investor, a distributor will only pay the distribution advance to a production company once the production is complete and the physical materials and relevant paperwork have been delivered to the distributor in accordance with the agreed delivery schedule for feature films or programme specifications for television programmes.

Distribution rights may be granted by the production company to distributors for all rights and all territories (for example if the distributor is a Hollywood studio) or for certain territories and certain rights (for example theatrical rights only in France). The distribution advance is an advance against receipts from the distribution of the production for the rights and in the territory granted by the production company to the distribution company. Once the distributor has paid the distribution advance to the production company, it will retain all receipts from the distribution of the production in the territory until the distribution advance and any distribution expenses are recouped (i.e. fully repaid to the distributor) after which further receipts (sometimes known as overages) are paid to the production company by the distribution company subject to the deduction of a distribution fee. The distribution advance is effectively an advance of receipts and royalties from the distribution company to the production company. If the production budget of the feature film or television programme is unrecouped (i.e. the production finance has not been repaid to the financiers) the distribution advance paid to the production company will be used by the production company to repay the financiers in accordance with the recoupment schedule. The distribution company will usually try to recoup its advance prior to repayment of any equity investment to financiers, although after repayment to the bank.

Unless any portion of the distribution advance is due to the production company before delivery of the physical materials (for example payment of 10 per cent of the distribution advance on signature of the distribution agreement) distribution advances by way of pre-sales to distributors will not assist the production company to cash-flow the production. As a result, production companies very often take signed distribution agreements to a bank that specialises in lending to the film and television industry in order to borrow finance from the bank to cash-flow the production against the right to receive the distribution advance from the distributor.

Only a limited number of banks are involved in lending against distribution advances as it is a risky investment – if the feature film or television programme is not produced and delivered, or the delivery materials are rejected by the distributor, the distribution advance will not be paid and the bank will have to sue the production company, which usually has limited assets, to recover the loan. The bank will assess the creditworthiness of the distributor and will 'discount' the value of the distribution advance in accordance with the risk of the loan (i.e. will only pay a percentage of the distribution advance to the production company) according to the rating given by the bank to the distribution company. For example, a Hollywood studio or a large independent distributor will be rated more highly by a bank than a small overseas distribution company, as a studio or large independent distributor will have a track record of making payments or will be known to the bank. The production company will receive, for example, 75 per cent of the value of the distribution advance on financial closing in order to cash-flow the production.

The bank will take a full assignment from the production company of the right to receive the distribution advance which will be used to repay the bank loan (normally repaid first) in accordance with the recoupment schedule, as well as charging the production company a fee, interest and costs for providing the discounting service. The bank will also wish to be a party to the collection agreement or may wish to collect the receipts from the distribution and exploitation of the production itself. The bank will also require an assurance in the form of a completion guarantee that the production will be completed on budget and delivered to the distributors on time and in accordance with the delivery schedule or programme specifications. A completion guarantee (sometimes known as a bond) is a form of insurance provided by a specialist insurance provider called a completion guarantor in exchange for a fee, which is usually the equivalent of 5 per cent of the budget. The completion guarantor will ask the individual producer and individual director of a feature film to sign inducement letters in relation to the production that entitle the completion guarantor to remove them from the production and replace them with someone else if they fall behind budget or schedule.

If a production company is able to make several pre-sales for the production from various territories it will be able to raise a considerable percentage of the production budget by taking the distribution agreements to a bank for discounting. Any distribution rights and territories that remain unsold after production is complete will continue to be sold by the production company to distributors on an ongoing basis in order to generate further receipts.

For further details on distribution, see **Chapter 13**.

12.2.3 Sales agents, gap finance and bridge finance

A sales agent is a specialist organisation engaged by the production company to find and appoint distributors for the feature film or television programme for those rights and in territories where distributors have not already been engaged by the production company. The sales agent may pay the production an advance against future receipts that can be used to cash-flow the production. Alternatively, the sales agent may provide the production company with sales estimates of likely distribution advances in unsold territories which the production company may take to a bank in order to request that the bank lend 'gap finance' to the production company against the value of the sales estimates. Gap finance is provided by only a limited number of banks or specialised film industry organisations due to the risk of the investment and will usually only be loaned if the sales estimates are two to three times the value of the actual loan.

The sales agent will recoup the advance from receipts received from the distribution and exploitation of the feature film or television programme and will also deduct a sales fee from distribution advances payable by any distribution companies appointed by the sales agent. In the same way as distribution companies, sales agents will try to recoup their advances prior to repayment of any equity investment to financiers but after repayment to the bank. The appointment of a sales agent takes the problem of seeking distribution and exploitation of the feature film or television programme out of the hands of the production company but does introduce a further element of fees into the recoupment schedule, which will delay repayment of the production finance to any bank and investors and reduce the level of any profits.

Gap finance should be distinguished from bridge finance, which is a specialised type of equity (i.e. cash) loan used by a production company in circumstances where the commencement of principal photography of a feature film or television programme is imminent but there is a shortfall in the budget and it is not possible to seek further finance by way of equity, distribution advances or tax breaks. Bridge finance is provided by certain specialised organisations for a short period of time sufficient to enable the production company to close the financing and commence principal photography of the production. It is an extremely risky investment as it is unlikely to be repaid if the production collapses prior to principal photography. As such, providers of bridge finance charge a high interest rate and require repayment of the loan from the first drawdown of production finance rather than taking a position in the recoupment schedule. The production budget will increase when bridge finance is borrowed, with the consequence that the production company must seek the approval of the lending bank, the other financiers and the completion guarantor to order to purchase the loan.

12.2.4 Tax breaks and co-productions

Tax breaks and co-productions are an important aspect of financing independent feature films. Tax breaks are available to film makers in the UK, throughout Europe and in North America and can fill a large part of a feature film budget if the film is produced as a European or international co-production.

Policy and regulations relating to UK tax relief for feature film makers is under the remit of HM Revenue and Customs. In the 2005 Budget the Chancellor of the Exchequer announced that the Government would introduce a new tax relief for feature film production in the UK to replace the existing legislation. Section 42 of the Finance (No.2) Act 1992 and s.48 of the Finance (No.2) Act 1997 had for several years facilitated sale and leaseback and film tax partnerships to UK film makers as a UK production or part of a co-production structure which resulted in a boom in feature film production activity in the UK. However, the Government felt that the intermediaries providing sale and leaseback and tax funds were problematic as a percentage of the tax breaks were directed into fees for their services. The Government therefore determined that the existing legislation should be replaced by a tax credit in order to deliver the tax benefit directly to feature film makers. The tax credit is set out in Chapter 3 of Part 3 and Scheds.4 and 5 to the Finance Bill 2006 and is available in respect of British feature films intended for theatrical release which commence principal photography on or after 1 January 2007.

At the time of writing the practicalities of the new tax credit are still subject to final clarification by the Government. However, production companies responsible for the pre-production, principal photography and post-production of feature films that are intended for theatrical release and that pay corporation tax in the UK spending 25 per cent of total core film production spend in the UK will be offered an enhanced deduction of up to 80 per cent of total production expenditure or the total UK spend (whichever is the lower) which can be surrendered for a payable tax credit. For feature films with a budget of less than £20 million the payable tax credit is 25 per cent of the production expenditure surrendered and for feature films with a budget of more than £20 million the credit is 20 per cent. The production expenditure that may be surrendered is limited to production finance only and not development, marketing or distribution finance. In order for the tax credits to be of any real benefit to production companies they are likely to be banked by either a bank or an intermediary at a discount in order to cash-flow the production of the feature film in the same way that distribution advances are discounted by banks. The level of discount will be based upon the likelihood of the tax credit not being received, which may occur if the production company's corporation tax return is investigated by HM Revenue and Customs or there is an outstanding tax liability.

Feature films must be certified as a British Film under Sched.1 to the Films Act 1985 or as a co-production in order to qualify for the tax credit. The Department for Culture, Media and Sport (DCMS) is the Government department responsible for certifying British feature films produced by way of UK finance or as a European or international co-production. The DCMS issues two types of certificate to production companies in respect of British feature films: an EC Certificate of Nationality or a Certificate of a British Film. A Certificate of a British Film may be granted under the revised Sched.1 to the Films Act 1985 that introduces a new 'Cultural Test' for British Films. A feature film will pass the Cultural Test if it is awarded 16 out of a possible 31 points based on cultural content (UK subject matter), cultural hubs (use of UK film-making facilities), cultural practitioners (UK personnel) and cultural contribution.

Tax breaks in the form of sale and leaseback, tax credits and tax rebates for use of local facilities and crew are available in several countries in Europe including the Isle of Man, Ireland, Luxembourg, Belgium, Germany, France, as well as in Canada and some States in the US such as New York and New Mexico. UK film makers can access these tax breaks by entering into a co-production agreement with a production company in a country where the tax breaks are available. When structured carefully this can bring a great deal of the budget to the production, although the availability of tax breaks should not dictate the shooting location, the screenplay and the casting of performers as it can result in feature films commonly known as 'Euro-puddings' with many disparate locations and accents.

The UK has entered into bilateral co-production agreements with Australia, Canada, France, Germany, Italy, New Zealand and Norway, although treaties with Italy and Germany terminated in 2006. It has also entered into negotiations to sign a bilateral treaty with India and there are proposals to enter into further bilateral treaties with China, South Africa, Jamaica and Morocco. The bilateral treaties are designed to encourage co-producers from different countries to pool their finance and film-making resources. The co-producers must contribute a minimum financial and film-making contribution to the film, which for Canada, France and Italy is 40 per cent, Australia and Germany 30 per cent, and New Zealand and Norway 20 per cent. For example, if the production was a UK–Canada co-production, the UK co-producer must bring at least 40 per cent to the film and the Canadian co-producer 60 per cent or vice versa.

The UK is also a signatory to the European Convention on Cinematographic Co-production (the European Convention) to which numerous countries are signatories including The Netherlands, Spain, Russia and Ireland. The European Convention is based upon a points system whereby a feature film will qualify as European if it achieves at least 15 points out of a possible total of 19 from the 'creative', 'performing' and 'technical craft' groups. It can be used to formulate a multi-lateral co-production with several different countries (for example a UK–Austria–Greece co-production) or can be used as a bilateral co-production if the UK does not have a direct bilateral treaty with a country that is a signatory of the European Convention (for example a UK–Russia co-production). The minimum financial contribution is 10 per cent, although if the European Convention is used to replace a bilateral treaty the minimum bilateral contributions apply.

When entering into a co-production under a bilateral treaty or the European Convention the co-producers must enter into a co-production agreement which will divide the ownership of the copyright in the film and the master negative, the right to distribute the film in certain territories and the right to receive receipts and profits from the distribution and exploitation of the film in proportions equal to their respective contributions.

Each co-producer must also submit documentation relating to the film such as the option agreement, screenplay, co-production agreement and collection agreement to the relevant authority in their respective country (such as Telefilm in Canada or the CNC in France) in order to receive a certificate equivalent to a British Film Certificate as granted by the DCMS in the UK. Provisional certificates based on the budget are usually granted, with a final certificate granted upon completion of the feature film and provision of a fully audited budget and statement of spend by a firm of accountants who specialise in feature films. It is in the interests of the production companies involved in the co-production and the completion guarantor to ensure that the budget does not deviate substantially from that upon which a provisional certificate was granted in order to avoid a final certificate being refused and the tax break being withdrawn, thereby leaving a hole in the production budget.

12.2.5   Product placement and sponsorship

In relation to feature films, product placement is becoming more common in assisting production companies fill any gaps in the production budget or reduce the level of the budget. Manufacturers of products such as watches, cars and clothes are increasingly prepared to invest equity in the budget of a feature film or provide products for no fee in exchange for prominent product placement in the film. This also avoids the need for the production company to clear the trade mark or logo of the product in order to include it in the film.

In relation to television programmes, the Ofcom Broadcasting Code which came into effect on 25 July 2005 prohibits product placement although this probition may be relaxed in the future. Sponsorship is permitted and the Ofcom Broadcasting Code sets out guidelines, including for advertiser-funded programmes. News and current affairs programmes may not be sponsored. Where sponsorhip is permitted there must be no promotional reference to the sponsor, its name, trade mark or products and it must have no other direct or indirect interest in the editorial content of the sponsored programme. Non-promotional references are permitted only if incidental and justified editorially.

12.2.6   Full commission with cash-flow for television programmes

A full commission from a UK broadcaster where the broadcaster provides all the production finance is a much more straightforward way of funding a television programme. The production is cash-flowed and, as long as it is on

211

schedule and within budget, the production company has fewer financial concerns than if it were employing production finance and recoupment schedules. The commissioning broadcaster will, however, impose strict terms upon the production company when providing production finance, including approval of the script, cast and crew and budget as well as the right for the commissioning broadcaster to take over or abandon the production in certain circumstances. In return for finance the commissioning broadcaster will be granted copyright including distribution rights in the production, a production fee and profits.

12.2.7 Net profits and producer's net profits

An important term in any financing agreement is the definition of profits. Profits are receipts payable after all production finance including interest and fees have been repaid to the financiers who have invested in the budget of the feature film or television programme. Profits can be either net profits or producer's net profits. As there is a significant difference between the two it is important to establish which have been granted. Net profits are a percentage of 100 per cent of all profits due, whereas producer's net profits are 100 per cent of all profits due to the production company. If the production company typically grants 50 per cent of net profits to financiers with the remaining 50 per cent to the production company, 10 per cent of net profits will be 10 per cent of 100 per cent of net profits whereas 10 per cent of producer's net profits will be 10 per cent of 50 per cent of net profits.

Profits are normally granted to the writer, director, lead cast and any financiers. However, production companies should be careful not to give too many net profits away as this will eat into the amount available to financiers and may result in financiers being less interested in investing in the production. Any party who is entitled to a share of net profits or producer's net profits should be named in the recoupment schedule and should be a party to the collection agreement. The definition of net profits or producer's net profits should be checked carefully to ensure it does not contain any unusual deductions which would reduce the share payable to the profit participant.

Profit participation should be distinguished from deferments. A deferment is a fee that is contractually payable as a line item in the production budget to a participant in the production such a producer or a member of the cast or crew which should have been paid from the cash-flow but which must be deferred (i.e. paid at a later date) if it transpires that there are insufficient funds in the production budget to meet the payment. The deferred fee will be inserted into the recoupment schedule to be paid by the production company after the production budget has been recouped. As the impact of deferrals is to delay the payment of profits, the bank, financiers and completion guarantor involved in a production must agree to the payment of any deferments and the redrafting of the recoupment schedule.

12.2.8   Example of a film financing structure

The following example illustrates the complexity of a typical arrangement for financing a feature film.

An independent production company seeks finance for a feature film with a completed screenplay and a budget of £5 million that is intended for theatrical release in the UK. Producer's net profits have been granted to the writer and the director of the film.

The production company will have to raise the finance for the production budget from a number of sources.

An equity investor invests equity of around 20 per cent of the budget to be advanced during production, used as cash-flow and recouped from the film's receipts in accordance with the recoupment schedule for the film. The production company enters into a loan agreement with the equity investor and grants the equity investor a share of net profits. The equity investor will require that the production company grants security to the equity investor over the rights of the production company in the underlying rights (including the screenplay), the film and the assets of the production company.

The production company then enters into a co-production agreement with a Canadian co-producer in order to access tax credits in the UK and in Canada amounting to around 30 per cent of the budget of the film. The production company submits relevant documentation to the DCMS in the UK and the Canadian co-producer to Telefilm in Canada. The co-producers own the copyright, the distribution rights and the right to receive income in proportions equal to their contribution to the film. The production company is granted the distribution rights in the UK and the Canadian co-producer is granted the distribution rights in Canada under the terms of the co-production agreement.

The co-producers raise finance from pre-sales of distribution rights in the film to distributors in the UK, Spain, France, Germany and the US. The distribution advances payable by the distributors amount to around 40 per cent of the budget payable upon delivery of the delivery materials of the completed film to the distributors.

For territories where the co-producers are unable to find a distributor, they appoint a sales agent who pays an advance of 10 per cent of the budget. The sales agent is granted net profits and requires the co-producers to enter into a charge by way of security over the rights of the co-producers in the underlying rights (including the screenplay) and the film and the assets of the co-producers.

The distribution advances agreed with the distributors and the advance agreed by the sales agent will be recouped from receipts derived from the distribution of the completed film in accordance with the recoupment schedule.

As the distribution advances payable by the distributors are only payable on delivery of the delivery materials for the completed film to the distributors, the co-producers approach a bank active in lending in the film and television industry to 'discount' the advances in order to cash-flow the production.

Once a bank is involved, the co-producers must:

- enter a loan agreement with the bank which will grant security over the rights of the co-producers in the underlying rights (including the screenplay), the film, the assets of the co-producers and the production account to the bank and assign the right of the co-producers to receive the distribution advances to the bank;
- send a notice of assignment to each distributor stating that the co-producers have assigned the right to receive the distribution advances to the bank;
- engage a completion guarantor to guarantee that the film is delivered on budget and on time;
- enter into an IPA with the bank, the equity financier and the sales agent setting out the rights and obligations of each party to the financing structure and the order of priority of charges (the bank's charge will always take priority over other security);
- enter into a laboratory pledgeholder's agreement which holds the delivery materials for the film to the order of the bank until the bank has been repaid but allows the distributors and the sales agent to order prints of the film for distribution; and
- enter into a collection agreement for payment of receipts in accordance with the recoupment schedule agreed between the parties.

Once the film is completed and delivered to the distributors, the distribution advances will be paid direct to the bank pursuant to the notices of assignment. Assuming that the production was brought in on budget and on time in accordance with the completion guarantee, this should cover the bank's loan, including interest and costs. The bank will then release its security and rights in the film.

The collection agent will continue to pay receipts in accordance with the recoupment schedule which first pays the sales agent its commission and then the equity investor and the sales agent their investments together with interest pro rata and pari passu. However, the equity investor and the sales agent will not receive anything until the distributors have recouped their distribution advances. At the point where the distributors are recouped, they will pay receipts (overages) less distribution expenses and the agreed distribution fee to the collection agent. Once repaid, the equity investor and the sales agent will release their respective security over the film.

At this stage, the co-producers will have repaid all the finance to the investors. The remaining receipts will then be applied by the collection agent as net profits to be paid to the equity financier and the sales agent. Remaining net profits belong to the co-producers and it is from this share of producer's net profits that the writer and director are paid producer's net profits.

12.3 PRODUCTION AGREEMENTS

The production agreement entered into by the production company with those providing production services or a co-producer sets out all the rights and obligations necessary to produce the feature film or television programme itself. The terms of a production agreement can vary enormously depending upon the way in which the feature film or television programme is to be produced, although terms common to most such agreements are set out below.

The terms of the production agreement will be taken into account by the financiers involved in the financing structure for the feature film or television programme. There is also a direct relationship between the terms of the production agreement and the distribution agreements, which set out the delivery materials or programme specifications that must be delivered by the production company to the distributors (see further **Chapter 13**). The terms of the production agreement will always be subject to the governing agreement for the financing of the feature film or television programme, which is the PFD agreement or, if a bank is involved, the IPA (feature films) and the production agreement or acquisition agreement (television programmes). The governing agreement will set out the circumstances in which the bank or financiers (in agreement with the completion guarantor or commissioning producer) may take over or abandon the production. This will normally be in the event of breach by the production company which is not remedied within a specified period of time, exceeding the budget or shooting schedule, failing to comply with the specifications of the feature film or television programme or insolvency.

12.3.1 Rights and ownership

If the production is a co-production with another producer in the UK or a co-producer (pursuant to one of the UK's bilateral treaties or under the European Convention for feature films), ownership of the copyright in the underlying rights (such as the screenplay or script) and the feature film or television programme itself, the distribution rights and the right to receive receipts should be apportioned between the parties in accordance with their respective contributions.

If the production agreement is for the provision of production services only (for example another company provides or facilitates use of locations, a studio, crew or post-production services to the production company) the production agreement should ensure that all copyright in any contribution is assigned to the production company and all moral rights are waived.

A commissioning broadcaster in respect of a television programme may require a full assignment of copyright in the television programme in return for which the production company will receive a production fee and profits.

12.3.2 Budget and cash-flow

The production agreement should set out the locked final budget as approved by the bank and completion guarantor or commissioning broadcaster and the cash-flow schedule. There should be specific provisions relating to the opening of a production bank account, signatories to the production bank account and the keeping of accurate accounts and records for any production spend. This is particularly important because the bank and other financiers involved in the financing structure will take a charge over the production bank account by way of security. If a completion guarantor is involved the completion guarantor's representative will oversee payments made from the production bank account during principal photography of the feature film. The production spend will be audited by an accountant who specialises in film and television production or the commissioning broadcaster at the end of the production in order to reconcile cash-flow and spend. Limits may be placed upon the amounts the production company can spend during each week of production in accordance with the budget and the production company will be asked to provide regular reports relating to spend.

Provision for spending over the locked budget (overspend) should be set out and if there are savings (underspend) the allocation of such moneys by the production company to the recoupment schedule should also be clear.

12.3.3 Specifications

The production and technical specifications of the feature film or television programme such as the writer, director, lead cast and crew, length, rating, materials and delivery date should be set out in order to ensure that the production company is contractually obligated to deliver the completed feature film or television programme in the form approved by the financiers or commissioning broadcaster. Time will be of the essence for delivery.

If the feature film or television programme delivered by the production company does not fit the specifications, the production company will be in breach and the distributors or commissioning broadcaster will refuse to pay any moneys due upon delivery. The distributors or the commissioning broadcaster must approve the delivery materials within a certain time specified in the distribution agreements or the commissioning agreement. If changes are required, the production company will usually be required to bear the cost of any such changes.

12.3.4 Warranties

The production company and the co-producer or the company providing production services will be required to warrant that the production will be completed on time and delivered in accordance with the screenplay or script, locked budget, cash-flow and specifications. Warranties will also be required that all fees will be paid and insurances maintained and that the feature film or television programme will not breach any third party rights and is not defamatory or obscene.

12.3.5 Insurance

The production company will be required to maintain a number of insurance policies during the course of the production including:

- insurance for the principal cast and the director;
- medical insurance;
- public and employer's liability insurance;
- prop and special equipment insurance;
- negative and faulty stock insurance;
- power failure insurance; and
- errors and omissions (E&O) insurance.

The financiers or commissioning broadcaster will wish to have their interest noted on the policies. This means that if there is any claim under any of the policies they will be entitled to take a proportion of the benefit of that particular policy.

CHAPTER 13

Distribution and exploitation

13.1 INTRODUCTION

Independent production companies rarely have sufficient resources available to distribute their own feature films or television programmes, or exploit any ancillary rights related to the feature film or television programme such as merchandising. Theatrical distribution is an expensive undertaking which requires a considerable amount of finance in order to undertake prints and advertising (P&A) spend (i.e. striking the prints and paying for advertising in relation to the film) and book cinema space.

The Hollywood studios (The Walt Disney Company, Twentieth Century Fox, Paramount Pictures, Warner Bros Entertainment, NBC Universal and Sony Pictures Entertainment) distribute their own films and are able to invest large sums of money (often at the same level of investment as the budget of the film itself) on P&A in order to release the film on as many cinema screens as possible and draw it to the attention of as many members of the public as possible. This strategy increases the likelihood of the studio recouping the budget and often involves releasing a film on as wide a number of screens as possible during the first weekend of release in order to generate the maximum amount of box office receipts before the film has had the opportunity to be reviewed by the critics. The number of screens will then usually be reduced over the following weeks throughout the theatrical release window, although if the film is a critical success or a sleeper hit a wider platform of screens can occur.

Independent production companies do not have this luxury. Although some UK independent production companies have tried to self-distribute their own feature films, this is rarely successful. Independent production companies therefore usually enter into distribution deals with several smaller independent distribution companies to distribute their films throughout the world territory by territory. In each case it is necessary for the production company to enter into a distribution agreement with the distribution company for a licence of the distribution rights for the relevant formats (for example theatrical, home video, television) and territories. The distribution company will in turn enter into agreements with cinema operators (such as

Odeon or Vue) to exhibit films theatrically and with sub-distributors to release the film on DVD and exhibit it on television.

When calculating box office revenues for a feature film, the fee payable to the exhibitor (sometimes known as the 'house nut', i.e. the cost of running the cinema) will always be deducted first. Although this can often be a large percentage of the box office receipts, cinema operators actually make most of their revenue from screen advertising and concessions such as popcorn and soft drinks. Further down the release window there are also distribution expenses payable to sub-distributors such as the manufacturing and release of DVDs and for certain television or Internet exhibition such as pay-per-view or video-on-demand. Although the cost of manufacturing DVDs has reduced considerably in recent years, it is still a relatively expensive exercise for independent production companies to manufacture and ship DVDs and book shelf space in retail outlets, which is why these arrangements will usually be left to the distribution company and its sub-distributors.

Television distribution in the UK is exclusively the remit of several main broadcasters such as the BBC, the ITV network and BSkyB and a number of smaller satellite and cable broadcasters. It is also unusual for an independent production company to directly exploit ancillary rights such as merchandising, publication or soundtrack rights spun off from a feature film or television programme. The production company will usually enter into licence agreements with specialist manufacturers, publishers or record companies in exchange for a royalty.

The physical projection of feature films in cinemas is still carried out by way of projectors using 35mm film. However, in the UK and elsewhere the move has begun towards the digital distribution and exhibition of feature films, sometimes known as D-cinema. The UK Film Council has created a fund via the Digital Screen Network to install digital projectors and screens in several hundred cinemas throughout the UK. At the moment digital copies of feature films are delivered to cinemas by way of physical delivery of hard drives, although it is anticipated that in the future they will be delivered by Internet or satellite delivery. This will mean that the delivery materials for a feature film may also change considerably; the long list of physical materials currently set out in the delivery schedule appended to the distribution agreement may be reduced to a list of just a few files that are subject to copyright protection software.

Similarly, the UK Government has announced that analogue television signals will be switched off in the UK between 2008 and 2012. The move to digital television means that all viewers will need a digital receiver for their television sets and video/DVD recorders in order to watch television.

13.2 DISTRIBUTION AGREEMENTS

13.2.1 Specifications and grant of rights

The distribution agreement between the production company and the distribution company will set out the specifications for the feature film or television programme, such as the title of the feature film or television programme, director, lead cast, the length or number of episodes and (if a feature film) the proposed BBFC rating.

The grant of rights in the distribution agreement to the distribution company can vary considerably, although it is usual for distribution companies to take the widest grant of rights possible.

The usual grant of rights to a distribution company is:

- theatrical rights (the right to exhibit in a cinema);
- non-theatrical rights (the right to exhibit in hotels, motels, airlines and ships);
- video rights (the right to exhibit on video in screening rooms, for educational purposes and home video rental and sales);
- pay-per-view rights (the right to exhibit by television broadcast from a menu of times specified by the broadcaster for a specific fee payable by the viewer);
- video-on-demand rights (the right to exhibit by television broadcast and new methods of distribution such as the Internet and via mobile telephones at a time specified by the viewer for a specific fee payable by the viewer);
- pay television rights (the right to exhibit by television broadcast where the film is shown as part of a package on a channel for which the viewer pays a subscription fee); and
- free television rights (the right to exhibit on free terrestrial channels such as the BBC or the ITV network).

Rights are usually licensed to the distribution company on an exclusive basis for a specific territory or territories (for example the UK and Germany) for a term of 15 or 20 years. The ownership of the feature film or television programme remains with the production company. The production company will usually be entitled in the distribution agreement to terminate the distribution agreement in the event of material breach or bankruptcy on the part of the distribution company, in which case the licence of distribution rights will come to an end and the rights will revert back to the production company in order that they may be licensed to another distribution company. It is unusual for distribution rights to be assigned in perpetuity to a distribution company, unless the distribution company was directly involved in the financing of the feature film or television programme (for example the distribution rights in the UK may be assigned in perpetuity to the distribution company in exchange for a distribution advance that is used to cash-flow the production).

There are often 'holdbacks' in the grant of theatrical, non-theatrical, video and television rights set out in the distribution agreement that prevent the distribution company from releasing the film in certain formats before others have been released. These holdback periods tend to be industry standards set by the Hollywood studios in order to preserve their revenues in each individual 'window' of exploitation and maintain the status of theatrical releases ('straight to video' films are still not regarded as being of the same quality as a film that has had a theatrical release). Theatrical release is still therefore the driving force for the P&A for a feature film even though most films make the majority of their revenue from DVD sales and rentals. The usual 'holdbacks' or period of time between theatrical release of a feature film and its release on DVD is four to six months, with a further four to six month exclusive period whilst the film is only available on DVD before it may be shown on pay-per-view television or video-on-demand.

These distribution models are however changing as a direct result of the threat of piracy and the onset of digital and Internet distribution of feature films and television programmes to personal computers, mobile telephones and handheld devices. In addition to taking legal action to prevent secondary infringement of copyright (the Hollywood studios successfully sued Grokster and Kazaa, providers of free software that allowed users to share electronic files of copyright material) a considerable number of Hollywood blockbusters are now released 'day and date' (i.e. on the same day throughout the world rather than staggered release dates through different territories) in order to reduce unauthorised duplication and illegal DVD sales. Internet distribution is widely regarded as likely to overtake DVDs in the future as the main source of revenue for feature films. Many feature films are now available to rent (streaming or temporary downloading) and buy (as a permanent download) online. This new method of distribution aims to prevent illegal file sharing of films by making them available legitimately online, as well as take advantage of the increase of broadband Internet in residential homes in order to generate additional revenue for the film. Online exploitation is authorised by the Hollywood studios through their own Movielink service and by several independent distributors of feature films. The BBC now broadcasts certain feature films and television programmes simultaneously on the Internet and also offers an Internet catch-up service for programmes that viewers have missed. Any licence of online rights in a distribution agreement by a production company to a distribution company should contain terms that ensure specific Digital Rights Management (DRM) software is employed in the streaming or downloading of the feature film or television programme that prevents the file containing the feature film or television programme being copied, burned to disc or forwarded to third parties and only allows the feature film or television programme to be viewed if an encryption software key is activated by a legitimate subscriber in residential premises in the territory.

The distribution company is also usually granted the right to:

- arrange for the feature film or television programme to be passed by the censors or broadcast within the terms of the Ofcom Broadcasting Code;
- cut, alter and edit the feature film or television programme to meet with any censorship requirements and to insert advertising breaks on television, as long as any contractual credits (for example the name of the director or the lead cast) are not removed;
- dub or subtitle the feature film or television programme into local languages of the territory;
- advertise and promote the feature film or television programme; and
- institute and prosecute proceedings in the name of the production company for piracy or infringement of rights in the feature film or television programme in the territory.

13.2.2 Distribution expenses and distribution fees

The distribution agreement will set out the distribution expenses that the distribution company is entitled to recoup and the distribution fees that it is entitled to deduct from receipts in exchange for providing a distribution advance and/or arranging the distribution of the feature film or television programme.

Distribution expenses usually include all reasonable direct out-of-pocket expenses paid by the distribution company relating to the promotion, marketing, advertising and distribution of a feature film or television programme, including:

- creation of prints, masters, DVDs and trailers;
- advertising, marketing and publicity costs relating to the distribution of the feature film or television programme including posters, film festivals, screenings, star tours and Internet website costs;
- freight and shipping charges for prints, masters, DVDs and trailers;
- custom and import costs and other taxes;
- the cost of preparing foreign language and subtitled versions of the feature film or television programme;
- censorship and editing costs;
- storage costs and insurance premiums;
- legal costs incurred in taking action on behalf of the production company;
- costs of securing any copyright registration; and
- costs and expenses for the packaging of DVDs.

The production company should check the terms of the distribution agreement to see whether any sub-distribution expenses are included in the distribution expenses of the distribution company (i.e. they are borne by the distribution company and not passed on to the production company). Sometimes distribution expenses are capped at a certain figure in the distribution agreement in order that the distribution company may not exceed an agreed level of expenses without the approval of the production company. Alternatively, the production company may sometimes require that the distribution company spend a minimum amount on P&A in relation to the feature film in order to ensure that it is shown on a minimum number of cinema screens and advertised to a wide section of the public.

The distribution agreement will also set out the distribution fees the distribution company is entitled to. The balance of receipts payable to the production company after deduction of the distribution fees is known as the 'royalty'. However, any distribution advance that the distribution company has paid to the production company as part of the financing of the feature film or television programme and the distribution expenses are usually deducted from the production company's royalty in each window of exploitation (i.e. theatrical through to free television) until the distribution advance and any distribution expenses are fully recouped by the distribution company. This can considerably delay the time before the production company receives any receipts from the feature film or television programme. Once the distribution advance and any distribution expenses have been repaid, any further royalty payments are paid to the production company. These payments are sometimes referred to as 'overages'. Usual distribution fees payable to a distribution company are in the region of 30–50 per cent for theatrical rights, 60–80 per cent for home video rights and 30–50 per cent for television rights.

The distribution company will also deduct withholding tax from the distribution advance and any royalties due to the production company. Withholding tax is payable when the production company and the distribution company are incorporated in different countries. However, the UK has entered into treaties with other countries in order to prevent double taxation and in such circumstances it is possible to file a certificate with the relevant authority in order to claim credit for the amount of tax deducted.

Payment terms

If the distribution terms involve payment of a distribution advance (sometimes known as a minimum guarantee) to the production company, the amount of the distribution advance and the payment terms of the distribution advance to the production company will be set out in the distribution agreement. The distribution advance is usually paid in instalments, for example a percentage upon signature of the distribution agreement, a percentage upon delivery of delivery materials and a percentage upon technical acceptance of the delivery materials. This allows the distribution company the option of withholding payment of part of the distribution advance if the delivery materials delivered to the distribution company by the production company are not technically acceptable. The distribution company may also pay box office bonuses to the production company if the box office receipts of the feature film reach a certain level. These will be added to the distribution advance and will, as set out above, be deducted from the production company's royalty share until the distribution company is fully recouped.

The distribution advance and any royalty will be paid by the distribution company to the production company into a nominated bank account at periods specified in the distribution agreement. If the distribution advance has been used to raise production finance for a feature film (as set out in **para.12.2.2**), the bank providing production finance to the production company in order to cash-flow the production will require the distribution company to sign a notice of assignment redirecting the payment of the distribution advance and any box office bonuses or overages to the bank until the loan to the production company has been repaid to the bank.

The distribution company will usually be obligated to send statements to the production company for specified periods of time during the term of the distribution agreement showing the receipts generated from the distribution of the feature film or television programme, for example the box office receipts from the theatrical release of the feature film and sales figures for DVDs. Statements are usually sent monthly for the first six to 12 months, then quarterly for a period of two to three years and thereafter annually. The distribution company must maintain a separate account for the feature film or television programme unless the receipts can be cross-collaterised (i.e. shared with) other feature films or television programmes. If a feature film or television programme is cross-collaterised, this means that a successful production may not produce any overages if it is accounted along with an unsuccessful production. The production company will usually be entitled in the distribution agreement to examine the distribution company's books and records once or twice a year on notice with any underpayments and costs of the audit to be paid by the distribution company.

Delivery materials

The delivery date for delivery materials relating to the feature film or television programme will be set out in the distribution agreement. Time will usually be of the essence for this date as failure to meet the delivery date will have serious implications for the distribution or broadcast of the feature film or television programme. The cost of delivering the delivery materials will usually be at the expense of the production company. Sometimes the distribution company will require only loan of or access to materials other than the major delivery items. The distribution agreement will usually set out a specific period of time for technical acceptance of the delivery materials. If the delivery materials are rejected by the distribution company, and if this is a contractual term of the distribution agreement the dispute may go to arbitration. If the delivery materials are not rejected by the distribution company within the specified time for technical acceptance they will be deemed to be accepted and any distribution advance instalment must be made.

The delivery materials required by the distribution company or broadcaster will be set out in a delivery schedule attached to the distribution agreement. Delivery to the distribution company of some or all of the delivery materials may be guaranteed by the completion guarantor to the distribution company if the distribution advance has been used as part of the production finance (see **para.12.2.2**). For a feature film, the most important delivery materials are:

- original negative;
- answer print and check print;
- interpositive and/or internegative of the original negative;
- title materials;
- optical soundtrack negative;
- music elements;
- video masters;
- interpositive and/or internegative of the trailer;
- post-production, legal and marketing elements including dialogue list, music cue sheet, music licences, promotional stills and publicity materials, credit requirements and approvals and the chain of title (as set out in **Chapter 11**).

13.3 BBFC CLASSIFICATION

The British Board of Film Classification ('BBFC') is an independent non-governmental body that has classified feature films distributed theatrically since its inception in 1912, and videos or DVDs since the Video Recordings Act in 1984. Its purpose is to bring a degree of uniformity to feature film classification although statutory powers remain with local councils which may overrule any decision made by the BBFC, for example banning a feature film that the BBFC has passed or making new cuts. Similar organisations exist in other countries worldwide.

The BBFC will, upon payment of a small fee, produce a classification for a feature film submitted to it by a production company or distribution company. The current categories of feature film classification are:

U or Uc — Universal: should be suitable for audiences aged four years and over.

PG — Parental guidance: some scenes may be unsuitable for young children.

12 or12A — No one under the age of 12 may see a 12 or 12A film in a cinema unless accompanied by an adult. No one under 12 may buy or rent a 12 rated DVD.

15 — No one under the age of 15 may see a 15 film in a cinema. No one under 15 may buy or rent a 15 rated DVD.

18 — No one under the age of 18 may see an 18 film in a cinema. No one under 18 may buy or rent an 18 rated DVD.

18R — To be shown to adults only in specially licensed cinemas or supplied to adults in licensed sex shops.

The classification applied by the BBFC can have enormous commercial impact, for example a 15 certificate may mean a larger audience than an 18 certificate. With this in mind, the distribution company will seek as part of the rights granted by the production company under the terms of the distribution agreement the right to edit the feature film in order to meet BBFC requirements.

PART 4

Computer games

Vincent Scheurer

CHAPTER 14

An overview

14.1 INTRODUCTION

14.1.1 Computer games industry

The computer games industry is the youngest sector of the entertainment industry. It is one of the fastest growing sectors. It is also subject to more disruption, due to rapidly changing technology and business practices, than the other entertainment sectors. At the time of writing, the sector is worth approximately $30 billion.

The computer games market is divided into three sectors of roughly equal size: North America, Japan and Europe. While the markets of North America and Europe share similar tastes in games, the Japanese market is noticeably different from the other two; and games which sell well in North America and Europe often fail commercially in Japan.

14.1.2 Types of games

Computer games themselves may be divided into the following types:

- *PC games*: games designed to function on home computers.
- *Console games*: games designed to function on a particular game console, such as the 'Nintendo Wii' or the Sony 'PlayStation'.
- *Arcade games*: games designed to function on hardware located in public areas, rather than in the home.
- *Handheld games*: games designed to function on game-specific handheld devices, such as the 'Nintendo DS' and the Sony 'PSP'.
- *Mobile games*: games designed to function on mobile telephones.

In general terms, PC and console games form the largest category in the games industry. Arcade games are somewhat in decline as the processing power of PCs and game consoles has increased, whilst mobile and handheld games are increasing in importance as mobile telephones and handheld devices become smaller and more powerful. Each of the above types of computer games may have 'online' features in as much as they may be played against other users over a local network or the Internet, or they may be updated or expanded by downloading additional content.

The game types above can be divided into two further groups:

1. *Licensed games*: games which require a licence from a third party licensor, such as a sporting body or film studio. Licensed games include sports simulation games and games based on films.
2. *Original games*: games based wholly on internally developed intellectual property, which do not require a licence from a third party. Original games include games in the 'Super Mario' and 'Tomb Raider' series.

14.1.3 Developing games

The size and complexity of a computer game, and consequently the development time and cost required to develop it, vary according to the type of game in question. In general, PC and console games now take between one and two years to complete. The development costs are measured in single digit millions of dollars, with a typical 'PlayStation2' game costing perhaps $2 million to develop. However, development costs tend to rise as technology evolves, and it is currently estimated that the development costs for 'PlayStation3' games will be at least two to three times greater than those of 'PlayStation2' games.

14.1.4 Exploiting games

Computer games are commercially exploited through a variety of methods, often depending on the type of computer game.

PC, console, handheld and arcade games

Arcade games generate income through players paying to play on a game-by-game basis in an arcade.

PC, console and handheld games are usually exploited in the same way as a DVD of a film: buyers pay a fixed fee to acquire a copy of the game on a disc or cartridge, and are able to play it as often or as little as they like for no extra cost. Patches or bug fixes developed after the release of the game may be made available for download to registered owners free of charge, while additional ('add-on') or episodic content may be supplied for an extra fee.

MMOGs

One exception is the 'massive multiplayer online game' or 'MMOG', typically a PC game which resides on the publisher's own servers. Players are allowed to access those servers and play directly with (or against) other players. These games may be commercially exploited by way of subscription revenue: players pay a defined sum per month, during which they can access the game as little or as much as they like.

Mobile games

Mobile games are often sold by direct download to the end-user in electronic format, rather than purchased on a disc. However, some mobile games are provided to players on a subscription basis: in return for payment of a subscription fee, a player has access to a number of games (which may be regularly updated) for a limited period of time.

The future

As distribution and billing technologies evolve, PC, console and handheld games will increasingly be sold by direct download. For the foreseeable future (which is a very short period of time in the computer games industry) it is likely that PC, console and handheld games will continue to be sold primarily through retail outlets.

14.1.5   Retail

PC, console and handheld games together make up the largest part of the computer games industry. Since these are usually sold as retail products, the retail industry has a very important role to play in the computer games industry as a whole. Large retail organisations like supermarkets have substantial bargaining power, and are often able to negotiate the purchase of games on beneficial commercial terms, including full sale or return and price protection (both further described at **para.16.2**). As computer games begin to be distributed through other routes, including direct download and on a 'pay per play' subscription basis, it is possible that the power of retail may begin to wane. However, at the time of writing, the retail industry can make or break a PC, console or handheld computer game.

14.1.6   Importance of 'franchises'

One central feature of the computer games industry is the importance of 'franchises'. This term is generally applied to a series of games which are connected in some way. For instance, they may share the same principal character, or the same title, or use the same concept. Within a 'franchise' one can distinguish:

- 'sequels' (games released in sequence, often for play on the same device, but with different contents); and

231

- 'ports' (games with very similar contents but released for play on different devices, often simultaneously or near-simultaneously).

The computer games industry evolves very rapidly. In particular, the devices on which computer games can be played increase in power at an astonishing rate. This allows computer games publishers the opportunity to recreate new versions of successful games for new gaming devices (or 'platforms') with dramatically improved graphics. This has resulted in a far greater reliance on sequels than one finds in, for instance, the film industry; with successful game franchises such as the 'Super Mario', 'Zelda' and 'Final Fantasy' franchises generating countless iterations without any suggestion of a diminishing appetite within the buying public. The true value of a successful computer game, then, often lies more in its capacity to generate further games within the same franchise, than simply in the net profit generated by that game alone.

Indeed, the successful franchise is the key to success in the computer games industry. The sales figures of new games based on established franchises are much more predictable than those of new games based on entirely new concepts. A game based on an established franchise is much less likely to fail commercially, and is therefore much more attractive from a business perspective. As the costs of developing games continue to rise, so too do the financial risks associated with the commercial failure of a game; and this naturally leads to a greater reliance on established franchises. This may yet result in a stifling of innovation within the computer games industry.

14.2 SHORT HISTORY OF THE COMPUTER GAMES INDUSTRY

14.2.1 The early days

The computer games industry began in 1971. Although computer games have existed since as early as 1958, the first games were developed by computer scientists and students to test the limits of their new, room-sized big budget supercomputers. It was not until the arrival of cheap, mass-produced processors that the computer games business became viable.

From the outset, the business evolved in distinct markets. That year, 1971, saw the mass production of the first computer game device for the home (or 'console'), a simple paddle and ball game built into a special piece of hardware called the 'Odyssey'. At the same time, 1971 saw the first computer game device for public spaces such as bars, amusement arcades and the like: 'Computer Space'. Its creator set up Atari in 1972. Atari released an arcade game, 'Pong' during the same year, and it followed this with a home version of Pong during 1974. Both were commercially successful.

The early successes of home and arcade devices prompted a rash of similar hardware products, and in the absence of any clear market leader or innovation the industry crashed in 1977. Many of the original game manufacturers left the business. Atari, however, remained, and developed a popular home console which used cartridges and could therefore play many different games. This in turn allowed other companies to create games for Atari's machines, starting with Activision, founded in 1979 as the first software-only games publisher.

14.2.2 The modern era

The computer games industry crashed again in 1983, this time due in part to a glut in undifferentiated software products, rather than hardware devices. It was rescued by Nintendo, which introduced its first cartridge-based game console, the 'Nintendo Entertainment System' (or 'NES'), into the US in 1986. This signalled the beginning of the '8-bit' era (named after the console's 8-bit microprocessor). Sega soon followed Nintendo into the US market.

Thereafter, game consoles began to emerge in cycles, with the rest of the computer games industry forced to follow suit.

16-bit era

The next cycle, the 16-bit era, began in 1989 with the launch of the Sega 'Genesis'. This was soon followed by the launch of Nintendo's new console, the 'Super Nintendo Entertainment System' (or 'SNES') in 1991. The handheld games industry also began in earnest in 1989 with the launch of Nintendo's 'Game Boy'.

During this time, the PC also emerged as an increasingly popular games playing device. The arrival of the PC CD-ROM in about 1994 allowed PC game developers to create richer, more detailed visual effects for their games. This came a year after a small game development company called Id Software had released 'Doom', innovating both on a technical level and on a business level – most units of the game were not sold through retail outlets, but directly to end-users by post or digital download.

32-bit/64-bit era

The 32-bit/64-bit era began in 1994, when Sony entered the game console market with the 'PlayStation'. This rapidly became the most popular console, outselling both Sega's 'Saturn' and Nintendo's 'N64' (released in 1995 and 1996 respectively). Nintendo continued to dominate the handheld market, however, with the launch of the 'Game Boy Colour' in 1998 and the 'Game Boy Advance' in 2001.

From PlayStation2 to the next generation

Sony maintained its new-found dominance in the console market during the following console cycle, which began with the launch of the 'PlayStation2' in 2000. This was followed by the launch of Nintendo's 'GameCube' in 2001 and the arrival of Microsoft, which launched its 'Xbox' console during the same year. Neither managed to overturn Sony's market dominance. Nintendo maintained its lead in the handheld market with the launch of the 'Nintendo DS' in 2004, followed later that year by Sony's first foray into the handheld market with its 'PlayStation Portable' (or 'PSP').

At the time of writing, this cycle is about to yield to the 'next generation' – the new Microsoft 'Xbox360', Sony 'PlayStation3' and 'Nintendo Wii' have launched recently. At the same time, online games are proving increasingly popular with the growing broadband infrastructure, and the ubiquitous mobile telephone is now also capable of supporting sophisticated games.

14.3 THE PRINCIPAL ACTORS

14.3.1 Four categories of actors

The principal actors in the computer games industry may be divided into the following four broad categories:

- *Game developers*: organisations which actually create computer games. These are often small, independent studios based in a single location with between 20 and 100 employees.
- *Game publishers*: organisations which market and publish computer games. These are often large multinational companies with many hundreds of employees.
- *Retailers and distributors*: organisations which distribute and sell computer games to the public. These include specialist shops, specialist chains and generalists such as supermarkets.
- *Console owners*: organisations which own game consoles. These organisations develop and sell the devices on which console games function. Typically, they also monopolise the replication of games for use on their consoles. These tend to be global multinationals and include Nintendo, Microsoft and Sony.

These categories are not completely distinct. Console owners also publish games and develop games using internally owned studios. Almost all publishers use their own internal studios to develop some of their games; the extent to which these studios are independent from their owners can differ substantially. Equally, almost all publishers work with independent developers even if they also own development studios of their own.

14.3.2   Other participants

Contractors

In contrast to the film industry, most individuals involved in developing games are employees of the game developer rather than contractors. Equally, game developers have typically tended to develop the whole game in-house, while nevertheless contracting out specialist and 'modular' tasks, such as the production of audio (including music, sound effects, speech and commentary), 'FMV' (full motion video) and motion capture.

However, console and PC games are becoming more complex to develop and are requiring increasing manpower. As a result, game developers are increasingly turning to individual contractors and outsourcing companies in order to provide additional manpower at particular stages of the development process.

Middleware providers

Historically, a game developer would create the whole game in-house. This would comprise all of the underlying technology, including artificial intelligence routines, the technology required to render a three-dimensional world in real time and the technology required to mimic the laws of physics in real time (often known as AI engines, 3D engines and physics engines, respectively). As this technology has become increasingly sophisticated, specialist technology providers have emerged to license this software to many different game developers. This software is generally known as 'middleware'. Many games now share the same middleware.

Agents and intermediaries

Some game developers rely on agents to assist them in finding game publishers and funding for their proposed games. Most agents are appointed on an exclusive basis.

An agent is usually responsible for:

- identifying and contacting suitable publishers on behalf of the developer;
- negotiating with publishers; and
- assisting in managing the parties' relationship both during and after the conclusion of the game project.

In return, the agent is usually paid a commission on all of the sums received by the developer from the publisher in relation to the project. This may also include a commission on any further income paid by the publisher to the developer in respect of future projects, as well as the project in respect of which the agent provided its services.

External finance providers and completion bonds

As noted in **para.15.1**, the development costs of computer games are usually funded by game publishers. However, as game projects become more expensive, new sources of capital are emerging to fund them. These include general project finance providers (including high street banks), as well as game-specific funds. This is true notwithstanding that the computer games industry does not benefit from many of the favourable tax regimes available to film producers.

Game production is still perceived to involve substantial risks. Accordingly, banks and other financial institutions which provide project finance often ensure that they do not bear the production risk in any project. This may require a third party to guarantee that a particular game will be completed by a certain date – a process which can be described as providing insurance against non-delivery of a game (the policy being known as a 'completion bond' or 'completion guarantee'). These guarantees are usually given by organisations which already provide similar services in the film industry.

14.4   THE PRINCIPAL RIGHTS

14.4.1   Introduction

The two principal classes of property rights which underpin a computer game are copyright and trade mark rights. Almost all other intellectual property rights and related rights are relevant to computer games, but the true value of a computer game, and particularly of a computer game franchise, resides in copyright and trade mark rights.

14.4.2   Copyright

Copyright subsists in different components of a computer game. As noted below, different parties may own copyright in different components of the same game. In general, the components in a computer game which are protected by copyright are divided into two broad groups: the underlying technology on the one hand, and the visible and audible elements on the other.

Underlying technology

Much of a computer game is comprised in a series of computer programs. The computer programs within a computer game include programs which:

- simulate artificial intelligence in characters controlled by the relevant game playing device;
- generate the images seen by the player as the game progresses;
- allow the player to play against other players on different game playing devices; and
- create believable animations in on-screen characters.

Computer programs are considered 'literary works' (CDPA 1988, s.3(1)(b)).

As noted above at **para.14.3.2**, some of these programs may have been acquired commercially from a middleware provider, in which case the copyright in those programs will remain the property of the middleware provider. In other cases, the game developer's own employees will have created all of the relevant programs, in which case the copyright in those programs will usually remain the property of the game developer.

Visible and audible elements

In general, a person playing a computer game is oblivious to the nature of the underlying technology used in that computer game. Instead, the player is conscious of the visible and audible elements of the computer game. These visible and audible elements are also generally protected by copyright. They can usually be broken down into the following distinct components:

- the graphic images used in the game (including characters, scenes, locations, buildings and backdrops);
- the text used in the game;
- the music used in the game (both the composition and the recording will be protected by copyright as further described in **Chapter 2**);
- the sounds used in the game;
- any video sequences shown during the game;
- static loading, options and menu screens;
- the 'heads up display' of the game, being the combination of the primary game screen during play together with the additional information shown to the player (such as health and ammunition meters).

In general, and provided they are sufficiently original to meet the test described in **para.2.4.1**, many of these components may be considered as individual copyright works. The game as a whole can be treated as a separate copyright work, combining all of these components in its own distinctive manner.

In addition, copyright will usually subsist in two additional categories of work:

- preliminary work, being work created as part of the game-making process, but not forming part of the final game; examples include concept art, game design documents and the like; and

237

- ancillary work, being work created in order to market and sell the game; examples include box art, poster art, disc art and the like.

Clearly, the ownership of a computer game 'franchise' is related much more to ownership of copyright in the visible and audible elements of a game, than it is to the ownership of copyright in the underlying technology in a game.

'Game play' and 'look and feel'

It is not uncommon for game development contracts to refer to the nebulous concepts of 'game play' or of the 'look and feel' of a game. In general, these terms are not helpful and add little, if anything, to the broad copyright dichotomy outlined above. The extent to which 'game play' and 'look and feel' can be protected by copyright, in addition to the other components described above, is very unclear.

Often, a game will benefit from an unusual art style, and many of the visible elements of the game will be considered artistic works and protected by copyright accordingly. Reproducing the 'look and feel' of such a game by copying these artistic works may well amount to actionable copyright.

In contrast, the 'look and feel' of a game, or (more usually) the 'game play' of a game, may refer instead to the manner in which the game is played, or in which the game functions. These concepts, or ideas, may not be protected by copyright at all. Many fundamental game innovations fall into this category, and as a result have proven very hard to protect.

14.4.3   Trade marks

Trade marks are used to distinguish the goods or services of one person from those of another. In general, the owner of a trade mark can prevent other persons from selling the same goods or services under that mark. As noted above at **para.14.4.1**, trade marks form an essential component of a game franchise.

When applied to computer games, the title of each computer game, together with the name of the publisher and/or the developer of that game (and the associated logo(s) of each) will generally be treated as trade marks by their respective owners.

If any particular trade mark is registrable (broadly speaking, if it is distinctive, rather than descriptive of the relevant game; and not immoral or similar to an existing trade mark), then the relevant owner will often register the relevant mark with one or more of the principal trade mark registries. Registration makes it easier for the owner of the registered trade mark to prevent others from selling similar goods or services under that mark.

Since computer games are sold worldwide, this usually means securing protection in North America, the EU and Japan.

Trade marks relating to computer games are usually registered in one or more of the following classes:

- class 9 (computer game programs);
- class 16 (printed matter such as books and posters);
- class 28 (handheld computer games other than those adapted for use with television receivers);
- class 38 (provision of access to games over the Internet, and the provision of related communications services including message sending and e-mail);
- class 41 (games services provided online); and
- class 42 (provision of technical information and support relating to computer games).

Of these, class 9 is the principal class and it is difficult to conceive of a computer game trade mark being registered in other classes but not class 9.

14.4.4 Registered designs

The owner of a registered design is granted a monopoly over the appearance of the whole or part of the product which is the subject of the registered design.

The designs of computer game consoles and their associated hardware, including controllers and accessories, are typically protected as registered designs, in addition to other forms of protection (including copyright and unregistered design rights).

In addition to hardware, the law relating to registered designs now allows for the registration of 3D computer game characters and even game logos as registered designs.

14.4.5 Other rights

Computer games are complex works. In particular, they feature an unusual combination of technological and aesthetic features. They often feature facsimiles of real people, such as recognised sporting personalities or actors, in increasingly realistic fashion. As such, computer games touch on almost all intellectual property rights in the widest sense of the term (including 'personality rights'). Since computer games are generally sold internationally, and are rarely created for just one market, they will usually be subject to the multitude of different intellectual property rights rules as they apply in different countries.

Two important intellectual property rights become relevant in this context: patent rights and personality rights.

239

Patent rights

A patent grants a monopoly over an invention. Under English law, neither computer programs nor literary or artistic works are patentable. As a result, computer games themselves (including their underlying technology) are not usually patented under English law. English patents in the computer game industry are usually confined to the hardware relating to computer games, particularly to the computer games consoles.

However, the law relating to patents in the US is generally less restrictive and, as a result, certain elements of computer games may be protected by US patents when they would not be patentable in England. An example is US patent number 6,935,954 (covering a 'sanity system' in a computer game).

From an English perspective, even if a feature of a game is not patentable in England, it may well be patentable in the US. This means that the English developer and publisher of a game will have to consider two additional issues: whether to obtain patent protection for one or more features of a particular computer game in the US; and whether their computer game infringes any other person's patent in the US. Given the significant costs of obtaining patent protection, together with the long lead time to the grant of a patent, it is unusual for developers or publishers to seek to register a patent of their own. However, disputes over existing patents are not uncommon, and are addressed in greater detail at **para.15.12.2**.

'Personality rights'

By 'personality rights', we mean the group of rights which permit any individual to object to or restrict the use of his image in connection with any good or service, including within a computer game.

'Personality rights' vary substantially from country to country and appear to be evolving at great speed. An example of a relatively recent personality right development in English law is the Eddie Irvine case (*Irvine & Ors* v. *TalkSPORT Ltd* [2003] EWCA Civ 423, CA, 1 April 2003, Lawtel, discussed at **para.5.2.9**).

The computer games industry has used the names, and increasingly the likenesses, of famous people since its earliest periods. This is particularly true of computer games which simulate real sporting events and which need to use the names of real sportsmen and women in order to maintain an up-to-date simulation.

Whilst the legality of using real names and accurate likenesses in computer games may be debated in certain jurisdictions, it is now generally accepted within the computer games industry that such use will be actionable by the individual concerned in at least one, and probably more, principal territories. As a result, it is now common practice to obtain a licence from any known individual before using that person's name or likeness in a computer game.

Licence agreements between developers and film studios for the production of a computer game based on a film, further described at **Chapter 17**, should state explicitly the extent to which the licence covers the use of its actors' likenesses or whether the developer will have to obtain the necessary rights separately.

Collective licensing of personality rights is now a common feature in sports. The governing bodies, league associations and player unions involved with the major sports have over the years developed licensing programs for computer games under which they have to varying degrees secured and are thus able to provide the rights to use the likenesses of sportsmen and women who are permitted to play in leagues and tournaments organised by that body.

Confidential information

Rights in confidential information, such as trade secrets, are not strictly speaking 'intellectual property rights'. However, they are relevant to any description of the principal rights in computer games. The technology of computer games evolves very rapidly, and many computer games are commercially successful in part because of a particular technological innovation which they alone feature.

Technological innovations in computer games are often buried within the underlying technology of a game. This technology is protected by copyright. However, copyright protection does not necessarily prevent another person from understanding and then reusing a particularly clever new idea or technique. Equally, although patent protection may be sought to protect a new idea, at least in the US, this is rarely done in practice as a result of the high costs and long lead times involved in securing patents.

As a result, in practice many commercially valuable ideas or techniques used in computer games are not protected by intellectual property law and the creators of these ideas or techniques have to ensure that they are kept as confidential as possible. This means restricting the disclosure of these ideas or techniques and ensuring that any person to whom they are disclosed first agrees, in writing, not to use them for their own purposes, or to further disclose them. Executing an agreement of this nature, often known as a confidentiality agreement or a non-disclosure agreement (or NDA), is an essential step in the process of preserving the confidentiality of any trade secret. However, it should be recalled that such an agreement is simply a contract, and thus it will be generally good against the other party to the contract, but not the rest of the world. Once a trade secret has ceased to be a secret, there is little that its creator can do to stop third parties from using it as they see fit.

CHAPTER 15

Commissioning and publishing

15.1 INTRODUCTION

This chapter deals with the relationship between the developer of a computer game and the publisher of that game. As noted in **Chapter 14**, some computer games are created by studios which are wholly owned and controlled by a publisher. However, many computer games are created by independent developers, and the relationship between an independent developer and a publisher is one of the principal commercial relationships of the computer games industry. It combines money and aesthetics, and as such it can be one of the most fraught commercial relationships that either party will have. It can also prove to be one of the most lucrative.

Creating a computer game costs money. Most of the money is allocated to the wages of the developer's staff involved in creating the game, together with related overheads such as office costs. An increasing amount is allocated to third parties, particularly licensors of middleware or sub-contractors and outsourcing companies (see **para.14.3.2**). In the case of licensed games (further addressed in **Chapter 17**), substantial up-front advances may be payable to the owner of the property on which the game is based. As noted above in **para.14.1.3**, the total costs of creating a console game are measured in the millions of pounds.

Creating a computer game is also risky. In particular, the rapidly evolving technological background imports technology risks which are not present in most of the other creative industries. A developer may find itself working with a wholly new piece of hardware, or trying to do something which has not been done before on an existing piece of hardware. A competitor may be first to market with a computer game incorporating a new feature which immediately becomes a 'must have', requiring other developers to restructure their own development plans in order to incorporate that feature. Most developers lack the working capital to fund this level of investment, and will find it very hard to raise sums of this nature from ordinary commercial lenders such as banks.

In practice, then, most of the funding for game development projects of a certain size, including most PC, console and handheld games, originates with the eventual publisher of the game. This in turn dictates many of the commercial terms of the publishing relationship. The publishing relationship is centred around the contract under which the game is developed and funded (here known as a 'publishing agreement'), but this is rarely the first contract to be concluded between the developer and the publisher.

15.2 PRE-PRODUCTION AGREEMENTS AND NEGOTIATION

15.2.1 Non-disclosure agreement

Contractual relations between a developer and a publisher usually begin with the execution of a mutual non-disclosure agreement, since both the publisher and the developer will be disclosing commercially sensitive and confidential information to one another. The developer will be discussing its technology and new gameplay ideas, and the publisher will be discussing its marketing strategy and portfolio of games in development.

15.2.2 Due diligence

Assuming that the parties reach common ground on the broad principles of a game to be developed by the developer and published by the publisher (game type, overview, console, budget and release date), they may undertake a certain amount of due diligence. This is rarely a formal process and its importance to the parties will depend on their previous dealings (if any) and common knowledge within the industry as to whether the other presents a good or a bad risk. The publisher may enquire further as to the developer's ability to deliver a game on time and to budget, and is likely to concentrate on the developer's past record in creating similar games for a similar technological platform. The developer may enquire further as to the publisher's ability to maximise sales of the game worldwide.

In any event, each party should be advised to spend considerable time analysing the financial position of the other, since a game development project requires both parties to accept substantial exposure to the other's creditworthiness. The insolvency of one party to a publishing agreement is one of the most common reasons for the failure of a game development project.

15.2.3 Intermediate work and contracts

If the parties' due diligence enquiries proceed positively, the next stage is for the developer to begin work on the game. This sometimes requires the payment of money to the developer in order to fund this early stage work. At this stage, the game design (including the technical design) will not be complete, and one early task is to create a full-scale, detailed game design document outlining the game in detail.

In addition, the publisher will usually require the developer to create a single, playable level of the game (which may be known as a 'prototype' or a 'vertical slice'). This is required for two separate reasons:

- to prove that the principal technology of the game actually works (thus reducing the technology risk inherent in the project); and
- to create a visual, playable part of the game in order to prove that the gameplay is as good in reality as it may appear to be on paper.

If a publisher has agreed to fund the development of the prototype, it will often do so under a 'pre-production agreement' or another intermediate agreement such as a binding heads of agreement or a binding letter of intent. An agreement of this nature will usually contain a mix of legally binding terms and terms which are not legally binding, but which set out the principal commercial terms of the eventual publishing agreement.

The parties may of course opt to negotiate a full length publishing agreement straightaway. However this can take time and delay the development of the game, as the developer will be understandably reluctant to commence work without payment; and the publisher will be equally reluctant to make payment without a contract clearly describing what it will receive in return.

15.2.4 Legally binding terms

The legally binding terms of a pre-production or other intermediate agreement generally include the following terms, which relate principally to the creation of the prototype (and not to the creation of the complete game):

- a description of the prototype work to be carried out by the developer, including a description of the software and documentation to be created, and the date by which it is to be created;
- the payments to be made by the publisher to the developer in respect of this prototype work;
- whether any such payments are conditional upon the achievement of any particular task, and (if so) the mechanism for determining whether that task has been achieved or not;
- detailed divorce provisions, should the parties elect to abandon the project (or simply fail to conclude a full publishing agreement) when the prototype stage is complete;
- a statement of ownership of the intellectual property rights in the work created by the developer; and
- confidentiality terms.

The parties may also agree a form of exclusivity, under which one or both parties agrees not to undertake a competing project with a third party during the prototype phase.

15.2.5 Non-legally binding terms

The terms which are not legally binding generally include the following terms, which relate to the complete game, rather than to the prototype. These are generally statements of the principal terms which the parties now intend to incorporate into an eventual full-scale publishing agreement:

- a general description of the game to be created by the developer, including the game type, an overview of how it will work and the platforms on which it is to operate;
- the intended completion date for the game;
- an estimated total budget for completion of the game;
- a summary of the royalties to be paid to the developer on the proceeds of exploitation of the game, together with a reference to the recoupment model used;
- a description of the intellectual property rights in the various components of each game, including a statement of which party owns each component;
- a description of the publisher's rights to commercially exploit the game, including the territory of exploitation and the intended duration of these rights;
- a summary of the responsibilities of the publisher, which may include the publisher's obligation to procure a licence from a third party (such as a sporting body or a movie studio);
- a summary of the types of credits to be given to the developer and its staff;
- a summary of the parties' rights in respect of sequels and ports of the game; and
- a summary of the parties' eventual termination rights, and the consequences of termination.

Again, the parties may also agree in principle that one or both parties should not undertake a competing project with a third party during a predetermined period of time.

15.3 THE PUBLISHING AGREEMENT

If the prototype phase proceeds to the satisfaction of both parties, and the publisher's own sales and marketing teams approve the project (something which they may be reluctant to do before seeing a prototype), then the publisher will 'green light' full production of the game. At this stage, the parties will negotiate the publishing agreement, committing each of them (but particularly the developer – see **para.15.11.2**) to the final completion and commercial exploitation of the game.

While publishing agreements differ from project to project, almost all publishing agreements concerning a game to be developed by an independent developer for a publisher address the following key issues:

- the parties' obligations during and after development of the game;
- testing and acceptance;
- ownership and control of intellectual property rights;
- the payment of advances and royalties;
- termination; and
- risk allocation and risk transfer through warranties, indemnities and limitations of liability.

These key issues are discussed in more detail in the remainder of this chapter.

The publishing agreement forms the cornerstone of the legal and business relationship between the developer and the publisher.

15.4   OBLIGATIONS OF THE PARTIES DURING DEVELOPMENT

15.4.1   The developer

During development of the game both parties are focused on completing the game on time and on budget. This is the principal obligation of the developer, and most publishing agreements start with the core obligation to deliver the game, in pre-agreed stages, by pre-agreed dates.

Within this overarching obligation, a publishing agreement will often include the following obligations for the developer:

- an obligation to create the game and each component to an agreed standard of quality;
- an obligation to create marketing materials to assist the publisher in marketing the game prior to release, including playable 'demos' and graphic assets to be distributed to the press;
- an obligation to employ certain named individuals or 'key staff' in relation to the game, and often to require those individuals to work exclusively on the game and not on any other game being developed at the same time for another customer; and
- a prohibition against incorporating any form of hidden content in the game (often known as 'Easter eggs') without the express approval of the publisher.

15.4.2 The publisher

The publisher is also implicated in the development process and its funding and testing obligations are addressed in greater detail below. Its further obligations usually include the following:

- an obligation to provide certain assets during development (typically including translations of the text and voice used in the game, which the publisher can often acquire at lower cost than the developer); and
- an obligation to test the game for bugs during development, and particularly at the end of development.

15.4.3 Contingencies

The publisher will usually require that time be of the essence of the developer's obligation to deliver the game. The publisher's marketing campaign for the game will be planned and implemented many months prior to completion, and delaying the marketing campaign can be costly. Equally, most games are sold during short holiday sales windows, particularly Christmas, so a failure to meet one of those windows can result in a substantial reduction in sales and a corresponding loss of profit.

The consequences of a 'time of the essence obligation' are primarily connected to the ease of termination of the agreement for breach, addressed below. However, it is necessary for a developer to ensure that the publisher cannot cause the developer to be in breach by reason of the publisher's own failure to perform an obligation on which the developer's delivery obligation relies. As a result, the publishing agreement should contain a mechanism adjusting the developer's delivery dates if these are affected by the publisher's delay in performing any of its own obligations.

15.4.4 Quality assurance testing

Most publishing agreements are based on drafts created by the publisher and accordingly do not address many of the publisher's obligations in great detail. In particular, the publisher's obligations to test the game during development are often very contentious. The cost of recalling a game from the market because it contains a technical fault or bug can be extremely high. As a result, the publisher will usually seek to pass this risk to the developer, whether by including a covenant to create a bug-free game, or a warranty that the game will not contain any bugs, or both. At the same time, the publisher will seek to avoid sharing any of this risk by accepting an obligation, express or implied, to test the game to a particular standard prior to release. This is the case notwithstanding that the publisher is, in practice, often heavily involved in testing a game for bugs, as part of the quality assurance or 'QA' process.

As a result, many publishing agreements will simply ignore the practical fact that the publisher will be heavily involved in testing the game for bugs; and others will expressly state that any such testing will not absolve the developer of responsibility for bugs which might have been missed during the process. However, the developer will be keen to ensure that the publisher bears some contractual responsibility for locating bugs prior to release of the game.

15.4.5 Changes to the game

The developer's obligation to deliver the game and interim deliverables will be tied to a game design document which describes both the creative and the technical facets of the game. As the computer games industry evolves very rapidly, but the development of a game can take many years to complete, it is not uncommon for the parties to agree to change the game design. During development, this is usually fine, provided that both parties understand, and agree, all of the consequences of any proposed change, including the effect on the overall development budget and the delivery date for the game.

Many publishing agreements contain sophisticated change control provisions, requiring any changes to the game design or related matters (such as budget and timetable) to be agreed and recorded in accordance with a formal mechanism of proposal, counter proposal and written agreement. In practice, the parties rarely if at all follow these procedures. Accordingly, a 'light touch' in regulating the process by which changes to the game design are agreed is often preferable.

15.5 OBLIGATIONS AFTER DEVELOPMENT

15.5.1 The developer

The developer's obligations do not cease on completion of the game. Whilst the core obligation to create the game has been performed, the following obligations are also very important to the publisher and can be essential to the success of the project:

- an obligation to translate or 'localise' the game into foreign languages;
- an obligation to fix bugs which may have been missed during the QA process but which are reported by end-users; and
- an obligation to assist in post-release marketing of the game, which may include working with the press during the critical game review process, which takes place during or immediately after completion of the game.

15.5.2   The publisher

Once the game is complete, the publisher will naturally attempt to recover its investment to date by selling it. This requires substantial investment, both in manufacturing copies of the game and in marketing the game. As a result, the developer may require the publisher to accept a positive obligation:

- to manufacture and distribute a minimum number of units of the game within a defined period;
- to spend a minimum sum in marketing the game; or even
- to generate a minimum level of sales income.

If the game is a console game, then in general only the console manufacturer is entitled to manufacture copies of the game for sale. The console manufacturer charges royalties for every unit of a game manufactured to function on its console; and these royalties are paid on delivery of each game unit, irrespective of whether that unit is eventually sold to the public or not. Accordingly, manufacturing a console game involves a massive capital outlay immediately before launch – which coincides with the bulk of the publisher's marketing budget, also spent in the months and weeks leading up to launch.

Contractually, the publisher will be reluctant to accept any positive obligation to manufacture or market the game or to achieve a predetermined income from sales of the game. In taking this position, the publisher may cite the heavy investment it has already made in the game through payment of advances to the developer, meaning that it is already financially committed to the game, so additional contractual obligations are unnecessary.

Whilst true in many cases, this argument does not hold at all times. If the publisher is experiencing cash-flow difficulties at launch, or is simultaneously launching another game (developed internally, and therefore potentially more profitable), then it may be tempted not to allocate as much money to the launch of a game as it may originally have intended. This in turn is likely to adversely affect sales of the game, leading to reduced (or no) royalties to the developer.

The publisher's other core post-release obligation (i.e. to account and pay for royalties) is discussed further below at **paras.15.9** and **15.10**.

15.6   TESTING AND ACCEPTANCE

As noted below at **para.15.8.1**, if the publisher has agreed to pay money to the developer during development of the game, then this money is usually payable in defined tranches due when the game has reached pre-agreed stages of development, or 'milestones'. This in turn requires a mechanism allowing the parties to assess whether or not the game has reached a particular milestone – an issue which can be contentious, given the sums which may be at stake.

A workable mechanism for the publisher to test and (if appropriate) accept a particular deliverable requires the following elements:

- a commitment by the publisher to review the relevant deliverable within a specified time period, commencing on the date of receipt of that deliverable;
- a commitment by the publisher to notify the developer of its findings on or before the last day of that period;
- if a deliverable is rejected, a commitment by the publisher to provide reasons for that rejection;
- an obligation on the part of the publisher to accept the deliverable unless it fails to meet the agreed standards set out in the contract; and
- a set of objectively measurable standards which must be met by each deliverable.

15.6.1   Quality

The final element will be a set of objectively measurable standards, and this can be problematic. Ultimately, a game is as much a creative work as a technical work, and it can be difficult to apply objective standards to the assessment and evaluation of a creative work. It is not uncommon for publishers to seek to require the game (and each deliverable) to meet subjective quality criteria, by specifying that the game should be of the 'highest quality', or 'triple A', or 'state of the art'. Criteria of this nature should be rejected by the developer as they are too uncertain (and often impossibly high). Since they trigger payment of sums which the developer may need in order to pay its staff salaries and overheads, they should not be contingent on ill-defined or vague criteria.

15.6.2   Licensed games

If the game is a licensed game, the parties will need to consider how to incorporate the approval rights of the third party licensor into the process of testing and acceptance. Many licensors retain a relatively unfettered right of approval over a game which incorporates their intellectual property rights. However, unfettered approval rights are clearly incompatible with objective quality standards.

15.7   OWNERSHIP AND CONTROL OF RIGHTS

Publishing agreements generally distinguish between ownership and control of:

(i)   the underlying technology in a game; and
(ii)   the visible and audible elements in a game.

15.7.1   Underlying technology

All intellectual property rights in the underlying technology are generally reserved to the developer of the game or (in the case of middleware) to the developer's licensors. In order to permit the publisher to commercially exploit the game, the developer usually grants the publisher a licence to copy and distribute the underlying technology within the game.

This licence is generally non-exclusive, allowing the developer to use the underlying technology in other games; and indeed the ability to reuse technology is often critical to the survival of independent developers.

However, the publisher may require some form of restrictive covenant preventing the developer from reusing its technology in a similar (and directly competing) game during a fixed period of time, such as the crucial first six months of sales of the relevant game.

The developer's control over the intellectual property rights in the underlying technology can present the publisher with a problem where it wishes to have the game developed for a different platform or to have a sequel developed but is unable or unwilling to engage the original developer to do so. The publisher may request a non-exclusive licence to use the original underlying technology for such purposes and may agree to pay a royalty to the developer for this. Such terms are often agreed as a form of insurance for the publisher should such circumstances arise and are rarely invoked. In fact, it will often not be feasible for another developer to make use of the underlying technology without the original developer's support, since it will contain many features and routines with which only the original developer is familiar.

15.7.2   Visible and audible elements

As noted above at **para.14.4**, the principal intellectual property rights in the visible and audible elements of the game are copyright and trade mark rights.

Ownership of these intellectual property rights generally confers ownership of the game franchise as well (see **para.14.1.6**). Since these rights are the primary source of long-term value in any successful game, both the developer and the publisher are generally very keen to own them absolutely. Whether a particular party prevails depends on its negotiating strength at the time of negotiation of the publishing agreement.

Most of these rights will originate with the developer. In particular, in the absence of any agreement to the contrary, all copyright in the work created by the developer's employees will vest automatically in the developer. If the publisher is to own the intellectual property rights in the visible and audible elements of the game, it will require an assignment of all of those rights from

251

the developer to the publisher. An assignment must be in writing but can, under English law, be effective even if executed prior to the creation of the relevant work.

If the developer is to retain all intellectual property rights in the visible and audible elements of the game, then the developer will grant a licence of those rights to the publisher. This licence will usually be an exclusive licence and is often granted on a worldwide basis. It will usually last for the commercial life of a game, although it may be shorter; but licences for less than three years (commencing on the date of commercial release of the game) are unusual.

Unlike copyright, the trade mark and associated rights and goodwill attached to the game title (in all languages) will not automatically vest in the developer from the outset. Accordingly, if the developer is to own all of the intellectual property rights in the game, it will need to ensure that all rights attached to the game title are assigned to it, free of charge, on or before the final day of the licence term.

15.8 FINANCIAL PROVISIONS

The financial provisions of a publishing agreement generally operate in two stages: during development of the game and after conclusion of development.

15.8.1 During development

During development, the publisher will be required to pay money to the developer in order to fund the development of the game. This is usually paid in pre-agreed tranches, each payment usually being triggered by the developer reaching a certain stage of development of the game (or 'milestone'). Accordingly, staged payments of this nature are often referred to as 'milestone payments'.

The money paid by the publisher during development is often, but not always, treated as an advance against future royalties (see **para.15.8.3**). If it does form an advance, then provided that the game is commercially successful it will be refunded in full to the publisher. In practical terms, this means that the publisher is assuming a number of risks (principally the risk of non-delivery of the game and of the commercial failure of the game), but the publisher may not, ultimately, be paying for development of the game itself.

15.8.2 After development

Once the game is complete, the payments from the publisher to the developer generally take the form of royalties on the income generated by the publisher from sales of the game.

Royalties are usually paid on a receipts-based model, being the sum actually received by the publisher from the exploitation of the game, less certain deductions (principally the costs of manufacturing the game and certain adjustments relating to returns and price protection, further addressed below at **para.15.9**).

Instead of a percentage of receipts, the parties may agree a fixed sum of money per unit sold, although terms of this type are generally resisted by publishers.

15.8.3   Recoupment – the traditional model

If the parties have agreed that the funds paid by the publisher to the developer during development constitute an advance against royalties, then the publishing agreement will specify the mechanism for recoupment of these funds by the publisher. Usually, this is achieved by allowing the publisher to retain all of the royalties which it would otherwise be required to pay to the developer until the amounts so retained equal the total advances paid during development.

This usually results in the developer waiting for some months, or even years, before it receives any royalty from the exploitation of a game. This has obvious cash-flow implications for the developer, whose own cash outgoings (principally its staff salaries) are usually as constant as they are inflexible. If royalties do not exceed the total advances, then the developer will never receive a royalty payment at all. This does not mean that the publisher has not made a profit from the game – under the traditional recoupment model described here, the publisher will usually reach a break-even point well before it is due to pay any royalties to the developer.

15.8.4   Alternative models

The traditional model described above does not work in all game projects. In particular, if the cost of developing a game is high when compared to the total income which it is expected to generate, then the developer is unlikely to receive any royalty income at all. This does not necessarily benefit the publisher either, since the prospect of royalties is a key motivating factor ensuring timely delivery of a high quality game by the developer. If a developer does not expect any royalties, then its only income from a game will come in the form of advances during development – resulting in an incentive to keep development going for an indefinite period.

Accordingly, games developers and publishers sometimes adopt alternative models, including the following.

(a)   The 'break-even' model: the publisher pays the developer royalties as soon as all net income from the game exceeds the game development and marketing costs paid by the publisher (i.e. when the publisher has 'broken even').

(b) The 'day one' model: the publisher pays the developer royalties on all income generated from the game, without any recoupment (and usually at a much lower rate than after recoupment).

(c) The 'bonus' model: the publisher pays the developer a fixed sum, or a series of fixed sums, once certain agreed trigger points are met (these are usually predefined volumes of units sold, or predefined total net income; but the trigger can just as easily be achieving a particular review score).

15.8.5 Third party funding

The funding models addressed above presuppose that that publisher is funding the development of the game as described above at **para.15.1**. If funding is provided by a third party, the issue of recoupment does not arise in the same manner, and the parties are freer to structure royalty payments differently.

15.9 ROYALTIES

15.9.1 Calculating royalties

The income received by independent developers generally falls into two categories: advances and royalties. Since advances are only paid during game development projects, developers generally rely on royalties from completed games in order to survive during the inevitable quiet periods between projects.

In the games industry, royalties are usually calculated by reference to the income actually received by the publisher from the commercial exploitation of the game, rather than by reference to some other sum, such as the notional retail price of the game.

The calculation of royalties takes place in three distinct stages:

In stage 1, the publishing agreement describes the classes of income received by the publisher from which the publisher is to pay a share to the developer.

In stage 2, the 'gross' figure in stage 1 is reduced to a 'net' figure by the application of agreed deductions.

In stage 3, the applicable royalty rate is applied to the net figure reached in stage 2, resulting in the net royalty payment due to the developer.

15.9.2 Stage 1 – defining the gross

Stage 1 is essential, but is often overlooked. If any income is not included in stage 1, then none of this income will be shared with the developer at all. Sums which might be omitted generally comprise non-core income, including income received from selling merchandise or hint books based on the game, premium rate telephone charges generated by the publisher's customer helpline, or even rental income generated by the game.

Intra-group sales and licences

Intra-group transactions must also be taken into account at stage 1. It is not uncommon for international publishers to sell game units (or grant licences) to other companies in the same group. Accordingly, the price paid for game units or licences by the other company in the same group will not be negotiated at arm's length and may not therefore be as high as it could be, for entirely legitimate reasons. If, however, the developer is paid a percentage of the publisher's income, then any artificial reduction of that income (because it comes from a related party) will affect the developer directly. Accordingly, the publishing agreement must deal with the issue of intra-group sales or licences.

This can be done in a number of ways. The most common are to:

- provide that 'gross' sum at stage 1 is the total amount received by the publisher's group as a whole, rather than just the publisher; or
- provide that a notional 'arm's length' payment must be used where the publisher transacts with another member of the same group of companies; or
- prohibit intra-group transactions completely.

The first is to be preferred, if only because option two is impractical for both parties and option three will interfere with the publisher's ability to maximise revenue from the game.

15.9.3 Stage 2 – deductions

The deductions made at stage 2 are generally heavily negotiated, as in practice they may have a larger impact on the net sum payable to the developer than the royalty rate itself. Some deductions, particularly deductions for taxes such as VAT, are now practically universal. Other deductions are also generally agreed – principally those relating to payments paid by the publisher to third parties in order to transform a single master disc into a row of boxed products on a retailer's shelf, including:

- the costs of manufacturing each game unit;
- for console games, the per unit licence fee paid to the console owner;

- licence fees payable to an external licensor (such as a film studio); and
- carriage and insurance.

Payments made by the publisher to retailers in order to repurchase unsold game units ('returns'), or to compensate the retailer for a later reduction in retail price of the game ('price protection') are also generally deductible at stage 2. Equally, retrospective discounts given by publishers to retailers who have achieved agreed sales volumes are often deducted. However, in each of these cases it is likely that the publisher's negotiations with (and payments or credits to) the retailer concern many different games. Accordingly, it is important that the publisher should not be entitled to agree certain financial incentives in respect of one game, in order to benefit another (which may bear a higher profit margin than the first). For instance, if one of the publisher's own games is not selling well, but a game developed by the developer is selling well, then the developer should ensure that the publisher does not agree to reduce the price of the developer's game as an incentive for the retailer to keep selling the publisher's game.

Equally, many payments made by the publisher in connection with sales of the game are generally considered to be the sole responsibility of the publisher, and therefore not deducted in stage 2. These include most of the costs paid in relation to selling and marketing the game (the publisher's key obligation, after all), including:

- publisher staff salaries;
- sales incentives and bonuses; and
- advertising and marketing costs.

Some payments sit between these two categories, and are amongst the most heavily negotiated as a result. These generally include sums paid by the publisher to the game retailer in order to promote the game in-store (often termed 'marketing development funds' or 'co-operative advertising'). The publisher will argue that these payments represent the costs of getting the game on to the retailer's shelf and should therefore be shared by the parties; while the developer will argue that they are more in the nature of sales or marketing payments, and should be borne solely by the publisher.

Clarity of deductions

Since deductions can have a significant impact on the total sums actually received by the developer, it is essential to ensure that each deduction is clear, unambiguous and independently verifiable. It is easy to calculate the VAT rate in each territory. The costs of manufacturing game units are also relatively stable. However, it is much harder to measure or verify other terms often seen within defined deductions, such as 'rebates', 'marketing costs', 'commissions' and 'other adjustments'. Terms such as these should either be properly defined or at the very least subject to a maximum limit.

15.9.4 Stage 3 – the royalty rate

The royalty rates applied at stage 3 vary according to two factors: the relative negotiating strengths of the parties, and the type of income which is being shared.

The games industry has not adopted standard royalty rates, so the rate payable to a developer can vary from as little as 5 per cent to in excess of 35 per cent. Where the game has not been funded by the publisher, and accordingly the publisher has not incurred any production risk, the rate can reach or even exceed 50 per cent.

Some forms of revenue are considered 'easier' than others. Although most publishing agreements grant the publisher worldwide publishing rights, many publishers do not operate in all principal territories. If a publisher does not operate in a particular territory, it can simply appoint a local publisher to sell its game in that territory (under a 'gold master' licence as described in **para.16.4.2**). If it does this, the first publisher will incur little cost, expense or risk in relation to that territory: it simply sends one copy of the game to the local publisher, and it is the local publisher which then spends money manufacturing, distributing and marketing the game. The income paid to the first publisher – sometimes known as 'sub-licence income' – is often considered to represent relatively easy money, and the developer will usually ask for a larger share as a result.

Separately, the parties may agree to vary the royalty rate so that it is lower for game units sold at a very low price (often known as 'budget' price), and higher when total income derived from the game has exceeded a certain level (for instance, once it is a commercial 'hit').

15.9.5 Alternatives

The model set out above is the primary but not the only model used in the computer games industry. In some cases, the parties may agree that the royalty should be a fixed sum per unit (bypassing each of stages 1 to 3), or a share of the 'gross' without deductions (bypassing stage 2), or a share of the 'gross' after deduction of a single agreed percentage (simplifying stage 2).

15.10 PAYING ROYALTIES

The publishing agreement will contain extensive terms dealing with the reporting of royalties and the mechanics of payment of royalties.

15.10.1 Recoupment of advances

First, if the publisher has paid the developer an advance against royalties, the publisher will need to recoup this against the developer's royalties before actually paying any net royalty to the developer.

15.10.2 'Cross-collateralisation'

If the developer has made more than one game for the publisher, the publisher may require the advances paid in respect of those games to be 'cross-collateralised'. This generally means that the publisher can recoup advance payments made in respect of one game from royalties paid in respect of another game. The more games covered by such a term, the better for the publisher.

It is not uncommon for the parties to agree cross-collateralisation in respect of games developed and sold at the same time. For instance, if the developer creates a PC version of a game and a 'PlayStation2' version of the same game, then the advances for both are often cross-collateralised.

However, if the developer completes a game, and then starts to work on a sequel, the position is very different. The income from the first game may already have refunded all advances paid in respect of the first game whilst the second game is still in development. In that case, if the advances for both games are cross-collateralised, the second game is being funded entirely by the developer out of its own royalties, and the publisher is taking no risk at all. Accordingly, it is very unusual for the developer to agree to cross-collateralise the advances paid for successive products.

15.10.3 Reports

The publisher must be obligated to report all relevant income to the developer. This is usually done on a quarterly basis, with reports issued within one to two months after the end of each calendar quarter. Since the level of detail in royalty reports varies, the developer must ensure that each report contains at the least enough information to allow it to:

- know how much is due to the developer in respect of the relevant quarter; and
- independently verify the calculations applied by the publisher in calculating the royalties due.

The second requirement is essential but is often overlooked. It is important for the developer to be able to verify the calculations made by the publisher in order to double-check that the publisher has not made any inadvertent mistakes. This requires the statements to provide much more information about the sales of the game than a final total royalty payment due to the developer. The following categories of information are often requested by developers for inclusion within a royalty statement (with varying degrees of success):

- separate reports for all key territories, rather than a single global report;
- the total income generated by the game (stage 1 above);
- each deduction (from stage 2) identified in a separate line;
- the royalty rate applied to the net figure (stage 3), separately reported for each individual class of income;
- the total number of game units sold;
- the total number of game units manufactured;
- an analysis of credits for returns and price protection;
- an analysis and reconciliation of any returns reserves;
- an analysis of any unrecouped sums (such as advances);
- the exchange rates used;
- any sums withheld under withholding tax provisions; and
- the number of game units distributed free of charge, e.g. for promotional purposes.

15.10.4 Payment

Clearly, the publishing agreement must set out the date by which the publisher must pay accrued royalties to the developer.

15.10.5 Returns reserve

As noted at **para.16.2**, game units are generally sold by publishers to retailers on a 'sale or return' basis and are 'price protected'.

Both returns and price protection may result in the publisher having to refund sums to retailers many months after receiving those sums. If the publisher has already paid the developer royalties on those sums, then the publisher will have to recover those sums from the developer, which may be difficult in practice. Accordingly, the publisher will usually require a right to maintain a 'reserve' against potential returns and price protection payments which may be required at some stage in the future. This reserve is usually set at between 15 per cent and 20 per cent of the net royalty due to the developer in any quarter.

It is essential for the developer to ensure that the date for payment of the sums held in the reserve is clearly set out in the publishing agreement. It is common practice for a new reserve to be taken each quarter, and for the balance to be paid to the developer at the end of the next quarter.

15.10.6   Audits

The publishing agreement should include a right of the developer to appoint an independent auditor to review the publisher's records to confirm the accuracy of the publisher's royalty statements. Most publishing agreements provide that the publisher will reimburse the auditor's fees if the auditor finds underpayments in excess of a certain sum.

15.10.7   Miscellaneous provisions

The publishing agreement should include a set of additional ancillary terms relating to the payment of royalties and advances. These generally include the following:

* an obligation for the publisher to pay the developer interest on late payments;
* a term setting out the appropriate date on which any currency exchange rate is calculated, so that the rate used cannot be selected by the publisher with the benefit of hindsight;
* terms setting out the method for calculating the royalties due on game units which are sold bundled with other game units at a single price; and
* terms providing for a form of expert determination in the event of a dispute over royalties due.

15.11   TERMINATION OF THE PUBLISHING AGREEMENT

The publishing agreement should include terms allowing either party to terminate it on the occurrence of certain events. These generally add to the parties' existing common law rights to terminate the agreement, for instance for repudiatory breach.

15.11.1   Termination 'for cause'

It is common for publishing agreements to allow either party to terminate the agreement for the following reasons:

* if the other party commits a material breach of the publishing agreement which has not been remedied within a defined period (usually 30 days) from the date of notification; or
* if the other party becomes insolvent (or is subject to insolvency or quasi-insolvency measures, such as receivership).

15.11.2   Termination 'without cause'

The provisions allowing a party to terminate 'for cause' are commonly found in other types of commercial agreements. However, publishing agreements often include an additional right for the publisher to terminate the publishing agreement at any time during development, for no reason.

This termination right has evolved as a result of the parties' respective bargaining strengths. It also reflects the fact that while it can take up to two years to create a computer game, the industry itself moves very quickly. As a result, by the time a computer game is half-way through production, it may already appear to be obsolete. In these circumstances, it is often preferable for both parties to 'cut their losses' at that stage.

Clearly, the publisher should not be entitled to terminate at will without paying the developer any sum on termination. The developer needs to ensure that, at the least, it is paid enough to pay for its staff and overheads while it tries to find a new project (or, on another view, that it is paid enough to honour its redundancy obligations).

As a result, the parties rarely negotiate whether or not the publisher is entitled to terminate the agreement without cause during development, whilst the sum payable on such termination is one of the most heavily negotiated elements of the whole publishing agreement.

15.11.3   Consequences of termination

The publishing agreement should set out in detail the consequences of early termination. These will vary, depending on the reason why the publishing agreement was terminated.

If the publishing agreement was terminated by the developer for unremedied breach of contract by, or insolvency of, the publisher, or by the publisher under its right to terminate 'without cause', then all of the publisher's rights relating to the game should terminate at that stage. Any terms restricting the developer's right to work on other projects should also end immediately.

If, however, the publishing agreement was terminated by the publisher for unremedied breach of contract by, or insolvency of, the developer, then the publisher should be entitled to try to rescue the project. Accordingly, the publishing agreement should normally provide an express right for the publisher to complete the game itself; and the publisher's rights to commercially exploit the game as intended would survive termination of the publishing agreement.

15.12   WARRANTIES AND INDEMNITIES

15.12.1   Warranties

The publishing agreement should include a set of warranties by the developer to the publisher in respect of the game. These are often heavily negotiated, as the developer will be reluctant to accept risks, through the warranties, which are outside its control and cannot be managed by the developer.

The developer's warranties usually include warranties that:

- the developer has the right to enter into the agreement and to grant the licences and to make the assignments set out in the agreement;
- the developer owns all intellectual property rights in the game;
- the developer was the creator of the game; and
- the commercial exploitation of the game will not infringe the rights of third parties.

However, these warranties are often subject to exceptions.

1. If the publisher is responsible for, or has contributed to, any part of the game, then that part should be carved out of the developer's warranties. For instance, if the publisher is responsible for acquiring a licence from a film studio to base a game on a film, then the developer will not want to accept any risk of a defect in title or licensing in relation to the intellectual property rights in the film.
2. If the developer has used 'middleware' in the game, then the developer cannot warrant ownership of the middleware, but can only warrant that it has a valid licence to use it in the game.

15.12.2   US patents

In addition, the developer may also seek to dilute its warranty of non-infringement of intellectual property rights by excluding a warranty that the game does not infringe US patent rights. US patent law allows for aspects of gameplay and technology to be patented in a way which is not available in the EU. As a result, there are many US patents which may affect a particular game.

Unlike copyright, a patent can be infringed without any party knowing of its existence; and unlike trade marks, it is very hard (if not impossible) to perform a meaningful search of a patent register in order to reduce the risk of accidentally infringing a third party patent. As a result, neither the developer nor the publisher is in a position to know whether a game infringes a US patent, or to undertake any meaningful searches to understand its possible exposure to a US patent claim.

On that basis, the developer may argue that a patent suit is simply an inherent risk of game publishing, and should therefore be borne by the publisher. This is particularly true about patents which are alleged to cover aspects of gameplay which are present in many games, rather than only in the developer's game.

15.12.3 Publisher warranties

The developer may require the publisher to give its own warranties of non-infringement in respect of any part of the game which is contributed by the publisher, or for which the publisher has accepted responsibility.

15.12.4 Indemnities

The publishing agreement will usually include an indemnity by the developer in respect of a breach of warranty by the developer. An indemnity is akin to an insurance policy offered by the developer to the publisher. Accordingly, the developer will seek to reduce the scope of the indemnity as far as possible.

The developer will usually seek to ensure that the indemnity does not cover the consequences of the breach of *any* obligation of the developer, as these will include the costs of delayed delivery of the game, or of fixing bugs in the game which were not detected before commercial release – all of which could be substantial if refunded on an indemnity basis.

Instead, the developer will usually seek to ensure that the indemnity only applies to a breach of the developer's warranty of non-infringement (i.e. to valid claims of intellectual property rights infringement brought by third parties against the publisher, but resulting from a breach of the developer's warranties of non-infringement). The developer will also wish to ensure that it (rather than the publisher) retains control over the defence of any third party claim of infringement, and that the publisher does not compromise the defence of such a claim (by, for instance, making any admissions as to the validity of the claim).

Finally, if the publisher is giving warranties in relation to its own contributions to the game, the developer may require the publisher to back its warranties with an indemnity of its own.

15.13 LIMITATIONS OF LIABILITY

The publishing agreement may include a limitation of the liability of one or both parties. In general, the publisher tends to object to a limitation of liability of either party. Since the publisher's own obligations are relatively limited, and tend primarily to be centred around the payment of fixed sums to the developer, the publisher knows that in practice a limitation of liability is more likely to benefit the developer. In particular, the publisher will usually seek to ensure that the developer's liability in respect of infringement of third party intellectual property rights is not limited in any way.

15.14 MISCELLANEOUS TERMS

Finally, the publishing agreement will usually include the following terms.

15.14.1 Confidentiality

The development of a game involves both publisher and developer working closely together and disclosing to each other what is often very sensitive confidential information. The developer will often disclose the secrets of its technology to the publisher's staff, and the developer will acquire knowledge of the publisher's games and release schedule well before these are made public.

Accordingly, the publishing agreement will include a term requiring each party to keep confidential the terms of the agreement and any confidential information relating to the other party's business or products or technology, and prohibiting each party from using the other's confidential information for any purpose not related to the purpose envisaged in the publishing agreement.

15.14.2 Credits

There is no standard method of crediting a developer and its staff as the creators of a game. In general, the developer's logo is displayed on the packaging of the game, and the developer's animated logo is played as a 'splash screen' at the beginning of gameplay. The developer's staff are often credited in a 'credits' section of the game, which is usually only shown either when this is actively selected by the player, or when the player completes the whole game.

The developer may also require its logo to appear on the front of the packaging and on any advertising for the game. Whether these credits are given will depend in part on the parties' respective negotiating strengths and on the perceived value of the developer's reputation in selling games.

15.14.3 Customer support

Usually, customer support is provided by the publisher. However, as noted above at **para.15.5.1**, the publisher may require the assistance of the developer's staff in undertaking its support obligations. In particular, it may need the developer's staff to provide bug fixes in the forms of 'patches' which can be downloaded by game players to fix bugs detected after commercial release.

The publishing agreement should set out the parties' obligations in relation to customer support, particularly:

- the manner in which the support is to be given (hours, language of response, turnaround times and the like);
- the duration of the developer's post-release support obligation; and
- whether the developer is to be paid in respect of any post-release support given.

15.14.4 Boilerplate terms

The publishing agreement will usually contain standard terms addressing:

- the giving of notices;
- the invalidity of any 'agreed' terms other than those set out in writing in the publishing agreement;
- the invalidity of any agreed variation to the publishing agreement, unless it is made in writing;
- the prohibition of one or both parties from assigning or transferring any part of the publishing agreement;
- force majeure;
- the absence of a joint venture or partnership;
- the severance of terms which are declared unenforceable;
- whether value added taxes are included in the sums given or not;
- third party rights under the Contracts (Rights of Third Parties) Act 1999; and
- choice of law and jurisdiction.

15.15 SCHEDULES

The schedules to the publishing agreement usually include:

- the development schedule (with the dates for delivery of each agreed deliverable);
- the payment schedules (setting out the sums due on delivery of each agreed deliverable);
- the game design document; and
- a description of any software retained by the developer (see **para.15.7**).

CHAPTER 16

Distribution

16.1 INTRODUCTION

16.1.1 The worldwide market

The three principal markets for computer games are North America (the US and Canada), Europe (primarily the EU) and Japan. Each of these markets is roughly equal in size. In addition, PC games played online and mobile games are extremely popular throughout Asia. They are also growing in popularity in Europe and North America.

Although most PC and console game publishing agreements grant the publisher worldwide rights (see **Chapter 14**), in practice few games are truly sold throughout all of the three principal markets. In general, most computer games which sell well in North America will also sell well in Europe; and many successful Japanese games are equally successful in North America and Europe. However, few North American or European games ever succeed commercially in Japan.

Each territory is characterised by different tastes in games and different methods of marketing and selling games. Regulation differs from country to country, particularly with respect to the level of violence which can be shown in computer games.

Sales channels also vary between countries: some countries have established computer game retail chains, whilst in others computer games are sold through supermarkets or through CD and DVD retail channels. In some countries, computer games are sold through small high street kiosks.

16.1.2 The need for local knowledge

Varying market conditions, languages and legal and cultural norms usually require a local specialist to distribute a computer game in any particular territory.

The larger international publishers have their own subsidiaries or branch offices in each principal country of each territory, and can therefore distribute computer games throughout each territory themselves. However, if a smaller publisher is to sell a computer game outside its core territory, it usually has to appoint an independent local publisher to do this.

If a publisher wishes to appoint another, local publisher to sell a computer game in a particular territory, it can usually proceed in one of two ways. It can either manufacture every unit of the game and ship these to the local publisher, or it can send the local publisher a single copy of the game, and allow the local publisher to undertake the manufacturing of the game as well as the distribution. In each case, the parties need to allocate responsibility for the different types of marketing techniques that are to be used to sell the game. These are considered in further detail at **para.16.4** below.

16.1.3   Different roles

In understanding the distribution of computer games, it is essential to understand the different roles of the participants in the chain of distribution:

A *publisher* is responsible for manufacturing individual boxed game units, for selling those units to retailers and for managing the stock in the retail channel. This includes negotiating sale or return terms with retailers. It is also responsible for marketing the game to potential end-users. The publisher is generally also responsible for marketing the game to retailers ('trade marketing') which is arguably as important as marketing directed at end-users.

A *distributor* is responsible for shipping game units to each retail outlet in the relevant territory. It may also assume responsibility for managing stock levels in the retail channel. A distributor may also be responsible for trade marketing.

A *retailer* is responsible for selling game units to end-users in its shops. This includes stocking the game and displaying promotional materials for the game (posters, cardboard cut-outs and the like) within its shops (a practice known as 'point of sale' marketing).

As noted above, the publisher's role may be undertaken by two separate publishers if the game is to be sold in a territory where the principal publisher is not active. In that case, the principal publisher will appoint a local publisher in that territory, and the local publisher will undertake some or all of the principal publisher's responsibilities in that territory.

This chapter will consider the commercial agreements which underpin each of these roles in turn, starting with the retailer.

16.2   AGREEMENTS WITH RETAILERS

16.2.1   Introduction

Most PC games, console games and handheld games are sold to end-users as a boxed product by a high street or online retailer or a supermarket.

Developers and publishers rarely sell their products directly to their customers. This may change in the future, as games become more widely available for consumers to download over the Internet directly from console owners, developers, publishers and other intermediaries. In particular, while older games consoles were not designed to accept downloaded content, current and future games consoles are (or will be) designed to allow increasingly seamless content downloads (from entire games to single levels and even to individual items to be used in games), and simplified payment systems.

Since the retailers have the most direct contact with the customers, retailers have substantial commercial power in negotiating with publishers. If retailers refuse to stock a computer game, then that computer game is unlikely ever to make a profit, no matter how good it is. The large retailers, by their store layout and their staff's recommendations to buyers (who may be buying a game for somebody else, and know nothing about games themselves) can make or break a game. The retailer's commercial power is evidenced by the terms it is usually able to negotiate with a publisher.

The method by which terms are agreed between publishers and retailers differs from country to country and may be carried out on a more or less formal basis.

16.2.2   Returns

Game units are usually sold to retailers on a 'firm sale' basis, a 'sale or return' basis or a combination of both.

Units sold on an entirely firm sale basis can normally only be returned by the retailer to the publisher for a refund if they are defective.

Under a sale or return arrangement, the retailer pays the publisher on receipt of each unit; but if the retailer cannot sell that unit, it can require the publisher to repurchase that unit at any time at the price it originally paid for it. Accordingly, the publisher has a liability to refund sums it has received in respect of game copies until those copies have been sold to end-users.

The practice of permitting returns is widespread throughout most territories, but it is by no means the norm. Whether the retailer is able to negotiate a sale or return arrangement will depend on its buying power. As noted above, as the last participant in the distribution chain, the retailer often has substantial commercial power, particularly if it accounts for substantial sales. However, if there is a high demand among consumers for a particular game, the publisher may be able to negotiate specific firm sale arrangements for that game. Equally, on rare occasions where the publisher has not manufactured enough units to meet demand, it may be happy to accept returns so that it can allocate them to other customers.

If a game is expected to sell very well, the publisher will manufacture and sell a large number of units to retailers. If it is found that the game fails at retail, then, depending on a retailer's rights of return, the publisher may be required to repurchase a substantial number of copies which can in turn have a negative effect on the publisher's cash-flow. Managing a publisher's exposure to returns is one of the hardest aspects of video game publishing, as a single mistake can destroy a publisher's business.

If a publisher lowers its prices (in the absence of price protection, discussed at **para.16.2.3**), it may need to guard against retailers attempting to return units purchased at a discount for a refund of the original, higher, price.

Returns may be shop-soiled and require repackaging or may even be unsaleable and need to be destroyed. Accordingly, the publisher may attempt to impose terms under which only returns in mint condition are accepted.

16.2.3 Price protection

Game units are usually sold to retailers at a price determined by reference to the publisher's published recommended retail price. For instance, the price could be set at 50 per cent of the recommended retail price. If the publisher drops the recommended retail price at a later stage, then the sum paid by the retailer for game units still in the retailer's inventory will have been too high. Accordingly, in these circumstances the retailer is entitled to call for a refund of part of the purchase price paid, in order to ensure that the retailer has only paid the agreed percentage of the new, lower recommended retail price. This is generally known as 'price protection'.

Price protection is closely connected to the issue of returns. If a game is not selling at a particular retail price, the publisher will not want to have to repurchase it from retailers, assuming the retailer has a right of return. If it is not selling at retail, matters are unlikely to improve while the game is sitting in the publisher's own warehouse. In these circumstances, the retailer can lower the price at which the game is sold, in order to stimulate demand. Of course, the retailer will want to adjust the price it has already paid for any game which is ultimately sold at a lower price than the parties first expected. This usually means a retrospective reduction in the publisher's recommended retail price, rather than a reduction in the percentage discount from that recommended retail price agreed with the retailer.

If the publisher agrees a reduction of recommended retail price with one retailer, it will generally have to offer the same terms to the other retailers in the same territory. This will result in substantial refunds (or credits against future invoices) given to retailers throughout the territory with similar cash-flow implications to receiving heavy levels of returns. However, price protection is generally preferable for publishers than returns, as game units are still likely to finish in the pockets of end-users, rather than in the publisher's warehouse.

In practice, agreements over price protection can be very fluid and may not be formally recorded at the outset. Accordingly, price protection deals are often negotiated between publisher and retailer on a game-by-game basis.

16.2.4 Other key terms

Agreements with retailers are almost always non-exclusive. In addition to returns and price protection, the other principal terms of an agreement between a game publisher and a retailer are as follows:

- terms relating to the process of *placing orders*: principally how orders for game units are to be submitted and processed, and whether the publisher can refuse an order;
- terms relating to the *fulfilment of orders*: when and where game units are to be delivered;
- terms relating to *payment for orders*: when and how the publisher is to be paid for game units;
- the *price* for game units (generally expressed as a percentage discount from the publisher's recommended retail price or catalogue price);
- the *duration* of the agreement (most agreements can be terminated by either party on relatively short notice);
- how and when *title and risk* pass to the retailer;
- *warranties* relating to quality, non-infringement of intellectual property rights and non-infringement of local laws (including age-rating laws); and
- terms setting out any *in-store marketing* or promotional activity to be undertaken (or funded) by the publisher.

These terms will usually be supplemented by the standard 'boilerplate' terms which will generally mirror those in publishing agreements and are described at **para.15.14.4**.

However, the 'entire agreement' term will usually be more detailed than in an ordinary publishing agreement: in practice, a 'battle of the forms' (where the parties' terms of sale, terms of purchase, invoices and purchase orders often contain conflicting terms) is much more likely to occur in a relationship between a publisher and a retailer.

There may also be terms attempting to ensure that release dates (set by the publisher) are adhered to, regardless of when the retailer receives stock, to prevent some retailers releasing games early in order to take advantage of initial demand at the expense of other retailers.

16.3 AGREEMENTS WITH DISTRIBUTORS

A publisher will often deal directly with large retailers such as store chains and supermarkets. However, many game units are sold through smaller retail entities including independent retailers who are not part of any larger chain. In order to reach these retailers, it is often cost-effective for the publisher to deal with an intermediary, such as a specialist distributor.

Agreements between a publisher and a specialist distributor will usually be similar to those between a publisher and a large retailer, as noted above at **para.16.2**. Again, the principal negotiated terms will centre around the price paid by the distributor, and retrospective reductions to that price (principally through returns and price protection).

In addition, whilst an agreement with a retailer is necessarily limited to the territory in which the retailer has its shops, a distributor may have a much wider sphere of activity. Accordingly, a publisher's agreement with a distributor may need to limit the territory within which the distributor is entitled to distribute game units.

16.4   SUB-LICENCES

16.4.1   Introduction

As noted above at **para.16.1**, many publishers do not operate on a global scale. Accordingly, most will usually appoint one or more local publishers to publish a game in any territory in which they are not already established. The local publisher – or the local 'licensee' – will then undertake most, if not all, of the publisher's principal responsibilities in the relevant territory, principally manufacturing and distributing the game, and marketing the game both to end-users and to retailers. It will usually also be responsible for translating the game into the language(s) of its territory.

16.4.2   Two business models

Local licensees are generally appointed under one of two core business models. These models depend principally on whether the local licensee is allowed to manufacture units or not. Each can be summarised as follows:

Under the 'finished product' licence model, the principal game publisher will remain responsible for manufacturing game units. It will then ship these units to the local licensee in a foreign territory. The local licensee will then ensure that the units are sold into the retail channel, and will undertake most (if not all) of the marketing.

Under the 'gold master' licence model, the principal game publisher will simply send the local licensee a single copy of the game (often known as a 'gold master disc'). The local licensee will then manufacture game units locally, in addition to undertaking their distribution and marketing. It may also localise the packaging or the game itself, subject to the publisher's approval.

Under the finished product model, the principal publisher has the benefit of controlling inventory and knowing exactly how many units it has shipped to the local licensee. However, this model may require the principal publisher to tie up more working capital than in the gold master model. The cost of transporting game units may also be prohibitive, depending upon where the local licensee is located. In contrast, under the gold master model, the principal publisher has few up-front costs; however, it has less control over the number of game units manufactured and shipped in the relevant territory. In addition, the principal publisher's net income per unit will usually be less under the gold master model than under the finished product model.

The key terms of each commercial relationship will be considered separately.

16.4.3   Finished product

The finished product model shares many of the characteristics of an agreement with a retailer, and therefore includes the principal terms set out at **para.16.2**, with some key differences:

- the *duration* of the agreement will usually be expressed as a number of years, and might not be terminable at will by either party before the conclusion of a minimum term;
- the local licensee will usually have an *exclusive* right to distribute game units in the relevant territory;
- the local licensee will usually be required to undertake some minimum *marketing* obligations (including an obligation to carry out an agreed marketing plan, or to spend an agreed sum on marketing the game);
- the local licensee may be required to provide *customer support* for end-users in the relevant territory;
- the *territory* or *channels* into which the game may be distributed is expressly limited;
- the *price* for each unit is often set in a different manner – either as a single fixed price, or as a percentage of the price which the local licensee receives from distributors and retailers in the relevant territory; and
- the local licensee may not be entitled to *return* non-faulty game units.

The first two differences reflect the fact that the local licensee, in assuming responsibility for marketing the game, is making a substantial investment of its own in the game.

In addition, the principal publisher may be reluctant to give any warranty to the local licensee as to whether or not the game breaches local content laws, particularly laws relating to violent content. As noted at **para.16.1.2**, different territories can sometimes apply very different rules to computer games. The local licensee is in a better position to understand those rules and to gauge whether any particular game might infringe them; accordingly, the principal publisher may require the local licensee to accept the risk of breaking local content laws. Equally, the principal publisher may not wish to share the risk of infringing certain local intellectual property rights, principally patent laws, for the same reasons as those of the developer cited in **para.15.12.2**.

16.4.4 Gold master

In contrast to the finished product model, the gold master model tends to share many of the financial characteristics of a publishing agreement (noted at **paras.15.8** and **15.9**), as well as many of the characteristics of an agreement with a retailer.

Terms relating to:

- the duration of the local licensee's appointment;
- the exclusivity of the local licensee's rights;
- the local licensee's marketing obligations;
- the territory in which the local licensee can sell game units; and
- warranties of quality and non-infringement of intellectual property rights

will generally mirror those found in a finished product licence agreement.

However, payment usually comes in the form of a royalty, so the principal financial terms relating to:

- any advance payment or guarantee;
- calculating the royalty;
- recouping advances and guarantees;
- 'cross-collateralisation';
- royalty reports;
- dates for payment;
- a returns reserve; and
- audits

will generally mirror those found in a publishing agreement, and discussed further in **Chapter 15**.

If the local licensee is to localise the game or its packaging, terms covering the development and ownership of the localised elements will be included. In general, the publisher will try to ensure that it owns the copyright in any localised elements created by the local licensee.

16.5 MOBILE GAMES

16.5.1 Introduction

Mobile games are sold in a wholly different manner from PC, console and handheld games. Few mobile games are sold as packaged products in retail outlets; most are either pre-installed on mobile handsets or distributed by direct download to the end-user.

This difference in the method by which end-users acquire games translates itself throughout the distribution chain. Instead of a single publisher being responsible for worldwide sales and distribution (or, at the least, for sale and distribution within a single country), mobile games are often sold by many competing organisations in each territory. These are principally the mobile network operators on the one hand, and the content aggregators on the other.

As a result, the principal publisher of a mobile game often enters into multiple, non-exclusive agreements for each territory in which the game is to be sold. Each territory is often no larger than a particular country: the principal route to market is via local mobile network operators, and for historical reasons many of these are only established in a single country.

16.5.2 Direct download

Where the mobile game is to be sold by direct download, the agreement with the licensee (the mobile network operator or the content aggregator) will be similar in principle to a gold master agreement (described above at **para.16.4.4**). Network operators and content aggregators in each territory differ considerably in their approach to such agreements and may, for example, be more sensitive to issues such as age rating and other local regulation of content, depending on their location.

16.5.3 Pre-installation

Where the mobile game is sold 'pre-installed' on a particular handset, different considerations apply. Essentially, the agreement is in many ways a simplified form of the gold master agreement: there is usually a fixed fee paid by the licensee (often the mobile telephone manufacturer), either per copy of the game, or for an unlimited number of copies. However, the parties need to be aware of some additional commercial risks not found in other forms of mobile content distribution. In particular:

- if there is any form of bug or fault in the game, this can harm the public's perception of the telephone handset, resulting in massive losses to the handset manufacturer; accordingly, the parties need to ensure that the game is thoroughly tested on the relevant handset before release; and
- if there is any form of problem with the game, principally a bug or an infringement of local laws or third party rights, this will result in a product recall for all of the handsets with the game. A product recall has massive direct and indirect costs for the handset manufacturer.

These features require the parties to properly allocate the responsibility for detecting errors and for complying with local regulations and intellectual property laws. The parties should also consider carefully whether the liability of the publisher should be limited in any way, and in particular whether the publisher should be liable for indirect or consequential losses suffered by the handset manufacturer.

16.6 LOCAL TRADE MARKS

The importance of a game franchise has already been mentioned (see **para.14.1.6**), and a core component of most game franchises is the collection of trade marks associated with the game, particularly the title of the game. Accordingly, the principal publisher should ensure that its licence agreement expressly addresses registration and beneficial ownership of all trade mark and similar rights in the title of the game in all languages: while it may be more convenient for the local licensee to register the mark in its territory, the principal publisher may wish to ensure that any such registration is transferred to it at the end of the publishing relationship. Otherwise, it may find that the local licensee has registered the local language version of the game title as its own trade mark in its local territory. This will restrict the principal publisher's ability to commercially exploit sequels of the game in that territory.

CHAPTER 17

Acquiring rights from third parties

17.1 INTRODUCTION

In **Chapter 14** we defined 'licensed games' as games which require a licence from a third party licensor, such as a sporting body or film studio. Typical licensed games include sports simulation games and games based on films.

Licensed games have played, and continue to play, a fundamental role in the computer games industry. A review of the best-selling games at any particular time will show that many (and at some times, most) of the best-sellers are licensed games. Highly popular licences, such as the 'Harry Potter' and 'James Bond' licences, command licence fees measured in the tens of millions of dollars.

In this chapter, a 'licence agreement' is the agreement between the licensor (typically the owner of the licensed property) and the licensee (typically the publisher of the licensed game).

17.1.1 Early licences

One important reason for the early importance of licensed games is the comparative technological weaknesses of the early games playing devices. Games such as 'Pong' were highly abstract, with few graphics and no colour. Attaching a licence to a very basic game, such as a celebrity tennis endorsement for simple a bat and ball game, or a film licence for an action game, had many benefits:

1. The licence provided a link to a coherent background (such as a tennis championship) with which the player was already familiar. This helped players to recreate, in their imagination, that which the games console could not create on the screen.
2. In the case of a film licence, the licence could provide a rich background story which, again, the game could not deliver.
3. In an age when all tennis games tended to look the same, a licence could help to differentiate one game from another, even if the difference was

limited to the game title and packaging, and did not affect the game content at all.

17.1.2 Modern licences

Game console technology has evolved to such an extent that a game can now reproduce photorealistic scenes and provide a complete and coherent story-line for the player. Nevertheless, licences remain popular, but for different reasons:

1. The players of sports simulation games demand absolute authenticity. This necessarily requires the use of accurate depictions of famous individuals and known sporting events.
2. Consumers demand new ways of 'consuming' popular franchises, particularly book and film franchises. Computer games allow consumers to indulge or develop their interest in a particular franchise in ways not available via other media. For instance, a Harry Potter fan can indulge her passion for 'Quidditch' by playing the 'Harry Potter: Quidditch World Cup' game.

17.1.3 Quality

In addition to the commercial reasons for acquiring licences addressed above, one further aspect has held true throughout all stages of the computer games industry: a licence is often treated by the potential consumer as a badge of quality, bestowed by the licensor on one particular game, to the exclusion of the others.

Equally, licensors usually treat the quality of all licensed merchandise, including licensed games, as a reflection of the quality of the licensed property. As computer games have become more complex and more intricate, so differences in quality between different computer games have become more and more pronounced. As a result, issues relating to game quality have become increasingly important in licence agreements.

17.1.4 Future use

Ultimately, licences are valued as a means of increasing the income generated by a particular game, whilst reducing the risk that that game simply fails in the marketplace. As the costs and the risks associated with developing and marketing computer games increase, so too will the value of any process, including acquiring external licences, which can reduce these risks.

277

17.2 LICENSING IN CONTEXT

17.2.1 Categories of licences

One can divide licences in the computer games industry into two broad categories:

1. *Essential* licences are licences which are necessary for a particular game. Without the relevant licence, the game could not be made at all, or (if made) would fail in the marketplace. Typical examples include sport simulation games and games based on particular films or television programmes.
2. *Incidental* licences are licences which are desirable, but not necessary. Many 'product placement' agreements for video games are essentially incidental licences. A game set in the real world may look more authentic if the player sees a Coca-Cola billboard, but sales are unlikely to suffer without it. Typical examples include licences to use recognised brands within games set in the 'real world'.

Essential licences often command substantial licence fees, paid by the game publisher to the licensor. In contrast, incidental licences are often agreed without payment to the licensor. Indeed, in some cases, particularly product placement or other in-game advertising agreements, the licensor will pay the game publisher to associate the licensor's property with the game.

17.2.2 Types of licensed rights

A 'licence' is simply a contractual permission, given by the owner of certain intellectual property rights, to a third party to allow that third party to use some of the owner's rights in a defined manner.

In the computer games industry, the intellectual property rights which are the subject of a licence are usually taken from the following list:

- copyright;
- trade mark rights;
- personality rights; and
- design rights.

The precise nature of the rights licensed in respect of any particular game will often depend on the type of game. For example:

A sports simulation game will usually require licences to use:

- registered trade marks (of the clubs, the championship organisers, and even some of the individual players);
- copyright works (including club badges, the layout of racing tracks and the combination of logos on a racing car); and
- personality rights (of the individual participants).

278

A game based on a film will usually require licences to use:

- registered trade marks (including the film title);
- copyright works (including the film itself, together with its script, storyline and musical score); and
- personality rights (of the individual actors in the film).

In many cases, the rights to be licensed are owned by different entities, requiring the game publisher to negotiate and conclude a number of separate licence agreements in connection with the same licensed game.

17.2.3   Practical implications of acquiring a licence

Creating a licensed game has both creative and commercial implications for the licensor and the licensee.

Creative implications

Creative implications tend to centre on the creative restrictions which are often imposed by the licence agreement. The licensor will usually seek to ensure that the licensed game is consistent with, and does not detract from, or undermine, the licensed property. To achieve this, the licensor will usually require approval rights over the game and related marketing materials (further addressed below at **para.17.4.8**). It may also specify certain restrictions in the licence agreement itself.

However, the extent to which the licensed game creators are hamstrung by the terms of the licence can be over-exaggerated. Interactive games are fundamentally different from other forms of entertainment, and the task of adapting a licensed property to an interactive environment is a highly creative task. In addition, sophisticated licensors may be prepared to approve important changes to the licensed property if these are essential to the game player's experience.

Even sports simulation games, which are usually judged primarily by reference to the degree of realism offered to the player, cannot be absolutely realistic. Otherwise, a true Formula One game could only be played successfully by someone with the skills of a real Formula One driver.

Commercial implications

The commercial implications of creating a licensed game are primarily:

1. Increased costs for the licensee, including payments made to the licensor and increased costs associated with an extended development period.
2. Increased risks for the licensee and the licensor, including the risk (for the licensee) that the game is not released because the licensor does not

approve release, and the obvious risk that the underlying property is unsuccessful or quickly loses popularity, together with the risk (for the licensor) that the game is of poor quality and therefore harms the perceived value of the underlying property. In the case of a game based on a film which has yet to be completed, both parties also share the risk that the game will not be completed in time to ensure a contemporaneous, or 'day and date', release (which has been demonstrated to be crucial to the success of such games).

3. Increased revenues generated by the licensed game for the licensee.

17.2.4 Divergence of interests

One key aspect of a third party licence is the divergence of, and the potential conflict between, the interests of the licensor and the licensee. Essentially, the licensor's primary interest is the preservation and enhancement of the value of the underlying licensed property. It is unlikely to obtain most of its income from computer games. Accordingly, the licensor is usually more focused on ensuring that the game is of the highest quality – and is perceived by the market to be of the highest quality – than it is focused on ensuring a maximum financial return from sales of the licensed game.

In contrast, the licensee is focused purely on ensuring that the licensed game is profitable. As a result, it will wish to ensure that the development costs are kept under control. It may also desire to sell the licensed game at a lower retail price than the price charged for comparable games, in order to sell more units, and possibly to grow its market share.

17.3 THE LICENCE AGREEMENT

17.3.1 Introduction

A licence to use rights in a computer game is not, in itself, an intellectual property right. It is simply a contractual right, and as such it is good against the licensor as the other party to the contract, but not against the rest of the world. If the licensor loses the rights it had, or had already granted conflicting rights to a third party, or never had the relevant rights in the first place, then the licensee's sole remedy is usually a contract claim against the licensor. If the licensor is insolvent, then this is worthless. Equally, if the licensor is entitled to terminate or revoke the licensee's rights, and it does so, then again the licence is worthless.

In each such case, the licensed game project must be terminated. If the game has already been distributed, then it may have to be recalled. The costs associated with these events are likely to be substantial. Accordingly, the terms of the licence agreement, together with the due diligence to be undertaken by the licensor and the licensee, are essential to the success or failure of the project.

The licensor may conclude a number of merchandising agreements for a variety of products featuring the licensed property. A licensed game may, from the licensor's point of view, be no different in this respect from any other form of merchandise and the licensor may suggest that the parties contract on the licensor's standard merchandising terms. However, the complexity of the game development and publishing process is unlikely to be satisfactorily addressed by such terms.

17.3.2 Due diligence

As noted below at **para.17.4.10**, the licence agreement will often include representations and warranties made or given by the licensor and relating to the licensor's capacity to grant the rights which are the subject of the licence.

However, the licensee should undertake its own research to ensure that the licensor is in a position to grant the rights that it claims to grant. In particular, it should seek to ascertain whether the licensor owns those rights, or has simply licensed them from a third party (which may mean that it could lose those rights at a later date).

Where the licensor is not the original owner of the underlying property but is a marketing agent or a corporate vehicle whose purpose is to market the rights and receive royalty payments, the licensee will wish to ensure there is an unbroken and sufficiently robust 'chain of rights' between the original owner, the ultimate licensee, and any other licensees or sub-licensees in between.

The ownership and control of the personality rights of players of certain sports may be particularly unclear or complex, partly because the legal and commercial background surrounding these rights may vary from sport to sport, player to player and country to country. In such cases, it may simply not be possible for the licensee to establish a clear chain of title to the degree of certainty that it would normally require.

Finally, the licensee should ascertain the creditworthiness of the licensor. If the licensor has insufficient funds to compensate the licensee for a breach of warranty, then the warranty is of little practical value.

17.4 LICENCE AGREEMENT TERMS

The principal terms of a licence agreement are as follows.

17.4.1 The licensed property

The licence agreement should define precisely the intellectual property rights which are being licensed to the licensee. In many cases, this is more complex than it would first appear. A film licence, for instance, might include the right to use the name of the film in the title of the game (a trade mark licence), together with the right to copy and adapt the script and screenplay of the film (a copyright licence). It may also include the right to use extracts from the film as cut scenes within the game (again, a copyright licence). However, these rights alone will not necessarily cover:

- the right to use the music used in the film;
- the right to reproduce the film soundtrack;
- the right to reproduce the likenesses of the actors appearing in the film; or
- the right to use other third party intellectual property which appeared in the film, such as brands or product designs, within the game.

Indeed, these rights are often controlled by third parties, so the film licensor may not be entitled to grant these rights to a computer game publisher at all.

Finally, as noted below at **para 17.4.6**, the licence agreement should expressly address whether any rights are to be granted in relation to future changes or updates to the licensed property. A football simulation game featuring the real teams during a particular season will be out of date as soon as that season has ended, unless the licensed property extends to new players, badges and sponsors.

17.4.2 Licensed rights and permitted activities

The licence agreement should define exactly what the licensee is entitled to do with the licensed property. Clearly, the licensee has to be entitled to create and sell one or more games based on the licensed property. However, the licence agreement should also specify whether (and if so, on what conditions) the licensee can:

- use the licensed property in the packaging or marketing materials for the game; or
- use the licensed property in 'ports' of the licensed game for different game playing devices (including devices not yet in existence at the time of contracting).

The licence agreement should also define what the licensee can and cannot do with the licensed game. Clearly, the licensee must be entitled to manufacture, distribute and sell copies of the game. However, it may also require the express grant of the right to rent the game, or to exploit the game by providing time-limited access to it in return for a subscription payment.

In addition, the licence agreement should state whether (and if so, on what basis) the licensee can grant sub-licences in respect of the rights licensed to it. Sub-licensing of publishing rights forms an essential element of the distribution network in much of the computer games industry (see in particular **para.16.4**). In addition, it will be necessary for the licensee to be permitted to sub-license the rights to copy and adapt the licensed property where it sub-contracts the development of the game, and to sub-license the right to reproduce elements of the licensed property to the manufacturer of the finished product. However, many licensors are reluctant to grant their licensees complete freedom to sub-license their rights to any third party.

17.4.3 Exclusivity

The licence agreement should set out whether, and if so to what extent, the licence is exclusive. If the licence is exclusive, then it is essential that the parties agree what is meant by this term. In particular, the licensee should consider whether the licensor will remain free to permit another game publisher to:

- publish a similar game featuring the licensed property for use on a different game-playing platform; or
- publish a different game featuring the licensed property for use on the same game-playing platform; or
- publish another entertainment product for use on the relevant platform, which is arguably not a 'game', but which nevertheless competes with games (such as an interactive guide to the licensed property).

For instance, an exclusive licence to create a PC game based on the latest James Bond film may not prevent third parties from creating:

- similar games for the Xbox 360 platform; or
- games based on earlier James Bond films for the PC platform; or even
- a game based on exactly the same film, also for the PC platform, but of a different 'genre' (such as a massive multiplayer online game featuring a persistent world).

The licensee should also consider whether the licensor is free to grant exclusive rights at all. If the licensed property is based on an earlier work which is not protected by intellectual property rights – such as a novel which is no longer protected by copyright, or even a historical event – then third parties may be free to create their own games based on the same underlying story without infringing the rights of any person. For instance, if the licensed property is a film based on a particular historical character like Alexander the Great, then the licensor may grant exclusive rights to create a game which re-uses copyrights relating to the film; but it will not be entitled to grant any exclusivity over the character and historical storyline which underpin the film.

17.4.4   Platform

The licence agreement should define the platform on which the licensee's games should operate. This is particularly important if the licensor is granting exclusive rights to different publishers in relation to different platforms. As the computer games industry changes very rapidly, it is not uncommon for new platforms to emerge which either combine two previously distinct platforms (for instance, 'personal digital assistants' and mobile telephones), or which divide what used to be a single platform into two distinct platforms (for instance, the emergence of PCs and game-specific consoles as separate entities). While there is no simple way of specifying or describing platforms in order to avoid these difficulties, the licence agreement should define platforms as clearly as possible, and by reference to more than just the generic name for that platform. For instance, the definition could refer to all of the following variables:

- the *functions* of the platform;
- the *operating system* used by the platform;
- the *primary purpose* of the platform;
- the actual (or relative) *cost* of the platform;
- the *programming language* in which the game is written; and
- the *intended users* of the platform.

17.4.5   Term, territory and termination

The licence agreement should set out the duration of the licence and the territory in which it may be exercised. It should also describe the consequences of termination in detail. For instance, the licensee may require a 'sell off' period to commence on termination of the agreement, allowing it to continue to sell unsold copies of the game (but not to manufacture any further copies) on a non-exclusive basis for a limited period of time after termination.

In addition, the licence agreement should set out the conditions, if any, under which a party may terminate it before the intended termination date. It is not uncommon for the licensor to be entitled to terminate the licence agreement if the licensee becomes insolvent, or breaches a material term of the licence agreement and fails to remedy the breach within a defined cure period. Since termination of the licence agreement whilst the licensee is developing or selling the game will usually have disastrous consequences for the licensee, it is essential that the licensee ensure that the licensor cannot terminate the licence agreement on a whim, or as a result of a single mistake by the licensee (or one of its sub-licensees) – such as the publication of non-approved marketing materials – which may have resulted in little actual damage to the licensor.

17.4.6 Sequels

The licence agreement should state whether the licensee is entitled to (or indeed is required to) create sequels to the licensed game.

If the licensee intends to create sequels, it should ensure that the licence agreement accommodates future changes to the licensed property. All brands and franchises change over time, and if the licence agreement does not cover new versions of the brand or franchise, then the licensee's games may soon appear stale and outdated.

17.4.7 Obligations of the parties

The licence agreement should describe both parties' practical obligations during development and exploitation of the licensed game in detail.

The licensee's obligations will usually include the obligation to complete and commercially exploit the game by a certain date, and to comply with the agreed approvals regime, further described below at **para.17.4.8**. They will also include the obligation to make payments to the licensor (together with other payment-related obligations, such as the provision of royalty statements), further described below **at para.17.4.9**. They may also include an obligation to commit a minimum sum to marketing and promoting the game.

The licensor's obligations may include the following:

- the provision of assets or information relating to the licensed property (for instance, the provision of a film script if the licensed property is a film which has not been commercially released);
- the provision of physical access to specified locations for the purpose of creating the game (for instance, access to the teams, cars and tracks if the licensed game is a car racing simulation game based on a real championship); and
- assistance in marketing the game, for instance by including reference to it in the ordinary marketing materials for the licensed property.

17.4.8 The approvals process

As noted above at **para.17.2.3**, the licensor will usually require a right of approval over the game and, usually, the marketing materials relating to the game. This right of approval allows the licensor to prohibit the commercial release of the game, or the use of certain marketing materials, by the licensee, if these do not meet the licensor's standards. Clearly, the licensor needs to be satisfied that the game and the marketing materials are not of poor quality, in order to protect the integrity of the licensed property.

However, as noted above at **para.17.2.4**, the licensor and the licensee often have conflicting interests, and the licensor's approval rights often bring this conflict into sharp focus. This can be particularly problematic for the licensee if the licensor has no experience of computer games of the type which the licensee intends to create. If the licensor already has that experience, then it is less likely to approach the project with unrealistic commercial or creative expectations.

Accordingly, it is essential for both parties to ensure that the licence agreement properly protects their position. In practice, this means the following:

1. The licensee should ensure that the licensor's right to veto a game or marketing materials is not exercisable simply at the licensee's discretion. It should be exercisable only if the game or marketing material falls short of an agreed, objectively measurable benchmark. A measure of objectivity may be imported if the licence agreement refers to other games released at a similar date on the same platform (and made with a similar budget), or incorporates a detailed, agreed game specification.
2. It is in the interests of both parties that the licensor should be required to approve (or disapprove) the game and marketing materials at multiple stages during the development of the licensed game, rather than simply on receipt of the finished product.

The earlier a problem is identified, the easier it is to address it. Approvals may be given at some (or even all) of the following critical stages:

- preliminary game design document;
- final game design document;
- preliminary technical design document;
- final technical design document;
- prototype/demo;
- alpha build (usually the first time that the game is playable from beginning to end, albeit without some artwork and including bugs);
- beta build (usually the first version free of major bugs);
- final build;
- preliminary marketing plan;
- final marketing plan;
- draft marketing materials;
- final marketing materials.

The licensor should be required to provide reasons for any non-approval, so that the licensee can address or (if appropriate) challenge them. These reasons should be provided within an agreed time frame.

17.4.9   Financial provisions

Payment to the licensor usually takes the form of a royalty on income generated by the licensed game. In addition, the licensor will usually require an advance payment during the early stages of the parties' relationship. This may be expressed as:

- an *advance* on royalties;
- a *minimum royalty guarantee*, being a guarantee of the amount of royalties which will become due to the licensor during a specified period; or
- a *minimum sales guarantee*, being a guarantee of the number of games which the licensee will sell during a specified period.

Such payments are generally recoupable against royalty payments so that no royalty is actually payable until the total accrued amount due exceeds the advance or minimum guarantee. There may be one or a number of separate payments payable over a period of time, or triggered by the reaching of a specified number of unit sales. The way in which these early payments are expressed and structured will reflect the parties' relative priorities and bargaining power. The minimum sales guarantee is perhaps the most elegant method for a licensor to ensure that it receives a minimum amount of royalties while appearing to maintain some interest in the game's success. The licensee will of course wish to ensure that there is a reasonable prospect of these advance payments being recouped.

The royalty rate itself tends to vary dramatically depending upon the perceived importance of the licence to the game itself, together with the parties' respective negotiating strengths. Rates will start from as little as one per cent of the net income generated by the licensed game, but may ultimately exceed 15 per cent for a very popular exclusive licence.

The calculation of the royalty, together with the modalities of royalty reporting, and the licensor's right to audit the licensee, generally mirror those found in publishing agreements and further described at **Chapter 15**.

17.4.10   Warranties

The licence agreement should include the licensor's warranties relating to its right to grant the rights in the licensed property to the licensee. These would generally include:

- a warranty that the licensor owns or controls the rights which it is granting to the licensee; and
- a warranty that the licensee's use of those rights in accordance with the licence agreement will not infringe the intellectual property rights of a third party; and
- (if the licence is exclusive), a warranty that no third party is entitled to grant or exercise those rights.

However, the licensor may not be prepared to give any such warranties. Where the licensed property is made up of a number of different rights, including rights whose ownership or control may be uncertain, then the licensor may not wish to accept any risk that there is a gap in its chain of title. For instance, computer game rights relating to older films are usually very unclear. Equally, the wide collection of rights relating to a particular sporting event may not all be held by the same single body. In those circumstances, the licence may amount to no more than a confirmation by the licensor that it will not seek to enforce any of its own intellectual property rights against the licensee during the term of the licence agreement, but without any guarantee that a third party will not seek to do just that.

Boilerplate terms

The licence agreement will usually contain boilerplate terms which mirror those contained in publishing agreements, described at **para.15.14.4**.

APPENDIX A

Music

Management agreement

From   [   ] of [   ]

To   [   ] of [   ]

Dated   [   ]

Re: Management Agreement

As discussed I set out below the terms upon which you will engage me to be your Manager.

1. During the period of my engagement hereunder I will be your exclusive Manager throughout the world representing you in connection with all your activities in the entertainment industry and any other activities undertaken by you which are either procured by me at your request or in respect of which you request my involvement as your Manager. I will be entitled to appoint a representative for North America as sub-Manager or co-Manager and I will obtain your prior reasonable approval to his or her selection and I shall be responsible for paying any and all remuneration payable to any person so appointed.

2. The period of my engagement as your Manager will be a period commencing on the date hereof and ending on the release of a second album reproducing your performances and released by a Major Record Company following the commencement of the term. Major Record Company means any of the BMG Group, Sony Music Entertainment Group, EMI Group, Universal Music Group and Warner Music Group. Notwithstanding the foregoing if for a period in excess of six consecutive months during the term you are not the subject of a current recording agreement then you may give me notice terminating the term.

3. I agree to use all reasonable endeavours to manage you and to enhance and develop your career. I shall not be entitled to sign any Agreement on your behalf (except one-off live performance engagements in accordance with an agreed career plan) nor to engage booking agents or other third parties without your prior consent.

4. I shall be entitled to receive and be paid a commission of a sum equal to 20% of Net Income.

5. Net Income shall mean gross income derived from all activities the subject hereof after deducting VAT or similar tax and after deducting recording costs or video production costs and payments to third parties such as producers or mixers and any monies received or payable as tour support shortfall and bona fide debts and any monies arising from the exploitation of any musical composition written after the term and any sound recording recorded by you after the Term. Notwithstanding the foregoing the commission shall five years after

expiry of the Term be reduced to 10% and for a further five years shall be reduced to 5% and thereafter shall cease.

6. You will appoint an accountant who shall collect all your income, the subject hereof and who shall be irrevocably instructed and authorised to make up statements of account quarterly to the last day of March, June, September and December in each year and to pay me my commission together with my expenses subject to appropriate invoices and vouchers.

7. The expenses which I shall be entitled to recover from you will be those incurred by me solely in respect of fulfilling my obligations to you hereunder provided that you have approved those expenses but I shall be entitled to pay and recover expenses of up to £250 per calendar month without the need to obtain your prior approval.

8. We shall each keep or cause to be kept full and up-to-date and accurate books of account and record of all our dealings hereunder and we shall act in good faith towards each other and you shall not undertake any of the activities in respect of which you have appointed me to act.

9. You warrant and undertake that you have full right power and authority to enter into this Agreement and that you are over 18 years of age and that you have taken independent expert legal advice prior to entering into this arrangement so that you fully understand it.

10. In the event of any alleged breach of this Agreement the innocent party shall notify the defaulting party in writing of the specific nature of any claimed breach and if the same is not remedied (if capable of remedy) within 30 days then the innocent party shall be entitled to give notice to the other terminating this Agreement.

11. Notice is to be served hereunder and shall be in writing and shall be sufficiently served if sent to the party to be served at the address set out above by hand or by prepaid registered post and the date of delivery if by hand or the date of posting if by post shall be the date of service thereof.

12. Nothing in this Agreement shall give rise to a partnership between us and neither party shall be entitled to assign or otherwise deal with this Agreement without the other party's written consent. This Agreement shall be governed by the laws and procedures of England whose Courts shall be the exclusive Courts of Jurisdiction.

If you agree the foregoing correctly reflects our discussions please sign and return the enclosed copy of this letter.

Yours truly

. . . .

Manager

Agreed and understood

. . . .

Artist

APPENDIX A2

Net profit sharing agreement

DATED [2007]

_____

[   ]

and

[   ]

_____

NET PROFIT SHARING AGREEMENT

_____

THIS AGREEMENT is made the [   ] day of [   ] [2007]

BETWEEN:

(1)   [   ] of [   ] ("Company")

(2)   [   ] of [   ] ("Artist")

WITNESSETH as follows:

1.   Artist shall render his services to Company exclusively to the best of his ability as a recording artist and whether performing alone or with others (and including recording with vision intended primarily for promotional videos or home use) and throughout the world ("the Territory") for the duration of the Term hereof.

2.   Artist warrants to Company that he is entitled to enter into this agreement and to grant the rights as herein contained and that in so doing and in Company exercising its rights hereby granted neither Artist nor Company are or will be in breach of any third party rights nor will they infringe any third party proprietary right and Artist undertakes to fully indemnify Company in respect of any claim damage or expense that Company may incur as a result of any breach by Artist of his obligations and warranties set out herein.

3.   Company shall provide facilities to enable Artist to record his recording commitment hereunder and Artist agrees to make additional recordings in each period if Company so designates.

4.   (a)   The recording commitment shall be:

(i)   In the Initial Contract Period and as the First Option period sufficient recordings to comprise one double sided so-called single play record.

> (ii)   In each subsequent option period sufficient recordings to comprise one single play record and one long playing record at least 35 minutes playing time.

(b)   Company shall release or cause to be released in at least any one of Germany, England or the USA the minimum commitment in any period within six (6) months of the satisfactory final recording thereof. In the case of default Artist shall give notice in writing of default to Company and if the default is not cured within ninety (90) days this Agreement shall cease.

5.   The Term hereof shall commence on the date hereof and continue for a period of the longer of six (6) months or two hundred and seventy (270) days after satisfactory completion of recording of the recording commitment. Artist grants to Company [five] separate and successive options to renew and extend the Term (under the provisions of this Agreement save as specifically stated and save for additional options) for the period expiring two hundred and seventy (270) days of the minimum recording commitment for the relevant period. Notwithstanding the foregoing no period shall exceed three (3) years. Each such option shall be exercised by notice in writing in that behalf given to Artist prior to the expiry of the period immediately preceding the period to which the option is intended to relate. Any such option may not be exercised if Company has not released or caused to be released on commercial sale to the public records hereunder during the expiring period.

6.   (a)   Artist hereby irrevocably authorises Company to make records of his performances in accordance with the provisions of this Agreement and to license distribute and sell them in any configuration (whether now known or otherwise) and whether audio or audio-visual throughout the Territory. The copyright and all rights of a similar or proprietary right in all recordings hereunder shall vest in Company and in so far as is necessary this Agreement shall operate as an assignment by way of future assignment of such copyright.

     (b)   Artist hereby waives all moral rights save the right of paternity which is hereby asserted by Artist.

7.   (a)   Company shall after consultation in good faith with Artist designate the compositions to be recorded the individual producer and the place in England (unless otherwise agreed) where recordings shall take place and the manner and style of recordings and all backing musicians and Company shall designate and pay all recording costs and expenses and costs of making any videos but Artist shall immediately repay Company any costs unnecessarily incurred solely by the act or default of Artist.

     (b)   Company will use its reasonable commercial efforts to promote and exploit recordings hereunder.

     (c)   Company shall afford to Artist the appropriate credit on album sleeves and liner notes and Company shall be entitled to use and authorise others to use the name biography and a likeness of Artist for all purposes of in connection with records made hereunder.

8.   (a)   By way of remuneration for his services Artist shall be entitled to be paid and receive a sum equal to [   ] of the Net Profit (as hereinafter defined) and derived from the recordings the subject hereof.

(b) For the purposes of this Agreement "Net Profit" shall mean the actual income received by Company (net of VAT or similar tax) arising from the sale use or exploitation of recordings hereunder after deducting therefrom all proper and reasonable and direct costs charges and expenses incurred or suffered by Company in relation thereto including without prejudice to the generality of the foregoing recording and filming costs, musicians fees, individual producer royalties and manufacturing and distribution costs, copyright fees, advertising and promotion costs and travel and subsistence costs and expenses but it is specifically agreed and declared that Company shall not make any deduction in respect of its general expenditure within the nature of its overhead costs or otherwise.

(c) By way of advance in respect of such share and recoupable therefrom Company will pay Artist the following sums payable as to one half on commencement of recording of the minimum recording commitment of the minimum recording commitment for that period.

(i) First Option Period – £[   ]
(ii) Second Option Period – £[   ]
(iii) Third Option Period – £[   ]
(iv) Fourth Option Period – £[   ]
(v) Fifth Option Period – £[   ]

PROVIDED THAT in the event that Company shall itself receive advances from third parties for the right to exploit recordings hereunder then Artist shall receive a sum equal to [%] thereof after deducting any known or reasonably anticipated expenses in relation to the recordings of Artist hereunder and subject to recoupment from Artist's share any advances already made to him.

9. Company shall at all times use its reasonable endeavours to ensure prompt and accurate payment of all monies due to it relating to the sale use and exploitation of recordings hereunder.

10. Artist will not re-record any composition recorded hereunder until five (5) years after the expiration of the Term of this Agreement (as renewed and extended).

11. Artist will co-operate in a reasonable manner in performing for and appearing in any promotional video and shall appear for promotional appearances and photographic sessions. Company shall be entitled to receive any performance fees payable to Artist limited to the amount of expense incurred by Company with the balance payable to Artist. Both in relation to the making of recordings and promotional appearances and photographic sessions hereunder Company will pay for reasonable travel and accommodation. Artist shall use his best endeavours at all times to attend promotional activities organised by Company in a prompt and professional manner.

12. Company shall keep up-to-date books of account and record of all its activities hereunder which may be inspected by Artist or his professional accountant by appointment and at Artist's expense not more than twice during each calendar year and Company shall make up accounts showing Net Profit hereunder to 30 June and 31 December in each year and deliver the same to Artist with payment within ninety (90) days. In the event that any inspection by Artist or his accountant shall reveal any shortfall of ten per cent (10%) or more amounting to at least five hundred pounds (£500.00) the reasonable costs of the said inspection shall be reimbursed to Artist or paid by Company.

13. Artist acknowledges that he has been advised to seek independent advice upon the terms hereof from a solicitor or barrister conversant with Agreements of this nature.

14. (A) (i) Artist shall have the right to terminate this Agreement in the event that Company goes into liquidation (save where such liquidation is voluntary and for the purpose of reconstruction or amalgamation) or ceases trading in any way.

(ii) Either party may terminate this Agreement in the event that the other is in breach of any of the material terms of this Agreement and has failed to remedy such breach within thirty (30) days of receiving written notification of the said breach from the party wishing to terminate.

(B) In the event of such termination by Artist all rights of Company in recordings hereunder shall cease and copyright in the recordings shall vest in Artist. Company appoints Artist its attorney to execute any necessary documents to vest such rights in Artist.

15. This Agreement shall be construed under the laws of England whose courts shall be the exclusive courts of jurisdiction.

AS WITNESS the hands of the parties hereto the day and year first above written.

SIGNED by the duly authorised)

officer of **COMPANY** in the)

presence of:)

SIGNED by the duly authorised)

officer of **ARTIST** in the)

presence of:)

[Note: This agreement can be modified, if appropriate, to simply refer to specific named recordings of specific titles.]

296

Recording agreement

DATED [2007]

[   ]

and

[   ]

RECORDING AGREEMENT

THIS AGREEMENT is made this [   ] day of [   ] [2007]

BETWEEN:

(1) [   ]

(hereinafter called "Label") of the one part and

(2) [   ] (aka "   ") of [   ]

(hereinafter called "Artist") of the other part

WHEREAS:

(A) Label is in the business of producing and exploiting phonograph records of all types.

(B) Label has agreed to engage Artist to render Artist's exclusive recording services under the name [   ] as Label may reasonably require during the term hereof in connection with the production of master recordings to be used by Label and its successors licensees and assignees inter alia for the manufacture distribution and sale of records therefrom.

(C) Artist has agreed to accept such engagement and has agreed to render such services for Label to the best of Artist's ability.

IT IS HEREBY AGREED as follows:

1.   DEFINITIONS

In this Agreement unless the context otherwise requires the following terms shall have the following meanings:

(a) "Territory" shall mean the world.

(b) "Term" shall mean the period during which Artist is to be exclusively contracted to the label.

(c) "Product Commitment" shall mean the minimum number of records to be delivered hereunder.

(d) "Record" means and includes all conventional types of phonograph records now in use as well as tape recordings of all types and any other products and devices now known or unknown including without limitation compact disc (as defined below) by which sound may be recorded for later transmission to listeners whether in the immediate presence of a reproducing instrument or device or via radio television or any other medium intended primarily for home use or use in means of transportation and whether embodying (i) sound alone or (ii) sound synchronised with visual images by motion picture film electronic tape or any other device by which both picture and sound can be projected transmitted or played back simultaneously.

(e) "Master Recordings" shall mean the original sound recording or film or combination of sound recordings or films embodying Artist's performances alone or with others which have been recorded for Label and accepted as technically and commercially satisfactory in accordance herewith by Label for use in the manufacture of Records therefrom for sale to the public whether stored digitally or in analogue format on any substance or material now known or hereinafter to be discovered or devised and including any duplicates thereof.

(f) "Single" shall mean an audio only Record consisting of two (2) or more Master Recordings comprised upon one twelve inch (12″) 33 or 45rpm single play record or the equivalent thereof and having a combined playing time of not less than ten (10) minutes.

(g) "Album" shall mean an audio only Record consisting of not less than ten (10) Master Recordings comprised upon one twelve inch (12″) 33 1/3 rpm long-playing record or the equivalent thereof and having a combined playing time of not less than forty (40) minutes.

(h) "Multiple Albums" shall mean packages containing two (2) or more long-playing records (or their tape or compact disc equivalent) which are sold as one unit. Multiple Albums shall be considered hereunder for all purposes as one Album and Artist shall not produce or record or deliver Master Recordings for Multiple Albums without Label's prior consent.

(i) "Digital Record" shall mean a Record embodying a laser option digital system of sound reproduction and shall include digital audio tape ("DAT") digital compact cassette ("DCC") and "mini disc" and/or any other Record presently not but at any time in the future available for sale or hire to the public in any part of the Territory.

(j) "Contract Period" shall mean the longer of a period of twelve (12) months and a period expiring 180 days after Artist shall have fulfilled the Minimum Commitment in respect of the Contract Period provided always no single Contract Period shall extend beyond three (3) years.

(k) "Controlled Composition" shall mean a musical work which is wholly or partly written composed owned or controlled by Artist or by any person or entity in which Artist has a substantial interest or a musical work selected by Artist to be recorded.

(l) "Major Record Company" shall mean any company within the following groups of companies namely Chrysalis, Universal, Warners, EMI and Sony/BMG.

(m) "Major Territory" shall mean the territory or territories set out in the Fourth Schedule.

(n) "Act" shall mean the Copyright, Designs and Patents Act 1988 as the same may from time to time be amended or re-enacted.

(o) "Video" shall mean an audio visual Record.

(p) "Minimum Commitment" shall mean the minimum number of Master Recordings to be recorded in each Contract Period as specified in the Third Schedule.

(q) "UK" shall mean the United Kingdom of Great Britain and Northern Ireland.

(r) "USA" shall mean the United States of America and its territories and possessions.

(s) "Promotional Video" shall mean performances of Artist to be shot and recorded on film and/or video tape for the primary purpose of promoting Master Recordings.

(t) "Commercial Video" shall mean performances of Artist to be shot and recorded on film and/or video tape or electronic media for the purpose of commercial exploitation thereof.

(u) "Packaging Charge" shall mean a sum equal to twenty-five per cent (25%) of the dealer price in respect of all formats except singles when it shall be ten per cent (10%) thereof.

2. GRANT OF RIGHTS

(a) Artist hereby confirms there is vested in Label and to the extent it is not initially vested in Label Artist hereby grants and assigns to Label the copyright and all other rights of every kind and the complete unconditional exclusive perpetual unencumbered title throughout the Territory in and to all results and products of Artist's services and performances hereunder and any and all Master Recordings sound recordings photographs and other material of every kind made commissioned or authorised by Label hereunder or which include the voices instrumental or other sound effects names photographs likenesses services or performances of Artist the subject hereof including without limitation but subject to the provisions hereof the right to record reproduce broadcast exploit perform and use the same separately or in combination with any other material for any purpose in any manner under any label trade mark or other identification and by any means or method whether or not now known invented used or contemplated.

(b) Without prejudice to the generality of the foregoing Artist hereby grants to Label:

   (i) the exclusive right at such price or prices and under such trade marks as Label may from time to time determine to license manufacture distribute sell and otherwise dispose of and exploit throughout the Territory Master Recordings and/or Records produced therefrom;

(ii)   the exclusive right in all media and forms (whether now existing whereafter invented) to advertise publicise and exploit in the Territory Master Recordings and/or Records produced therefrom by any and every means including without limiting the generality of the foregoing the right to use the names including Artist's Name (as described in Sub-clause (d) below) and any other professional names photographs and likenesses of and biographical material concerning Artist for advertising publicising and otherwise exploiting Records and/or Master Recordings;

(iii)   subject to the interest of the appropriate performing right society the exclusive right to authorise public performances in the Territory of Master Recordings and/or Records produced therefrom for the purpose of exploiting the same;

(iv)   subject to the provisions hereof the exclusive right to control the use of the Master Recordings and the mothers matrices stampers and other copies or derivatives of Records produced from the Master Recordings and the performances embodied therein;

(v)   the right to permit and authorise others to exercise directly or through persons designated by them any or all of Label's rights hereunder;

(vi)   all rights necessary to enable Label to exercise the rights granted to it under this Clause 2.

(c)   Artist confirms that Label is the person by whom the arrangements necessary for the making of Master Recordings are undertaken.

(d)   Artist agrees warrants and undertakes that during the Term hereof Artist will not directly or indirectly appoint authorise or permit any person other than Label to manufacture distribute sell or otherwise exploit in the Territory Records containing or embodying the performance(s) of Artist under the name specified in the First Schedule ("Artist's Name") or under any name using any of the words comprising Artist's Name or under any acronym of Artist's Name or any other colourable similar name or words which indicates a close connection with Artist's Name or indicating a succession ("Connected Names") **PROVIDED THAT** this will not prevent Artist from recording under names other than Artist's Name or Connected Names as an unfeatured session musician for third parties or producing/mixing third parties **PROVIDED ALWAYS THAT** that such activities shall not interfere with the fulfilment of Artist's obligations hereunder which shall be on a first call basis and which shall always take priority over any other such activities. Artist further agrees warrants and undertakes that Artist will not for a period of five (5) years from and after the expiration of the Term perform or re-record any part of the material performed by Artist on any Master Recordings hereunder (nor allow Artist's names likeness voices biographical material or other identification to be associated with any such material) for the purpose of making Records therefrom for manufacture sale distribution or other exploitation by anyone other than Label. Without prejudice to any of Label's other rights in the event that Artist is in breach (whether directly or indirectly) of the provisions of this Clause 2(d) then Label shall be entitled as non-reducible liquidated damages to withhold sums payable or otherwise becoming payable to Artist hereunder in respect of exploitation by or on behalf of Label of the Master Recordings previously recorded for Label which contains Artist's peformance(s) the subject of the breach in question.

300

(e)   Subject to Clause 5 hereof Label shall be in sole and exclusive control of the sale of Records embodying Master Recordings hereunder and shall have the right to exercise the said rights in accordance with Label's reasonable business discretion either directly or through any licensee or assignee.

(f)   Label has not made and does not hereby make any representation or warranty with respect to the extent of the sale of Records embodying Master Recordings. Artist recognises and acknowledges that the sale of Records is speculative and Artist agrees that (subject to the provisions of Clause 5 hereof) the judgment of Label and its subsidiary and affiliated companies licensees or assignees with regard to any matters affecting the sale distribution and exploitation of Records shall having regard to the fact that it is Label or its relevant licensee or assignee which bears the costs of making marketing and promoting Records be binding and conclusive upon Artist. Artist agrees that Artist will not make any claim nor shall any liability be imposed upon Label or be based upon any claim merely or solely that more or better business could have been done than was actually obtained or done by Label or any of Label's subsidiary or affiliated companies licensees or assignees or that better prices or terms could have been obtained.

(g)   Save as otherwise herein provided to the contrary all costs and expenses in connection with Label's activities with respect to the recording manufacturing marketing distributing advertising and exploiting of Records embodying Master Recordings pursuant to this Agreement shall be the responsibility of Label and Artist shall not be responsible for any such costs and expenses.

3.   ARTIST'S REPRESENTATIONS AND WARRANTIES

Artist undertakes represents covenants warrants and acknowledges that:

(a)   Artist is and will remain entitled to enter and perform this Agreement and Artist has not done and will not during the period in which Label is entitled to exploit any material hereunder do or permit any person to do anything which conflicts or is incompatible with the terms of this Agreement.

(b)   Subject to the provisions of Clause 2(d) above during the Term hereof Artist shall render Artist's exclusive services as a recording artist in recording Master Recordings for Label.

(c)   Any contract entered into by Artist performing under Artist's Name during the Term hereof or thereafter for performances in cinematograph films television radio broadcasts and/or stage productions during the Term hereof or any extensions thereto (and in respect of any material recorded by Artist hereunder any contracts governing the performance by Artist of such material entered into by the Artist during the five (5) year period referred to in Clause 2(d) hereof) shall specifically exclude the right to use any recordings of such performances for the manufacture and sale of Records unless and to the extent previously authorised in writing by Label. Artist shall promptly deliver to Label copies of the pertinent provisions of each such contract and will co-operate fully with Label in any controversy dispute or litigation relating to the rights of Label under this Agreement.

(d) (i)   Artist shall appear at the times and places mutually agreed or failing such agreement reasonably designated by Label from time to time for all recording sessions required hereunder and at each such session Artist shall render Artist's professional services to the best of Artist's ability and shall rehearse record and re-record the chosen selections under the general direction of such individual producer as may be chosen. The aforementioned choice of selections and individual producer shall be carried out jointly after consultation between Artist and Label provided that in the event that Label and Artist fail to agree upon the designation of such selections and such individual producer Label shall be entitled to designate such selections and such individual producer as Label in its reasonable commercial discretion deems appropriate;

    (ii)   If Artist shall fail to appear or shall be late in appearing at the times and places agreed upon in accordance with Sub-clause 3(d)(i) above for recording sessions hereunder (other than for reasons of sickness or injury or otherwise beyond Artist's control) Artist shall pay to Label all costs and expenses incurred by Label by reason thereof.

(e)   In the event that Artist includes in Master Recordings so-called "sampled" extracts from other recordings ("Sampled Recordings") and/or utilises extracts from compositions other than Controlled Compositions ("Composition Extracts") such Sampled Recordings and/or Compositions Extracts shall only be used with Label's prior written consent **PROVIDED THAT** for the purposes of this clause Label's written consent to the use of Sampled Recordings and/or Composition Extracts shall be deemed not to have been given until Artist has secured all requisite licences and clearances in respect thereof.

(f)   Save as otherwise specified below the material recorded by Artist hereunder on Master Recordings will be available to Label for use in connection with the manufacture distribution sale and other exploitation of Master Recordings and Records in the Territory on the standard terms and conditions for the licensing of copyright material for Records in the Territory and shall not be obscene nor constitute a libel or slander of any person and shall not infringe upon or violate any other right of any third party.

(g)   The compositions recorded by Artist hereunder on Master Recordings are hereby licensed to Company for use in connection with the manufacture of records in the UK at the rate agreed by the recognised record industry association in the UK with any music publishing industry association or at the rate ordered by the Copyright Tribunal for the payment of mechanical royalties in respect of records sold in the UK provided that if there is no such rate agreed or ordered then the material shall be subject to the compulsory licence provisions in effect as at the date of abolition thereof.

(h)   All Controlled Compositions are hereby irrevocably licensed to Label and/or its licensees and/or its assignees for the USA and Canada at a rate equal to seventy-five per cent (75%) of the minimum compulsory rate imposed under the copyright law of the USA or Canada as the case may be on the date of commencement of recording of the Master Recording concerned.

(i)   Notwithstanding the foregoing the maximum aggregate copyright royalty rate in the USA and/or Canada shall be:

- (i) with respect to each Single released hereunder not more than two (2) times the rate set forth in Sub-clause (h) above;
- (ii) with respect to each Album released hereunder not more than ten (10) times the rate set forth in Sub-clause (h) above;
- (iii) notwithstanding anything to the contrary contained herein if different versions of a particular composition recorded hereunder are embodied on a particular record Label shall pay mechanical royalties in connection therewith at the applicable rate for such composition as though only one version of the composition was embodied thereon.

(j) Artist hereby undertakes to reimburse Label for any mechanical royalties paid by Label or its licensees and/or assignees in excess of the amounts specified in this clause and if Artist does not do so then Label shall be entitled to recover such excess from royalties and other payments due to Artist hereunder.

(k) Notwithstanding any contrary provision contained herein no copyright royalties shall be payable in respect of:

- (i) Records distributed for promotional purposes or to induce sales of other records by Artist;
- (ii) Records distributed in order to effectuate a bona fide discount;
- (iii) "bonus" or "free" Records distributed in reasonable quantities through record clubs or by mail order;
- (iv) Records sold as "cut-outs" or as scrap or upon deletion thereof from the catalogue of Label or its licensees or assignees.

(l) Any assignment made of the ownership of or copyrights in or the rights to license or administer the use of any Controlled Compositions shall be subject to the terms and provisions hereof.

(m) Notwithstanding the foregoing in respect of any Controlled Compositions Artist will do or procure all acts necessary grant all relevant licences and sign all relevant documents to enable Label to comply with its obligations to its licensees or assignees in the USA and Canada in respect of such compositions as aforesaid and Artist shall keep Label indemnified against any loss or damage arising to Label as a result of any breach of this provision.

(n) Artist owns (and insofar as may be required hereunder hereby grants to Label) all rights in and to Artist's Name. During the Term of this Agreement Artist will not authorise license or permit any performance by any person or persons who shall in any way be identified with Artist's Name (or any name substantially similar thereto) for the purpose of making Records other than for Label and during the period of five (5) years after the expiration of the Term of this Agreement for any reason whatsoever Artist will not authorise license or permit the performance by any person or persons who shall in any way be identified with Artist's Name (or any name substantially similar thereto) of any composition recorded hereunder for any person other than Label for the purpose of making Records.

(o) Artist is and will continue to be a member in good standing of either Equity or the Musicians' Union.

(p) None of the Master Recordings recorded hereunder will embody performances by Artist of musical works which at the date of delivery thereof have been recorded for release for sale to the public by a person firm or company other than Label.

(q)   Artist is and will remain at all times during the Term a "Qualifying Person" as defined in the Act.

(r)   Artist is not a minor.

(s)   Artist is a British Subject resident in the UK for the purposes of the Taxes Acts and any legislation amending or replacing them.

4.   TERM

The Term of this Agreement shall be for the period specified in the Third Schedule hereto.

5.   RELEASE COMMITMENT

Notwithstanding anything to the contrary herein contained Label shall use all Label's reasonable commercial endeavours to procure in any Major Territory the release for commercial sale to the public of Records embodying Master Recordings the subject hereof within four (4) months of acceptance by Label. Should Label fail to procure a release for commercial sale in any Major Territory within the period specified herein Artist shall be entitled to serve notice on Label requiring the commercial release of the Record in question within ninety (90) days thereof. In the event that Label fails to procure such release Artist shall have the right on notice to designate a Licensee in the Major Territory concerned for that and all further recordings hereunder and Label will in good faith negotiate the term thereof but on the basis that Label will receive in its own right a royalty of four per cent (4%) based on dealer price with the balance payable to Artist and those claiming through or under him **PROVIDED THAT** Label shall be entitled to receive any advances to recoup any monies expended by Label by way of recording costs and advances to Artist.

6.   RECORDING COSTS

In consideration of the rights and services granted and the obligations entered into by Artist hereunder Label agrees to pay all costs with respect to the production of Master Recordings to comprise the Minimum Commitment (provided that such costs have been approved in writing by Label before they have been incurred by Artist) including the costs of instrumental musicians vocalists conductors arrangers orches-trators copyists etc. payments to a trustee or fund based on wages (as opposed to any "per record" royalties) to the extent required by any agreement with any labour organ-isation or trustee studio tape editing mastering and other similar costs in connection with the production of the final Master Recordings and all other costs and expenses incurred in producing Master Recordings which are customarily recognised as recording costs in the phonograph record industry [and specifically as set out in the Fifth Schedule] ("Recording Costs").

7.   PAYMENTS TO ARTISTS

Subject to Artist fully and faithfully performing Artist's obligations hereunder in consideration of the rights granted and the services performed by Artist hereunder:

(a)   Label agrees to pay Artist the advances set out in Part I of the Second Schedule which shall be aggregated and chargeable and recoupable from remuneration becoming due to Artist hereunder;

(b)   Label shall pay or credit to Artist from time to time the royalties as set out in the Second Schedule hereto from all sales of Records derived solely from Artist's Master Recordings.

8.   ACCOUNTING

(a)   Accounting periods hereunder shall end upon 30 June and 31 December in each year and Label shall within ninety (90) days after each period render a statement of accrued remuneration earned under this Agreement during the preceding accounting period. Label will pay to Artist within thirty (30) days of rendering such statement the amount if any which may be due to Artist over and above the costs payments and advances deductible hereunder. Label and its licensees and/or assignees shall have the right to withhold a portion of the remuneration payable to Artist hereunder as a reserve against returns and credits of whatsoever nature. All royalties' statements and all other accounts rendered by Label to Artist hereunder shall be binding upon Artist and not subject to any objection by Artist for any reason unless specific objection in writing stating the basis thereof is given to Label within one (1) year from the date rendered.

(b)   Artist shall have the right at Artist's own expense to have a firm of independent professionally qualified accountants at reasonable hours and on reasonable notice but not more than once during each year conduct an examination and take copies and extracts of Label's books and records relating solely to the sale of Records sold by Label pursuant hereto. Artist shall free of charge provide Label with a copy of such accountants' report.

9.   WEBSITE

Artist grants to Label the exclusive right during the Term to create, host, manage, maintain, update and service website(s) or web pages on the Internet or sites accessed by mobile devices relating primarily to Artist's services and career and Label shall own Artist's sites in respect thereof. The cost of such activity up to a maximum of £10,000 per annum shall be recoupable from royalties payable hereunder.

10.   FORCE MAJEURE

If either party's material performance is hereunder delayed or becomes impossible or impracticable because of any act of God fire earthquake strike civil commotion act of government or any order regulation ruling or action of any labour union or association of artistes affecting Label or Artist or the phonograph record industry either party upon notice to the other party may suspend its obligations under this Agreement for the duration of such delay impossibility or impracticability and in such event a number of days equal to the number of such days of suspension shall be added to the Term hereof.

11.   INDEMNIFICATION

Artist shall indemnify Label its assignees and licensees and hold each of them harmless from and against any and all claims demands loss damage liability cost and expense including legal fees (on a full indemnity basis) arising out of or by reason of any breach by Artist of any of the representations warranties or agreements made by

Artist hereunder provided such claims are judicially awarded by a court of competent jurisdiction or settled with the consent of Artist such consent not to be unreasonably withheld. Upon notice of any such claim Label shall be entitled from time to time to withhold from the amounts payable to Artist under this Agreement such amounts as may be reasonably necessary to protect Label and as are directly related to the potential liability thereunder until liability upon any such claim has been finally settled determined and paid and Label has been reimbursed its actual out-of-pocket costs and expenses including legal fees on a full indemnity basis incurred in connection therewith provided such withheld money shall be liquidated if court proceedings are not commenced within six (6) months. Artist shall have the right to participate in the defence of any such claim at Artist's own cost and expense.

12. DEFAULT

(a) In the event of any default or breach by Artist in the performance of any of Artist's obligations hereunder Label may without prejudice to its other rights suspend its obligations hereunder for the duration of such default or breach and until the same has been cured and may at its option extend the Term of this Agreement for a period equal to all or any part of the period of such default or breach and in such an event the dates for exercise by Label of its options hereunder and the date of each subsequent Contract Period shall be extended accordingly.

(b) Save as otherwise provided in this Agreement no default hereunder on the part of either party shall entitle the other party to terminate this Agreement unless that party shall give notice in writing of such default to the party in default and the party in default shall fail to remedy the same within thirty (30) days after the service of such notice.

(c) It is acknowledged that the performance of Artist hereunder and the rights and privileges granted to Label under the terms hereof are of a special unique and intellectual character which gives them a peculiar value the loss of which cannot be reasonably or adequately compensated by damages in an action at law and that a breach by Artist of any provision of this Agreement will cause Label great and irreparable injury and damage. Accordingly Artist hereby expressly agrees that Label shall be entitled to the remedies of injunction specific performance and other equitable relief to prevent a breach of this Agreement. This provision shall not however be construed as a waiver of any rights which Label may have in the premises for damages or otherwise.

13. INCIDENTAL SERVICES

Artist undertakes represents covenants and warrants that Artist shall from time to time at Label's request appear for photography poster and cover art etc. under the direction of Label or its nominee; appear for interviews with representatives of the press and Label's publicity personnel; appear in promotional concerts and films; and advise and consult with Label regarding Artist's performances hereunder and similar matters. Artist shall also if requested by Label and subject to Artist's reasonable availability make personal appearances on radio television and elsewhere and record taped interviews spot announcements trailers and electrical transcriptions all for the purpose of advertising exploiting and/or "plugging" Records recorded by Artist hereunder. Artist shall not be entitled to any compensation from Label for such services other than reasonable per diems and out-of-pocket expenses.

14. AUDIO VISUAL

(a) Label shall be exclusively entitled to make commission or approve the making of Promotional Videos and Commercial Videos.

(b) Fifty per cent (50%) of all costs of Promotional Videos and/or Commercial Videos ("Videos") shall be deemed advances by Label to Artist recoupable from any and all remuneration due to Artist pursuant to this Agreement and the balance of such costs (i.e. to the extent not so recouped) shall only be recoupable from remuneration otherwise payable to Artist from the commercial exploitation thereof.

(c) In respect of Promotional Videos and Commercial Videos Label shall at all times have the sole and exclusive right of commercial exploitation including but not limited to the rights as more particularly set out in Clause 2 of this Agreement.

(d) In respect of Promotional Videos and Commercial Videos Artist shall attend at such places and times as Label and Artist shall mutually agree (each acting reasonably) and the choice of director shall be mutually agreed by Label and Artist.

(e) Artist will sign any documentation required by the Musicians' Union or other applicable union in respect of Artist's performances relating to Videos and as agent for Artist hereby gives on behalf of Artist all required consents pursuant to the provisions of the Act or any like enactment anywhere in the Territory.

(f) Subject to the provisions of Sub-clause (b) Label shall pay or credit to Artist fifty per cent (50%) of any sums from time to time received by or credited to Label (against a prior debit balance) from the exploitation of Videos after deducting any payment to any requisite independent third party arising from such exploitation subject always to Label's standard Packaging Charges from time to time for such Video and after deduction of a distribution fee (receivable by Label) of thirty per cent (30%) of such sums.

(g) Promotional Videos and Commercial Videos shall not be deemed to form part of Artist's Minimum Commitment hereto but shall be additional thereto.

(h) Artist will execute any documents that are necessary to give full effect to the provisions of this Clause 14.

(i) Whenever applicable whether now or in the future Artist will procure the granting to Label of any synchronisation or other licence required by Label (other than in respect of those synchronisation rights granted to Label hereunder) to enable Label to utilise any audio-visual device recorded by Artist hereunder in whatever way Label sees fit and without further payment.

15. NOTICES

(a) Any notice or other communication given or made under this Agreement shall be in writing and may be delivered by hand facsimile or prepaid letter addressed to the relevant party at the address shown in this Agreement or to such other address as the relevant addressee may hereafter substitute by notice hereunder.

(b) Any such notice or other communication shall be deemed to have been fully served:

(i)   if hand delivered at the time of delivery;

(ii)   if sent by prepaid post two (2) days after posting if posted to an address within the country of posting and five (5) days after posting if posted to any address outside the country of posting;

(iii)   if sent by facsimile (fax) when transmitted provided a hard copy is simultaneously sent by first class prepaid post.

(c)   A courtesy copy of each notice sent to Label shall be sent simultaneously for the attention of Label's legal advisers Messrs [   ] of [   ]. A courtesy copy of each notice sent to Artist shall be sent simultaneously for the attention of Artist's legal advisers [   ].

16. MISCELLANEOUS

(a)   The captions in this Agreement are for convenience and are not to be deemed a part of this Agreement or relied upon in the construction or interpretation thereof.

(b)   No waiver of any term or condition of this Agreement or any breach of this Agreement or any part thereof shall be deemed a waiver of any other terms or conditions of this Agreement or of any later breach of this Agreement or any part thereof.

(c)   Artist hereby gives all necessary consents and where necessary shall obtain all other necessary consents under the Act and any similar enactments anywhere in the Territory to enable Label to make the fullest use of Master Recordings recorded hereunder. Artist hereby irrevocably and unconditionally waives as against Label and/or its licensees and assignees any and all moral and like rights that Artist may have in Master Recordings and the performances and musical works embodied therein.

17. ASSIGNMENT

(a)   Artist grants to Label the right to assign this Agreement to:

(i)   any person firm or corporation purchasing all or substantially all of Label's assets or with whom Label may merge; or

(ii)   any Major Record Company;

provided that in each case the assignee is a reputable company engaged in the business of producing and exploiting records; or

(iii)   any company owned or controlled by Label or any parent affiliate associate or subsidiary corporation thereof;

it being understood and agreed that nothing herein contained shall be deemed to limit the right of Label to license and/or assign its rights in Master Recordings to its licensees associates tape producers record clubs or others in its absolute discretion. Wherever in this Agreement the word "licensees" appears it shall be deemed also to include Label's assignees where appropriate.

(b)   Artist acknowledges that Artist may be required and hereby agrees that Artist will sign a so-called "inducement letter" in connection with the assignment/licensing of Label's rights hereunder but such requirement shall be only to the extent of Artist's obligations herein contained.

18. LEGAL ADVICE

Artist by Artist's signature hereto confirms that Label has advised Artist to take and that Artist has taken specialist independent legal advice on the terms and conditions of this Agreement.

19. ILLEGALITY

(a) Illegality and unenforceability of any portions hereof shall not affect the legality or enforceability of the balance of this Agreement nor shall illegality or unenforceability of all or any portion hereof in any particular country or territory affect the legality or enforceability hereof in the balance of the Territory.

(b) The provisions set forth herein constitute the entire agreement of the parties. This Agreement may not be modified altered or changed except by an instrument signed by Artist and by Label.

20. SINGULAR AND PLURAL

In this Agreement the singular shall include the plural and vice versa and the masculine gender shall include the feminine and vice versa. Where Artist comprises more than one individual all covenants, warranties, undertakings, grants and acknowledgements on the part of Artist herein contained shall be joint and several unless otherwise specified and where Artist is a group all references to Artist shall include all members of the group collectively and each member of the group individually unless otherwise specified.

21. LAWS

The validity construction and effects of this Agreement and any or all modifications hereof shall be governed by the laws of England and any legal proceedings that may arise out of it are to be brought in the High Court of Justice in London.

22. CONSENT

Whenever in this agreement any matter shall require Label's consent approval or agreement Label shall be entitled to withhold such consent approval or agreement if Label is effectively precluded from granting the same by virtue of Label's arrangements with Label's licensee(s) notwithstanding that it is herein stated that such consent approval or agreement is not to be unreasonably withheld.

THE FIRST SCHEDULE

[Professional name of Artist]

THE SECOND SCHEDULE

PART I

Advances

In accordance with Clause 7(a) of this Agreement Label agrees to pay to Artist:

[   ]

309

PART 2

Royalties

"Royalties" shall be based upon the dealer price less the Packaging Charge and less discounts and VAT or sales or similar turnover tax and subject to the remaining provisions Label shall pay Artist:

(i) in respect of albums sold in the United Kingdom at full price a royalty of [%] and for album sold at mid price (a price of sixty per cent (60%) or less of full price) a royalty of [%] and in respect of albums sold at less than one half of full price a royalty of [%];

(ii) in respect of singles sold in the United Kingdom a royalty of [%] of the dealer price;

(iii) in respect of the sale of records abroad the royalties shall be eighty per cent (80%) of the foregoing but in any event shall not exceed seventy-five per cent (75%) of the actual receipts of Label;

(iv) in respect of sales by the Internet or mobile applications the royalty shall be the foregoing rates and calculated on the net receipt of the Label less a sum equal to the Packaging Charge;

(v) in respect of records sold in conjunction with TV or radio advertising, the royalty shall be one half of the foregoing rates;

(vi) no royalties shall be paid on records distributed as promotional records or in respect of which Label is not paid or which are sold as scrap deletions or over stocks;

(vii) if the laws of any country provide for a deduction in respect of taxation Label shall similarly deduct such sums from royalties otherwise payable hereunder;

(viii) In respect of any album which shall sell in excess of 500,000 copies the royalty shall be increased to [%] on sales in excess of such number.

THE THIRD SCHEDULE

(The Term)

A. The Term of this Agreement shall be for an initial period ("the Initial Period") of one Contract Period.

B. During the Initial Period Artist agrees to record the sufficient recordings to comprise at least:

(i) Master Recordings embodying performances of Artist to comprise one (1) Single (hereinafter called "First Single").

(ii) Label shall have the right to call upon Artist to record and deliver to Label further Master Recordings sufficient to constitute one (1) further Single (hereinafter called "the Second Single").

(iii) Label shall have the right to call upon Artist to record and deliver to Label further Master Recordings sufficient to constitute one (1) Album and up to three bonus tracks. For the avoidance for doubt it is agreed that the "A" side of each of the First Single and the Second Single may be embodied on such Album.

C.   Artist hereby grants to Label three (3) separate irrevocable options to extend the Term of this Agreement for an additional Contract Period commencing upon the date of expiration of the previous Contract Period ("the Option Periods"). The option shall be exercisable by Label giving to Artist written notice of its election to exercise the option any time prior to the expiration of the Term hereof.

D.   During the Option Period Artist agrees to record for Label and Label agrees to so record Master Recordings embodying performances of Artist sufficient for one (1) Album and up to three bonus tracks.

THE FOURTH SCHEDULE

("Major Territory") any of the United Kingdom or the United States of America or Germany or Australia.

THE FIFTH SCHEDULE

[Recording Costs]

AS WITNESS the hands of the parties hereto the day and year first before written.

SIGNED by   )

for and on behalf of **LABEL**   )

In the presence of:)

SIGNED by the said   )

For and on behalf of **ARTIST**   )

In the presence of:)

Songwriting agreement

DATED [2007]

[   ]

and

[   ]

EXCLUSIVE SONGWRITING AGREEMENT

THIS AGREEMENT is made the [   ] day of [   ] [2007]

BETWEEN:

(1)   [   ] whose registered office is at [   ] (the "Publisher") and

(2)   [   ] of [   ] (the "Composer" which expression shall be deemed to include the personal representatives executors successors and assigns of the Composer where the context so admits)

IT IS AGREED as follows:

1   **Definitions and Interpretation**

1.1   The following definitions apply in this Agreement:

"Advance" means the sums to be paid to the Composer hereunder as recoupable but non-repayable moneys.

"Agreement" means this agreement and any and all schedules annexures and exhibits.

"Composition(s)" means all the musical works and lyrics written and composed wholly or in part by the Composer heretofor or during the term and each of them.

"Copyright" means the entire copyright subsisting under the laws of the United Kingdom and all similar proprietary rights and all analogous rights subsisting under the laws of each and every jurisdiction throughout the world.

"Cover Record" means any commercial recording of a Composition other than an Original Record.

"Excluded Items" means Value Added Tax and any similar taxes and any taxes amending or replacing the same including expressly any and all levies and any remittance and/or withholding taxes from time to time applicable in any part of the Territory; the cost of conversion and transmission of currency; [all commissions fees and expenses paid to or deducted by sub-publishers and administrators] and fees commissions and charges made by **PRS** and by the mechanical rights societies and any other third parties collection agencies established in any part of the Territory for any purpose; any amounts paid or payable by way of remuneration to arrangers adapters and translators; advances and guarantees received by the Publisher unless and until earned; costs fees expenses and damages awarded to or against the Publisher arising from or in consequence of or in relation to the Compositions and any act or default of the Composer.

"Gross Receipts" means 100% of all sums actually received by the Publisher in sterling in the United Kingdom arising directly and identifiably from the use and/or exploitation of the Compositions in the Territory after the deduction of the Excluded Items. [*or*] [All income arising "at source" in each country of the territory less Excluded Items.]

"MCPS" means the Mechanical Copyright Protection Society Limited.

"Original Record" means any commercial recording of a Composition made by the Composer as a featured artist either alone or with others.

"Product Guarantee" shall mean at least sufficient of the Compositions newly recorded in each period and first released on record in each period of the Term hereof to comprise the equivalent of eighty per cent (80%) in playing time of one album and released by a major record company provided that any of the Compositions released as an "A" side of a single but additional to and not included in an album release shall be deemed to be one-tenth in playing time of an album.

"PRS" means the Performing Right Society Limited.

"Publisher Obligations" means the covenants herein contained on the part of the Publisher.

"Royalty" means the sums to be paid to the Composer hereunder.

"Term" means the period of this Agreement.

"Territory" means the world.

1.2 Any reference in this Agreement to any statute or statutory provision shall be construed as including a reference to that statute or statutory provision as from time to time amended modified extended or re-enacted whether before or after the date of this Agreement and to all statutory instruments orders and regulations for the time being made pursuant to it or deriving validity from it.

1.3 Unless the context otherwise requires words denoting the singular shall include the plural and vice versa and words denoting any one gender shall include all genders and words denoting persons shall include bodies corporate unincorporated associations and partnerships.

1.4 Unless otherwise stated time shall be of the essence for the purpose of the performance of the Composer's obligations under this Agreement.

1.5 Unless otherwise stated references to clauses sub-clauses sub-paragraphs schedules annexures and exhibits relate to this Agreement.

2 Grant of Rights

2.1 The Composer and each individual comprised within the definition jointly and severally with full title guarantee **HEREBY ASSIGNS** to the Publisher the entire copyright (whether vested contingent or future) and all rights of action and all other rights of a proprietary or similar nature in and to the Compositions **TO**

HOLD to the same unto the Publisher its successors assigns and licensees absolutely for the full period of copyright throughout the world including all reversions renewals and extensions free of any claim by any third party.

2.2 The Composer irrevocably and unconditionally waives all moral rights to which the Composer may be entitled under any legislation now existing or in future enacted in any part of the world.

2.3 The Composer undertakes to deliver to the Publisher copies of all scores lyrics vocal instrumental and orchestral parts demo tapes floppy discs magnetic tapes and other means of digitally or electronically or otherwise recording or storing information relating to the Composition(s) together with equipment specifications access codings and any other necessary or pertinent information promptly on their coming into existence.

2.4 If the Composer is a member of the PRS the rights assigned pursuant to this Agreement are assigned subject to the rights of the PRS arising by virtue of the Composer's membership of the PRS but include any reversionary interest of the Composer in those rights.

2.5 The Publisher its successors assigns and licensees shall have the right to use the name professional name likeness and biography of the Composer throughout the Territory in the Compositions for the purpose of exploiting the Publisher's rights under this Agreement.

2.6 The Composer undertakes to do any and all acts and execute any and all documents in such manner and at such location as may be required by the Publisher in its sole discretion to protect perfect or enforce any of the rights granted or confirmed to the Publisher pursuant to this Agreement. As security for the performance by the Composer of the Composer's obligations under this Agreement if the Composer shall have failed following [fourteen (14)] days' notice from the Publisher to execute any document or perform any act required pursuant to this Agreement the Publisher shall have the right to do so in the place and stead of the Composer as the lawfully appointed attorney of the Composer and the Composer undertakes and warrants to confirm and ratify and be bound by any and all of the actions of the Publisher pursuant to this clause and such authority and appointment shall take effect as an irrevocable appointment pursuant to the Powers of Attorney Act 1971 Section 4.

3 The Term of this Agreement

The term of this Agreement shall be the period of one year or if longer until six (6) months following fulfilment of the Product Guarantee together with three (3) additional periods of one (1) year or if longer until six (6) months following fulfilment of the Product Guarantee for such period. Such additional periods shall be separate and successive and shall come into being at the option of the Publisher by giving notice in writing to that effect to the Composer no later than the expiry of the then current period. No period shall in any event exceed four (4) years.

4 Composer's Warranties and Obligations

As a material inducement towards the Publisher to enter into this Agreement the Composer (and each party comprising the Composer jointly and severally) warrants undertakes and agrees with the Publisher that:

4.1 the Composer is not a minor

4.2 the Composer is free to enter into this Agreement and grant to the Publisher the rights granted in it and the Composer is not under any disability restriction or prohibition which might prevent the Composer from performing or observing any of the Composer's obligations under this Agreement

4.3 the Composer is the sole composer and writer of the Compositions and has not entered into and shall not enter into any arrangement which may conflict with this Agreement and is the sole absolute unincumbered and beneficial owner of all rights granted to the Publisher and is the sole "author" of the Compositions as defined by the Copyright, Designs and Patents Act 1988 Section 9

4.4 there are no restrictions relating to the Compositions which the Composer is legally able to write for the Publisher under this Agreement and the Compositions are not the subject of any prior licence grant or incumbrance other than to the PRS and the rights in the Compositions have not at any time been exploited by any person prior to the date of this Agreement

4.5 the Compositions are and shall be original to the Composer and are not and shall not be obscene blasphemous or defamatory of any person

4.6 the Compositions do not and shall not infringe any rights of copyright moral rights rights of privacy rights of publicity or any other right of any other nature of any person

4.7 the Composer shall sign at the request of the Publisher any separate agreement in respect of the Compositions including but not limited to any collection agreement and shall sign at the request of the Publisher the division of fees form of the PRS

4.8 the Composer shall allow the Publisher to have full and complete control over the manner and extent of the exploitation and advertisement of the Compositions throughout the Territory and the Publisher shall have the right without the Composer's consent to transfer assign or grant licences in and to any of the Compositions subject to assignees being bound by the terms and conditions hereof

4.9 the Composer irrevocably authorises the Publisher to make alterations in adaptations of and additions to the Compositions at the Publisher's discretion and to provide translations of new words or lyrics in other languages

4.10 the Composer is or shall become and remain a member of the PRS and agrees that this Agreement shall be regarded as a certificate for the purpose of Rule 1(o)(ii) of the PRS or any rule replacing it authorising the PRS to treat the Publisher as exploiting the Compositions otherwise than by publishing for the benefit of the persons interested in them and as an agreement to vary the division of fees pursuant to Rule 5(f) or any rule replacing it

4.11 the Composer was or will be at the time the Compositions were or are written a "qualifying person" within the meaning of the Copyright, Designs and Patents Act 1988 Section 154

4.12 the Composer shall not without the consent in writing of the Publisher disclose reveal or make public any information of whatever nature in connection with the business of the Publisher or the terms of this Agreement all of which shall be treated by the Composer on a strictly confidential basis

4.13 the Composer has taken advice from a solicitor experienced in agreements of this nature and that the Composer has read and fully understood all of the provisions of this Agreement

4.14 the Composer undertakes to indemnify the Publisher and keep the Publisher at all times fully indemnified from and against all actions proceedings claims demands costs (including without prejudice to the generality of this provision legal costs of the Publisher on a solicitor and own client basis) expenses awards and damages however arising directly or indirectly as a result of any breach or

315

non-performance by the Composer of any of the Composer's undertakings warranties or obligations under this Agreement.

5 Publisher's Obligations

The Publisher undertakes with the Composer that subject to and conditional upon the full and timely performance and observance by the Composer of all of the Composer's warranties undertakings and obligations in this Agreement:

(i)   the Publisher shall use all reasonable endeavours to procure the exploitation of the Compositions whether the exploitation shall be by the Publisher or any sub-publisher licensee or assign and

(ii) the Publisher shall pay the Advances and the Royalties.

6 Royalties

6.1   Subject to the full and timely performance by the Composer of all of the Composers' obligations warranties and undertakings in this Agreement and to recoupment of the Advance the Publisher undertakes to pay or procure the payment of to the Composer by way of Royalties sixty per cent (60%) of all Gross Receipts less the Excluded Items and derived from the Compositions save in respect of performing income and Cover Records.

6.2   In respect of Cover Records the share shall be fifty per cent (50%) and in respect of performing income the same shall be collected by the PRS which will pay fifty per cent (50%) to the Composer and fifty per cent (50%) to the Publisher for its own benefit.

6.3   The Publisher shall pay to the Composer a sum equal to twenty per cent (20%) of its receipts from the PRS relating to the Compositions.

6.4   Each individual comprising the Composer shall receive an equal share of moneys due hereunder.

7 Advances

7.1   By way of Advance in respect of the Royalty and recoupable therefrom the Publisher shall pay to the Composer the sum of £[   ] payable as to one-third on the execution of this Agreement and the balance upon fulfilment of the Product Guarantee.

7.2   In the event that the Publisher shall exercise its first option to extend the Term it shall pay an Advance in respect of the Royalty in the sum of £[   ] payable as to one-third on exercise of the option and the balance upon fulfilment of the Product Guarantee for that period.

7.3   In the event that the Publisher shall exercise its second option to extend the Term it shall pay an Advance in respect of the Royalty, in the sum of £[   ] payable as to one-third on exercise of the option and the balance upon fulfilment of the Product Guarantee for that period.

7.4   In the event that the Publisher shall exercise its third option to extend the Term it shall pay an Advance in respect of the Royalty, in the sum of £[   ] payable as to one-third on exercise of the option and the balance upon fulfilment of the Product Guarantee for that period.

8 Royalty Accounting

8.1 The Publisher shall render to the Composer within ninety (90) days after 30 June and 31 December in each year any positive statement of account relating to the preceding six (6) month period indicating all Royalties due to the Composer in accordance with the provisions of this Agreement and accompanied by the payment of the amount indicated by such statements to be owing.

8.2 The accounting statements shall be deemed to be binding on the parties hereto unless the Composer shall within one year specify any error in the same. The Composer shall have the right acting by a professional accountant and not more than once in any calendar year to inspect the accounting records of the Publisher relating to the Compositions and to take copies thereof. If such inspection shall reveal an underpayment of the greater of ten per cent (10%) of the sums accounted for or £5000.00 the Publisher shall reimburse the Composer with the cost of such inspection excluding and travel hotel or subsistence costs and excluding any contingency fee or success fee.

8.3 If the Publisher shall not have paid any Royalties to the Composer or shall have incorrectly calculated the amount due the Composer shall give notice in writing to the Publisher of this omission or error and the publisher shall have a further thirty (30) days following the receipt of such notice during which period the Publisher shall not be deemed to be in default of its obligations under this Agreement if the Publisher shall make payment of the Royalties due or make good any incorrect payment without interest.

8.4 The Composer expressly authorises the Publisher to deduct and withhold from all sums due to the Composer under this Agreement any sums which may be deductible in accordance with local laws or regulations from time to time.

9 Copyright Notices

9.1 The Publisher shall where possible print or cause to be printed on the outside cover or title page or first page of every printed copy of the Compositions published by or under the control of the Publisher pursuant to this Agreement a proper notice of copyright in accordance with the requirements of the Universal Copyright Convention and shall where possible accord to the Composer clear and legible personal credit as the Composer of the Compositions.

9.2 The Publisher shall not be liable for any neglect or default on the part of any sub-publisher to accord the notice or the credit referred to and no casual or inadvertent failure of the Publisher of its obligations in that regard shall constitute a breach of this Agreement and the Composer acknowledges that the Composer's only remedy for breach of the provisions of this clause shall be damages and not injunctive relief for any alleged failure of the Publisher or any third party.

10 Reversion

NOTWITHSTANDING anything else in this Agreement the Publisher shall re-assign to the Composer or his designee the copyright in the Compositions on request made at any time following the 15th anniversary of the expiry of the Term of the Agreement.

11 Notices

11.1 Any notice or other document required to be given under this Agreement or any communication between the parties with respect to any of the provisions of this Agreement shall be in writing in English and be deemed duly given if signed by or on behalf of a duly authorised officer of the party giving the notice and if left at or sent by prepaid registered or recorded delivery post or by telex telegram cable facsimile transmission or other means of telecommunication in permanent written form to the address of the party receiving such notice as set out at the head of the Agreement or as notified between the parties for the purpose of this clause.

11.2 Any such notice or other communication shall be deemed to be given to and received by the addressee:

11.2.1 at the time the same is left at the address of or handed to a representative of the party to be served

11.2.2 by post on the day not being a Sunday or public holiday two (2) days following the date of posting

11.2.3 in the case of a telex telegram cable facsimile transmission or other means of telecommunication on the next following day.

11.3 In proving the giving of a notice it should be sufficient to prove that the notice was left or that the envelope containing the notice was properly addressed and posted or that the applicable means of telecommunication was addressed and despatched and despatch of the transmission was confirmed and/or acknowledged as the case may be.

12 Severability

If any provision of this Agreement shall be prohibited by or adjudged by a court to be unlawful void or unenforceable such provision shall to the extent required be severed from this Agreement and rendered ineffective as far as possible without modifying the remaining provisions of this Agreement and shall not in any way affect any other circumstances or the validity or enforcement of this Agreement.

13 Assignment

The Publisher shall have the right to assign license sublicense or charge the whole or any part of its rights under this Agreement and the covenants undertakings and warranties of the Composer shall inure to the benefit of the Publisher's successors and assigns. In the event of the Publisher's successors or assigns covenanting to perform the obligations of the Publisher under this Agreement the Publisher shall not have any further liability to the Composer in respect of those obligations.

14 Agreement Final and Complete

This Agreement contains the full and complete understanding between the parties and supersedes all prior arrangements and understandings whether written or oral appertaining to the subject matter of this Agreement and may not be varied except by an instrument in writing signed by all of the parties to this Agreement. The Composer acknowledges that no representations or promises not expressly contained in this Agreement have been made by the Publisher or any of its servants agents employees members or representatives. The Composer acknowledges that he has been advised to and given the opportunity to obtain independent legal advice upon this Agreement.

318

15 Waiver

No failure or delay on the part of any of the parties to this Agreement relating to the exercise of any right power privilege or remedy provided under this Agreement shall operate as a waiver of such right power privilege or remedy or as a waiver of any preceding or succeeding breach by the other party to this Agreement nor shall any single or partial exercise of any right power privilege or remedy preclude any other or further exercise of such or any other right power privilege or remedy provided in this Agreement all of which are several and cumulative and are not exclusive of each other or of any other rights or remedies otherwise available to a party at law or in equity.

16 No Partnership

This Agreement shall not be deemed to constitute a partnership or joint venture or contract of employment between the parties.

17 Governing Law

This Agreement shall be governed by and construed in accordance with the laws of England and Wales the courts of which shall be courts of competent jurisdiction.

AS WITNESS the hands of the parties the date and year first above mentioned.

SIGNED by the duly authorised   )

officer of the Publisher in the   )

presence of:)

SIGNED by   )

in the presence of:)

SIGNED by   )

in the presence of:)

SIGNED by   )

in the presence of:)

SIGNED by   )

in the presence of:)

Sub-publishing agreement

DATED [2007]

[   ]

and

[   ]

SUB-PUBLISHING AGREEMENT

THIS SUB-PUBLISHING AGREEMENT is made this [   ] of [   ] [2007]
BETWEEN:

(1)   [   ] MUSIC LIMITED of [   ]

(hereinafter called "the Owner")

and

(2)   [   ] MUSIC LIMITED of [   ]

(hereinafter called "the Sub-Publisher")

WITNESSETH AS FOLLOWS:

1.   In this Agreement the following expressions shall have the following meanings:

   (1)   The "Catalogue" shall mean all musical compositions owned and controlled by the Owner during the term and each of them.

   (2)   The "Rights" shall mean the following rights in connection with the Catalogue in the Territory and during the Term:

      (i)   to print and reproduce copies of sheet music and to publish and sell such copies;

      (ii)   to grant non-exclusive licences to manufacture parts serving to reproduce the Catalogue mechanically and to make mechanical, electrical and electronic productions thereof;

      (iii)   (subject to any and all rights of any official performing right society in the Territory) to license public performance including broadcasting and television;

(iv) to grant worldwide perpetual synchronisation licences in respect of films and videos and similar originating within the Territory;

(v) (subject to prior written consent of the Owner) to make and publish new adaptations and arrangements of the Catalogue and to translate the lyrics thereof and on the basis that all new matter including but not limited to adaptations, translations and arrangements shall be copyrighted in the name of the Owner and shall be the Property of the Owner;

(vi) the exclusive right to collect in the all royalties monies and other income arising from the exploitation or existence of the Catalogue during the Term and in the Territory;

(vii) to license digital and electronic use of the Catalogue to servers situate within the Territory.

PROVIDED THAT all rights not expressly hereby granted are reserved to the Owner.

(3) The "Royalties" shall mean the sums payable by the Sub-Publisher to the Owner pursuant to this Agreement.

(4) The "Territory" shall mean the Territory of [   ].

(5) The "Term" shall mean the period of [   ] years.

(6) "Cover Record" shall mean any commercial recording of a composition comprised within the Catalogue embodying a performance of that composition by any artist other than the writer of that composition (whether as part of a group or otherwise) which has been procured demonstrably by the efforts of the Sub-Publisher.

2. In consideration of the covenants by the Sub-Publisher herein contained the Owner hereby grants to the Sub-Publisher the Rights for the Term and for the Territory.

3. Royalties
The Sub-Publisher shall pay to the Owner royalties computed as follows:

(a) In respect of each copy of each printed edition of the Catalogue and any song within it sold in the Territory in the sum of fifteen per cent (15%) of the selling price less sales turnover or similar taxes.

(b) A mechanical royalty in respect of each mechanical, electrical or electronic reproduction in the sum of [%] save that where the Sub-Publisher procures demonstrably any Cover Record then mechanical royalties shall be [   ].

(c) A sum equal to [%] of receipts in respect of any synchronisation licence.

(d) A sum equal to [%] of the publisher's share of performing income earned on the basis that it is agreed or understood that the so-called "writer's share" of performing income shall be 6/12s of all fees and shall be paid directly to the writer through PRS and its associates.

(e) A sum equal to [%] of all other income of whatever nature derived from the Catalogue received by the Sub-Publisher including undistributed income and so-called black box income **PROVIDED THAT** where so-called black box distributions are made and cannot be attributed to any particular songs then such share shall be based upon a sum equal to that proportion of unidentified distributions as the income of the Sub-Publisher in relation to the Catalogue bears to its overall income for the accounting period in which the unidentified distribution was received.

4. All sums to be paid to the Owner pursuant to this Agreement shall be computed upon actual receipts by the Sub-Publisher less only sales turnover or similar tax

required to be deducted and commissions and fees deducted by performing rights societies, mechanical rights societies or any other independent industry collecting agencies and amounts paid by way of remuneration to arrangers, adaptors and translators in accordance with the rules of the local collection society or if none, such as shall be fair and reasonable.

5. By way of advance on such share of income and recoupable therefrom the Sub-Publisher shall pay to the Owner forthwith on execution hereof and as a condition of this Agreement the sum of [   ].

6. Sub-Publisher's Obligations

(a) The Sub-Publisher shall ensure that the compositions are registered with the applicable performing and mechanical rights societies in the Territory and with any formal copyright registration requirements in the Territory on behalf of and in the name of the Owner.

(b) The Sub-Publisher shall use its best endeavours to promote and exploit the Catalogue.

(c) The Sub-Publisher shall use its best endeavours to provide all proper and appropriate credits and copyright notices.

(d) The Sub-Publisher shall at all times provide a efficient and first class administration and collection service to keep up to date and accurate and complete books of account and record of all its dealings hereunder and in relation to the Catalogue.

7. Accounting

The Sub-Publisher shall make up true and correct statements of account up to 30 March, 30 June, 30 September and 31 December in each year and render the same to the Owner within sixty (60) days of each such date and shall pay by bank to bank transfer on such dates the sum shown to be due.

8. Termination

8.1 The Owner shall be entitled to terminate this Agreement with immediate effect and all rights granted hereunder shall immediately revert to the Owner without formality in the event that:

(i) the Sub-Publisher shall default in the performance of any material obligation or duties hereunder and that such default shall continue for a period of thirty (30) days; or

(ii) if the Sub-Publisher is insolvent or incapable of paying its debts as they fall due or in administration or liquidation or otherwise is wound up or ceases to trade.

8.2 If ownership and control of the Sub-Publisher shall change the Owner shall have the right to terminate this Agreement upon thirty (30) days' notice.

9. Enforcement

The Owner grants to the Sub-Publisher for the Term the non-exclusive right to enforce and protect all rights in the Catalogue and the compositions and the copyright thereof throughout the Term. The Sub-Publisher shall notify the Owner if it becomes aware of any infringement of the rights in the compositions or the Catalogue in the Territory and the parties shall mutually agree any enforcement action to be taken. Any recovery obtained by settlement judgment or otherwise shall be divided between the parties in the same proportion as the mechanical royalty rate provided for above after deduction of reasonable legal fees.

10. Notices

All notices, accounting statements, payments and other documents shall be sent by mail postage prepaid or by facsimile or e-mail. Notices served by post shall be deemed served two (2) working days after dispatch and those by facsimile and e-mail shall be deemed served on the date of transmission of the message.

11. Miscellaneous

The Sub-Publisher shall not assign or transfer any of its rights under this Agreement. This Agreement shall be construed under the laws of England whose courts shall be the non-exclusive courts of jurisdiction. This Agreement contains the entire understanding of the parties and supersedes all prior and collateral Agreements and no modification, alteration, amendment or waiver of any of the provisions of this Agreement shall be valid unless in writing and signed by each of the parties.

AS WITNESS the hands of the duly authorised representatives of the parties hereto the day and year first above written.

SIGNED by the duly authorised)

officer of the **OWNER**)

in the presence of:)

SIGNED by the duly authorised)

officer of the **SUB-PUBLISHER**)

in the presence of:)

Film and television

APPENDIX B1

Option agreement

THIS AGREEMENT is made the [   ] of [   ] [2007]

BETWEEN:

(1)   [   ] of [   ] [c/o [*name of agent/publisher*]] (the "Owner") which expression shall be deemed to include the Owner's personal representatives; and
(2)   [   ] of [   ] (the "Purchaser") which expression shall be deemed to include its licensees, successors in title and assigns.

WHEREAS:

(A)   The Owner is the owner of the worldwide copyright and all other rights, title and interest in and to an original [un]published [*type of work*] entitled [*name of work*] (the "Work").
(B)   The Purchaser intends but does not undertake to develop and produce a feature film primarily intended for theatrical [television] exploitation based upon the Work (the "Film").
(C)   The Owner has agreed to assign and grant to the Purchaser the sole and exclusive option and, conditional upon exercise of the option, certain rights in and to the Work upon the terms, subject to the conditions of and for the consideration set out in this Agreement.

IT IS HEREBY AGREED as follows:

1.   Option

1.1   In consideration of the payment by the Purchaser to the Owner of the sum of [*first option fee in figures*] ([*first option fee in words*]) (the "First Option Fee"), the Owner hereby grants to the Purchaser with full title guarantee the sole and exclusive option (the "Option") to acquire the Rights (as defined at paragraph 2.2 of this Agreement) in the Work, the First Option Fee to be payable on signature of this Agreement by the parties.
1.2   The Option shall be exercisable by notice by the Purchaser in writing at any time within [*first option period in figures*] ([*first option period in words*]) from the date of this Agreement (the "First Option Period").
1.3   If the Purchaser shall pay to the Owner at any time prior to the expiration of the First Option Period a further sum of [*second option fee in figures*] ([*second option fee in words*]) (the "Second Option Fee"), the Purchaser shall be entitled to an extension of the First Option Period for a further period of [*second option period in figures*] ([*second option period in words*]) from the expiry date of the First Option Period (the "Second Option Period").

1.4 The Purchaser shall be entitled at any time prior to the expiry of the Option to write or cause to be written screenplays and/or other adaptations of the Work alone or combined with other source material relating to [*subject matter of screenplay*] owned or controlled by the Purchaser by any writer or writers engaged by the Purchaser to enable it to decide whether or not to exercise the Option.

1.5 In the event that the Purchaser shall not serve a notice exercising the Option within the First Option Period or the Second Option Period (as the case may be) this Agreement shall lapse and the parties shall have no further rights or obligations hereunder.

1.6 The sum paid to the Owner pursuant to paragraph 1.1 of this Agreement shall [not] be on account of the sums payable to the Owner under the terms of paragraph 3.1 of this Agreement.

2. Assignment of Rights

2.1 Subject to and conditional upon the Purchaser serving on the Owner written notice of its exercise of the Option and paying to the Owner the sum specified in paragraph 3.1 of this Agreement the Owner hereby irrevocably assigns to the Purchaser with full title guarantee the Rights (as defined at paragraph 2.2 of this Agreement) for the Purchaser to hold the same absolutely throughout the world for the full period of copyright in the Work and in any such other product produced hereunder and all renewals and extensions thereof and thereafter (insofar as may be or become possible) in perpetuity in any and all media now known or hereafter devised.

2.2 The rights which are the subject of this Agreement are all copyright (present and future), rental and lending rights, feature film, videogram, video-on-demand, television, Internet and other visual and/or audio-visual and other similar recording rights (whether now known or hereafter devised) and all rights incidental, ancillary or allied to any and all of the foregoing in and to the Work (as such terms are commonly used and understood in the film and television industry) including but not limited to merchandising rights and promotional rights (the "Rights").

2.3 The Owner hereby irrevocably and unconditionally waives in perpetuity all moral rights or "droit moral" or any similar law in any part of the world to which the Owner has become or shall become entitled in relation to the Work and agrees not to bring or permit any legal action in any part of the world on the grounds that the Film or any such other product produced hereunder constitutes an infringement of any such rights or are in any way a defamation or mutilation of the Work.

2.4 The Owner hereby confirms and agrees that the assignment of rights in and to the Work includes any and all lending and rental rights and satellite and cable retransmission rights in and to the Work and any adaptation and copies created pursuant thereto (whether now known or hereafter devised) and further agrees that the consideration payable to the Owner takes into account and includes a payment in respect of all such rights, that such payment constitutes full, equitable and adequate consideration for the grant and/or exercise of all such rights and that the Owner will not be entitled to any further payment of any kind in respect of all such rights nor be entitled to bring or permit any legal action in any part of the world to restrict or prevent the distribution and exploitation of the Work and/or any such adaptation or copies.

3. Consideration

3.1 The Purchaser shall as full and final consideration for the Rights and all other rights granted to the Purchaser hereunder pay or procure to be paid to the Owner on or before the first day of principal photography of the Film the sum of [*purchase price in figures*] ([*purchase price in words*]).

3.2 The Purchaser shall further pay or procure to pay to the Owner [*percentage in figures*]% ([*percentage in words*] per cent) of 100% (one hundred per cent) of [Producer's] Net Profits for the Film such [Producer's] Net Profits to be set out in the collection agreement or other contract governing the distribution of receipts of exploitation of the Film amongst all relevant beneficiaries.

3.3 In this Agreement [Producer's] Net Profits shall mean all profits derived from the exploitation of the Film in all media worldwide as defined, computed and accounted for in accordance with the definition of net profits as approved by principal financiers of the Film and the definition "[Producer's] Net Profits" accorded to the Owner shall be no less favourable than the definition accorded to any other contingent participant of the Film.

3.4 The Purchaser shall use its best commercial endeavours to provide the Owner with a copy of the definition of [Producer's] Net Profits and the collection agreement by no later than the first day of principal photography of the Film.

3.5 The Owner acknowledges that no further sums shall be payable by the Purchaser in respect of the Rights and all other rights granted hereunder or the exploitation of the Film or any other film or product produced hereunder whether by way of profits, repeat fees residuals, royalties or otherwise and that the sums specified herein represent a complete "buy-out" of all such rights throughout the world in perpetuity.

4. Credit

4.1 If the Purchaser produces the Film based wholly or substantially upon the Work, the Owner shall be accorded a customary source material credit the placement, size, position, duration and prominence of which shall be at the Purchaser's discretion:

(a) given on screen in the form ["Based on [*name of work*] by [*name of author*]"] on the negative and all positive copies of the Film; and

(b) in all major paid advertising and paid publicity relating to the Film and packaging of all ancillary products issued by or under the direct control of the Purchaser

made by or under the control of the Purchaser subject to the usual standard exclusions (including but not limited to group list or "teaser" advertising or publicity or special advertising or publicity) as commonly used and understood in the film and television industry.

4.2 The Purchaser shall use its reasonable endeavours to procure that the distributors of the Film accord to the Owner a credit in accordance with the provisions of this paragraph 4 on all prints of the Film issued by such distributors provided always that the Purchaser shall not be liable for the neglect or default of the distributors or any costs incurred in remedying such neglect or default if the Purchaser shall have notified the distributors of the credit to which the Owner is entitled and shall have used its reasonable endeavours to remedy any such neglect or default.

4.3 No casual or inadvertent failure by the Purchaser or any third party to comply with the provisions of this paragraph 4 shall constitute a breach of this Agreement by the Purchaser and the Owner acknowledges that the only remedy of the Owner for a breach of the such provisions shall be damages (if any) and in no event shall the Owner be entitled to injunct or otherwise restrain the distribution, exhibition, advertising or exploitation of the Film.

5. Warranties and Obligations

5.1 The Owner hereby warrants represents and undertakes to and with the Purchaser that:

(a) the Owner is the original author and sole owner with full title guarantee of the copyright and other rights in the Work;

(b) to the best of the Owner's knowledge having made all reasonable enquiries the Work does not contain any obscene or defamatory material, does not infringe the copyright or any other rights including any rights of confidentiality or privacy of any third party and shall not expose the Purchaser to civil or criminal proceedings;

(c) no film radio or television programme based on the Work has been developed produced or authorised and no agreements with respect to the Work have previously been entered into by or on behalf of the Owner which would operate to derogate from the grant of rights made pursuant to this Agreement;

(d) the rights hereby granted and assigned are vested in the Owner absolutely and the Owner has not previously granted licensed assigned charged or in any way dealt with or encumbered the same so as to derogate from the grant and assignment hereby made; and

(e) the Owner has full right, title and authority to enter into this Agreement and the Owner is not bound by any previous agreement which adversely affects this Agreement.

5.2 The Purchaser shall be entitled to use and authorise others to use the right at all times hereafter to use and authorise others to use the approved name, approved likeness, approved photograph and approved biography of [*name of author*] in whole or in part in connection with the advertisement, publicity, exhibition and commercial exploitation of the Film and in association with the advertisement, publicity and commercial exploitation of any products produced hereunder provided (except with the Owner's prior written consent) the name of [*name of author*] is not directly or indirectly used to suggest that the Owner personally uses or recommends any such other commodities other than the Film itself.

6. Indemnity

The parties hereby indemnify and agree to keep the other fully and effectually indemnified from and against all claims costs proceedings demands losses damages and expenses (including reasonable outside legal costs and expenses and Value Added Tax thereon) and liabilities suffered or incurred, directly or indirectly, by the parties in consequence of any breach or non performance of any of the warranties conditions material obligations representations undertakings and agreements made by the parties in this Agreement.

7. No Obligation

Nothing in this Agreement shall obligate the Purchaser to exercise the Option or to develop or produce the Film and the Purchaser shall not be liable to the Owner for any loss or damage (including but not limited to loss of opportunity on the Owner's part to enhance the Owner's reputation) which the Owner may suffer as a result of the Purchaser's failure to develop, produce, release, distribute, advertise or otherwise exploit the Film or to utilise the Work.

8. No Injunction

The Owner acknowledges that in the event of a breach of this Agreement by the Purchaser any application to enjoin or restrain the production, distribution, exhibition, advertising or exploitation of the Film or any film produced hereunder or any rights therein or derived therefrom would be excessively disruptive and unreasonably damaging to the same and the Purchaser's interests therein and the Owner expressly agrees not to apply for any such relief and accepts that the recovery of damages, if any, in an action at law will provide a full and appropriate remedy for any loss or damage incurred by the Owner as a result of any such breach.

9. Termination

9.1 Either party shall be entitled to terminate this Agreement in the event that the other party has committed a material breach of its obligations under this Agreement and does not rectify the position within fourteen (14) days of being required to do so by the non-breaching party.

9.2 In the event of termination in accordance with paragraph 9.1 of this Agreement the Purchaser shall have no further obligation to the Owner. This shall not prejudice any rights and/or claims which the Purchaser shall have against the Owner hereunder at the time of such termination, including but not limited to any claim the Purchaser may have in damages arising from any failure, refusal or neglect of the Owner to observe the terms of this Agreement or arising from the rights hereby granted or assigned to the Purchaser.

9.3 In the event of a breach by the Purchaser of any of its obligations under this Agreement or pursuant to statute, law or common law, the rights and remedies of the Owner shall be limited to the Owner's rights (if any) to recover damages.

10. Turnaround

In the event that principal photography of the Film does not commence within [*turnaround period in words*] ([*turnaround period in figures*]) years after the date the Purchaser has served on the Owner written notice of its exercise of the Option and paid to the Owner the sum specified in paragraph 3.1 of this Agreement, all rights granted and the Work shall revert to the Owner on written notice by the Owner to the Purchaser subject to a lien in the amount of one hundred per cent (100%) of the sums paid by the Purchaser to the Owner under this Agreement, all of which shall be repaid by the Owner or a third party on the Owner's behalf to the Purchaser on the first day of principal photography of any film produced by a third party elsewhere.

11. Miscellaneous

11.1 This Agreement supersedes all previous agreements or representations made in relation to the subject matter of this Agreement and contains the entire agreement of the parties and may only be varied by written instrument signed by both parties.

11.2 Nothing in this Agreement shall be construed or deemed to create or constitute any relationship partnership by joint venture between the parties.

11.3 Any notices required to be given under this Agreement shall be in writing by registered post and shall be sent to the parties at their addresses set forth above and unless otherwise agreed shall be deemed to be received two (2) working days after posting.

11.4 All sums payable under this Agreement are exclusive of Value Added Tax.

11.5 The parties agree to execute and deliver all such further documents as the parties may require in relation to this Agreement and if the Owner shall fail to execute, acknowledge or deliver the same the Purchaser is hereby irrevocably appointed the attorney-in-fact of the Owner with full right, power and authority to execute, acknowledge and deliver the same in the name of and on behalf of the Owner.

11.6 The Purchaser shall be entitled to assign, charge, license or grant this Agreement in whole or in part to any third party.

11.7 Each party shall bear its own costs and expenses in relation to the preparation, completion and implementation of this Agreement.

11.8 No term of this Agreement shall be enforceable under the Contracts (Rights of Third Parties) Act 1999 by a person who is not a party to this Agreement.

11.9 This Agreement shall be construed under and performed in all respects in accordance with and governed by the laws England and Wales and the parties hereby submit to the exclusive jurisdiction of the English courts.

SIGNED BY a duly authorised signatory)

for and on behalf of)

[*name of owner*])

SIGNED BY a duly authorised signatory)

for and on behalf of)

[*name of purchaser*])

Director's agreement

THIS AGREEMENT is made the [   ] day of [   ] [2007]

BETWEEN:

(1)   [   ] of [   ] (the "Company") which expression shall be deemed to include its licensees, successors in title and assigns; and

(2)   [   ] of [   ] (the "Director") which expression shall be deemed to include the Director's personal representatives.

WHEREAS:

The Company wishes to engage the Director to direct the feature film primarily intended for theatrical [television] exploitation provisionally entitled [*name of film*] (the "Film") which the Company intends but does not undertake to produce and the Director has agreed to do so for the consideration upon the terms and subject to the conditions hereinafter appearing.

It is hereby agreed as follows:

1.   Definitions and Interpretation

In this Agreement unless the context otherwise requires the following words have the following meanings:

"Final Budget"
      shall mean the final locked cash cost of the production of the Film as approved by the principal financiers of the Film [excluding any overhead charged by a financier or the Company, finance fees, producer fees, completion guarantee fees, legal fees, audit fees, any deferred fees, contingency and all payments made to the Director hereunder];

"Producer's Net Profits"
      shall mean all profits derived from the exploitation of the Film in all media worldwide as defined, computed and accounted for in accordance with definition of producer's net profits as approved by the principal financiers of the Film such Producer's Net Profits to be paid on a pro rata pari passu basis with all other participants in Producer's Net Profits to be set out in the collection agreement or other contract governing the distribution of receipts of exploitation of the Film amongst all relevant beneficiaries; and

"Reserved Rights" shall mean [live stage rights, radio rights, merchandising rights, publication rights including in graphic novel and volume form, music publishing and soundtrack album rights as commonly defined in the film and television industry].

2.   Conditions

2.1   This Agreement and the Company's engagement of the Director hereunder is subject to:

(a)   receipt by the Company of fully executed copies of this Agreement;
(b)   receipt by the Company of all forms and documents necessary to enable the Company to effect payment to the Director including tax and/or identification [and immigration] forms; and
(c)   qualification by the Director for insurance pursuant to paragraph 21 of this Agreement.

2.2   In the event that the conditions set out at paragraph 2.1(a) and (b) above are not met in a timely fashion the Company shall have the right to terminate this Agreement without any further obligation to the Director.

3.   Engagement

The Company hereby engages the Director and the Director hereby agrees to render the Director's services as the individual director of the Film upon the terms and subject to the conditions of this Agreement.

4.   Term of Engagement

4.1   The Company shall be entitled to the non-exclusive but first priority services of the Director from [date] and the exclusive services of the Director from [date] until delivery of the Director's Cut (as defined at paragraph 10 of this Agreement).

4.2   Thereafter the Company shall be entitled to the services of the Director on a non-exclusive but first priority basis until Delivery of the Film (as defined at paragraph 8 of this Agreement).

4.3   The Company shall also be entitled to make use of the services of the Director subject to the Director's prior professional commitments notified to the Company in writing in advance without additional remuneration in connection with the publicity of the Film including the giving of press and publicity interviews and the making of personal appearances in the major territories of the Film's release.

4.4   In this Agreement time is of the essence.

5.   Approvals and Controls

5.1   Subject to the Director not being in material uncured breach of any of the Director's material obligations under this Agreement the Director shall be entitled to consult in good faith with the Company in connection with the:

(a)   final shooting script (the "Final Shooting Script");
(b)   shooting schedule (the "Shooting Schedule");
(c)   key creative decisions including but not limited to the selection of principal cast, department heads and key crew members;

(d)   choice of locations for principal photography and post-production;

(e)   theatrical version for distribution worldwide;

(f)   initial release pattern; and

(g)   location and timing of previews and festivals

for the Film provided that in the event that the parties are unable to reach agreement the decision of the Company shall be final.

5.2   The Company in its sole discretion shall have all other rights of approval and control in connection with the Film.

6.   Services

6.1   The Director shall perform the Director's services hereunder:

(a)   where and when required by the Company diligently willingly conscientiously and to the standard skill and ability expected of a first class director of feature length sound and colour cinematograph films and soundtracks;

(b)   in any manner that may be required by the Company in accordance with the reasonable directions given by the Company or the agents of the Company; and

(c)   in collaboration with such persons and in such places as the Company shall designate from time to time.

6.2   The Director shall:

(a)   render all those services usually rendered by a first class director of feature length sound and colour cinematograph films and soundtracks during the continuance of the Director's engagement hereunder;

(b)   do all things, supply all information at the Director's disposal and co-operate wholeheartedly with the Company to enable the Company to prepare a proper comprehensive and detailed Shooting Schedule;

(c)   during the pre-production of the Film assist in all necessary preparations for the shooting of the Film in accordance with the Final Budget and the Shooting Schedule if requested by the Company including but not limited to selection of designs for the sets and costumes, scouting and selection of locations, attendance at casting conferences, selection of cast and crew, selection of materials and equipment, attendance at screen and recording tests, readings and rehearsals, consultations and discussions with studios, publicity stills, interviews and all such other supervisory work required of a first class director of feature length sound and colour cinematograph films and soundtracks;

(d)   direct the photography and recordings of the Film in the manner of a first class director of feature length sound and colour cinematograph films and soundtracks as efficiently and economically as possible and unless otherwise specified by the Company in accordance with the Final Budget, Final Shooting Script and Shooting Schedule with no material deviation by the Director from the same without the prior written approval of the Company except for minor changes to the Final Shooting Script due to production exigencies and which do not materially alter the characters, storyline or plot;

(e)   do all things that may reasonably be required by the Company to ensure that the photography and recordings of the Film shall be of the highest quality;

(f) both during and after the completion of the principal photography and recording of the Film assist in and supervise the cutting, editing, post-synchronising, scoring, dubbing, special and optical effects and titling and direct any retakes, added or substituted scenes of the Film as may be required by the Company in order to make due and proper delivery of the Film to the Company's distributors and sales agent in a first class condition and suitable for exploitation to the public in first class theatres; and

(g) from time to time to select for exhibition to a representative or representatives of the Company and its nominees daily rushes of the Film and assemblages thereof.

7. Remuneration

7.1 Subject to the Director not being in material uncured breach of any of the Director's material obligations under this Agreement and if the Company produces the Film the Company shall as remuneration and as full and final consideration for all services rendered and for all rights granted to the Company hereunder pay or procure to be paid to the Director:

(a) the sum of [*director's fee in figures*] ([*director's fee in words*]) (the "Fee") payable as follows:

(i) [*first instalment in figures*] ([*first instalment in words*]) upon the first day of principal photography of the Film;

(ii) [*second instalment in figures*] ([*second instalment in words*]) upon Delivery of the Film (as defined at paragraph 8 of this Agreement);

(iii) [*third instalment in figures*] ([*third instalment in words*]) to be paid as a deferral in last position on a pro rata pari passu basis; and

(b) such further sums equal to [*percentage in figures*]% ([*percentage in words*] per cent) of Producer's Net Profits for the Film.

7.2 The sums set out in paragraph 7.1 of this Agreement shall be deemed to be a buy-out throughout the world in perpetuity for all services rendered and for the Rights (as defined at paragraph 9.1 below) granted under this Agreement and the Company shall be fully and freely entitled to exploit the Film and the Rights without the need for any further payment to be made to the Director inclusive of all use fees, reuse fees, repeat fees or residuals by reason of the exploitation of the Film to which the Director may be entitled pursuant to any other applicable collective bargaining agreements and no further sums whatsoever shall be payable to the Director.

7.3 All payments pursuant to paragraph 7 of this Agreement shall be exclusive of Value Added Tax ("VAT") and if and to the extent only that VAT is or becomes payable on any such payment the Director shall render to the Company a VAT invoice in respect thereof upon receipt of which the Company shall make payment to the Director of the amount thereby shown to be due.

7.4 The Company shall use its reasonable endeavours to ensure that the Director is accounted to in respect of the Director's share of Producer's Net Profits under the terms of the collection agreement no less frequently than every six (6) months. If the Company does not engage a collection account manager in respect of the Film the Company shall send statements of account to the Director within fourteen (14) days of receiving statements from the distributors of the Film.

8. Delivery, Length and Rating

8.1 "Delivery" shall be deemed to have occurred only upon the Director's delivery to the Company or a designee of the Company of an answer print which conforms to all of the approved delivery schedule requirements including without limitation the following:

(a) the Film shall be filmed in colour in 35mm with an aspect ratio of 1.85:1 and shall have a running time of not less than ninety (90) minutes and not more than one hundred and twenty (120) minutes inclusive of main and end titles;

(b) the Film shall be an original feature length sound and colour cinematograph film and soundtrack that adheres to the Final Shooting Script and there shall be no material deviation by the Director from the same without the prior written approval of the Company except for minor changes to the Final Shooting Script due to production exigencies and which do not materially alter the characters, storyline or plot; and

(c) the Film shall be fully edited titled synchronised and assembled in all respects for first class technical release in any and all media and in territories throughout the universe and be recorded (not dubbed) in the English language.

8.2 The Film shall qualify for a BBFC rating no more restrictive than [U].

9. Rights

9.1 In consideration of the Fee:

(a) the Director hereby irrevocably assigns to the Company with full title guarantee free from all third party rights the products of the Director's services hereunder and all copyright (present and future), rental and lending rights, feature film, videogram, video-on-demand, television, Internet and other visual and/or audio-visual and other similar recording rights (whether now known or hereafter devised) and all rights incidental, ancillary or allied to any and all of the foregoing in and to the Film (as such terms are commonly used and understood in the film and television industry) for the Company to hold the same absolutely throughout the world for the full period of copyright in the Film and all renewals and extensions thereof and thereafter (insofar as may be or become possible) in perpetuity in any and all media now known or hereafter devised (the "Rights") but excluding the Reserved Rights;

(b) the Director hereby irrevocably and unconditionally waives in perpetuity all moral rights or "droit moral" or any similar law in any part of the world to which the Director has become or shall become entitled in relation to the Film and agrees not to bring or permit any legal action in any part of the world on the grounds that the Film or any such other product produced hereunder constitutes an infringement of any such rights or are in any way a defamation or mutilation of the products of the Director's services hereunder;

(c) the Director hereby confirms and agrees that the assignment of rights in and to the products of the Director's services hereunder includes any and all lending and rental rights and satellite and cable retransmission rights in and to the Film and any adaptation and copies created pursuant thereto (whether now known or hereafter devised) and further agrees that the consideration payable to the Director takes into account and includes a payment in respect of all such rights, that such payment constitutes full, equitable and adequate consideration for the grant and/or exercise of all such rights and that the Director will not be entitled to any further payment of any kind in respect of all such rights nor be entitled to bring or permit any legal action in any part of the world to restrict or prevent the distribution and exploitation of the Film and/or any such adaptation or copies.

9.2 The Company shall have the right but not the obligation at its discretion at all times hereafter to use and authorise others to use the Director's name photograph likeness recordings of the Director's voice taken or made hereunder and the autograph and biography of the Director (which the Director shall supply immediately upon request failing which the Company shall be entitled to use its own biography) in whole or in part:

(a) in connection with the advertisement, publicity, exhibition and commercial exploitation of the Film and all and any ancillary rights connected therewith; and

(b) for the purposes of and in association with the advertisement publicity exhibition and commercial exploitation of the Film and of any other commodities provided always that (except with the Director's prior written consent) the Director's name photograph or likeness is not directly or indirectly used to suggest that the Director personally uses or recommends any such other commodities

in any and all media now known or hereafter devised throughout the universe and in perpetuity without further consideration or payment to the Director and the Director hereby grants the Company all consents to make the fullest use of these rights.

9.3 The Company may also at its sole discretion make films and sound recordings of the Director's physical likeness and voice for "behind the scenes" promotional films and to reproduce the same and exploit the same in any and all media now known or hereafter devised throughout the universe in perpetuity without further consideration or payment to the Director.

9.4 Within two (2) days of the expiration of the Director's engagement hereunder the Director agrees to hand over to the Company at the Company's offices at [address] all physical materials relating to the Film or the products of the Director's services hereunder (including but not limited to set designs, costumes, photographs, books, plans, drawings, sketches, papers, files and any other effects whatsoever) belonging to the Company which are then in the Director's possession or are under the Director's control.

10. Director's Cut and Cutting

10.1 The Director shall complete and deliver a fine cut of the Film (the "Director's Cut") for screening by the Company in accordance with the approved production schedule it being understood that the Director's Cut may not be a dubbed version of the Film. The Director shall cause the Director's Cut to conform to the specifications set out in paragraph 8 of this Agreement. The Director's Cut shall not be performed on the original negative of the Film.

10.2 After delivery by the Director of the Director's Cut the Company shall make arrangements to view the Director's Cut as soon as practical thereafter. After such viewing the Company the principal financiers of the Film and the Director shall mutually agree upon any cuts additions changes amendments alterations or other editing of the Film it being agreed that in the event of any dispute the decision of the Company and/or the principal financiers of the Film shall prevail.

10.3 If the Director is prepared to make the cuts additions changes amendments alterations or other editing of the Film requested by the Company and/or the principal financiers of the Film then the Director shall carry out all such work in accordance with the requirements of the Company and/or the principal financiers of the Film and complete the same in accordance with Company's schedule it being understood that any subsequent cuts of the Film including without limitation the final cut thereof shall remain under the sole control of the Company.

10.4 If the Director refuses to make any such cuts additions changes amendments alterations or other editing of the Film required by the Company and/or the principal financiers of the Film the Company shall be free to engage another party to complete the cutting and dubbing of the Film in such manner as the Company shall in its absolute discretion determine it being understood that any subsequent cuts of the Film including without limitation the final cut thereof shall remain under the sole control of the Company.

10.5 In the event that the Director does not comply with this paragraph 10 the Company may (without prejudice to the Company's rights and remedies in respect of such failure to comply) take such steps in its discretion to cut edit and complete the Film in order that delivery of the Film may take place in accordance with the approved production schedule.

11. [First Opportunity to Direct Sequel, Prequel, Remake, Spin-Off

In the event that the Company decides to produce a sequel prequel remake or television spin-off based substantially on the same story incidents and characters in the Film the Director shall have the exclusive irrevocable first opportunity to be engaged by the Company to direct one or more of the same on terms to be agreed in good faith between the parties in accordance with the Director's then precedents and status in the film and television industry.]

12. Travel and Expenses

The Company shall provide the Director with [business class] accommodations and living expense allowance as pre-approved and agreed by the parties and with [business class] roundtrip air transportation for the Director plus [number] members of the Director's family.

13. Credit

13.1 Subject to the Director not being in material uncured breach of any of the Director's material obligations under this Agreement and if the Company does produce the Film and the Film is theatrically released the Company shall subject to the customary exclusions and exceptions set out at paragraph 13.3 below accord to the Director on the negative and all positive copies of the Film made by or to the order of the Company a single card credit on screen in the main titles of the Film and in all major paid advertising and paid publicity relating to the Film in the form:

["Directed by [name of director]"]

13.2 All references in this paragraph 13 to the title of the Film refer to the so-called "regular" title thereof and not to any "artwork" title used in connection therewith. Except as specifically set out in this paragraph 13 all other decisions with respect to credit including without limitation the position size prominence style placement duration colour and form of any and all credits shall be determined by the Company in its sole and exclusive discretion.

13.3 The provisions of this paragraph 13 shall not apply to:

(a) "group" "list" "special" or so-called "teaser" advertising pre-release publicity of exploitation;

(b) by-products of any kind (including but not limited to sheet music and gramophone records);

(c) "trailer" or other advertising on the screen or radio or television;

(d) institutional or other advertising or publicity not relating primarily to the Film;

(e) advertising of ten column inches or less;

(f) advertising or publicity material in narrative form;

(g) twenty-four (24) sheets and six (6) sheets;

(h) special advertising, publicity or exploitation of the Film relating to any member or members of the cast producer or other personnel connected in its production or to Academy Awards, BAFTAs or other prizes or similar matters; or

(i) roller credits at the end of the Film

any and all of which said items may be issued without mentioning the name of the Director therein.

13.4 The Company shall inform its licensees and distributors of the foregoing credit obligations. No casual or inadvertent failure by the Company to comply with the provisions of this paragraph 13 and no failure of persons other than the Company to comply therewith or with their contracts with the Company shall constitute a breach of this Agreement by the Company. The rights and remedies of the Director in the event of a breach of this paragraph 13 by the Company shall be limited to the Director's rights (if any) to recover damages in an action at law and in no event shall the Director be entitled by reason of any such breach to enjoin or restrain the distribution, exhibition, advertising or exploitation of the Film.

13.5 The Company shall use all reasonable endeavours to procure that the distributors of the Film accord to the Director credit in accordance with the provisions of this paragraph 13 (except as specified in paragraph 13.3) on all prints of and paid advertising for the Film issued by such distributors provided that the Company shall not be liable for the neglect or default of any such distributor or the cost of rectifying the same so long as the Company shall have notified the distributors of the credit to which the Director is entitled.

14. Videocassettes and DVDs

Subject to the Director not being in material uncured breach of any of the Director's material obligations under this Agreement and if the Company does produce the Film and the Film is theatrically released the Company shall upon the Director's written request furnish the Director with [number] DVD version of the Film if and when such DVDs are commercially available and subject to Director's signing any customary forms required by the distributor of the Film.

15. Premieres

In the event that the Company does produce the Film and the Film is theatrically released the Company shall use its best commercial endeavours to cause the distributor of the Film to provide an invitation for the Director and [*number*] guest[s] to the [United Kingdom and the United States] premiere and to [*number*] European festival screening[s] of the Film (if any) and shall use its best commercial endeavours to cause the distributor to provide the Director and [*number*] member[s] of the Director's family with [business class] roundtrip air transportation to and from such premieres or festival (if any) and a reasonable living expense allowance for the Director in connection therewith.

16. Suspension and Termination

16.1 Notwithstanding anything to the contrary contained elsewhere herein the Director's employment and Director's compensation hereunder shall automatically be suspended on written notice during any and all periods that:

(a) the Director does not render services hereunder because of the Director's illness or incapacity;

(b) the Director does not render services hereunder because of the Director's material default including but not limited to material default in respect of any of the obligations set out at paragraph 6.2 of this Agreement;

(c) production of the Film is prevented interrupted or delayed because of force majeure events including any labour dispute fire war or governmental action or any other disruptive event beyond Company's control; or

(d) production of the Film is prevented interrupted or delayed by reason of the death illness or incapacity of any key production personnel or a principal member of the cast.

16.2 Unless this Agreement is terminated pursuant to this paragraph 16 the periods set forth in paragraph 16.1 above shall be deemed extended by a period equivalent to all such periods of suspension.

16.3 Except with respect to Director's default if the Company requests the Director to remain on location during any such period of suspension the Company shall continue to provide for the Director as set out in paragraph 7 of this Agreement.

16.4 If:

(a) any matter referred to in paragraph 16.1(a) or (d) above continues for longer than ten (10) consecutive days (to be reduced to five (5) days during principal photography);

(b) there is a material default on the part of the Director under paragraph 16.1(b) or any matter giving rise to termination of the Director's services under the terms of the Company's bond agreement in relation to the Film including but not limited to failure by the Director to deliver the Film on time or on budget;

(c) the Director is guilty of conduct calculated or likely to prejudicially affect the interests of the Company including but not limited to creative differences with the Company or with any member of the cast or crew engaged by the Company in respect of the Film which conduct continues for longer than five (5) consecutive days (to be reduced to two (2) days during principal photography); or

(d) any matter referred to in paragraph 16.1(c) above continues for more than four (4) consecutive weeks or six (6) weeks in the aggregate, the Company may terminate this Agreement on written notice with immediate effect.

16.5 In the event that this Agreement shall be terminated hereunder by reason of the disability of the Director to perform any term of this Agreement the Director shall be entitled to receive such material sums as shall have accrued due at the date of such payment pursuant to this Agreement.

16.6 Notwithstanding the above, the transfer of rights to the Company under this Agreement shall survive the expiration or other termination of this Agreement.

17. No Injunction

All rights granted and assigned pursuant to this Agreement shall be irrevocable under any and all circumstances and shall not be subject to reversion, rescission or termination. The Director acknowledges that in the event of a breach of this Agreement by the Company any application to enjoin or restrain the production distribution exhibition advertising or exploitation of the Film or any rights therein or derived therefrom would be excessively disruptive and unreasonably damaging to the Film and the Company's interests therein and consequently the Director agrees not to apply for any such relief and accepts that the recovery of damages (if any) in an action at law shall provide a full and appropriate remedy for any loss or damage incurred by the Director as a result of any such breach.

18. Representations and Warranties

18.1 The Director hereby represents and warrants that:

(a) the Director shall perform the Director's services hereunder where and when required by the Company diligently willingly conscientiously and to the best of the Director's artistic and creative skill and technical ability and in any manner that may be required by the Company in accordance with the reasonable directions given by the Company or the agents of the Company in collaboration with such persons and in such places as the Company shall designate from time to time;

(b) the Director has and shall continue to have the right to enter into and to perform this Agreement to perform all of Director's obligations to be performed hereunder and to grant all rights granted hereunder;

(c) all material written composed prepared or submitted by the Director in connection with the preparation production and post-production of the Film shall be wholly original to the Director and shall not be copied in whole or in part from any other work except that furnished to the Director by the Company as a basis for such material;

(d) to the best of the Director's knowledge and belief (or such knowledge and belief as the Director would have acquired in the exercise of reasonable prudence and enquiries) none of the material set out in paragraph 18.1(c) above shall infringe or violate any third party rights including but not limited to intellectual property rights, defamation, rights of privacy publicity or confidence of any person firm or corporation; and

(e) from the date hereof until completion of the services required of Director hereunder in connection with production of the Film the Director shall not travel in an airplane or other vehicle which travels by air other than at the Company's request or as a passenger on a regularly scheduled commercial airline without the Company's prior written consent.

18.2 The Company hereby represents and warrants that it has and shall continue to have the right to enter into and to perform this Agreement.

19. Indemnities

19.1 The Director hereby indemnifies and agrees to keep the Company fully and effectually indemnified from and against any and all losses costs actions proceedings claims damages expenses (including reasonable legal costs and expenses) or liabilities suffered or incurred directly or indirectly by the Company in consequence of any breach non-performance or non-observance by the Director of any of the agreements conditions obligations representations warranties and undertakings on the part of the Director contained in this Agreement. The Director hereby expressly acknowledges that this indemnity shall survive the completion of the Director's services hereunder.

19.2 The Company hereby indemnifies the Director with respect to all claims arising in connection with the production distribution and other exploitation of the Film provided that such claims do not arise from the Director's breach of this Agreement.

20. Assignment

20.1 The Company and any subsequent assignee may freely assign this Agreement in whole or in part to any party provided however that the Company shall not be released from any of its obligations hereunder to the Director unless such assignee assumes in writing all of the Company's executory obligations hereunder.

20.2 This Agreement is not assignable in whole or in part by the Director except that the Director may assign his right to receive moneys hereunder provided the Director executes any documentation required by the Company or its assignee to effect such assignment.

21. Insurance

21.1 The Company may secure life health accident cast or other insurance covering the Director. Such insurance shall be for the Company's sole benefit and the Company shall be the beneficiary thereof and the Director shall have no interest in the proceeds thereof.

21.2 The Director shall assist in procuring such insurance by submitting to required examinations and tests and by preparing signing and delivering such applications and other documents as may be required. The Director shall to the best of [his/her] ability observe all terms and conditions of such insurance.

21.3 The Company shall name the Director as an additional insured party on the Company's general liability and Errors and Omissions insurance policies in connection with the Film (if and to the extent such policies are acquired) subject to the limitations restrictions and terms of such policies.

22. General Restrictions

22.1 The Director shall not:

(a) order goods or incur any liability on the Company's behalf or in any way pledge the Company's credit or hold the Director out as being entitled to do so;

343

(b) without the prior written consent of the Company at any time hereafter either personally or by means of press or publicity or advertising agents or agencies make any statement or disclosure or supply any information photographs or physical material to any person firm or corporate body (other than the Director's agents and professional advisers) or to the public relating to the Film any matter arising hereunder or to the general affairs of the Company coming within the Director's knowledge by reason of the rendering of the services of the Director hereunder or otherwise howsoever; or

(c) make any statement or carry out any act that is damaging injurious or unfavourable to or about the Film.

23. No Obligation

Notwithstanding and irrespective of any advertisement or announcement which may hereafter be published nothing in this Agreement shall be construed as to impose upon the Company any obligation to make use of the services of the Director or of the Film or any part or parts thereof and the Company shall not be liable to the Director for any loss or damage for or in respect of loss of publicity advertisement reputation or the like due to the Company's failure to develop produce release distribute advertise or otherwise exploit the Film in whole or in part.

24. Working Time

The Director agrees to work such hours as are necessary to fulfil the Director's obligations under this Agreement and the Director accepts that this may involve working an average of more than forty-eight (48) hours per week. The Director agrees that the maximum weekly working time specified in Regulation 4 of the Working Time Regulations 1998 (the "Regulations") shall not apply to this Agreement and this paragraph shall constitute an agreement in writing for the purposes of Regulation 5 of the Regulations. The Company shall not require the Director to work any hours in excess of the maximum weekly working time if to do so would cause any safety or health risks. The Director agrees to comply with the Company's request and do all things required of the Director by the Company (including maintaining a timesheet of the Director's working hours) to assist the Company in complying with its obligations under the Regulations to maintain a record of the number of hours worked by the Director.

25. Notices

Any notices to be given or served under this Agreement shall be in writing and shall be delivered or sent by first class (airmail if posted to another country) prepaid registered or recorded delivery (if available) post or by facsimile or other print-out communication mechanisms to the party to be served at the address set out herein (or such other address as either party may from time to time notify in writing to the other) and in the case of the Company marked for the attention of [name] and shall be deemed to have been served:

(a) if hand delivered at the time of delivery;

(b) if sent by facsimile or other print-out mechanisms within eight (8) hours of transmission if during business hours at its destination or within twenty-four (24) hours if not within business hours but subject to proof by the sender that it holds a transmission report indicating uninterrupted transmission to the addressee; or

(c) if sent by prepaid post as aforesaid on the expiration of the second business day following the date of posting (the fifth business day if posted to another country).

26. Additional Documentation

The parties agree to execute acknowledge and deliver such further instruments or documents as may be necessary or reasonably requested to fully effect the rights privileges and property which are the subject of this Agreement. If the Director shall fail to execute, acknowledge or deliver the same within two (2) weeks of receipt of a written request by the Company, the Company or its nominee is hereby irrevocably appointed the attorney-in-fact for the Director with full right power and authority coupled with an interest to execute acknowledge deliver and record the same in the name of and on behalf of the Director.

27. Miscellaneous

27.1 No waiver by either party hereto of any breach of any of the terms or conditions of this Agreement in a particular instance shall be deemed or construed to be a waiver of any preceding or succeeding breach of the same or any other terms or conditions. All rights, remedies, undertakings and obligations contained in this Agreement shall be cumulative and none of them shall be in limitation of any other rights, remedies, undertakings or obligations of either party.

27.2 If any paragraph or any part of this Agreement or the application thereof to either party shall for any reason be adjudged by any court or other legal authority of competent jurisdiction to be invalid such judgment shall not affect the remainder of this Agreement which shall continue in full force and effect.

27.3 Nothing herein contained shall be construed or deemed to constitute a partnership or joint venture between the parties hereto and save as expressly herein provided no party shall hold itself out as the agent of the other.

27.4 The Director acknowledges that his services are being rendered to the Company as an independent contractor and that at no time shall the Director become an employee of the Company.

27.5 This Agreement contains the entire agreement of the parties and may only be varied by written instrument signed by all parties.

27.6 This Agreement may be executed simultaneously in one or more counterparts each of which shall be deemed to be an original but all of which together shall constitute one and the same instrument.

27.7 Except insofar as this Agreement expressly provides that a third party may in his own right enforce a term of this Agreement, a person who is not a party to this Agreement has no right under the Contracts (Rights of Third Parties) Act 1999 to rely upon or enforce any term of this Agreement but this does not affect any right or remedy of a third party which exists or is available apart from that Act.

27.8 This Agreement shall be construed under and performed in all respects in accordance with and governed by the laws of England and Wales and the parties shall submit to the exclusive jurisdiction of the courts of England and Wales.

SIGNED BY a duly authorised signatory)

for and on behalf of)

[*name of company*])

SIGNED BY [*name of director*])

in the presence of)

Witness signature: . . . .

Name (block capitals):   . . . .

Occupation: . . . .

Address: . . . .

                              . . . .

                              . . . .

APPENDIX B3

Co-production agreement

THIS AGREEMENT is made the [   ] day of [   ] [2007]

BETWEEN:

(1) [   ] of [   ] United Kingdom (the "UK Producer") which expression shall be deemed to include its successors in title and assigns; and

(2) [   ] of [   ] (the "[*country*] Producer") which expression shall be deemed to include its successors in title and assigns

(together the "Co-Producers").

WHEREAS:

The Co-Producers wish to enter into an agreement whereby the parties will co-produce a feature film primarily intended for theatrical exploitation based wholly or substantially upon an original [un]published screenplay written by [*name of writer*] entitled "[*name of screenplay*]" (the "Screenplay") provisionally entitled "[*name of film*]" (the "Film") under the terms of the [European Convention on Cinematographic Co-Production] (the "Treaty") subject to the conditions of and for the consideration set out in this Agreement.

It is hereby agreed as follows:

1. Term

This Agreement shall commence on the date [set out on page 1 above] and shall continue unless terminated earlier in accordance with the other provisions of this Agreement.

2. Services and Role of Each Party

2.1 In consideration of the mutual covenants and obligations set out in this Agreement the parties hereby agree to:

(a) co-produce the Film in accordance with the terms of this Agreement and within the framework of the Treaty based up on the work written by [*name of writer*] ([*country*] Citizen) and to be directed by [*name of director*] ([*country*] Citizen);

(b) distribute and exploit the Film in its original version or any and all other versions, whether dubbed or subtitled, in any and all media whether now known or hereafter devised throughout the world; and

(c) share all revenues and profits to be derived from such distribution and exploitation of the Film.

2.2 The parties shall consult with each other in relation to the principal decisions relating to the Film as a co-production to be mutually agreed by the parties such agreement not to be unreasonably withheld.

2.3 The parties acknowledge that irrespective of the position of the [UK] Producer as minority co-production participant if the parties are unable to reach agreement the decision of the [UK] Producer shall be final subject always with the requirements of and the responsibilities of the parties to the government agencies of the United Kingdom being the Department for Culture Media and Sport (the "DCMS") and [country] being [name of relevant authority].

2.4 The parties hereby declare that there is no common ownership between the two entities.

3. Managing Producer

3.1 [Name] of the UK Producer shall be appointed and act as the Managing Producer of the Film (the "Managing Producer") during the Term of this Agreement.

3.2 In the event that [name] is no longer able to act as Managing Producer the parties shall consult with each other to mutually agree a replacement such agreement not to be unreasonably withheld but if the parties are unable to reach agreement in respect of the same the decision of the [UK] Producer shall be final.

4. Production Budget and Finance

4.1 The Film shall be produced in accordance with the agreed total budget provisionally estimated to be [budget in figures] ([budget in words]) (the "Budget") appended to this Agreement at Schedule A.

4.2 Any change to the Budget shall be agreed in writing by the parties, such agreement not to be unreasonably withheld.

4.3 The parties shall each respectively contribute to the financing of the Budget in the following proportions:

UK Producer: [percentage in figures]%

(the "UK Contribution")

[country] Producer: [percentage in figures]%

(the "[country] Contribution")

4.4 The drawdown payments of the financing for the Budget shall be mutually agreed by the parties in accordance with the agreed cash flow schedule such agreement not to be unreasonably withheld but if the parties are unable to reach agreement the decision of the Managing Producer shall be final.

4.5 The parties hereby agree that any currency exchange rate fluctuations between the UK Pound Sterling and the [currency] shall be the responsibility of the UK Producer.

5. Production Specifications

5.1 The parties shall consult with each other in relation to the completion of the final shooting script for the Film (the "Final Shooting Script") but if the parties are unable to reach agreement the decision of the UK Producer shall be final.

5.2 The Film shall be produced in the English language to a running time of approximately ninety (90) minutes and shall be shot in and about [location].

5.3 The quality of the finished Film shall be technically and pictorially of first class quality and meet international standards. The parties hereby agree to use only first class material and equipment and to hire only qualified and experienced production and technical personnel.

6. Copyright and Ownership of the Film

6.1 The UK Producer shall renew or exercise the option or assign the copyright in respect of the Screenplay.

6.2 The UK Producer shall acquire all worldwide copyright and all other rights, title and interest including but not limited to rental and lending rights and moral rights waivers and all other rights of a similar nature necessary for the production of the Film and its distribution and exploitation throughout the world in respect the agreements appended to this Agreement at Schedule B (the "Rights Agreements").

6.3 The UK Producer shall pay all amounts due pursuant to the Rights Agreements and hereby undertakes that the Rights Agreements are and shall be in full force and effect in accordance with their terms throughout the Term of this Agreement.

6.4 The UK Producer hereby irrevocably assigns to the [country] Producer [percentage in figures]% ([percentage in words] per cent of the Rights (as defined at paragraph 6.5 of this Agreement) with full title guarantee to the [country] Producer for the parties to hold the same absolutely in the proportions set out at paragraph 6.6 below throughout the world for the full period of copyright in the Film and in any other product produced hereunder and all renewals and extensions thereof and thereafter (insofar as may be or become possible) in perpetuity.

6.5 The rights which are the subject of this Agreement are all copyright (present and future), rental and lending rights, feature film, videogram, video-on-demand, television, Internet and other visual and/or audio-visual and other similar recording rights (whether now known or hereafter devised) and all rights incidental, ancillary or allied to any and all of the foregoing in and to the Film (as such terms are commonly used and understood in the film and television industry) including but not limited to merchandising rights and promotional rights, the right to make, distribute and exploit the same by any and all media now known or hereafter devised, the benefit of all moral rights waivers and all other rights of a similar nature and the Rights Agreements (the "Rights").

6.6 Ownership of the Film by the parties shall be in the following proportions:

UK Producer: [percentage in figures]%

[country] Producer   [percentage in figures]%

6.7 Neither party may without the written consent of the other, transfer, assign, sell to a third party or encumber the Rights in whole or in part.

7. Accounting

7.1 The parties shall each maintain separate, full, complete and accurate written books of accounts relating to all aspects of the Film and the distribution and exploitation of the Film. Such books shall be maintained in accordance with generally accepted accounting principles which are in force in the country of the party in which such books are maintained. The UK Producer shall have access to the books of accounts of the [country] Producer and the [country] Producer shall have access to the books of accounts of the UK Producer.

7.2 The parties shall exchange a financial report giving the final audited costs of their respective proportions of the Budget within [ninety (90)] days after delivery of the answer print or copy of the master videotape of the Film in a form similar to the accepted form of the Budget or a mutually agreeable form.

8. Bank Accounts

8.1 A production bank account shall be opened in a recognised banking institution chosen by the UK Producer from which are to be made all payments of all expenses in respect of which the UK Producer is responsible in relation to the Film.

8.2 A production bank account(s) shall be opened in [country] in a recognised banking institution chosen by the [country] Producer, from which are to be made all payments of all expenses in respect of which the [country] Producer is responsible in relation to the Film.

9. Completion Guarantee

9.1 The UK Producer undertakes to obtain a completion guarantee in respect of the Film (the "Completion Guarantee") from a recognised completion guarantor on terms acceptable to the [country] Producer (the "Completion Guarantor").

9.2 To the extent that the Completion Guarantor is not responsible for any over-budget expenditure in the Budget such over-budget expenditure shall be the responsibility of each party in the same proportion as they are responsible for financing the Budget. In the event of any readjustment of the Budget the Film shall continue to be a UK/[country] [percentage in figures]%/[percentage in figures]% co-production.

10. Distribution and Exploitation – Revenues, Profits and Territories

10.1 The UK Producer shall have the exclusive distribution and exploitation rights at its own cost in the [countries] Territories as follows:

(a) until recoupment by the UK Producer of the UK Contribution, 100% of Net Revenues to the UK Producer; and

(b) after recoupment by the UK Producer of the UK Contribution [percentage in figures]% of Net Revenues to the UK Producer and thereafter [percentage in figures]% of Net Profits to the UK Producer.

In this Agreement the [countries] Territories shall mean the [countries], their bases throughout the world, respective territories and possessions, armed forces installations and governmental and similar installations wherever situated and aircraft and ships throughout the world flying the flag of [countries].

10.2 The [country] Producer shall have the exclusive distribution and exploitation rights at its own cost in the [countries] Territories as follows:

(a) until recoupment by the [country] Producer of the [country] Contribution, 100% of the Net Revenues to the [country] Producer; and

(b) after recoupment by the [country] Producer of the [country] Contribution, [percentage in figures]% of Net Revenues to the [country] Producer and thereafter [percentage]% of Net Profits to the [country] Producer.

In this Agreement the [countries] Territories shall mean the [countries], their bases throughout the world, respective territories and possessions, armed forces installations and governmental and similar installations wherever situated and aircraft and ships throughout the world flying the flag of [*countries*].

10.3 All Net Revenues and Net Profits earned from the distribution and exploitation of the Film from all sources in all territories other than those specified in paragraphs 10.1 and 10.2 above shall be allocated to the parties as follows:

To the UK Producer [*percentage in figures*]%

To the [*country*] Producer [*percentage in figures*]%

10.4 In this Agreement:

(a) Net Revenues shall mean all gross revenues actually received from the exploitation of the Film after deduction of all distribution fees and distribution expenses in accordance with the [*countries*] Territories or the [*countries*] Territories terms of any distribution agreement and all sums advanced by the principal financier(s) of the Film, together with interest thereon and all deferments;

(b) Net Profits shall mean all profits derived from the exploitation of the Film in all media worldwide as defined, computed and accounted for in accordance with the Film's principal financiers' standard definition of net profits.

10.5 Any source of financial assistance not constituting Net Revenues available to either the UK Producer or the [*country*] Producer in the UK or [*country*] respectively may be retained by the party receiving such financial assistance with the exception of UK Tax Credits which shall constitute revenue in the UK Territories.

10.6 The parties and the principal financier(s) of the Film shall enter into a collection account management agreement with [*collection agent and address*] (the "Collection Agent") in respect of the Film whereby a collection agreement or other contract shall specify the recoupment schedule in respect of the Film and shall govern the distribution of receipts of exploitation of the Film amongst all relevant beneficiaries.

10.7 The UK Producer shall grant the distribution rights in the [*countries*] Territories and the [*country*] Producer shall grant distribution rights in the [*countries*] Territories only to distributors that are acceptable to the parties.

11. Distribution and Exploitation – Agreement and Records

11.1 All distribution and exploitation agreements in all territories from which revenues and profits are to be shared between the UK Producer and the [*country*] Producer as set out in paragraphs 10.1 to 10.3 above shall be mutually agreed by the parties such agreement not to be unreasonably withheld.

11.2 The parties shall use their best commercial endeavours to provide the documentation set out in paragraph 7 of this Agreement to the Collection Agent.

12. Third Party Contracts

12.1 The benefit of all contracts concluded by either party in relation to the Film with the exception of those set out in paragraphs 6.1 and 6.2 above shall be held by that party for the benefit of parties jointly.

12.2 All contracts concluded by either party in relation to the production of the Film shall be in a form usual to the film and television industry and shall be consistent with this Agreement and with the requirements of the principal financiers

351

of the Film and the Completion Guarantor. Such contracts shall contain a grant of rights to permit the widest legally possible exploitation of the Film including but not limited to rental and lending rights and moral rights waivers.

13. Insurance

13.1 The parties shall obtain in a timely manner and maintain in good standing at all material times after the commencement of principal photography of the Film for the benefit of the parties jointly policies of insurance for the Film in a form usual to and in accordance with the standards of the film and television industry and as required by the principal financiers of the Film from an organisation specialising in film and television entertainment insurance. Such policies shall name the parties as additional insured and shall insure against among other risks:

(a) death or other incapacity of the director or principal cast;
(b) loss or destruction of the original master negative or master copy of the Film, faulty stock, camera, editing and processing and of the sets, props, wardrobe or equipment used on the Film;
(c) liability for death, personal injury or damage to property;
(d) pre-production, third party property damage and production, office contents;
(e) employers and public liability insurance; and
(f) liability for errors and omissions in respect of the chain of title of the Film, infringement of copyright, defamation or invasion of privacy.

13.2 Any moneys paid by an insurer shall be deposited in the Film bank account as set out in paragraph 8 above in the event of a delay or other interruption of the production of the Film.

13.3 The parties hereby agree that they shall not do or permit to be done anything that may cause the policies of insurance to lapse or become wholly or partially void or voidable by the insurers.

13.4 In the event that it shall be impossible to resume the production of the Film for any reason the policies of insurance shall provide that the insurance proceeds shall be paid to the UK Producer and [country] Producer on a pro rata basis based on their respective financial participation in the Film or subject to the requirements of the Completion Guarantor.

14. Production Schedule

14.1 Principal photography of the Film is scheduled to begin on or about [date] for a duration of [number] production days in and about [location] as required by the Final Shooting Script.

14.2 Editing of the original version of the Film shall take place in [country] and is scheduled to be completed on or about [date].

14.3 Sound for the original version of the Film shall take place in [country] and is scheduled to be completed on or about [date].

14.4 The Film shall be edited by an individual to be determined (Nationality: [United Kingdom]). The music shall be composed and music performed by individuals to be determined (Nationality: [United Kingdom]).

14.5 The answer print of the Film is scheduled to be completed on [date].

14.6 If either party requests or causes an unscheduled delay in the start of principal photography or taping thereby causing the other because of contractual obligations to incur additional expenses, the party so causing such a delay shall reimburse those additional expenses to the other party in full.

14.7 The UK Producer shall be responsible for obtaining the final approval of the DCMS for the qualification of the Film as an official co-production under the terms of the Treaty.

14.8 The [country] Producer shall be responsible for obtaining the final approval of [name of relevant authority] of the qualification of the Film as an official co-production under the terms of the Treaty.

15. Publicity

15.1 During the production of the Film the parties shall be responsible for publicity for the Film in their respective territories as set out in paragraph 10 above.

15.2 The party responsible for the distribution and exploitation of the Film from all sources in all territories other than those specified in paragraphs 10.1 and 10.2 above shall be responsible for the publicity in such territories. The other party not so responsible for such distribution and exploitation shall make available its publicity materials for that purpose.

15.3 The parties shall inform each other of their respective publicity commitments and hereby undertake to respect the publicity commitments of the other and shall use their reasonable commercial endeavours to ensure that their respective distributors respect such publicity commitments.

15.4 The parties hereby agree that each shall have access to the publicity materials of each other and all third parties.

16. Credits

16.1 The master negative and/master videotapes and all positive copies and prints and videotapes used in the distribution and exploitation of the Film shall include the following on screen credits and all printed material relating to the same shall include the following credits:

A United Kingdom-[country] Co-Production

Copyright 200[   ] [UK Production Company] and [[country] Production Company] All Rights Reserved

16.2 All other credits shall be in accordance with all contractual requirements including those of guilds and unions and shall be subject to requirements of the principal financiers of the Film or any distributors or sub-distributors. Neither party to this Agreement shall grant credits to any third party without the written consent of both parties.

17. Original Master Negative and/or Master Videotapes of the Film

17.1 The original master negative and/or master videotapes of the Film shall be kept at a laboratory to be determined in the [United Kingdom].

17.2 The parties hereby agree that the original master negative and/or master video-tapes of the Film and all other Physical Materials from or relating to the Film (the "Film Materials") shall be owned by the parties jointly in [equal] shares throughout the world in perpetuity and shall be kept at the said laboratory and/or a storage vault under the names of both parties.

17.3 The parties hereby undertake to make available to the other and hereby grant access to the other to the original master negative and/or master videotapes of the Film and the trailer of the Film (if any) and the Physical Materials for the purpose of taking copies of the same or as applicable.

17.4 The parties shall have the right to grant the security over the original master negative and/or master videotapes of the Film to the principal financier(s) of the Film.

17.5 The laboratory or custodian of the storage vault shall require written authority from both parties to release or dispose of any of the Film Materials to the parties or one of the parties or otherwise.

17.6 The parties shall inform the laboratory or custodian of the storage vault of the requirements set out in this paragraph 17 and shall obtain confirmation from such laboratory or custodian that it is aware of and shall respect such obligations.

17.7 The parties shall obtain from the laboratory or the custodian of the storage vault an undertaking to provide any of the Film Materials to the parties notwithstanding that legal proceedings have been undertaken by a creditor with regard to either party.

17.8 In this Agreement Physical Materials shall mean the materials of and all other physical properties of every kind relating to the Film now in existence or made in the future including without limitation positives, negatives, prints, soundtracks, recordings, audio and videotapes and discs and all duplicates, versions and copies thereof.

18. Validity

18.1 This Agreement shall be executed subject to the grant of final approval of the Film as an official co-production by the DCMS and [name of relevant authority] and the agreement of the same that the Film meets the requirements of the Treaty and that the parties are eligible to all benefits contained therein.

18.2 The parties hereby undertake to submit this Agreement and all relevant documentation to the DCMS and [name of relevant authority] in a timely fashion in accordance with prescribed deadlines.

18.3 This Agreement is subject to the respective regulations, if any, of the competent authority of the country of each party.

19. Arbitration and Judicial Proceedings

If either party disagrees with the interpretation of any term or condition of this Agreement such disagreement may be settled either at the choice of the party bringing the complaint [by independent arbitration or] through judicial process in the United Kingdom.

20. Censorship

The approval of the Film by the DCMS and [name of relevant authority] shall not be interpreted as binding such authorities to grant any licence of whatever kind to exhibit the Film.

21. Procedure on Non-approval by Relevant Authorities

21.1 In the event that the Film is not accepted by the DCMS the UK Producer and/or [name of relevant authority] the [country] Producer as the case may be shall be responsible for any and all the contracts and commitments that party has undertaken or expenses it has incurred in relation to the same.

21.2 In the event that the Film does not receive approval for public exhibition in either United Kingdom or [*country*] all distribution, financing and security contracts relating to the Film shall remain in full force and effect.

21.3 All costs related to the matters set out in this paragraph 21 shall be the responsibility of the party found to be in default, if any.

22. Warranties and Indemnity

22.1 The parties hereby warrant, represent and undertake that:

(a) they shall perform their obligations hereunder diligently, willingly, conscientiously and to the best of their skill and ability;

(b) they have the full power and authority to enter into this Agreement and to grant the rights herein;

(c) they shall promptly pay all amounts payable and due to any and all third parties in respect of their services and any rights granted by them provided the same is in accordance with the terms of this Agreement; and

(d) there are not and shall not be any claims, liens or encumbrances of any nature affecting the Screenplay or the Film or any part thereof with the exception of those in favour of third party financiers.

22.2 The parties hereby indemnify and shall at all times keep each other fully and effectually indemnified from and against all actions, proceedings, costs, claims, damages and losses whatsoever suffered or incurred directly or indirectly in consequence of any material breach or non-performance of any of the agreements, representations, material obligations, warranties and undertakings contained in this Agreement.

23. Termination

23.1 Without prejudice to its other rights and remedies, either party may terminate this Agreement forthwith by notice in writing to the other if the other party commits any material breach of any term of this Agreement which (in the case of a breach capable of being remedied) shall not have been remedied within [thirty (30)] days of a written notice by the notifying party giving full particulars of the breach referring expressly to this clause and requesting the other to remedy the same.

23.2 Without prejudice to its other rights and remedies, either party may terminate this Agreement forthwith by notice in writing to the other if the other party shall not contribute its respective proportion of the Budget under paragraph 4.3 above.

23.3 Without prejudice to its other rights and remedies, either party may terminate this Agreement forthwith by notice in writing to the other upon the occurrence of any act of insolvency by the other party, including but not limited to the appointment of a receiver, administrator or liquidator, or the effecting of an arrangement with creditors, whether in relation to part or whole of the defaulting party, or if the other party ceases trading or threatens to cease trading.

23.4 Existing rights of ownership on termination of this Agreement for whatever reason will not affect any accrued rights or liabilities of either party and upon any such expiry or termination all outstanding payments due from any party to the other shall be made in full.

24. Force Majeure

24.1 In the event that this Agreement cannot be performed or its obligations fulfilled for any reason beyond the reasonable control of either party (including but not limited to war, industrial actions, floods or acts of God), then such non-performance or failure to fulfil such obligations shall be deemed not to be a breach of this Agreement.

24.2 If a party (the "Affected Party") is unable to perform any of its obligations under this Agreement as a result of such a force majeure event for a continuous period of more than [thirty (30)] days, the other party shall be entitled to terminate this Agreement at any time and without any further liability, upon giving written notice to the Affected Party.

25. Confidentiality

The parties mutually agree in good faith and undertake to keep and maintain any information relating indirectly or directly to the business of the parties, the Screenplay and the Film that has been received from the other party and is not already in the public domain confidential at all times and to use such information only for the purpose of developing, financing, producing and/or exploiting the Film unless otherwise required by law or any applicable regulations.

26. No Injunction

All rights granted and assigned pursuant to this Agreement shall be irrevocable under any and all circumstances and shall not be subject to reversion, rescission or termination. The parties acknowledge that in the event of a breach of this Agreement by the other, any application to enjoin or restrain the production, distribution, exhibition, advertising or exploitation of the Film or any rights therein or derived therefrom would be excessively disruptive and unreasonably damaging to the Film and the interests of the other party therein and consequently the parties agree not to apply for any such relief and accept that the recovery of damages, if any, in an action at law will provide a full and appropriate remedy for any loss or damage incurred by the parties as a result of any such breach.

27. Assignment

The parties shall not be entitled to assign and charge the benefit of this Agreement to any third party without the prior written agreement of both the parties.

28. Notices

Any notice or communication to either party for the purpose of this Agreement must be in writing and shall be deemed to have been served on and received by the parties in the normal course of business if it is sent by prepaid delivery post to that party at the address stated above in this Agreement or such other address as is notified to the other party during the Term or, if sent by facsimile transmission, receipt shall be deemed received on the close of business of the addressee on the following business day subject to proof by the sender that it holds an acknowledgement from the addressee confirming receipt of the transmitted notice in readable form.

29. VAT

All sums payable under this Agreement are stated exclusive of any Value Added Tax that may be payable by either party. Invoices will include Value Added Tax at the relevant rate on the date of invoicing.

30. Miscellaneous

30.1 No waiver by either party hereto of any breach of any of the terms or conditions of this Agreement in a particular instance shall be deemed or construed to be a waiver of any preceding or succeeding breach of the same or any other terms or conditions. All rights, remedies, undertakings and obligations contained in this Agreement shall be cumulative and none of them shall be in limitation of any other rights, remedies, undertakings or obligations of either party.

30.2 The parties agree to execute and deliver all such further documents as the parties may require in relation to this Agreement and if either of the parties shall fail to execute, acknowledge or deliver the same the other party is hereby irrevocably appointed the attorney-in-fact of the defaulting party with full right, power and authority to execute, acknowledge and deliver the same in the name of and on behalf of the defaulting party.

30.3 If any paragraph or any part of this Agreement or the application thereof to either party shall for any reason be adjudged by any court or other legal authority of competent jurisdiction to be invalid such judgment shall not affect the remainder of this Agreement which shall continue in full force and effect.

30.4 Nothing herein contained shall be construed or deemed to constitute a partnership or joint venture between the parties hereto and save as expressly herein provided no party shall hold itself out as the agent of the other.

30.5 This Agreement contains the entire agreement of the parties and may only be varied by written instrument signed by the parties.

30.6 Each party shall bear its own costs and expenses in relation to the negotiation, preparation, execution and implementation of this Agreement, including the fees and disbursements of their respective legal, accountancy and other advisers.

30.7 No term of this Agreement shall be enforceable under the Contracts (Rights to Third Parties) Act 1999 by a person who is not a party to this Agreement.

30.8 This Agreement shall be construed under and performed in all respects in accordance with and governed by the laws of England and Wales and the parties shall submit to the exclusive jurisdiction of the courts of England and Wales.

31. Counterparts

This Agreement may be executed in counterparts, each of which shall be deemed to be an original, but both of which together shall constitute one and the same instrument. A facsimile of a party's signature shall be deemed and comprise an original signature for all purposes hereof.

AS WITNESS the hands of duly authorised representatives of the parties the day, month and year first above written.

SIGNED BY [*name*]   )

As an authorised signatory for and   )

on behalf of [UK Production Company]   )

SIGNED BY [*name*]   )

As an authorised signatory for and   )

on behalf of [*name of overseas production company*]   )

SCHEDULE A

BUDGET

SCHEDULE B

RIGHTS AGREEMENTS

APPENDIX C

Interactive entertainment

Model publishing contract

MODEL CONTRACT

FOR PUBLISHING AND DEVELOPING INTERACTIVE ENTERTAINMENT WORKS

PUBLISHING AGREEMENT

[*Insert intended name of product.*]

THIS AGREEMENT is made on the [   ] day of [   ] [2007] (the "Effective Date").

BETWEEN:

(1) [   ] a company registered in [   ] under registered number [   ] whose principal place of business is at [ ] (the "Publisher"); and

(2) [   ] a company registered in [   ] under registered number [   ] whose principal place of business is at [   ] (the "Developer").

BACKGROUND:

(A) The Developer develops interactive entertainment products and the Publisher publishes interactive entertainment products.

(B) The Developer has agreed to create a game to be published by the Publisher on the terms and conditions of this Agreement.

IT IS AGREED THAT:

1. DEFINITIONS

1.1 In this Agreement, unless the context otherwise requires, the following words shall have the following meanings:

"Accounting Period"	means a three month period ending on 31 March, 30 June, 30 September or 31 December;
"Advance Payments"	means the payments set out in Schedule 1;
"Affiliate"	means any associated company of the Publisher (as defined in Section 416 of the Income and Corporation Taxes Act 1988);
"Deliverable"	means the works further described in Schedule 1 including the Game;
"Delivery Date"	means the delivery date for each Deliverable and set out in Schedule 1, as such date may be amended in accordance with clause 2.4;

"Game"	means the interactive entertainment game provisionally entitled [*title*] and described in the Specification;
"Intellectual Property Rights"	means copyright, registered and unregistered designs, database rights, registered and unregistered trade marks and trading names, patent rights, know-how, performance rights, goodwill and applications for any of the same and other rights of a similar nature enforceable anywhere in the world;
"Key Staff"	means the individuals listed in Schedule 6 or their replacements appointed in accordance with clause 2.6;
"Net Revenue"	means all sums received by or credited to the Publisher (or an Affiliate, if earlier) in respect of the sale, distribution or other exploitation of the Game (including by granting sub-licences, renting the Game or making the Game available for play over a computer network) less, to the extent actually credited or paid by the Publisher (or the Affiliate, if applicable) in respect of the Game: [*insert agreed deductions*];
"Publisher Assets and Information"	means the assets and information described in Schedule 2;
"Publisher Elements"	means the Publisher Assets and Information together with [the Game title(s)] [and] [any element of the Game which incorporates any Intellectual Property Rights of the Publisher's licensor(s)];
"Retained Technology and Assets"	means the technology [and tools] described in Schedule 3 and includes the Third Party Software;
"Specification"	means the specification for the Game contained in Appendix 1 as amended from time to time in accordance with clause 2.7;
"Third Party Software"	means the software so described in Schedule 3.

1.2 In this Agreement, unless the context otherwise requires:

(a) words in the singular include the plural and vice versa and words in one gender include any other gender;

(b) a reference to:

(i) a "person" includes any individual, firm, body corporate, association or partnership, government or state (whether or not having a separate legal personality); and

(ii) a "clause" or "schedule" is a reference to a clause or schedule of this Agreement; and

(iii) "includes" or "including" is to be construed without limitation.

2. OBLIGATIONS DURING DEVELOPMENT

2.1 The Developer shall create the Deliverables and deliver each Deliverable to the Publisher on or before the Delivery Date for that Deliverable.

2.2 The Developer shall create each Deliverable in accordance with its description in the Specification and in Schedule 1 and shall do so to the standards of skill and care expected of a professional interactive entertainment software developer as at the date of creation.

2.3 The Publisher shall deliver the Publisher Assets and Information to the Developer on the date(s) specified in Schedule 2. The Publisher shall comply with its obligations (if any) set out in the Specification by the dates provided in the Specification. If the date for performance of a particular obligation is not specified in the Specification, the Publisher shall perform that obligation by such date as is reasonably required by the Developer in order for the Developer to comply with its own obligations in this Agreement.

2.4 Subject to clause 2.5, if the performance of any obligation of the Developer is delayed by reason of the delay or failure of the Publisher to comply with any of its obligations by the date(s) provided in this Agreement ("Publisher Delay"), then without prejudice to any other right of the Developer the date for performance of that obligation of the Developer shall be postponed by a period equal to the period of Publisher Delay and the Delivery Date for any affected Deliverable shall be amended accordingly.

2.5 The Developer shall use all reasonable endeavours to mitigate the effect of any Publisher Delay and shall notify the Publisher of the probable consequences of any Publisher Delay notwithstanding such endeavours as soon as reasonably practicable after becoming aware of that Publisher Delay.

2.6 While available to work for the Developer, the Developer shall assign the Key Staff to work exclusively in relation to the Deliverables unless otherwise provided in Schedule 6. If a member of the Key Staff is unavailable for such work the Developer shall notify the Publisher accordingly as soon as is reasonably practicable and the Developer shall use its reasonable endeavours to replace that person with another person of equal or greater skill as soon as is reasonably practicable.

2.7 The Specification and the definitions of each Deliverable shall not change without the [written] agreement of both parties.

2.8 The Developer shall not incorporate in the Game any hidden content which is not described in the Specification without the prior approval of the Publisher.

3. TESTING AND ACCEPTANCE

3.1 The Publisher shall review each Deliverable within [   ] working days of receipt of that Deliverable (the "Testing Period"). The Publisher shall notify the Developer that it either accepts or rejects each Deliverable on or before the last day of the Testing Period for that Deliverable.

3.2 The Publisher shall accept each Deliverable unless either: (i) that Deliverable fails materially to conform to the standards described in clause 2.2; or (ii) the Developer is in breach of any of its warranties in respect of that Deliverable.

3.3 If the Publisher notifies the Developer that it rejects a Deliverable, the Publisher shall at the same time inform the Developer of the reasons for such rejection in sufficient detail to allow the Developer to attempt to correct the Deliverable so that it complies with the terms of this Agreement. Without prejudice to the Developer's obligations under clause 2.1 or to the Publisher's right to terminate this Agreement under clause 7.2, the process described in clauses 3.1 to 3.3 shall apply to any rejected Deliverables which are resubmitted to the Publisher for acceptance while this Agreement remains in force.

3.4 The Developer shall send the Publisher a Value Added Tax invoice in respect of each Advance Payment. The Publisher shall pay each Advance Payment within [ ] working days of the date on which the Deliverable to which that Advance Payment applies has been accepted by the Publisher.

4. INTELLECTUAL PROPERTY RIGHTS

4.1

Model A [all intellectual property rights are retained by the Developer]	Model B [certain intellectual property rights are assigned to the Publisher]
All Intellectual Property Rights in or relating to the Specification and each Deliverable (including the game title) shall belong to the Developer. Subject to clauses 4.2 and 4.3, the Developer hereby grants to the Publisher an exclusive, worldwide, perpetual [(subject to clause 7.5)] right and licence to copy, manufacture, distribute, sell, rent, license and commercially exploit the Game. [However, the Developer reserves to itself all rights to create and commercially exploit sequels, prequels, ports, expansion packs or other products using some or all of the Intellectual Property Rights in the Game and no such rights are licensed to the Publisher.]	Except for the Retained Technology and Assets, all Intellectual Property Rights in or relating to the Specification and each Deliverable (including the game title) shall belong to the Publisher. Subject to clauses 4.2 and 4.3, the Developer hereby assigns to the Publisher (by way of a present assignment of future rights) all Intellectual Property Rights in or relating to the Specification, the Game and each Deliverable (except for the Retained Technology and Assets). All Intellectual Property Rights in or relating to the Retained Technology and Assets shall remain the sole property of the Developer.

4.2 The Publisher is responsible for obtaining all necessary rights and licences required in order to incorporate the Publisher Elements into the Game and to exploit commercially the same within the Game. Accordingly, the Developer makes no guarantee as to the underlying title in respect of those parts of the Game which incorporate or reproduce the Publisher Elements. The Publisher hereby grants to the Developer a non-exclusive royalty-free worldwide licence to incorporate the Publisher Elements into the Game in the manner contemplated in the Specification.

4.3 The Developer hereby grants to the Publisher a non-exclusive, worldwide licence (with the right to grant sub-licences) to copy, manufacture, distribute, sell, rent, license and commercially exploit the Retained Technology and Assets [(excluding any tools)] in object code format only and solely within and as a part of the Game (the "RTA Licence"). The RTA Licence shall commence on the date of completion of the Game and shall remain in force in perpetuity [unless earlier terminated in accordance with clause 7.5].

4.4 Each party shall at the request and reasonable expense of the other perform such acts and execute such documents as the other may reasonably require in order to effect or confirm the provisions of this clause 4 and of clause 7.4(d).

5. MARKETING, SUPPORTING AND PUBLISHING THE GAME

5.1 Save as further provided in this clause 5, the Publisher shall be free to market, publish and commercially exploit the Game in any way it sees fit through any channel and in particular the Publisher shall be free to set the price(s) for the Game at its discretion [and to choose such title(s) for the Game as it sees fit]. The Publisher shall be free to appoint such sub-licensee(s) as it sees fit, provided that the Publisher shall remain responsible to the Developer for the actions or omissions of its sub-licensees as if they were the actions or omissions of the Publisher.

5.2 During the six month periods both prior to and immediately following the date of first commercial release of the Game, the Developer shall provide the Publisher with such assistance in marketing the Game as is specified in Schedule 7. The Publisher shall pay all of the reasonable out-of-pocket expenses incurred by the Developer in connection with such assistance within [   ] days of receipt of an invoice, provided that the Publisher has approved such expenses in writing in advance. If the Publisher does not so approve any proposed expense then the Developer shall not be required to provide the assistance connected to that expense.

5.3 The Publisher shall credit the Developer as the developer of the Game in the manner set out in Schedule 4. An accidental failure to comply with the terms of this clause 5.3 shall not entitle the Developer to terminate this Agreement. However, the Publisher shall take all available steps to correct any such failure at the next print run of any material so affected. The Developer hereby grants to the Publisher a non-exclusive, worldwide, royalty-free licence to use and reproduce the Developer's logo (in the format delivered by the Developer) in accordance with this clause and Schedule 4.

5.4 The parties shall use reasonable endeavours to describe the Developer as the [sole] developer of the Game for the purposes of any commercial statistics (including retail sales statistics) concerning the Game. However, this clause shall not impose any positive obligation on either party to correct any third party who does not describe the Developer as the [sole] developer of the Game.

5.5 The Publisher shall provide reasonable end-user support for the Game in accordance with the prevailing standards within the interactive entertainment publishing industry. The Developer shall provide the Publisher's support staff with prompt reasonable technical support relating to the Game free of charge during the first year following the date on which the Game is first commercially released by any person. Such reasonable technical support shall be provided in English during the Developer's ordinary office hours and (to the extent reasonably required) shall include providing software patches to remedy faults detected in the Game after commercial release of the Game.

6. FINANCIAL PROVISIONS

6.1 The Publisher shall pay the Developer a royalty in respect of all Net Revenue derived from the Game at the rate(s) in Schedule 5 and in accordance with the further provisions of this clause 6.

6.2 The Publisher shall pay the Advance Payments to the Developer in accordance with clause 3.4. The Advance Payments shall constitute advance payments in respect of the royalties that may arise under this Agreement. Accordingly, the Publisher shall not be required to pay any royalties to the Developer in respect of the Game unless and until the total royalties derived from the Game exceed all of the Advance Payments paid to the Developer by the Publisher. However, a failure of the Publisher to recover all of the Advance Payments under this clause 6.2 shall not of itself oblige the Developer to make good any shortfall in the sums so retained by the Publisher.

6.3 Within thirty (30) days of the end of each Accounting Period during the Audit Period (as defined in clause 6.6 below), the Publisher shall send the Developer a statement setting out: (i) the Net Revenue received or credited during that Accounting Period, together with (ii) the royalties due to the Developer in respect of that Accounting Period. Each statement shall contain the information set out in Schedule 5 [and shall be in the form of the sample statement annexed to Schedule 5].

6.4 Following the receipt of each statement referred to in clause 6.3, the Developer shall send the Publisher an appropriate Value Added Tax invoice in respect of the royalties due to the Developer. The Publisher shall pay those royalties to the Developer within forty-five (45) days of the end of the Accounting Period in which they accrued.

6.5 The Publisher shall be entitled to retain [   ]% of the royalties which accrue to the Developer under this Agreement in respect of each Accounting Period, as a reserve in respect of possible adjustments to such royalties which may arise after the closure of that Accounting Period (a "Reserve"). The Publisher shall pay the Developer the balance of each Reserve (after any adjustment made in connection with that Accounting Period) at the conclusion of the Accounting Period immediately following the Accounting Period in respect of which the Publisher made that Reserve.

6.6 The Publisher shall keep separate records and complete and accurate accounts of all Net Revenue sufficient to calculate the royalties due to the Developer under this Agreement. The Publisher shall retain all such records and accounts at its principal place of business [in the United Kingdom] while the Game is being commercially exploited by any person and for [two (2)] years thereafter (the "Audit Period").

6.7 During the Audit Period, the Publisher shall provide any independent qualified accountant or accounting company instructed by the Developer with access to the records and accounts referred to in clause 6.6 during normal working hours in order to inspect and copy such records and accounts. If the Developer requests such an inspection, it shall give the Publisher not less than fourteen (14) days' notice of the day on which the Developer wishes such inspection to commence. All information disclosed by the Publisher during such inspection shall be treated by the Developer as the confidential information of the Publisher and shall be subject to the terms of clause 10.

6.8 If any inspection carried out on behalf of the Developer under clause 6.7 correctly identifies that the Publisher has made any underpayment under this Agreement, then the Publisher shall promptly pay to the Developer a sum equal to the amount of that underpayment. If any such inspection identifies that the

Publisher has made any underpayment under this Agreement in respect of any period amounting to [ten per cent (10%)] or more of the total sums actually due in respect of that period then the Publisher shall also reimburse the Developer for the reasonable charges of the independent qualified accountant or accounting company which carried out such inspection.

6.9   The Publisher may withhold from payments of royalties due to the Developer any tax which the Publisher is required by law to withhold, provided that the Publisher shall as soon as reasonably practicable: (i) provide full details of any sums so withheld to the Developer; and (ii) complete and execute such document(s) as the Developer may reasonably require to be completed and executed for the purpose of obtaining any available tax credit.

6.10 For the purposes of calculating the royalty due to the Developer, if the Publisher or an Affiliate receives any Net Revenue in a currency other than [sterling], such sums shall be deemed to have been converted to [sterling] at the rate for the purchase of [sterling] with such other currency prevailing upon the last working day of the Accounting Period in which the Net Revenue was received.

7.   TERMINATION

7.1   This Agreement shall commence on the Effective Date and shall remain in force in perpetuity unless earlier terminated in accordance with this clause 7.

7.2   Without prejudice to any other right or remedy available to either party under this Agreement or at law, either party (the "Innocent Party") may terminate this Agreement at any time and with immediate effect upon giving notice to the other party (the "Party in Breach") if:

(a)   the Party in Breach has committed a material breach of this Agreement and has failed to remedy such breach within thirty (30) days of receipt of a notice from the Innocent Party describing the breach and requiring its remedy; or

(b)   the Party in Breach passes a resolution for its winding up or a court of competent jurisdiction makes an order for the winding up or dissolution of the Party in Breach; or

(c)   an administration order is made in relation to the Party in Breach or a receiver or administrative receiver is appointed over the Party in Breach or any of its assets; or

(d)   the Party in Breach makes an arrangement or composition with its creditors or makes an application to a court of competent jurisdiction for protection from its creditors; or

(e)   an event substantially similar to an event in clauses 7.2(b) to 7.2(d) inclusive occurs in respect of the Party in Breach in any country in which the Party in Breach is located.

7.3   The Publisher may terminate this Agreement at any time prior to [cut-off date] for any reason (or for no reason) on notice to that effect to the Developer. Within seven (7) days of termination of this Agreement pursuant to this clause 7.3 the Publisher shall pay all Advance Payments then due to the Developer, together with an additional sum of [insert].

7.4   If this Agreement is terminated by the Publisher in accordance with clause 7.2 before the Developer has complied with all of its development and maintenance obligations in this Agreement, the Publisher shall be entitled to complete the Deliverables and maintain the Game. Accordingly, with effect from the termination of this Agreement in such circumstances:

(a) the Developer hereby grants to the Publisher a non-exclusive worldwide royalty-free licence to use and modify the Retained Technology and Assets for the sole purpose of completing the Deliverables and maintaining the Game (but for no other purpose); and

(b) the Developer shall deliver a copy of all of the Retained Technology and Assets and all work in progress connected to the Deliverables to the Publisher; and

(c) the Publisher shall treat the Retained Technology and Assets as the confidential information of the Developer and subject to clause 10; and

(d) the Publisher hereby assigns to the Developer (by way of a present assignment of future rights) with full title guarantee all Intellectual Property Rights in or relating to any modifications made to the Retained Technology and Assets in connection with the completion of the Deliverables as contemplated in this clause ("Modifications"); and

(e) the Publisher shall deliver to the Developer a copy of each Modification promptly upon creation; and

(f) this clause 7.4 shall not apply to any Third Party Software comprised within the Retained Technology and Assets.

7.5

Model A	Model B
[If this Agreement is terminated by the Developer in accordance with clause 7.2 [prior to the commercial release of the Game] or is terminated by the Publisher in accordance with clause 7.3 then the exclusive licence granted to the Publisher in clause 4.1 and the RTA Licence shall both terminate on the date of such termination.]	[If this Agreement is terminated by the Developer in accordance with clause 7.2 [prior to the commercial release of the Game] or is terminated by the Publisher in accordance with clause 7.3 then the RTA Licence shall terminate on the date of such termination.]

7.6 The termination of this Agreement howsoever arising shall not affect:

(a) any right or obligation of either party which accrued on or prior to the termination of this Agreement; or

(b) any term which is expressly or by implication intended to survive the termination of this Agreement, including those in clauses [1, 4, 5.1, 5.3, 5.4, 6–11].

8. WARRANTIES AND INDEMNITIES

8.1 The Developer represents and warrants to the Publisher that:

Model A	Model B
(a) it has the right to enter into this Agreement and to grant the licences set out in this Agreement;	it has the right to enter into this Agreement and to make the assignment and grant the licences set out in this Agreement;

Model A	Model B
(b) the Developer is the sole and exclusive owner of all Intellectual Property Rights subsisting in the Deliverables (except the Publisher Elements and the Third Party Software) free and clear of all liens, charges, encumbrances or claims;	were it not for the assignment in clause 4.1, the Developer would be the sole and exclusive owner of all Intellectual Property Rights subsisting in the Deliverables (except the Publisher Elements and the Third Party Software) free and clear of all liens, charges, encumbrances or claims;
(c) the use and exploitation of the Game by the Publisher and its licensees in accordance with this Agreement shall not infringe the Intellectual Property Rights of any person;	the use and exploitation of the Game by the Publisher and its licensees in accordance with this Agreement shall not infringe the Intellectual Property Rights of any person;
(d) the Developer is and shall at all times remain entitled to use the Third Party Software in the manner contemplated in this Agreement and to permit the Publisher and its licensees to use and commercially exploit the Game (incorporating the Third Party Software) as contemplated in this Agreement; and	the Developer is and shall at all times remain entitled to use the Third Party Software in the manner contemplated in this Agreement and to permit the Publisher and its licensees to use and commercially exploit the Game (incorporating the Third Party Software) as contemplated in this Agreement; and
(e) the Developer has not entered into (and shall not enter into) any agreement or arrangement and has not done (and shall not do) any act or thing which shall (or might) inhibit, restrict or impair the exploitation of the licences it has granted in this Agreement.	the Developer has not entered into (and shall not enter into) any agreement or arrangement and has not done (and shall not do) any act or thing which shall (or might) inhibit, restrict or impair the exploitation of the licences it has granted and the rights it has assigned in this Agreement.

However, this clause 8.1 shall not apply to any actual or alleged infringement of a US patent if the patent owner also alleges that that patent is also infringed by other interactive entertainment products which were not developed by the Developer.

8.2   The Publisher represents and warrants to the Developer that:

    (a)   it has the right to enter into this Agreement and to grant the licence in respect of the Publisher Elements in clause 4.2 and to assign the Intellectual Property Rights described in clause 7.4(d); and

    (b)   the use by the Developer of the Publisher Elements as permitted in clause 4.2 shall not infringe the Intellectual Property Rights of any person.

8.3   Each party (the "Indemnifying Party") shall indemnify (and shall keep fully indemnified) the other (the "Indemnified Party") from and against all claims, demands, costs, liabilities, losses, expenses and damages (including legal fees and expert witness fees) arising out of or in connection with any third party claim (a "Claim") which, taking the claimant's allegations to be true, would result in a breach by the Indemnifying Party of any of the Indemnifying Party's representations, warranties or covenants set out in this clause 8, provided that the Indemnified Party (and each Affiliate of the Indemnified Party):

(a) takes all reasonable steps to mitigate its loss and:
(b) promptly notifies the Indemnifying Party if the Indemnified Party receives notice of any Claim (or the possibility of any Claim) and provides the Indemnifying Party with all available details of the nature of that Claim;
(c) co-operates with the Indemnifying Party in all reasonable respects in connection with the defence of that Claim at the reasonable expense of the Indemnifying Party; and
(d) shall not make any admission of liability, agreement or compromise in relation to that Claim without the prior approval of the Indemnifying Party (such approval not to be unreasonably withheld).

9. LIMITATIONS OF LIABILITY

9.1 Save as provided in clause 9.3, neither party shall be liable for any consequential or indirect loss or damage however caused.

9.2 Save as provided in clause 9.3, each party's entire aggregate liability arising under or in connection with this Agreement shall be limited to a sum equal to £[*insert*].

9.3 Nothing in this clause shall limit the liability of either party for:

(a) death or personal injury caused by its negligence; or
(b) any misrepresentations made fraudulently; or
(c) any liability arising under clause 6 [and clause 8.3].

10. CONFIDENTIALITY OF BUSINESS INFORMATION

10.1 Except as referred to in clause 10.2, each party shall treat as strictly confidential all information of a confidential nature received or obtained as a result of entering into or performing this Agreement which relates to the provisions or subject matter of this Agreement, the other party or the negotiations relating to this Agreement ("Confidential Information"). Neither party shall use the Confidential Information of the other party for any purpose not envisaged in this Agreement.

10.2 Each party may disclose information which would otherwise be Confidential Information if and to the extent that:

(a) it is required to do so by law or any securities exchange or regulatory or governmental body to which it is subject wherever situated;
(b) it considers it necessary to disclose the information to its professional advisers, auditors and bankers provided that it does so on a confidential basis;
(c) the information has come into the public domain through no fault of that party; or
(d) the information was previously disclosed to it without any obligation of confidence.

11.   MISCELLANEOUS PROVISIONS

11.1   *Notices.* All notices, approvals and other communications to be given under this Agreement shall be in writing and shall be sent by letter posted [for overnight delivery] with an internationally recognised courier or facsimile (such facsimile notice to be confirmed by letter posted [for overnight delivery] with an internationally recognised courier within twenty-four (24) hours of the transmission of the relevant facsimile) to the address of the other party set out at the top of this Agreement (or to such other address as either party may notify to the other under the provisions of this clause).

11.2   *Entire Agreement.* This Agreement supersedes all prior agreements and undertakings (whether oral or written) between the parties and constitutes the entire agreement between the parties relating to the Game. Each party acknowledges that it has entered into this Agreement in reliance only on the representations, warranties and promises expressly contained in this Agreement. Save as expressly set out in this Agreement, each party disclaims any further representations (save fraudulent misrepresentations), warranties, conditions or other terms, express or implied.

11.3   *Variation.* No addition to or modification of any provision of this Agreement shall be binding upon the parties unless made by a written instrument signed by a duly authorised representative of each of the parties.

11.4   *Assignment and Sub-Licensing.* Save as expressly provided herein, neither party may assign, transfer or sub-license any of its rights under this Agreement without the prior written consent of the other (which shall not unreasonably be withheld).

11.5   *Force Majeure.* Neither party shall be deemed to be in breach of this Agreement, or otherwise liable to the other, by reason of any delay in performance or non-performance of any of its obligations under this Agreement to the extent that such delay or non-performance is due to any event beyond the reasonable control of that party.

11.6   *No Joint Venture or Partnership.* Nothing in this Agreement shall create, or be deemed to create, a partnership, joint venture or relationship of principal and agent between the parties.

11.7   *Waiver.* No failure on the part of either party to exercise or to enforce any right given to it by this Agreement or at law or any custom or practice of the parties at variance with the terms of this Agreement shall constitute a waiver of either of the parties' respective rights under this Agreement or operate so as to prevent the exercise or enforcement of any such right at any time.

11.8   *Severability.* If any provision of this Agreement is held to be invalid or unenforceable, in whole or in part, that provision or part shall to that extent be deemed not to form part of this Agreement. However, the validity and enforceability of the remainder of this Agreement shall not be affected.

11.9   *Value Added Tax.* All sums due under this Agreement are exclusive of any applicable Value Added Tax (or other sales tax). Each party shall pay any applicable Value Added Tax (or other sales tax) with the relevant sum at the rate and in the manner from time to time prescribed by law, subject to receiving an appropriate Value Added Tax (or other sales tax) invoice from the other party.

11.10 *Law, Jurisdiction and Third Party Rights.* This Agreement shall be governed by and construed in accordance with English law and the parties submit to the exclusive jurisdiction of the English courts. No term of this Agreement is enforceable pursuant to the Contracts (Rights of Third Parties) Act 1999 by any person who is not a party to it.

This Agreement has been executed on [the date appearing at the top of page 1].

[Publisher]   [Developer]

Signed . . . .   Signed . . . .

Print name. . . . .   Print name. . . . .

Title. . . . .   Title. . . . .

SCHEDULE 1

DELIVERABLES, DELIVERY DATES AND ADVANCE PAYMENTS

[*Here insert a list of all Deliverables and their delivery dates, together with their associated Advance Payments.*

The Deliverables should include all interim deliverables (including demos) and the final version of the Game.

All agreed languages should be set out here.

All agreed technical specifications, including compliance with the requirements of Nintendo, Microsoft and Sony, and the absence of certain bug types, and any limitations imposed by any licensor should also be set out here.]

SCHEDULE 2

PUBLISHER ASSETS AND INFORMATION

[*Here insert a list of all assets and information required from the Publisher, and the dates by which those assets and that information should be provided. The assets include localisation assets (the Developer should specify the required format) and assets and style guides provided by a licensor (if any). The information may include the final title(s) of the Game.*]

SCHEDULE 3

RETAINED TECHNOLOGY AND ASSETS

[*Here describe the technology and assets which are retained by the Developer.*]

THIRD PARTY SOFTWARE

[*Here list any third party middleware or other software which does not belong to the Developer.*]

SCHEDULE 4

CREDITS

[*The following are relatively common credit provisions. The parties can bypass the detail in this Schedule by simply referring to an existing game (which may or may not have been developed by the Developer or published by the Publisher) which features developer credits acceptable to both parties.*]

The Developer shall be credited as the [sole/principal] developer of the Game as follows:

1. *Splash Screen.* The Developer shall be credited in a "splash screen" featuring the Developer's animated logo within the opening section of the Game. The splash screen shall be created by the Developer but is subject to the approval of the Publisher which approval shall not unreasonably be withheld.
2. *Credits.* The Developer and its nominated staff shall be credited within the credits section of the Game.
3. *Packaging [and advertising].* The Developer's logo shall be included in colour on the [reverse/front] of the packaging for the Game, in the Game manual [and on the CD or DVD for the Game] [and on any advertising material referring to the Game]. The logo shall be in full colour and of no less than [*insert minimum size(s)*].
4. *Legal text.* The following legal text shall be included within the Game, on the packaging for the Game [and on all advertisements for the Game] wherever the Publisher's own similar text is printed:

[*Insert developer copyright and trade mark notices, e.g.* Game [*Technology*] © [*name of Developer*] [*date of first publication of Game*]. All Rights Reserved.]

SCHEDULE 5

ROYALTY RATES AND ROYALTY STATEMENTS

The royalty rates in respect of the Net Revenue the Game shall be [   ]% of Net Revenue [but shall be no less than £[   ] per copy].

[*or*]

The royalty rates in respect of the Net Revenue for the Game shall be calculated by reference to the sale of copies of the Game in accordance with the following table:

Total number of copies of the Game sold	Royalty Rate
0 – [ ],000	[ ]%
[ ],001 – [ ],000	[ ]%
[ ],001 – [ ],000	[ ]%
[ ],001 +	[ ]%

[Fixed Fee
£[   ] per copy of the Game [sold by the Publisher to a retailer or distributor in the [EU]]
[unless that copy was sold to an end user in a particular country at Budget Price, in which case the fixed fee shall be £[   ] per copy. "Budget Price" means a price of no more than [   ]% of the lowest retail price charged to end users in the relevant country during the first [   ] months of commercial exploitation of copies of the Game in that country].

[*Insert list of requirements for statement contents*]

SCHEDULE 6
KEY STAFF

[Here insert the key staff required to work on the Game. If any staff will not be working full time on the game, or will not be required during part of the development process, this should be specified here.]

SCHEDULE 7
MARKETING ASSISTANCE

[Here describe any marketing assistance required of the Developer, such as participation in press events. Under clause 5.2, the Publisher is required to refund the Developer's expenses incurred in connection with this assistance.]

APPENDIX 1
SPECIFICATION

Index